'ELIZABETH'

'ELIZABETH'

THE AUTHOR OF
Elizabeth and Her German Garden

Karen Usborne

THE BODLEY HEAD
LONDON

For Ashley and Susanna

British Library Cataloguing
in Publication Data
Usborne, Karen
'Elizabeth'
The Author of *Elizabeth and Her German Garden*
I. Title
823'.912   PR6035.U8Z
ISBN 0-370-30887-5

© Karen Usborne 1986
Printed in Great Britain for
The Bodley Head Ltd
32 Bedford Square, London WC1B 3EL
by The Bath Press, Avon
Set in Baskerville
by Wyvern Typesetting Ltd, Bristol
First published 1986
Second impression 1987

Contents

Illustrations

ILLUSTRATIONS

The caravan tour. Billy the dog became their symbol: 'Nature with dignity'.
Liebet and Evi at Blue Hayes in the summer.
Passport photograph of Elizabeth aged forty.
Elizabeth at fifty-seven.
H. G. Wells.
Wells and Elizabeth at the chalet, answering to 'no authority of any kind'.
Frere at about the time of his first meeting with Elizabeth.
The Chalet Soleil and Little Chalet.
The chalet from the iris walk. Frere is standing in the porch.
The chalet taken in 1922 by Thelma Cazalet from the opposite mountain.
Francis, Earl Russell in middle age on his yacht *Royal* soon after his marriage to Elizabeth.
From left to right: Bertrand Russell, Elizabeth and Frere on the terrace to the chalet.
Katherine Mansfield at the period when a 'thousand devils' sent Elizabeth without her German garden to tea with her in Hampstead.
Left to right: Victor Cazalet, Hugh Walpole, Elizabeth, Rudyard Kipling and Mrs Cazalet at the Cazalets' house, Fairlawn in Kent, 1928.
Elizabeth and her son-in-law Tony von Hirschberg.
Le Mas des Roses from the back in 1932. Unfortunately there is no hint in the photograph of the spectacular view down the valley to the sea beyond.
Elizabeth on the roof of Le Mas des Roses with her puppies in 1932. Her family referred to her at that stage as being 'all dog'.
Elizabeth at the Golden Eagle Hotel in Beaufort, South Carolina, 1940. 'I'm going to stay here till driven away by agile alligators and snakes,' she wrote to Liebet.
Elizabeth in the early 1920s.

'ELIZABETH'

Introduction

'Elizabeth' anonymously published her first novel, *Elizabeth and her German Garden*, in September 1898. It went into eleven reprints by the end of the year, and by then the book had earned her £10,000—over £300,000 in today's money. It was the cause of the greatest literary mystery of the period, and full-page articles appeared in the English papers demanding to know the identity of the author. She was, at that time, thirty-two, a countess, married to a Prussian *Junker* who was an ex-army officer, banker and an experimental farmer close to ruin.

Born in New Zealand, the daughter of a prosperous shipping merchant, Elizabeth had travelled to England with her family when she was three. She was educated in Europe and England, and by her mid-twenties she was an accomplished concert pianist, violinist, organist and a formidable and original feminist thinker. She then married Count Henning von Arnim-Schlagenthin who had the status of an English earl in *Hochgeboren* society and was the son of Count Harry von Arnim, Bismarck's former rival for the Chancellorship of the new German Empire.

She lived a life of hard work and seclusion alternating, after her first novel was published, with periods of intense socializing on her visits to England where she was lionized by literary hostesses and adored by her public. In time her scandalous affair with H. G. Wells, her disastrous second marriage to Francis, Earl Russell, the so-called 'wicked Earl' and elder brother of Bertrand, as well as the ruthless and comic depictions in her novels of friends and family, caused her to be ostracized by the society which had once so assiduously courted her.

An urbane and witty woman—some thought her one of the great wits of her time—she was on intimate terms with many of the most creative people of a fascinating era. H. G. Wells, who was her lover and lifelong friend, considered her the most amusing, engaging and original letter writer of her generation. Her correspondence with her daughter Liebet rivals that of Madame de Sévigné. Tiny, dynamic and highly active, her long and well-documented life was filled with dramatic episodes. Hugh Walpole and E. M. Forster were tutors to her numerous children; both used her as a model for characters in their writings, as did some of her other friends, who included George Bernard Shaw, George Moore, Michael Arlen, Max Beerbohm, George Santayana and Katherine Mansfield, who was also her cousin. Katherine's last letter was written to Elizabeth. In it she said, 'Goodbye, my dearest . . . I shall never know anyone like you. I shall remember every little thing about you for ever.'

Elizabeth's life and work were dedicated first and foremost to exploding the complacency she encountered everywhere, most particularly that of England in regard to Prussian military ambition, which she was in a unique position to understand. Many of her books contained warnings, and it was cold comfort when her prophecies came true. She brought her children, who were German citizens, to England before the First World War, and towards the end of her life Hitler came to represent for Elizabeth everything that was evil. She was living near the border of France and Italy prior to the outbreak of the Second World War and fled, reluctantly, to America where, ill and alone, she died, conscious that, as far as she was concerned, Hitler had won, that 'his long black claws' had reached her even as far away as South Carolina. Her last novel and twenty-second book was completed only months before her death in 1941 and was made into a Hollywood film, *Mr Skeffington*, starring Bette Davis and Claud Rains.

Although artistic merit is rarely accorded to best-selling authors, Elizabeth was a rare and happy exception to this rule, an author whose books were enjoyed and appreciated by the finest minds of her day as well as by a huge popular audience. She never allowed herself to be swayed by the success of each publication into repeating a formula and every book that she wrote was an experiment in form.

The only book about her that has been published to date was written by her daughter Liebet. Elizabeth had made her executor of her estate and there emerged in 1958 a biography called *Elizabeth of the German Garden*, published by William Heinemann and written under the pseudonym of Leslie de Charmes. I have referred to this book throughout as Liebet's memoirs.

My own interest in Elizabeth was kindled unexpectedly one afternoon many years ago when I picked up a copy of *The Enchanted*

April and idly read a few sentences here and there. Immediately I was fired with an uncharacteristic desire not only to know more of the author but to acquire all of her books. The research for this biography took me five years and to California twice to work in the archives at the Huntington Library in San Marino where Elizabeth's papers and diaries are lodged. Within a few days of my arrival I realized I had struck gold. New material, not just of Elizabeth's but of Francis and Bertrand Russell, George Moore, Katherine Mansfield, H. G. Wells and many others, was waiting to be excavated.

Such is the influence of the West Coast of America that it all seemed very much what one might have expected. It was only when, like Aladdin, I had stuffed my pockets with treasure and returned home to write the book that I realized what I had found. I had also unearthed *Remembrances of the Authoress of Elizabeth and her German Garden* by Teppi, governess to the von Arnim children and lifelong friend of Elizabeth's, the diaries and unpublished memoirs of another of Elizabeth's daughters, Evi, the journals of Henry Herron Beauchamp, Elizabeth's father, as well as the recollections of members of Elizabeth's family who live in California.

After the publication of her first book, she was known to her readers, eventually to her friends, and finally even to her family as Elizabeth. She will become Elizabeth in this book when *Elizabeth and her German Garden* has made her name, but she was christened Mary Annette Beauchamp when she was born in 1866, and her family called her May. She will remain May here for her first thirty-two years.

K.U.

April, 1986.

· 1 ·

Mary, Mary

Mary Annette Beauchamp, known to her family as 'May', was born in New Zealand shortly before the dark and stormy winter dawn of 31 August 1866. If natural and unnatural events on the day that a child is born are in any way portentous, then May's life was certainly to reflect the omens around her birth. There was a solar eclipse which was total in Rome; earthquakes shuddered along the coasts of the Mediterranean basin. Closer to home May's father, a hitherto wealthy shipping merchant, lost most of his money. He had speculated in shares which crashed in the panic of that year, and the news of this coincided with the information that two of his cargo ships had sunk in the Indian Ocean, and reached him when his daughter was only a few hours old. The joy of her safe arrival was somewhat blighted by these events.

1866 was also the year in which Bismarck ensured the supremacy of Prussia in the newly confederated German states. At the battle of Sadowa, fought only a few months before May was born, the Prussian guards, armed with the new needle guns, completely routed the gorgeous but out-of-date Austrian hussars. The European stage was, after the signing of the Treaty of Prague on 22 August, set for the whole drama of the two world wars which were to dominate May's life. In England Lord John Russell, her future grandfather-in-law, was Prime Minister.

It was a large family that welcomed May into the world. She shared the nursery with two-year-old Harry, who clearly resented her arrival. Sydney who was five and Walter who was a year younger were as 'thick as thieves'[1] and were soon to lead the two younger ones into all kinds of mischief. The beautiful Charlotte, who helped to care for the infant while her mother indulged in a lengthy Victorian convalescence, was eight. She already had Ralph, the elder by a year and a little simple-minded, firmly under her thumb.

Their father, the handsome Henry Herron Beauchamp, had emigrated to Australia from England via Mauritius when he was a young man in 1850. His forebears had come over to England with William the Conqueror and his father, John Beauchamp, had inherited the family firm of silversmiths which is mentioned in Pepys's diaries. He invented a new method of plating which might have made him a wealthy man had he exploited it, but he preferred the romantic life of his artist friend Constable and the painter's biographer, Charles Robert Leslie, to the constraints of a business-man's life. He lived in Highgate, foxhunted in Highgate woods, and married one of the fashionable 'Precious Stone' sisters, Ann.[2] He wrote doggerel by the yard and was known affectionately by his friends as the 'Poet of Hornsey Lane' and by succeeding generations as 'the original pa-man'.[3] But his neglect lost him the family firm and his seven sons were obliged to seek their fortunes in Australia with nothing more than a good grammar school education to their names. Henry, the fourth son, was a wiry, energetic young man of slightly less than medium height. He put his faith in a 'stout heart and a thin pair of breeches'[4] and did very well for himself in the boom years of imperial growth. In the course of his work he met a young man whose sister, Annie Powell's, quiet charms Henry admired. They did not marry, for another business associate, Frederick Lassetter, also had a sister, Elizabeth, who was the most popular girl in Tasmania (where the family lived) and was 'surrounded at all times by friends and admirers',[5] of which Henry quickly became one of the most devoted. It was said that she was so beautiful she was obliged to wear a heavy veil when she went out rather than inflame the young men of the town.

Henry announced his intentions towards the young woman within a few days of meeting her but this alarmed the Lassetter family, for her father was a Baptist minister and Henry was, it appeared, 'non-committal about theology'[6] and only a lukewarm Christian. In the Lassetter household the family and servants met for communal worship four times a day—four times too often for Henry. Frederick, in answer to a request from his father to sound out this potential brother-in-law as regards his faith, reported back: 'He appears to think that as long as his actions accord with the Ten Command-ments he is all right . . . I can make nothing more of his religion than this.'[7] This lamentable want of Christianity distressed the Lasset-ters. Henry eventually held out a thin hope for his salvation by assuring them that he was progressing in faith but opined it would be the work of time before he became entirely devout. His persistence, however prevailed: he finally obtained the family's consent to the marriage.

Elizabeth Lassetter was known as 'Louey' to her family and friends. She was accustomed to being the centre of attention and to getting her own way. She did not enjoy the propriety expected of her during their engagement and confessed, in a note to her intended the day before the wedding, to having allowed 'every little thing'[8] to annoy her and hoped that marriage would cure her shortness of temper.

Over the years Henry was to become a deeply religious man, while his wife, once she was removed from the direct influence of her family, became a worldly woman with little time for a personal religion. Her inclination was for clerics rather than the Church, and she introduced them into her house just as her daughter, later, introduced them into her novels so that 'the twinkle of gaiters' became the novelist's trade mark.

As the Beauchamp family grew they moved from address to address in and around Sydney. Eventually they settled in a spacious mansion called 'Beulah' in Rose Bay, one of the smartest suburbs. It was a long, low, white house with slender-pillared verandas surrounded by smooth lawns and well-kept flowerbeds, while through the tall eucalyptus there was a fine view of the harbour. It was the house of every successful Australian's dream. There was also a family holiday home in Kiribilly Point on the west coast of New Zealand towards Paremata where May was born. Here the lilies grew so high that her father had to mow them down with a scythe.[9]

Frederick Lassetter and his wife Charlotte, May's uncle and aunt, had produced children at about the same rate as the Beauchamps, and the Beauchamp and Lassetter children were playmates for each other. The attachment was so close, indeed hermetic, that for a time when one family moved house the other was quick to follow, and Charlotte, having far more girls than boys, sent her eldest daughter, Emma, to live permanently with the Beauchamps to help with their offspring. In spite, or perhaps because of the closeness of the family ties, there was fierce competition between the two women centred on the affluence of their husbands and the number and gender of their children. The financial loss that Henry suffered when May was born set the Beauchamps at a disadvantage. As if to underline this the Lassetters, distancing themselves, moved to England later in the same year. It was to be three years before the Beauchamps could afford to follow.

During this time they were far from happy. Louey resented her repeated childbearing. She was not a strong woman, and her fecundity was no less an emotional than a physical strain on her. She had managed to keep her figure throughout six pregnancies (Charlotte Lassetter had not), but Louey knew there was a limit to the effectiveness of will-power and youthful elasticity. She decided that little May was to be her last child. Because there was no socially countenanced form of birth control at that time, the natural conse-quence of this decision was an estrangement between Louey and her husband on the sexual level of their married life. Henry was not pleased.

He had discovered, too late, that 'the cries of babies maddened him'. As his youngest daughter was later to write: 'He wasn't a man who ought ever to have had any children except grown-up ones.'[10] Added to this the whole family suffered repeated and sometimes severe illnesses and the house was more often like a children's hospital than a home. It is not surprising that Henry remained long hours at his office, renewed his friendship with Miss Annie Powell and was occasionally, especially after May's birth, seen in the company of the rather more boisterous ladies of the town.

As soon as the Lassetters had settled in England Frederick wrote to his brother-in-law urging him to bring his family there too, if only for a holiday.

> You cannot shut your eyes to the fact that both your own and Louey's health is unsatisfactory, [he wrote] and that your children have had more than their average share of indispositions ... You and I could occupy our time travelling. Louey and Chad [Charlotte] would enjoy themselves immensely together. You would find yourself a new man.[11]

By the time May had passed her third birthday Henry decided that a move to England would be feasible. If things went well he could set up an office in London and conduct his business just as, if not more, effectively from there. Louey was in favour of seeing more of the world. She missed her brother and sister-in-law and, besides, being a bigger fish than everybody else in Sydney had lost its glamour. She longed for that larger pond, England, in which she and her husband could make a splash.

In January 1870 Henry Beauchamp, his 'darling wife', his chil-dren, niece Emma Lassetter, Miss Miles the governess, Nurse Hoolohan and his father-in-law the Reverend Lassetter, set sail in the *Hogue*, a small, yellow, English sailing ship of 1,331 tons. Henry started writing a ship's log journal of events on the same day. He had taken the precaution of bringing with him, as Frederick had suggested, more than 'a few pint bottles of champagne' in case any of them should become low-spirited on the voyage.[12]

May was in sole care of Nurse Hoolohan, while Miss Miles attempted to keep charge of the other five children. May was fed, napped and promenaded according to a rigid Victorian schedule while her brothers were 'like so many monkeys over the ship', at least until they met heavy weather when all of them suffered badly from sea-sickness except 'May, the honest heart who never knew distress'.

In a few days the family began to recover and spoke facetiously of their 'growing retentive powers'. Soon they were able to eat without 'chucking up'. Their appetites grew so heartily that they found all of them could comfortably consume the less than generous rations provided, even to first-class passengers, on the long voyage, without quite dismissing the pangs of hunger. Henry was scandalized to discover that ham sandwiches were laid out last thing in the buffet for the ladies only. It was not long before the females in his party were provided with empty sponge bags and instructed to smuggle out as many sandwiches as they could to Henry and the ravenous boys waiting on the deck.

The weather turned extremely cold as they travelled eastward over the Pacific towards Cape Horn. The Suez Canal had only just been completed and was not yet in general use. The oldest child, Ralph or Rally as he was known, was just thirteen. Henry noticed that he was 'not entering into the spirit of things' at all but was quite doubled up with the cold and was crawling about, 'the picture of passive suffering'. Sydney, who was nine, looked in worse shape than Rally with a white face and glassy eyes, but his naturally high spirits buoyed him up. 'There must be something wrong with him,' his father noted in his journal. Henry was himself suffering from home-sickness more than anything else and longed repeatedly for 'an hour on the sunny side of George Street on a hot day'.

When Louey recovered her sea legs she regained much of her premarital vitality. The captain remarked to Henry his hope that her 'health would not improve further lest she should become unmanageable'. The day before, at dinner, she had lightheartedly fired off her napkin across the captain's table right into Miss Miles's face. But Louey continued to recover and engaged in ostentatious flirtation with the male members of the crew, to the point where an outraged elderly matron, a Mrs Plomers, openly accused her of improper relations with the captain. When challenged the matron protested, 'Well, certainly, Mrs Beauchamp, I thought it not improbable, considering your playful disposition.' Mrs Beauchamp's playful disposition had led her, the day before at the dinner table, to say out loud to the red-faced captain who had been indulging in some undercover footwork, 'If you love me say so, but don't dirty my stockings.'[13]

Henry's attention was taken up with the pursuit of Miss Annie Powell who, by chance or so it appeared, was also travelling on the same ship with two women friends. He was observed assiduously to cultivate their company, and Louey, pretending to be oblivious of her husband's friendships, enjoyed being 'perched' on the ship's railings and monopolized by the captain. Of Louey's behaviour, Henry commented in his journal: 'The less said about that the better.' Of Henry and Annie there is no comment available to the biographer, but there commenced during the voyage an irregular liaison between them which was to have repercussions for some years to come.

As the ship rounded Cape Horn it passed what looked, from a distance, like a small island covered with snow. On closer inspection it turned out to be a dead whale covered in seagulls. At the same time the Beauchamps were attending a burial service for a young man called Mr Butler. He had been sent to Australia by his family and had caught a cold on the voyage out which became severe and developed into pneumonia as soon as he arrived in Sydney. It was felt the best thing for him would be to return home and die, as he was clearly going to do, in the arms of his mother. Unfortunately the return voyage was too much for him, and the crew and first-class passengers watched him weaken and perish. Champagne eased him on his way. 'I have just had two nice little naps, my last on earth,' he announced and, to nobody's surprise, expired a quarter of an hour later 'without any struggle or pain'. At the burial service, while the body, declared by the second mate to look 'every inch a corpse' was consigned to the deep, six-year-old Harry turned to his father and cried cheerfully, 'He's gone.' Sydney was more solemnly impressed and little May piped her first recorded words over the silent prayers for the young man's soul, 'Pa, are him bellied?' She was somewhat indignant for, to her, a burial had something to do with holes in the ground. More than sixty years later she was to write, 'My life has been dotted with tombstones.'[14] This was her first experience of death.

After the funeral the usual evening card games were, by common consent, suspended out of respect for the deceased Mr Butler. More serious methods of passing the time were contemplated 'so as to be comparatively unhappy and proper'.[15] The captain therefore had an uproarious wrestling match at his end of the table instead which resulted in bruises for Louey, and her daughter Charlotte nearly had her arm broken.

Three days later Harry caught scarlet fever. There was no way of isolating him from the other children other than by keeping him in his cabin, but the passengers took the situation calmly. Mrs Plomers was certain that her grandson Shakto had caught it and was overheard to say that she would be thankful if he 'took the disease off a respectable child'. On whether she considered Harry to be respectable or not she did not comment, but her respect for the charismatic Henry Beauchamp clearly overrode her disapproval of his wife's conduct. She demonstrated her feelings by strapping herself, one stormy night, to his cabin door handle, declaring that she only felt safe when she was near him. Henry remained meanwhile fearfully in his bunk hoping she wasn't going to insist on joining him there for the duration of the tempest. Eventually she was escorted back to her cabin by the captain and the first mate.

May took very little part in all these shipboard dramas but spent her time playing with another little girl of her own age called Toady. So close did Toady become to the Beauchamps that she soon began to call Henry 'Pa'. She came from a family of staunch Roman Catholics and was 'remarkably quick'. Henry was incautious enough to ask her, after the funeral, whether she considered that Butler's soul would be judged at once or would it stand over till the Final Resurrection, and if the latter, would it be conscious of the intervening time? (Henry considered this a more pleasant way of starting a conversation than a remark about the weather.) Toady opined that Butler's soul would remain in Purgatory 'quite a good time' before it would be ready for judgement. She then expatiated about the Roman Catholic faith in general and suggested a few Protestant objections which had not occurred to Henry, answering them herself. She talked 'like a book' on the Pope's infallibility, immaculate conception, transubstantiation, celibacy of the priesthood and Purgatory. Henry was dumbfounded. The first mate, seeing that he was getting the worst of the conversation, tried to stand up for Henry. The poor man was told by Toady that she was not arguing with *him*, and she recommended him 'not to talk on subjects of which he was evidently ignorant'. After about an hour they all concluded by exchanging compliments. Henry said that he hoped that he and Toady might meet again in the next world as he felt they already must have done 'in some other'.

May witnessed this exchange with amazement. Although she was by far the most intelligent child in her family, she was to suffer all her life from an inexplicable sense of intellectual inferiority and it is possible that this may have had its origin on the voyage to England. The experience of spending more than three months in the company of such a stupendously precocious child of her own age may have left an indelible mark on her budding personality.

As if to underline Toady's opinion about the fate of Butler's soul, strange and unaccountable noises were heard round the mizzen mast on two successive nights. The ladies flew into a state of hysteria and the children declared their intention of lying in wait for the ghost to appear the following night. But the noises were never heard again.

At the end of March, with still four weeks to go before the ship was due to dock in London, one of the passengers in steerage produced a female child. May was profoundly puzzled that such a thing could happen at sea. Boats were not equipped with parsley-beds (the Beauchamp equivalent of the gooseberry bush). Her perplexity was assuaged when it was explained to her that the baby had arrived in the night on the back of an enormous flying fish. This, she was told, was the custom at sea.

'Ships do arrive home sometimes, and perhaps ours will,' she remarked when they were still a week away from docking. So long had they been at sea that she had despaired of ever seeing land again.

One miserable afternoon, a few days before disembarkation, the group at the captain's table drifted into riddle-making. One of them in particular May was to remember and puzzle over. Henry recorded it in his journal: 'When is a ship wisely in love, foolishly in love and insanely in love? Answer: When she is tender to a man of war; when she is attached to a buoy, and when she is hankering after a swell.' It is significant that in later life May was to fall in love three times: with a soldier, with a young man nearly thirty years her junior, and with an earl.

· 2 ·

Cinderella

The Beauchamp family had been at sea for three and a half months when the *Hogue* docked in the Thames on a bitterly cold day in April. The family disembarked and were delighted, after such a long sea voyage, to be back on dry land. They travelled through London to Belsize Park, where they had been invited to stay with the Lassetters until they had found a place of their own. The cabs went in procession through miles of 'astonishing streets'[1] trimmed, as they came out of the city, with trees and shrubs decked in their spring leaves. Nobody but Henry had ever seen anything like it before.

A few days later Rally came down with scarlet fever, and Chad Lassetter despatched her own children to lodgings in Blackheath. Henry began to wish they were all back in Sydney: 'We feel ourselves like cuckoos having taken possession of other birds' nests,' he wrote in his journal. Louey drew some comfort from the fashionable theory that the diseases one was likely to contract depended on the class one travelled: first class provided the risk of scarlet fever, which was considered, therefore, a respectable disease, and second class that of measles. Third-class travellers caught smallpox.

In the second week of May the family officially took possession of a furnished house at 1, New West End, Finchley Road, Hampstead, where they bought a twelve-month lease for £250.* As none of the other children caught the fever, they quickly settled down to enjoy a perfect English spring. Henry was able to explore the countryside which he had known so well as a boy, and May accompanied him on these nostalgic rambles when she was invited. None of the boys had any desire to take more exercise than was necessary and she soon became her father's sole and preferred companion, developing a taste for exploration which was never to leave her. Sometimes their

*£5,600, in today's terms.

walks took them in the direction of the nearby home of Miss Annie
Powell and May enjoyed these visits.

In June Henry took the family to church at Child's Hill where the
preacher appeared in a skull cap which made little May stare. In
answer to her father's inquiry, as they walked home, as to how she
had liked him, May quietly replied, 'Him's a rum one, Pa.' This was
certainly, in her father's opinion, as good a definition as could be
given of 'the queer looking, lugubrious old frog' whose discourse was
almost entirely made up of assurances that the congregation were
intended to groan through their three score and ten years on this
earth.

Louey rarely accompanied her husband on these family outings
for she was afflicted with a series of mysterious infirmities. The fact
that Henry had openly set up his mistress, Miss Powell, in a house in
Hampstead did nothing to improve his wife's health. She was
constantly attended by doctors but her ailments were never
diagnosed to her satisfaction. On the contrary, the doctors could
hardly ever find anything wrong with her and were unanimous in
declaring her to be ten years younger than her age and healthier than
most. Henry noted in his journal, 'Our coming is a fine thing for the
medical profession . . . Dr Brown called this morning and I succeeded by brilliant strategic movements in keeping him off Louey
and saved me [sic] various guineas.' His suspicions as to the
imaginary, if not strategic, nature of her indispositions deepened
when one Sunday evening they left 'poor Louey' at home too ill to
accompany the family to St Paul's and then out to dinner. When they
returned home unexpectedly they found her in 'full fig' and waiting
for a brougham she had ordered to drive out in herself. 'Much
pleased by such a change for the better,' was her husband's ironic
comment. But Louey, for all her wilful behaviour, was always able to
placate him. May recalled that her father 'couldn't for long with-
stand her sweet twining ways and found the prospect that she should
ever, even temporarily, cease to twine intolerable'.[2]

If Louey suffered from hypochondria, May, in reaction, was to be
remarkably free from this condition or indeed indispositions of any
kind. Her own or, later, her children's she treated with recommenda-
tions to vigorous exercise. In extreme cases she prescribed a liberal
dose of castor oil. Resorting to sofas as a method of dealing with the
problems of life was a habit she energetically opposed and in her
novel The Pastor's Wife, which was published in 1914, May was to
expose the relationship between a married woman and her sofa with
her mother in mind: 'It was respectable; it was unassailably effec-

tive; it was not included in the Commandments. All she had to do was to cling to it, and nobody could make her be or do anything.'

One morning May, snuggled in her mother's bed, calmly requested her to turn over a new leaf and get better. Her startled parent asked her who had taught her that expression. 'Well, Ma,' May replied, 'Pierce [a former nurse] said "You must turn over a new leaf and be better children," so, Ma, I got a new leaf and turned it and turned it, but I never got any better at all.' Persevering, she asked her mother to get up and go to church with them. Louey said she would stay in bed and nurse herself. 'But Ma, how can you do that? How can you nurse yourself better?'[3] said May, her sole idea of nursing being to be a baby in another's arms. To May as a child her mother was mysteriously frail, an object of solicitude by whose helplessness all others were rendered helpless also.

Louey worried her youngest daughter with her undiagnosable indispositions, but there were other times when she would recover with astonishing rapidity, for her natural gaiety could not remain dulled for very long. With the selective memory of adulthood May recalled that her mother was 'a happy, adorable little creature' and described her affectionately as 'singing through the years, always crowded round with friends and admirers'.[4] There were parties and outings and both Henry and Louey often disappeared on visits to the country to stay with friends or simply to explore while the children remained behind under the iron rule of Miss Miles. When their parents returned, Henry declared 'a solemn general holiday' and the children, accompanied by Miss Miles and sometimes by their father, would be taken to visit a museum or the Houses of Parliament or the Zoo. Once they went to the Cattle Show and were delighted and charmed with the 'immense, comfortable, warm, fat things', especially the pigs, 'both ends alike'.[5]

There were always jokes currently in favour. During the summer of 1871 all of the children were marched around the Royal Academy summer show. One riddle that caused special merriment was: 'Why do Royal Academicians surpass Solomon in Glory? Answer: Because Solomon in all his glory was not R A'd like one of these.'

Every so often Henry used to gather all of his children around him, close his eyes and pretend to be dead. They would then have to prove that they would know exactly what to do if he actually had died, finding his will and the relevant papers. As he was an exceedingly neat man this was not very difficult. Even in the dark he could find anything he wanted in his tidy desk.

The winter of that year was a hard one and Henry confessed to feeling pinched and inclined to think of orange groves in Australia. The Thames disappointed the children by not freezing over entirely, but there were dangerous ice floes which they enjoyed watching from Tower Bridge. The whole family skated on Hampstead Pond and were delighted to observe the jollity with which an unusual weather condition infected the phlegmatic British soul. Henry had not been skating since boyhood when he and his brothers had occasionally slithered round on the same pond. Now he sustained minor tumbles and one serious one which bruised his hip, elbow and temple. His anxiety that his ribs might be broken elicited scant sympathy from the others. To see such a normally very upright man as Henry Beauchamp sprawled with helpless indignity on the ice was an awesome sight. 'Louey, Chad and the children were vastly amused with the scene on the pond,' he recorded painfully in his journal that evening.

The following August the children helped to rake in the hay from the fields that surrounded their house, and May worked alongside the others trying her best to keep up with them. She sometimes came home feverish after her long hot day in the blazing sun, a condition her father described as 'hay fever'. It was then that she began to have nightmares and irrational fears which were to torture her young mind for three years. She woke up every night 'and shivered for two or three hours, sick with fright and very cold'. She feared 'The Crack of Doom' which her nurse had told her would usher in the Last Day. 'And the Last Day,' said the nurse, 'might be expected to begin any night.'[6] May lay awake, trembling in abject misery, waiting to hear the Crack, sure it would be the most horrible bang, her ears stuffed with as much of her stockings as would go in besides her fingers. For ever after thunder storms were the only things that could profoundly frighten her.

The other children teased May once they realized that she believed everything she was told. She quickly discovered that her only defence lay in inventing even more fabulous stories with which to confound them. Miss Miles's strict guardianship of the Truth prevented this game from leaking out of the schoolroom and into their everyday lives, but even so May was inclined, in later years, to indulge herself in what E.M. Forster was to describe as 'an enlarged bunkum of one kind or another'.[7] She would insist, lightheartedly, that something was true even though it was clearly absurd, often prolonging the joke for days.

Henry and May continued on their rambles and these often included visits to two Stone aunts, sisters of Henry's mother. Both were extremely elderly but as spry as twenty-five-year-olds, and they still lived in Highgate, though Henry's parents were long since dead. These aunts pronounced May to be 'a quaint . . . peculiar little thing . . . an objectionable . . . pert, unlovable child.'[8] One day May and her father came home from their house damp from a sudden rain shower and the following morning both had developed croup. They remained 'crouped up and unhappy'[9] for the better part of a week. It was then that Henry decided that the family needed clear mountain air for their general health, which was still bad, and their well-being, which was unstable. The lease of the Finchley Road establishment was due to expire the following spring and the winter was spent in intermittent European studies. They planned to spend a year in Switzerland and, if their health improved, the following year in France and the year after that in Germany. Louey was overjoyed, for Miss Powell was to remain behind in Hampstead.

Henry decided that travel was to be tutor to his children; it had broadened his own mind and he was determined that it should do the same for his sons. His education had taught him nothing that had ever come in useful in his business but had on the contrary, he considered, caused him much unnecessary misery. He determined that his own sons should not suffer in the same way. The fashionable public schools of the rich, he decided, produced men 'too learned for any business avocation'. His sons should not be hampered by such unwanted baggage in the merchant careers he had chosen for them. The education of Charlotte and May did not, of course, concern him. They would marry no doubt and for that no learning was required, indeed it was a hindrance in the acquisition of a suitable husband. It was mere luck that because Henry chose to educate his sons at home, May was exposed to a higher standard in the schoolroom than the average middle-class daughter of the Empire.

Europe was at peace and a treasury of the culture that Henry was determined his children should have an opportunity to absorb. New railways had recently been completed, making family travel in Europe considerably easier. Money was running low but Henry had the financial optimism of a self-made man: he assumed that having made one fortune, he could easily make another. Louey, though by nature extravagant, was more practical. She had many natural anxieties about the future and was not slow to put them up for discussion.

The family, niece Emma, Miss Miles, three maids and a friend of Sydney's set out for Switzerland in May 1872. The fourteen of them, baggage-laden and high-spirited, made their way to Cannon Street

Station in a convoy of horse-drawn hansom cabs. Henry described in his journal a 'thrilling scene' when the train very nearly left without Louey, and she was cheered by the whole party as she leapt on to the moving train. They had a safe passage to Ostend although most of them were sick, and arrived at Brussels in the evening 'in fairly good order'. The next day at Heidelberg they dogged the German station-master, who could not speak a word of English, up and down the long platform looking for a carriage. The train was full of people who 'appeared greatly amused'. Henry stuck close behind the belea-guered official, repeating continually in his ear *'Basel—direkt—Familie'*, with the rest of the tribe following in a file. Every few minutes he shouted over his shoulder, 'Family, back me up.' The wretched station-master finally got tired of it and turned an old lady out of a first-class carriage, in which the party travelled comfortably to Basel in spite of having only second-class tickets.

When they at last arrived in Lausanne they quickly found and moved into an old wooden-balconied chalet on the outskirts of the town. It was called Mont Rhynchite and was rented, fully staffed, for 5,500* Swiss francs for the year. Louey, happy and braced by the powerful mountain air, departed from tradition by remaining upright during the move and supervised the allocation of rooms and the unpacking of bags. Four days later the Lassetters, with their six children, arrived to stay. When the bustle of settling in had died down Henry concluded in his journal that they were 'not in at all a bad place'. The atmosphere was delightful, the temperature was hot during the day but wonderfully cool in the evenings and they were surrounded by charming fields, trees, hedges and wild flowers.

They enjoyed unbroken views of the lake and mountains and unbroken health for exactly two weeks, when Rally, Charlotte and 'poor little May' were put to bed with a rash. The next day the doctor found them with swollen throats, 'more or less deaf' and the rash red and irritable. The swollen throats and deafness were diagnosed as resulting from chills and the rash from eating too many cherries. Having delivered himself of this verdict the doctor pocketed his fee and left.

Almost every day the children who were not indisposed went out on hilarious sightseeing excursions and it was only on wet days that they were forced to absorb some learning in the schoolroom. Miss Miles, in sole charge of the overstimulated crowd of youngsters, fought a losing battle to gain their attention. The Lassetters eventu-

*= £400 in today's terms.

ally moved into a chalet nearby but even so the rioting did not cease. The general holiday atmosphere made the children boisterous and to teach them anything at all was almost impossible. Miss Miles complained loudly to Henry and pointed out that Ralph and Sydney were the worst offenders. This normally patient and devoted woman was prepared to resign her post unless the boys were sent elsewhere to be educated. Faced with a governess in such a distraught condition, Henry was obliged to swallow his theories and agreed to send the boys to school. They were enrolled without delay in a Swiss day school in Lausanne called L'Ecole Industrielle Nationale.

The unhappiness of the brothers, who were forced to attend school every day and acquire an education in a language they hardly understood under a regime which they comprehended not at all, was a warning to the others. The Lassetter family moved further away, to the Château de Coppet, a much grander place than the Beauchamps could afford, and Charlotte, Walter and Harry were alone in the schoolroom. It was agreed that May should join them. Although she was nearly six, she had had no formal schooling at all until then. Soon, learning to write, she 'was seen concentrating for the first time her ability on strokes'. The rest of the time she was extremely naughty and nearly made up, in nuisance value, for the departed troublemakers. Her brother Harry's cry of *'Poonisez-la,'* at regular intervals became a family joke.

As a tribute to Henry's theories, or perhaps because of them, L'Ecole Industrielle Nationale was nearly fatal for the two older boys. Rally refused to eat and began to waste away, while Sydney, the most sensitive of the boys, collapsed. The doctor diagnosed 'brain fever' and was doubtful if the boy would survive. Henry, who was away in London at the time arranging some business affairs, also became critically ill with rheumatic fever, and was nursed with great care and devotion by Miss Annie Powell at her house in Hampstead. As soon as Louey's frantic telegram arrived containing the bad news, Henry and Annie drove to his doctor who absolutely forbade Henry to travel. Louey, who had got wind of Annie's devotions, began to fire off a battery of letters and telegrams full of scoldings and dire warnings of what would become of them all if Henry did not get back soon to Switzerland. When at last his doctor allowed him to travel he arrived to find his wife 'not worn and thin' as he had feared, and Sydney very much on the mend. In fact there was no reason at all for him to have cut short his stay in London which had been undertaken in the first place to allay Louey's anxieties about money. But Louey 'never tired of recounting poor dear little Sydney's tortures, ravings and resignations and how they all prayed for his death [*sic*] which seemed so imminent'.[10]

When Sydney was out of danger Henry and Louey set off for a prolonged tour of Europe accompanied by Fred and Chad Lassetter. The quartet explored Italy thoroughly and arrived in Naples in time to witness the eruption of Vesuvius. Henry made for Pompeii while the others fled to the safety of Naples. He found the ossified town much enhanced 'by the red glow and perpetual roar of the volcano close by' as it threw up a 'great column of smoke and stones and ashes while hissing jets of steam burst forth from various parts of the cone'. That night the four travellers arranged themselves to sleep in heroic attitudes so that when they were dug up after eighteen centuries or so they might make 'a creditable show for their generation'.[11]

The party arrived back to discover the family in an apprehensive state. Charlotte had some momentous news to impart. She was, she confessed through tears and hysteria, expecting a baby. For a fifteen-year-old unmarried girl to become pregnant would be distressing in the latter part of the twentieth century, but in the 1870s it was a calamity. When Louey had recovered from the shock she joined Henry and Miss Miles in their deep distress and could only be thankful that they were not in England and that the family shame could be hidden from the wagging tongues of her friends. The identity of the father was obviously confessed along with the stupendous news of their beautiful daughter's downfall, for there is no perplexity on that point in the family papers, but neither is it revealed. The probability is that one of the Lassetter boys or their friends was the culprit. The acute little May was aware of the crisis that the family was suffering but was merely puzzled that such a natural event could cause such an unnatural reaction in her beloved parents. A riddle rather cruelly in vogue in the family was: 'Why do modern young women resemble Pharisees? Answer: Because they appear unto men too fast.'

Not wishing to be a witness to his daughter's shame, Henry made immediate plans to travel around the world, a long-cherished and now convenient ambition. For the following year the family continued entirely 'unsupervised and unregimented'. May remembered this time some sixty years later when she was writing her autobiography, *All the Dogs of My Life*, where she remembered that the moment he had left everything and everybody relaxed: 'Queer how sprightly life became, how roomy, with what wide margins.' Instead of worrying about her manners and watching her p's and q's she 'ceased to mind or watch anything'. Louey bloomed in her grass widowhood, for Annie Powell had remained safely in Hampstead. Whatever May asked for her mother simply laughed and kissed her and gave her, for she knew that her husband was still receding and not going to turn his face homewards for another six months. Her letters to him gave no hint of the sudden ease that everyone in the household was experiencing while he was away. They contrived to make him believe that while he was enjoying himself, she was left weak, lonely and defenceless, bravely shouldering the heavy burden of all the domestic responsibilities. But May's effervescent and mercurial mother had a strong practical side to her nature which her youngest daughter was, fortunately, to inherit. Louey's anxieties about the financial future of the family increased and she was not slow to put this to her husband in her letters. She had not been gifted with his optimism which appeared to grow as the money decreased. Her upbringing had been that of a careful cleric's daughter while Henry had grown up in cheerful poverty. Carelessness for material wealth and the glorification of the romantic vagabond life had been cultivated by his father, and fostered by his friendship with painters and writers. Paradoxically Henry put it forward as one of the explanations for his own success in life, which was an unusual view of the world for a well-to-do Victorian middle-class merchant. In answer to his wife's pitiful letters he wrote urging her not to be despondent about their uncertain future: 'I say it is brightly, gloriously and delightfully uncertain.' He chided her for not yet being 'a properly converted woman' and promised, generously, that as soon as he had 'sown his wild oats' he would settle down and make his way in the world. 'Do not imagine,' he told her unnecessarily, 'that wealth confers happiness.'[12]

May, in the meantime, was in a state of blissful happiness. Those times she was turned out at eleven o'clock in the morning to romp among the buttercups and daisies, a piece of bread sprinkled with sugar in her hand, were the most exquisitely and intensely happy moments of her childhood, indeed of her whole life. These two simple flowers became for her emblems of freedom and happiness. She rarely did any school work, and perfected the art of seeming to have spent all morning learning her French verbs or doing her copy-book work when she had been romping, writing stories or simply dreaming. She practised her scales in the last twenty minutes of each afternoon so that when Mademoiselle arrived in the school room from her rest she would find her pupil at the piano, 'pigtails vibrating with diligence'.[13]

Charlotte produced a baby boy in March. As soon as Henry received the news in a doleful letter from his wife he set his sights for home. Whether the child died or lived to be fostered is not on record. He was never mentioned again. Most likely, as was the custom, he was reared by a peasant family who were glad of a small income for their pains. It was not until after the event that May realized something was very wrong. Charlotte had been a gay, fearless young woman. She was also beautiful, much more beautiful than May would ever be, with red-gold hair that reached to her heels. '[Charlotte] was [May] grown tall, grown exquisite, [May] wrought wonderfully in ivory and gold,' she was to write of her sister in *The Pastor's Wife*. 'No man could possibly fall in love with [May] while there before his very eyes was exactly the same girl, only translated into loveliness.' Many people were drawn to Charlotte for this reason and because of her sweet nature. May knew from a very early age that she herself would have to rely on wit and an unusual attitude to life to be noticed at all. Now that Charlotte had lived through the ordeal of bearing an illegitimate child and of having to part with it she had changed. She became tentative, nervous and unable to make up her mind about anything. Her faith in herself had been shattered, and she appeared then to her young sister like a rudderless ship adrift, without sails or an anchor. Her manner became cloying and sugary-sweet to hide a deep bitterness within her.

Henry arrived back in September 1873. He was delighted to be home again and decided 'Lausanne is, after all, the true earthly paradise.'[14] Louey's anxieties about the baby, money and the family were evidently laid to rest on the night of the reunion. At three o'clock in the morning they stirred up poor Emma to get them cold chicken and claret which she served in their bedroom and afterwards they unpacked trunks till dawn.

The family settled back into the paternally dominated structure with p's and q's being minded by all of them. There were more parties and expeditions and everybody enjoyed the winter-sporting for which Switzerland was not yet famous. The idyll could not last, however, and in February the Beauchamp children and three of the Lassetters went down with measles. Henry's dislike of illness, which had grown steadily over the years, sped him on a journey through France, while Louey, her friends gathering around her like moths to a flame, yet again played her part of the abandoned wife and noble mother to the full.

When Henry returned he took the family back to London. He had sown his wild oats, as he put it, and a more mature look at the family fortunes caused him at last to have some qualms. Louey was so delighted that her husband was showing signs of taking life, or anyway money, seriously again that any objections or reservations she might have had about the proximity of Miss Powell were put to one side. August 1874 was the last month of their stay in Switzerland. It passed in a frenzy of last-minute sightseeing, farewell parties and visits. At the end of it Louey left for England with the women of the party, Charlotte, May, Emma and a French maid, and Henry and the boys followed a few days later. All were exhausted by pleasure-seeking and ready, at last, to apply themselves to sterner business.

The family settled into Mayfield Lodge in Southgate, on the outskirts of north-west London. The Lassetters, as always, took a house nearby. Sydney, or 'Sinner' as he was now called because he was so good, Harry and Walter were sent to University College School in Frognal where their father had been a student before them. Charlotte, who was sixteen, and May, who was eight, went to Blythwood House. Here they learned Latin, French, German and Italian and were able to attend lectures on natural philosophy, geology and botany. Also on the curriculum were pianoforte, harp, American singing, elocution, drawing, dancing and callisthenics. May, who had perfect pitch, took violin lessons privately.

In October it was May's turn to come down with scarlet fever. It was a mild attack but she had to be isolated and Emma Lassetter was to act as her nurse. Henry took four rooms at 6, Mount Vernon, at 35/- (shillings) a week furnished. Henry noted in his journal: 'We are surprised and amused at the horror people have of contagion. We are tabood [sic] and shut out from all our friends. We can visit no one and nobody visits us. We begin to feel quite ashamed of ourselves.' May was at first delighted with her new status. Her mother went with her to the isolation ward, kissed her 'violently' and then came home and kissed all the other children. May and Emma were away three whole months during which time her father saw May only once, gloomily gazing through the window as he passed by. When they returned, May was mercilessly teased by the boys because she had become extremely fat. She was so mortified that she concentrated all her energies on regaining her original slimness and in future she was to regard being fat, whether in herself or others, as akin to, if not worse than, being wicked. That Christmas the family sent out cards which said, 'A merry Bronchitis to you and a happy Scarlet Fever when it comes.' Henry recorded in his journal: 'Merry Christmas and friends and relatives is all humbug here. It is the season par excellence which nearly all elderly, long-loved relations, and many young ones, choose for dying, or at least for getting alarmingly ill.'

During May's absence Charlotte had been presented at court and was caught up in the 'season'. She began to entertain a gentleman caller called George Waterlow, the son of Sir Sydney Waterlow of Waterlow & Son, City stationers.* He was an eccentric young man but very much enamoured of Charlotte. He would one day be very rich and it was considered that he and Charlotte would make a fine match, he being kept ignorant of her previous amorous adventure.

When Ralph was eighteen and ready to be inducted into the world of business, he began work in the offices of Shepheard & Co., tea brokers of Great Tower Street for 'nothing a week and find himself'. In other words he was paid nothing in wages and had to pay for his own food and travel.

Henry began to contemplate plans to set up an office in the City for a new shipping business and it soon became clear that he would have to return to Australia to look up his old business contacts. On the way there and back, since there was no great urgency, he decided that he might as well make another round-the-world odyssey, this time from North to South as his previous one had been from West to East. He was away for nine months. May remembered his return vividly, possibly even to the point of exaggeration.

Unfortunately, the first letter Henry opened after his homecoming was a bill for a hundred pounds from Marshall & Snelgrove—for ribbons. The house vibrated with his 'frenzied incredulity' and even Louey, 'the adventurous little buyer of ribbons', found it advisable to take to the tips of her toes. But even in an atmosphere 'thick with sulphur'[15] she managed more quickly than most wives would have to clear it away.

A week later, having by that time recovered from the contents of his mail, Henry announced his scheme for 'settling to business' in London.[16] There was great consequent joy. Life began to move at a more sedately suburban pace, with Henry attending his office in the City, Louey passing the time with female acquaintances, and regular family musical evenings. George Waterlow, in an uncharacteristic fit of generosity, gave May a dog. In her autobiography, *All the Dogs of my Life* she remembered that for the short time that it took him to court and marry Charlotte, she was allowed to keep it. Why it was allowed into the family circle she did not know, except that in the

*Waterlow & Son were later to print bank notes for the Bank of England. Both Sir Sydney and his son George were knighted for their services in this field.

general atmosphere there was 'extreme good will and indulgence'. May was not allowed to keep the dog for much beyond the wedding day. Her father did not like dogs and her mother was 'too pretty, too busy with her admirers' to have any time left over for noticing, or even being aware of, 'such of her fellow-pilgrims' that had more than two legs.

In old age Charlotte was to remember with horror how May had been neglected by her parents and downtrodden, ignored and teased by the rest of the family. May was the Cinderella: always last; always forgotten and always wearing the cast-off clothes from her sister and the Lassetter girls. When the time came for May to 'come out', an expensive and wearisome business for the mother involving much chaperoning, Louey decided she could give no time to it. It was assumed that 'poor lonely little May', with her quaint ideas, would never make a brilliant match and therefore little was done then to find her a husband. May stayed at home and sat by the fire.[17]

May was later to attribute her 'slender little talent', as she always referred to her writing ability, to having been the youngest member of a large and noisy family. She called it her 'apartness in the family' and, being a girl after three boys who were 'as thick as thieves' with each other, she had every reason to feel separate and different.[18] She found that however arresting she contrived her comments and jokes to be, no one wanted to listen, and she perfected her art of lightning repartee at this early stage in her life. She was teased so much by her brothers, all but Sydney whom she adored, that she became a private child. Her life was thick with secrets like that of many other writers, for there is an eloquence which arises directly from a passion for concealment.

Charlotte and George married in August 1876, and took a house called Beaufort in Edmonton. A month later the Beauchamps moved into a house nearby called Tanner's Hall. That same year Sydney was apprenticed to the Waterlow firm 'to learn the art and mystery of a stationer'. Before this he had been taken to a Harley Street doctor to be tested for 'weakness of the brain', a condition his parents feared he may have sustained as a result of his brain fever because he found it difficult to remember things. The specialist pronounced him 'fit and sound',[19] but he left the stationery business a year later. He had set his heart on becoming a doctor and, encouraged by May, he began his medical training in Cambridge. Because of his difficulty and his erratic early education, his first years of medicine were painful and his frequent failures to pass preliminary exams heart-breaking. May's faith in him gave him the strength to persevere and he eventually became one of the most sought-after doctors in London, and finally gynaecologist to Queen Victoria.

Harry, the youngest boy in the family, was employed in his father's firm, but it was not a happy arrangement. He thought of returning to Australia, but his health was delicate and his parents decided that he should go to the country and work on a farm to build up his strength. He took a 'cello along with him and practised enough, for want of other distractions, to be able to join in the family musical evenings when he came home. May, then eleven years old, accompanied him on the piano and discovered he had a beautiful singing voice. She took him to sing before Sir Walter Parratt, who was at that time teaching her the organ, and Sir Walter passed him along to sing to Sir George Grove, musician and author of the dictionary. Sir George sent him to Signor Visetti at the Royal College of Music. So, 'Harry abandons his intention of emigrating to Australia and will stay at home and cultivate his voice. General joy consequent on his not leaving us,' Henry wrote in his journal. He was to become a professor at the London Academy of Music and was teaching there when his cousin Katherine Mansfield attended for 'cello lessons during her school days at Queen's College in Harley Street. Finally Harry was to become head of the London School of Music.*

Charlotte, meanwhile, made legitimate grandparents of Henry and Louey by producing a baby girl in May 1877, a previous child, born a few weeks after the wedding, having died at birth. In June this baby, christened Zoë, also died, having ailed with an illness that none of the doctors could identify. 'Suppressed scarlet fever' and 'something else' was as near as any of them could agree upon as a diagnosis.

Walter was apprenticed to a wool broker's office in London and finally went back to Australia. May emerged as the steadying force in the family at this time. By 1880 she was the only child still at school. In 1881 the Beauchamps moved house again to a spacious Georgian residence called East Lodge in Acton. It was situated on the Uxbridge Road opposite Twyford Avenue, then little more than a country lane. It was a square brick house with a prominent double-storey bow at the front. Full-length sash windows on the ground floor looked on to a wide stone terrace shaded by Regency wrought-iron balustrades. The spacious garden was encumbered with dilapidated

*Harry was known in the family, for some mysterious reason, as De Monk and was Katherine's official guardian in England while she was under age.

greenhouses, outbuildings and rotting fences when they first moved in. On three sides was a park newly planted with young trees.

Life became relatively staid and dull for the fifteen-year-old May. Her father was almost completely occupied with his business affairs and her mother was surrounded by a circle of friends now exclusively female. Henry called them her 'feminines' and fled from them into his study whenever he could. May was taken out on visits to elderly relatives, flower shows and galleries. There is an intriguing entry in her father's journal: 'Had race with May. She kept up most pluckily but on the tenth round we were stopped by the police [Louey].' The parent for whom p's and q's had to be minded appears now to have been her mother. There is no further mention of Miss Annie Powell.

Louey progressed from female friends to a revived interest in the Church, and May and Sydney were, at the same time, passing through an intensely religious phase. Henry found the house swarming with clergy, 'attendant frumps', choir boys, mission meetings and Sunday-school infants who were given their religious instruction by May. It was during this period that May became the authority on the clergymen who were to make so many comic appearances in her novels. Her own religious feelings grew profound, and as they did so the worldly ambitions of the local clergy came to appear to her ridiculous. 'If ever she wanted to write about someone and make fun of them, she would turn him into a pastor or a bishop,' was the opinion of one of her friends, 'she was influenced by Trollope in that way.'[20] But her religious fervour at this time could not be dimmed even by the clergy. She began then and continued for the rest of her life, according to her daughter later, to respond to:

> . . . the inexplicit aspirations of cathedral buildings, the
> dimly felt assurances of sacred music, and those vaguer
> portions of the scriptures that are equal inspiration to poet
> and saint. It was from their inherent, impersonal beauty
> rather than any message they might convey that she
> would, in later years, draw consolation in times of indeci-
> sion and despair.[21]

When May was an elderly woman she revisited the church, All Saints, in Acton where the family had worshipped: 'Really a little jewel of a church, and quite worth the ecstatic joy I poured into it from fourteen to seventeen,' she wrote. 'It seemed beautiful to me with memories of youth and quivering holiness.'[22] She knelt and tried to pray in each of the places in which she had formerly sat, but the exaltation and joyful piety she had experienced as a young girl eluded her.

Side by side with these sublime and spiritual yearnings worldly passions began to make themselves felt. She describes her first infatuation thus: 'I only began to be shocked by the blackness of my nails the day I began to lose the first whiteness of my soul by falling in love, at fifteen, with the parish organist . . .'[23] It was the first glimpse, so she says, of surplice and Roman nose and fiery moustache, all she could see of him from where she sat in church, that did the trick. She loved him 'to distraction' for at least six months. She declared that it was her own snobbery which terminated the attachment, for meeting him in the street one day when she was with her governess she was so shocked by his unofficial garb—a frock coat combined with a turn-down collar and a bowler hat—that she never loved him again. It is much more likely that her parents got wind of the affair and put a stop to it. May's astrological chart indicates that the man she became fond of at that time in her life was the one she should have married, and several of her novels deal nostalgically with the plight of a young woman such as herself married to a parson or a lowly cleric.

In 1882, when she was sixteen, May was sent to Queen's College School in Horn Lane, Acton, run by a Miss Summerhayes. She was thought to be a generally indifferent, easily distracted student until then, but Miss Summerhayes was an inspiring teacher and soon May started to take a real interest in her studies. A school friend, Miss Celena Joscelyne, who was two years younger than May, developed a *Schwärmerei*, or crush, for her. She remembered her as being 'a very small person with long fair hair tied at the nape of the neck with a ribbon. She had blue eyes and a brilliant colour.' She also recalled that a particular essay May wrote about flowers in the Senior Certificate public examination of 1883 moved her examiner to outspoken enthusiasm. In July Henry entered in his journal: 'May glorified by coming out first in a history examination against all Ealing schools.' He added that compared with her three brothers, of whom at any one time only one was able to attend school, 'May was hardly ever ill.' One of the jokes currently in vogue in the family was: 'Why is a woman's wit like a telegraph? Answer: Because it is ahead of the mail in intelligence.'[24] Henry had never insisted that his children attend school if they could come up with a plausible excuse not to. May's robustness of health, however, was a reality. She was hardly ever ill during her adult lifetime and rarely visited a doctor. She often attributed this and her high spirits to a sound stomach and a clear conscience.

In 1883 the lease of East Lodge was renewed for another five years, for the Beauchamps found they were very happy there. The 'feminines' were going 'rather violently to church' and May still taught a Sunday school. One of her queries to the class, 'Why did they strew palm in the way before Christ?' produced an answer from a boy of five: 'I suppose to keep Jesus's boots clean, teacher.'[25]

In November, to everybody's astonishment, May caught various diseases and was in bed for nearly three weeks. She should have been sitting her university entrance examination, and was dreadfully disappointed at being excluded through this illness, from all chance of passing the exam. It was a bitter blow for she had set her heart on going to Cambridge and Miss Summerhayes had assured her that she stood a very good chance. She never referred to this episode again, although she rarely had a good word to say for bluestockings and often despaired that the education two of her daughters received at Cambridge was less than useful in their everyday lives. She always had a particularly soft spot, though, for anyone who had been or was being educated there.

May left Queen's College at Christmas the following year, 1884. She was eighteen and expected to stay at home and be a comfort to her parents until in due time she became a comfort to her husband. She continued with her studies at the Royal College of Music and intermittently with 'Old Poll' Parratt, by then organist at Windsor Castle. She would always be grateful to him for teaching her to play Bach fugues on the organ of St George's Chapel.[26] She had grown to her full height by this time, not much over five feet and A. S. Frere, a lover in her middle age, recalled watching her play: 'Coping with all the pedals gave her as much exercise as a person of ordinary height might get from a work-out in a gymnasium.'[27]

The shortness of May's stature is not mentioned in the family reminiscences. Neither the Beauchamps nor the Lassetters were tall: as the youngest child it was probably considered fitting that she should be small. Growing up as she did with the minimum of parental strictures and the maximum of competition for their attention she developed an original and forthright nature.

This, added to her quickness and the sweet twining ways inherited from her mother, was an invincible combination and the strongest men in her life were to be no match for her. She enjoyed then and always would the astonishment aroused in others when they realized that this small body contained such a forceful and quietly dramatic personality. For a motto she chose *Parva sed Apta* (small but effective).

Her wit and telling barbs were delivered in a soft, high, slightly mewing voice, and her friend Frank Swinnerton later described it as sounding like that of a 'choir boy with a sore throat'.[28] In her early teens her speech had nearly lost its Australian twang, and by the time she published her first book she had developed a 'society drawl' which entirely concealed her origins.

The family celebrated May's coming of age on the 31st of August 1887. Her father noted the event with: 'Our baby's the bright, industrious, good May's birthday'. She received many notes, cards and telegrams and the day was generally festive and happy — 'very different from that of her birth', wrote Henry, still remembering with some trepidation the days of the 'great panic' which, combined with his losses at sea, had nearly ruined him.[29] A party was organized to which Laura* and the two Kelly sisters, Annie and Posy, were invited. Laura was May's particular friend and was quiet and bookish by contrast to the sisters and everybody called her 'Mouse'. It was she who encouraged May to read, for the Beauchamp household left books severely alone. Mr Hunter Dunn, the vicar (who was also to be the grandfather of Sir John Betjeman's tennis-playing beauty, Joan), was invited with his satellite 'frumps'. Sydney came down from Cambridge where he had stayed on during the vacation to study and he brought with him some young doctors and students. East Lodge was again, as it had been so often in the past, 'gay and lawn tennisy'.

*Laura was for many years to be May's closest friend and confidante, but nowhere is her second name recorded. It is possible that she was a Beauchamp cousin.

· 3 ·

An Invitation to the Ball

May continued single for nearly three more years. She had no lack of attentive beaux but she 'sometimes made remarks of a cynical nature to her admirers, who took fright at such symptoms of advancing age and fell considerably in number', as does the heroine of *The Benefactress*, her first full-length novel. It was Louey who suffered most from what she considered May's wilful refusal to go out of her way to attract a suitable husband. It was generally feared that she was well on the way to becoming a 'frost-bitten virgin'.[1] Chad Lassetter's daughters had all married appropriately and early, which circumstance Louey was not allowed to forget. Henry mellowed as the number of children living in his house decreased. He began to take an interest in his garden and May joined him in this passion. 'Bills instead of being for boots were for bulbs,' she wrote of him then, and nobody who adored his garden as Henry did minded paying for bulbs, but it was a rare quality not to mind having to pay for somebody else's boots. As his children gradually left home, he was to be seen, finished with his paternal role, sitting 'peaceful and unruffled among his roses'.[2] He enjoyed May's company and she enthusiastically shared his new passion for horticulture. She was content to stay at home whenever she could and relax in the ease and tranquillity that now pervaded East Lodge. Her brothers, those who lived there still, were mostly away, but her beloved sister lived nearby with her new baby boy, Timothy, later called Sydney, and destined to become knighted and British Minister in Athens for the period just before the Second World War.

By the time she was twenty-four, nearly all the girls May knew of her own age were married. She felt as though she was 'a ghost haunting the ball-rooms of the younger generation'.[3] Disliking this feeling, she stiffened and became unapproachable. She invented excuses for missing most of the functions to which she was invited and 'began to affect a simplicity of dress and hair arrangement that was severe'. It was bad enough for Louey to have a spinster daughter in the house but the spinster was turning into a feminist, and feminists, as everybody knew, were dangerous and unstable creatures inclined to write novels and often of a Sapphic orientation. May worried the family by talking of getting a job sweeping crossings. Then she was going to go away and live by herself in a cottage, keep a cow, grow vegetables and generally stand on her own feet.

> I would preach independence. Only that, always that.
> They would be sermons for women only; and they would
> be warnings against props . . . shake them off, the props
> tradition and authority offer you, and go alone, crawl,
> stumble, stagger, but go alone.[4]

Henry and Louey decided that drastic action must be taken and, as before, travel abroad appeared to offer a solution. Henry did not renew the lease of East Lodge and plunged the family once more into the nomadic way of life which had been a normal one for the Beauchamp family since the 1850s when the brothers had left England for the swagman's life in Australia. There was a saying in the family that the hens lay on their backs with their legs in the air waiting to be tied when the sound of packing was heard in a Beauchamp household. May was to move her home over thirty-five times during her lifetime, not counting the long periods during which she travelled on the Continent and in America.

In January 1889 May and her father 'bade adieu to many sorrowing relatives at Victoria Station'[5] and departed for the Continent. Louey was to join them later when she had seen to the storage of the furniture and settled Sydney, Harry and Ralph into digs in Wandsworth. She was staying with the Lassetters and inclined to postpone her departure for as long as possible.

The crossing from Dover to Calais was smooth but the journey by train to Milan was made awkward for Henry by the pressing attentions of a German officer who took a great liking to May and quickly became an annoyance to her father. Once the Beauchamps had arrived in Italy they managed to shake him off. In Milan they went to mass in the cathedral and the opera at La Scala before proceeding to Genoa. Here they took an excursion to Pegli to see the gardens of the Villa Pallavicini. Henry, regretful of his garden in Acton, noted in his journal: 'Shown round by a sturdy little gardener—seventy-eight years old and as active as I. Could any existence be more envied!' They wandered with him under the blue sky and warm sun and looked out on to the calm Mediterranean among varied and glorious vegetation, colourful birds and butterflies, and spent 'two hours well remembered'.

By the beginning of February they had reached Rome. Unemployment demonstrations which had turned into riots and looting were noisily in progress when father and daughter arrived. Henry paid them scant heed and hurried May from garden to ruin to church. She was allowed to play the organ in St Peter's. Amongst the visitors there was a cavalry officer who had fought in the Franco-Prussian War, Count Henning von Arnim, who sought out and thanked the small organist and asked to be presented to her father.

Henry hired an Italian tutor who visited May every day at tea time and conversed with her in Italian on general topics. In the evening they paid calls on people to whom they had letters of introduction. Sir George Grove had recommended May to a celebrated Italian musician, Signor Sgambacti. She and her father were invited to dinner and just as they were about to leave, Count Henning von Arnim, 'dressed up to the eyes',[6] called on his way to a ball at the Quirinal Palace. He was enchanted to meet May so soon again and stayed over an hour.

The next day Henry snatched May away like a fly from a hungry trout, planning to spend a Prussian-free March in Naples. His attitude to any man that showed an interest in his daughter was the reverse of his wife's and contrary to her instructions. He chose to forget that the main reason they were abroad was to expose May to potential suitors, and as long as Louey was not there to stop him, he did his best to keep May to himself. When they returned to Rome in April the Sgambactis held a reception. Count von Arnim spent the entire evening paying court to May and quite turned the young woman's head with his attentions.

Graf Henning August von Arnim-Schlagenthin was fifteen years older than May and had recently become a widower. He was above average height (and therefore towered over May), broad and bald. He claimed that this last condition was due to his hair having been shot off by the enemy during the Franco-Prussian War. He was the only son of Count Harry* Kurt Edward von Arnim who had studied law when he was young, an unusual step for a *Junker* of his social position, and rose in the diplomatic service under the patronage of Bismarck to become German ambassador in Rome and Paris. Harry

*'Harry' appears to have been Henning's father's given name, not Henry.

von Arnim's friends variously described him as a brilliant and gifted statesman and as an incompetent and irresponsible intriguer. While he was a diplomat he witnessed the rise and unification of Germany, and his friendship with the imperial family lent him the power, he imagined, to challenge Bismarck. He was seen by the Conservative Party (*Alt Konservitive*), who were trying to overthrow Bismarck, as the Chancellor's natural successor, and it was no secret that Harry coveted the position.

They fought each other in the political arena but Count Harry proved, in the words of G. O. Kent, the chronicler of the contest, to be 'a deficient David challenging a brilliant Goliath'. He attempted to bring Bismarck into disfavour by arranging the publication of a newspaper article which relied for its information on papers that had been smuggled out of the German Embassy in Paris. He was requested to return them but refused, claiming that they were his own private papers to do with as he liked, and there then ensued a lengthy battle in the courts commencing with his arrest. The *Junker* classes were shocked that Bismarck should have resorted to criminal law against someone of Count Harry's social position and the case later became something of a *cause célèbre*. The count broke his bail and fled to France to avoid a sentence to three months' imprisonment and for this the sentence was commuted to nine months. He and his son, Henning, published a pamphlet, *Pro Nihilo*, which stated their case and which stimulated Bismarck into bringing a new case, and Harry was eventually sentenced to five years penal servitude should he ever set foot on German soil again. The von Arnims remained in exile, in Nice, for the brief remainder of his life.

Bismarck had confiscated the von Arnim estates in Pomerania and when Harry died in 1881 he left his son Henning nothing but heavy debts. When Henning met the Beauchamps in 1889 he was petitioning the Kaiser to return his estates, having acknowledged, somewhat quixotically in the opinion of Henry Beauchamp, all of his father's debts, most of them to family and friends.

May's musical talent did not go unnoticed during her return visit to Rome. A few days after the reception, Signor Sgambacti arranged for May to give an organ recital to a selected audience at the American Church—if Henry refused to play Pandarus to his daughter, Signor Sgambacti was only too happy to oblige. May was to play Bach fugues and the count, who had of course been invited, loved music—he was a close friend of the Wagner family and had been taught the piano by Liszt—and was particularly devoted to German music.

After the recital, which impressed the audience, Henning proudly introduced May to all his friends as if he had invented her himself. Henry was not pleased by what he considered this gross flattery; it could only end in tears in his opinion, and it would be best for May if they got away as soon as possible. It seemed to him unnatural that such an august personage as Count von Arnim should be making a fool of himself (and that, in Henry's eyes, was what he was doing) over such an insignificant person as his daughter. True, she played well and was rarely at a loss for a word to say, but her father could not imagine that she was in any way eligible for serious courtship by a *Junker* count. His journal became loud in its irritation at the way the count kept turning up and at May's tendency to lag and spend time with him in cake shops and generally interfere with her father's sightseeing.

May recalled that time in her memoirs: 'The child must be fed, [Henning], who was immensely older than I was, would say when, passing a pastry cook's in the course of sight-seeing, I would sniff wistfully.'[7] Quickly she learnt to turn her nose from side to side when she smelt anything she wanted to eat. Her father, who discouraged eating between meals, looked on 'with pursed lips' as his daughter greedily gulped down the cakes provided for her by the attentive Henning. Unknown to Henry, who retired early as a rule, May slipped away in the evenings and the couple met in the dim salons of old palaces in Rome, with their painted ceilings and faded tapestries, where foreign diplomats and Italian beauties gathered for tea and intelligent conversation and a little scandal. May, a vivacious child, or so she appeared, with her mop of fair hair and pretty little English face, looked fresh and childish by comparison to the other women in Henning's circle.

May and the count were not yet betrothed but Henry, who was impatient with the dalliance, inadvertently put that right. He found two English spinsters in Florence who took in paying guests and, with relief, deposited May with them to await her mother while he sped on to Lucca. Henning dogged May like a shadow, and thus they were alone together for a week before Louey arrived with her half-sister Jessie to take up the serious business of chaperoning her daughter. Henning was a person who knew what he wanted, and had marked down the little English girl as a suitable wife and mistress of his estates as soon as he saw her. He proposed at the top of the Duomo in Florence, his breath short and face glistening from the effort of getting there. 'All girls like love. It is very agreeable. You will like it too. You shall marry me and see,' he said and embraced the startled young woman 'voluminously'. She struggled. This was an entirely new experience for her and she did not like it. When he finally let her go he explained that that was merely a beginning, which alarmed rather than reassured as it was meant to do. He then pulled out of his pocket a diamond and sapphire ring which had belonged to his first wife and put it on May's finger, 'clinching thus the business'. To have been given such a ring by the impressive count delighted May, but she was even more delighted by her sudden importance. 'Up to then I had been nobody, and suddenly to be somebody, or indeed, for a time everybody,'[8] was an extremely pleasant experience.

The count was in a great passion of love for May. They were 'privately engaged'[9] and this only because Henning had not yet had the opportunity formally to request Henry for his daughter's hand. Louey was astonished to find that her 'lonely little May' was, very probably, to become a countess. She chose, for the time being, to ignore the disadvantages of the match, such as Henning's age (he was nearly forty) and his nationality (none of the Beauchamps spoke German). 'In those days we didn't mind Germans,' May wrote in her autobiography in the 1930s, 'and my parents saw me being turned into one without a flickering of an eyelash.'[10] Louey delighted herself, instead, with the contemplation of the envy of her friends, particularly her sister-in-law, Chad Lassetter, who had recently been lording it over the Beauchamps because her husband had become extremely rich.

In June Henning made arrangements for the family to take rooms at the best hotel in Bayreuth for the Wagner opera festival at the end of July. He was impatient to introduce May to the Wagners, for, since his father's death, they had adopted him as a member of the family, and it was important that Cosima Wagner should approve his choice. While Henry continued with his sightseeing, Louey moved May to the shores of Lake Como where she concentrated on refurbishing her daughter's wardrobe. May received long, passionate letters from Henning daily. They were in French, a language that lends itself to love, and May's mother reported home to Jessie, who had by that time departed, 'Miss Mary grows fonder'—one of the family taunts which had been in currency for a long time was the couplet, applied to May, 'Mary, Mary quite contrary, how does your garden grow?'[11]

After a few weeks they travelled to Baden where the count joined them for several days. Louey wrote to Jessie that May had had a 'good cry' after he left. She was much amused on their last morning at the hotel to be presented by the landlord with bunches of flowers. He bowed when he gave Louey hers and said, 'For Madam,' and giving May hers said, 'For the Countess.' May blushed, but the man, thought Louey, was only being kind. 'I shall have to part with my little May,' she mused, 'the very sunshine of my life.'[12]

When they arrived in Bayreuth, Henning met them at the station and conducted them to their rooms at 4, Alexandrastrasse. Bayreuth was full of people who knew the count and Louey was slightly put out that she was expected to go everywhere with the happy couple since it was not thought proper that they should be seen alone. And a fine dance, she considered, she was led. The night May was presented to the Wagners Louey was astonished by the brilliance of the house and the people there. She had spared no effort to 'get herself up' and 'looked very nice, some said'. May, who was wearing a cream silk evening dress handed down to her by Charlotte Lassetter and a bunch of pink roses given to her by Henning, looked like a girl of thirteen. The count stayed close to her for the whole evening and introduced them to the other guests. Louey noticed that everybody seemed fond of him, but that night she had anxieties about 'the whole set' into which, if the marriage took place, May would be inducted. She felt that they were all 'far too swell' for her. When she saw the lovely, clever, highly educated women that Henning habitually associated with she wondered why he preferred May, as he most clearly did.

This meeting with the Wagners and his other friends was supposed by Henning to reassure the parents of his beloved that he was earnestly intending to make May his wife. He could not have guessed that it would have quite a different effect on them and alarm them into wondering if he wasn't far too grand for their insignificant little daughter. Louey continued her reports home in a rather more thoughtful vein, reiterating that she had thought from the first that it would have been better if May married one of 'her own set'. She could not believe that her daughter would ever be happy living among such people, though Henning was all devotion and did not imagine for a moment that there were times when May 'did not feel quite sure of herself'. On the other hand, if he was away from her for more than a few hours at a time May felt 'lonely and wretched'.[13]

Those few weeks were the most trying of May's young life. She had been accustomed during her childhood to being 'poor, lonely little May' in the back line of the chorus of a large family. Now she found herself cast as a leading lady and with no time in between to learn her lines. Those receptions and parties were often an agony for her and it says much for her courage that her mother noticed that she felt unsure of herself only some of the time. Both May and Louey were beginning to realize what marriage to the count would mean. She would have to live far away from the security of the family and everybody she knew. She would have to transform herself into a grand lady in a German society that was riddled with protocol; learn the ins and outs of their unfamiliar and elaborate rituals as well as the language, which she found ugly and difficult to pronounce. Worse still, Germany was going through what they hoped was only a temporary phase of Anglophobia. Queen Victoria's condescension to her nephew Kaiser Wilhelm in 'giving' him two useless territories in Africa so that 'Willy can have an Empire too' had roused nothing but fury in the average German heart.

Louey was also worried by the expense of money and energy for the furtherance of what now seemed to her a dubious courtship. 'This Bayreuth caper has nearly ruined us,' she wrote home. But they were to be there for another two weeks. May was having a rich musical treat, and every evening Henry and Louey had to take her to the opera house, leave her with the count during the performance and then go back at seven-thirty to order their supper and sit with them while they ate it 'so as to be proper'. After that the couple went back and enjoyed the rest of the opera while May's parents sat up and waited for them to come home, usually not until eleven o'clock. 'So you see what we are reduced to,' complained Louey in an unenthusiastic letter to her half-sister.[14]

Henning arranged for May to give a recital of Liszt's music to an invited audience. This, he explained, was the sure way to Cosima Wagner's heart. To be accepted by her was to be accepted by his world, for as well as being Richard Wagner's widow, she was Liszt's daughter and had been previously married to Hans von Bülow, one of the greatest conductors of his day. In Cosima the pivot of German culture rested, and the Liszt–Wagner musical coterie, which also had strong connections with the court of the Kaiser, was not just a 'swell set' in a purely social sense as Louey perceived them to be. It was an understandably apprehensive May who stepped up on to the rostrum and played those dramatic, technically demanding works. Cosima sat in the front row, an ominous figure, heavily veiled and dressed in black. If she did not find fault with the pianist, May would be accepted as a member of the most exclusive and artistically influential group of people in the world. Fortunately the concert was a success and Madame Wagner was impressed.

During those weeks in Bayreuth May had her first taste of the total

Wagnerian experience. In later life she became so familiar with the lush, chromatic harmony and the extravagant productions that she came to know every note and every word by heart. After listening to only a few bars she could tell exactly which work it was from and who was singing. She knew at last every note, and every note got on her nerves. In 1925 when her friend Hugh Walpole invited her to join him in Bayreuth to see *Parsifal*, she wrote declining the invitation, saying that she was 'heartily sick of *Parsifal*' and that she agreed with George Moore that it was 'like a sadist preaching chastity to choir boys'. She asked him not to tell the Wagners and to think of her sometimes in the middle of it, for her first husband had courted her at Bayreuth, and there was not a tree anywhere within five miles that she had not been kissed under. On that occasion Walpole was to regret the absence of a companion for he was obliged to share his box with a 'curious tenth-rate fellow', one of Winifred Wagner's lame ducks, called Adolf Hitler. The man distracted him by continuously bursting into tears. Walpole thought that a few terms at an English public school would have cured the odd creature of that sort of behaviour.[15]

By June of 1889 Louey had begun to wilt from the exertion of making sure her daughter was respectable. Henry decided that he had had enough of the whole business and set out on a tour of South Germany leaving Louey to soldier on. But she managed to extract one grain of comfort from the ordeal. Chad Lassetter, green with envy, wrote to her regularly and repeated, unconvincingly, that she was glad that 'May was not one of her girls' as she wouldn't have been able to stand the late evenings and the worry.[16]

It took time, Louey realized, for a courtship of this nature to blossom into marriage, and once Henry had left it did not take long for Henning to persuade her that her daughter need not be chaperoned between the acts. He could easily see to it that May was fed, he told her. The lovers took this opportunity to stroll round the city. They kissed under trees and swore the kind of undying love that Siegfried and Brünnhilde were singing about in the opera house that they were not attending.

Henning told May about his sad and romantic life. His father the ambassador had first married Elise von Prillwitz who was the daughter of August, Prince of Prussia, by a morganatic marriage to a Polish ballet dancer called Marie Arndt. Elise was Henning's mother and had died when he was only three. Harry had then married a distant cousin, Sophie Adelheid Gräfin von Arnim-Boitzenburg, who was an unloving stepmother to Henning and his four older sisters. He told her about their life in exile when they were forced by Bismarck's revenge to live in the South of France. And then there was his own first marriage and his great grief when his wife died soon after the birth of his first child, a girl who had soon followed her mother to the grave. What he did not tell May was that Harry had become engaged to an English girl soon after the death of his first wife, and that he had jilted her for Sophie Adelheid. That history was repeating itself was certain. How far it would continue to do so remained, at that time, to be seen.

In July the Beauchamps received the 'joyful' news that Sydney had at last passed his final examinations in London and was able to write after his name B. A. (Cantab). 'God be praised and thanked for this well earned reward of our dear boy's steady perseverance,' Henry wrote in his journal.[17]

By August the Wagner season was over and the Beauchamps went to Berlin to arrange for May to take German lessons. Louey regained her optimism and wrote home:

> Henry went to the Count's town house. He says it is magnificently furnished, really valuable things. And he brought the Count back with him last night. We did not expect him and I wish you could have seen the meeting. May rushed into his arms. He is so sweet to her. I think they will marry before many months and I shall feel perfectly happy in leaving May with such a man. May is so funny about getting married. She says she absolutely refuses to be present at her own wedding as she could not endure the agony of it.[18]

Henry left for England and Louey and May settled for a time in Dresden. May, who was concentrating all her energies on her studies, was not much company for her mother who soon began to feel sadly isolated. Henning was busy trying to settle the debts inherited from his father, mortgaging some of the land in North Germany inherited from his mother and continuing to petition the Kaiser for the return of his father's estates in Pomerania. The date of the marriage depended on the result of his efforts. As an honourable man, he did not feel he could marry May until he was solvent.

Meanwhile gloom exuded from Louey's letters to Henry. She was 'fretting, ill and miserable', and Henry finally set off to rescue them. The family left Dresden at the end of October, stopping off briefly to call on Henning in Berlin. They left for England with the date of the wedding still not fixed. Henry thought that it was an extremely unsatisfactory state of affairs and both of the women were profoundly depressed.

The next few months were as unsettled as any they had spent on the Continent. With no home base they stayed for a time in Sydney's new flat in the Cromwell Road. The trains passing underneath their windows made it impossible to sleep so they moved into hotels. Henry eventually took the lease of 91 Addison Road, Holland Park, an ugly new stuccoed house with three floors and a basement looking out at the back on to a narrow, walled yard with no horticultural potential, and combining all the disadvantages of suburbia without the then rural advantages of Acton. Sydney became engaged to a young lady called Miss Sharp, and the whole family thoroughly approved his choice. Louey decided that Henning's slowness in clinching the business begun in Rome might be because May had not been presented at court, so on the 14th of March 1890 May 'honoured Her Most Gracious Majesty by being presented by Lady George Hamilton at the Queen's drawing-room at Buckingham Palace'.[19]

The family lived in hope and settled down to await the outcome of Henning's petitions. They were startled when Henning himself appeared in London keen to continue his friendship with May but still unwilling to enlighten her father as to the date of the wedding. He pleaded poverty and honour but spent all his time with May when her father considered it would be better if he spent it putting his finances to rights. By November Henry had had enough. After a family consultation, both Henry and May sent letters to the count saying they had decided that the engagement should be broken off, a move intended to spur the indecisive Romeo into action. They were shocked to receive a letter in return coolly stating that it would be some months before his affairs would be in order and in the interval he begged to be informed if May should marry someone else.

At this point May took matters into her own hands and went to see Henning. She told him she had arranged to spend a few weeks at a cottage in Goring, on the Thames, where she would be scantily chaperoned. Why did he not come and stay nearby? Henning soon managed to overcome his scruples and May lost her virginity with the waters of the river lapping beneath her window. When the couple sheepishly returned to London, Henry insisted that Henning make an honest woman of May. The date for the wedding was fixed, and a dove descended Henry's dressing-room chimney which he 'interpreted as a good omen'. Certainly a free spirit had voluntarily entered into domestic captivity, and not by the most impeccable route.

· 4 ·

Quite Contrary

The couple were married at the Church of St Stephen, Gloucester Road, on 21 February 1891. After the ceremony they and their guests drove to Laura's new house for the reception. Everything went smoothly in spite of May's misgivings, and Henning and she caught the afternoon train to Paris, 'going off most merrily, as did everything',[1] wrote the bride's father. May wore a costume of heliotrope habit cloth trimmed with black rib velvet in the style of Louis XI. On her head perched a small black bonnet trimmed with heliotrope beaver while around her neck she wore a bear-skin boa and in her hands she held a matching muff. She looked like a child in the guardianship of a kindly uncle.

The Graf and Gräfin von Arnim spent the first two nights of their married life in Paris, then the world centre of sybaritic luxury. The *fin de siècle* naughtiness of the city failed to cast the appropriate spell and the honeymoon was far from successful. Now that they were married Henning's attitude towards May changed. She had become his property and a German. German wives were not supposed to think or act for themselves and were entirely under the domination of their husbands, as May was to discover painfully over the following weeks. She was suddenly no longer his 'little lamb'[2] but had become, it seemed in the twinkling of an eye, a sheep. A little sheep, but still no longer a lamb, as she was to point out in *The Pastor's Wife*. In this novel the heroine opines that 'probably she has no gift for honeymoons'. Indeed, from an entry in Henry's journal, it appears that May had a poor opinion of them. Many years later, after Henning's death, May confided to her lover, H. G. Wells, that her husband did not smell quite right.

When they arrived in Berlin May was further shocked to find that the sumptuous house that she and her parents had visited, so full of 'really valuable things', had been sold. The couple lodged in a rented

42

apartment which was noisy. As for the city itself: 'It just blared away at you . . . it is about as comforting and loving as the latest thing in Workhouses . . .'³ The German people were going through an intensely political phase in their newly united German Empire. Xenophobia was endemic and the Berliners talked of nothing but politics: 'They blaze with interest,' May was to write in a later novel, *Christine*, 'they explode with it, they scorch and sizzle.' She was aware of 'a sort of fever' in the people that she met. There was also an antipathy to herself because she was English. About the German people she commented, 'There is the oddest mixture of what really is brutal hardness, the kind of hardness that springs from real fundamental differences from ours and their attitude towards life, and a squashiness that leaves one with one's mouth open . . . One feels more alone in Berlin than anywhere in the world, I think.'

Henning compounded May's loneliness by becoming daily less attentive and spending the whole day from just after breakfast till dark seeing to his business affairs. In compensation he gave her a small dachshund which had belonged to his first wife, and May and the dog fell in love at first sight. Her opinion of the late Gräfin, which had been favourably coloured by the sapphire engagement ring, 'leapt to heaven' when she saw 'the blessed little low-geared dog . . . her whole body one great wag of welcome'.⁴ The dachshund was called Cornelia and May picked it up and kissed the silky brown fur on its neck. 'Do not,' interrupted her husband, 'kiss the dog. No dog should be kissed. I have provided you, for kissing purposes, with myself.'

Dealing with the servants was a further trial for May. Orders had to be given in German and she was still unfamiliar with the language and unused to telling people what to do. She wrote, 'It wasn't really to be expected of me whose life until then had been spent receiving orders, that I should suddenly turn around and give them.' Six months earlier her Mademoiselle had been calling her a *'petite sotte'* and sending her upstairs to wash her face. 'How could a person used to that sort of thing all of a sudden start looking lofty and issuing orders to people manifestly twice her age?'⁵ She discovered that the temperament of German servants was entirely different from their English counterparts: German staff functioned only to direct orders. Never lazy but entirely lacking initiative, once a job was finished they sought out the Gräfin to ask for further instructions. May had to invent tasks for them to do or escape from the flat if she were to get any peace. She took up bicycling and in the mornings when most *Hausfrauen* were in the kitchen organizing their households, May was pedalling away from her responsibilities. Her most fervent wish then and later was that there should be no servants in Heaven.

Within weeks of the von Arnims settling themselves in Berlin doctors confirmed that May was expecting a baby. In her account of this experience in *The Pastor's Wife* she transcended the whimsy and mawkish sentimentality of most contemporary female writing of the time and conveyed the physical and mental stresses with a simple and dreadful accuracy:

> As the months went on her body became fastidious even about daily inevitable smells such as the roasting of coffee or the frying of potatoes . . . She had little spirit. She was more tired every day. Just the difficulty of keeping herself tidy in dresses that seemed to shrink smaller each time she put them on, took up what strength she had. There was none left over . . . She felt humiliated, ashamed of her awkward, distorted body . . . It was as though she had suddenly grown old . . . She would have been transfigured by her shining thoughts if anything could have transfigured her. But her thoughts, however bright, could not pierce through the sad body. Her outlines were not the outlines for heroic attitudes. She not only had a double chin, she seemed to be doubled all over.

Both morning- and home-sickness combined to colour further May's distaste for this strange city, and she was panic-stricken when her request to return to England for the birth was peremptorily dismissed by her husband. She had not yet perfected the 'sweet twining ways' with which her mother was able to get her own way, and Henning was not Henry. It was considered unpatriotic for a young Gräfin to want to have a child anywhere but on German soil. It was also generally believed that the Emperor Frederick, who had died that year, had been hastened on his way by the criminal neglect of his English doctor, Queen Victoria's personal physician, so that English doctors in general were held in deep suspicion by all patriotic Germans.

May could neither protest nor complain. In Germany for a woman to express dissatisfaction was not only in bad taste, it was unheard of. May was enjoined by her female acquaintances to consider herself blessed to have the honour of carrying a German child: she should feel privileged to be in a position to produce sons for the Fatherland. It is not surprising that she withdrew into herself, and looked for consolation, at this and later times of loneliness and distress, to the works of Goethe. It was through him that she discovered the works and letters of her famous predecessor, Bettina, sister of the poet Clemens Brentano, and friend of Heine, Beethoven and the Brothers Grimm. Bettina had married another poet, Ludwig Achim von Arnim, whose cousin Ernst was Henning's grandfather. Her attitude to being pregnant was, to May, refreshingly un-Germanic and echoed May's own feelings:

> A woman who is pregnant carries in the first half death in her heart and everything on which she casts her eye arouses nausea and exhaustion within her, and everything which she touches sends the shudder of death through her nerves and bones . . . A woman is very good and very enlightened who does not hate the man who put her in this state.[6]

May came to the end of her term in early December 1891. The labour was hard and long, lasting for two days, for the baby's head was exceptionally large. In those days, because of the risks, Caesarian section was only resorted to *in extremis* and the birth was agonizing. The pain experienced by a mother was considered by German doctors (all of whom were men) to be an integral and even necessary part of childbearing, and the doctor who attended May showed the greatest possible indifference to her feelings, explaining that so natural a process as giving birth called for no particular management and that German women glorified in bringing forth their young with unimpaired consciousness. 'The whiff of anaesthetic for which she begged seemed to be denied her on moral and patriotic grounds.'[7] The experience was shattering and it was followed by a painful inflammation of the breast and high fever. She experienced a 'thin but hurrying confusion high up in the treble, high up at the very top where all the violins were insisting together over and over again on a thin, quivering anxious note.'[8]

She recovered rapidly from the fever but remained depressed for months. In retrospect she perceived that everything had been normal except her own mental state: 'There, in the black recess, crouched fear.' She became suspicious of life, for in that awful thirty-six hours of labour she had lost her confidence in it: 'She knew it now. It was all death. Death and cruelty.'[9]

The child was a girl and a disappointment to Henning who, naturally, looked for an heir, though he was relieved that the sturdy little May had survived the experience which his first wife had not. The baby was christened in the Lutheran church Eva Sophie Louise

Anna Felicitas von Arnim-Schlagenthin. One of Henning's sisters, Tante Lotte, was her godmother. For some time the child was referred to as Ottolina, but finally the family settled on Evi as an appropriate name for her.

Cornelia, the dachshund, with true canine solidarity, produced a litter at the same time. After a week she was running around and as full of life as ever. May knew that she herself was never going to be the same again: 'lively, yes, but not as ever . . .' she recalled in her memoirs, *All the Dogs of my Life*.

The proud grandfather wrote:

> My dear Arnim,
> Your kind letter of the 11th instant is before me and we are all greatly rejoiced at getting such a favourable account of darling May and the young lady. We are much babied just at present. Babies who are born dead, disappointing to the poor little expectant mother, causing little or no trouble to the world in general. Babies that behave themselves decently for a week or so and then make themselves generally noxious, disturbing family arrangements right and left, requiring many doctors, nurses (wet and dry), donkeys etc. Babies that are not yet seen, but cast their shadow (and substance) before, causing distraction, nervousness and unrest. Finally there is the natural well-disposed baby, such as you appear to be blessed with and for which you ought to feel thankful to Heaven. But fond parents! You must not give it all it cries for, from the moon down. But rather teach it early to economize its wants if you wish it peace and happiness in this transitory life.

He declined the invitation proffered by Henning at May's insistence to come to Berlin for the christening.

Had he gone he would have been appalled at his daughter's tendency to hang dotingly over the cradle. May had received scant sympathy from her husband for all her suffering, and her illness was dismissed by her father in his journal as 'awkward' only because she was unable to breastfeed her baby and a wet nurse had to be called in. But as soon as she regained some of her spirit Evi became the centre of her universe. The baby was taken everywhere and shown off as if she were the first of her kind as her name implied. May's delight in her made up for Henning's lack of interest in a mere daughter. Evi was pretty and quickly learnt how to make people

46

laugh. At the circus, when she was only two, she stood up and bowed graciously to the audience, assuming that the applause was meant for her.

Five months after the birth, May and Henning went for a short visit to England to show the child to the Beauchamps and May's friends. May's pleasure at the reunion was marred, however, when she discovered she was pregnant again. Henry and Charlotte travelled back to Berlin with them when they left, for Henning could not be persuaded to let May have her second baby in England and they were concerned for her well-being. Her tight-lipped silence about the birth of Evi was utterly unlike May's usual open, frank nature and Henning's own account had not been reassuring. In February 1892 another girl was born in exactly the same circumstances as the first. The labour was prolonged, no chloroform was administered and the doctor and nurse once again showed no consideration for May's feelings. But there was no inflammation afterwards and of all the babies this one was the only one to be suckled by her mother. She was christened Elizabeth Irene after her maternal grandmother and was always known as Liebet.

Before May had entirely recovered from her second confinement she was bitterly rebellious to discover that she was expecting yet a third. This time she insisted that she go to England, and Henning grudgingly capitulated to her demand. She took Evi and Liebet and a 'full sized nurse'[10] and arrived to stay with her parents in Holland Park at the beginning of November. She wanted Sydney to attend the birth and while she was waiting went to see Sarah Bernhardt who was playing a season in London in the wake of her highly successful American tour. May was enthralled by the great one-legged actress's performance of the consumptive courtesan, Marguerite Gautier, in *La Dame aux Camélias* by Alexandre Dumas. She went night after night, sometimes in the company of a new friend whom she had met through the Waterlows, Maud Ritchie, daughter of a future Chancellor of the Exchequer, Lord Ritchie of Dundee. On one occasion they met a friend of Maud's, Miss Maude Stanley, who was with her nephew John Francis Stanley, Earl Russell, grandson of the former Prime Minister, Lord John Russell. He was the same age as May, tall, handsome with blond curly hair which he wore unfashion- ably long. He was 'quite wonderfully lordly'[11] in his manner and spoke with the assurance of a natural orator. He wore a shabby but expensive tweed suit, a battered tweed hat and smoked a well- seasoned briar pipe. He appeared to May the perfect romantic hero of fiction and every inch an earl. His friends called him Frank, and so, very soon, did May. Francis wrote of their friendship in his memoirs:

> In 1894 I had become well acquainted with a very charming and attractive lady of artistic tastes who stimulated my admiration for Sarah Bernhardt. We constantly went together to see her magnificent performances, and in that emotional atmosphere we very soon thought we were in love. At any rate, she wrote the most charming love letters, and I thoroughly enjoyed her society which I found most exhilarating.[12]

Though little is known about May's relationship with Francis at this early time, he was later to play an important role in her life, and it is certain that she continued to see something of him whenever she came to London. It is therefore appropriate to cover aspects of his unusual background in some detail at this point.

Francis Russell had been brought up in the free and easy atmosphere of a country house called Ravenscroft, three miles from Tintern Abbey. His father was Viscount Amberley, son of Lord John Russell who had distinguished himself during his two terms of office by passing the Second Reform Bill, and as a reward for his services an hereditary earldom was bestowed upon him. Amberley married Kate Stanley and they pursued an idealistic life. Their best friend was John Stuart Mill and Amberley had stood for Parliament and used for his platform the unmentionable practice of birth control. He was an unbeliever in reaction to his parents' oppressive religiosity and, because Kate's family were fierce freethinkers, their first born, Francis, did not ever recall having 'the name of God inflicted'[13] on him and he did not have to go to church. He was allowed to run about barefoot and ride on his pony without a saddle. A 'brain fever' in infancy had caused a doctor to dictate that he should never be crossed and so when he called his mother a 'she-devil' and a 'beast'[14] he was lightly punished by being given only dry bread for his supper, a situation he quickly remedied by blandishments to the cook. If a visitor or a lesson displeased him he would climb up on to the roof and stay there until the crisis had passed.

He saw more of his parents, when they were at home, than was normal in those days and his mother taught him his letters in her bedroom. He was nine when she died of diphtheria, taking her five-year-old daughter, Rachel, with her. Francis was more than distraught by this double tragedy for he had been the carrier of the infection. When his father died of a broken heart eighteen months later, Francis remained in the room sobbing and crying so that his father's hand was wet with tears. Amberley's last words to him were, 'My poor boy, now you are indeed an orphan.'[15] Bertrand Russell was six years younger than Francis and was less obviously scarred by the tragedy of his parents' deaths.

Evidently Kate had placidly allowed herself to be 'available'[16] to a tutor called Spalding who had been forbidden to marry by his doctor because he was consumptive and there was madness in the family: Amberley apparently felt that he would be doing good all round by providing him with such a service. Obviously Spalding, who was writing a book on behaviourism and to which end he contributed to the general chaos by keeping chickens on the ground floor of the house and a beehive in his bedroom, had some emotional hold over the Amberleys, for he appeared to do more or less what he liked in their house. When the viscount died he left the two boys in the guardianship of the Darwinian Spalding and a briefless barrister whom Amberley had known at Oxford called Thomas Sanderson who had been in love with Kate and was a great favourite with the boys. He later became the bookbinder and co-founder of Doves Press, Cobden-Sanderson, and incidentally a great friend of May's.

The horrified Russell family, who lived in a grace-and-favour house in Richmond Park called Pembroke Lodge, fought for and gained custody of the boys. Many of the private papers of the Amberleys were then carefully destroyed by the family and the social conclusions of the unconventional couple were hushed up as far as possible. The influence of the argumentative Stanleys was held to blame for pulling their son off the straight and narrow, for as a family the Stanleys could not have been more at variance with the Russells who rarely spoke above a reverent whisper. The boys' aunt, Lady Georgiana Peel, wrote a description of what it was like to have dinner with Kate's family at Alderley:

> The firing off of generally ironical questions on every subject, the quick replies, generally involving an argument in which everyone would have a different opinion, and uphold it with tremendous spirit. Such a clatter of tongues, as there was all round the table at any meal, and such a clashing of brilliant wits . . .[17]

The boys' Stanley grandmother and her daughter Maude were devoted to the children and they loved going to stay there, but the Russell grandparents did not approve and made visits a rare treat.

Aunt Maude Stanley told Francis that he had been a 'very naughty little boy', and his adored grandmother that he had been an 'unwashed, ill bred, impertinent little child dressed in rags'[18] when he was finally rescued from his unsuitable guardians.

The inhabitants of Pembroke Lodge took it upon themselves to convert the heathens. Francis quickly grew to hate the hushed, apologetic tone of voice in which everything was discussed in that house, finding there an 'atmosphere of insincerities, conventions, fears and baited breath'[19] which he deplored. He told his father's brother Rollo that he would kick him if he did not speak like a man. Above all the Russells professed to a mournful and deadening Christianity that neither of the brothers could ever embrace. Francis became completely unmanageable and spent much time on the roof. He did not bother to hide his feelings from the family and his grandfather's only and reiterated comment whenever he saw the boy was 'Frank by name and frank by nature'.

The young viscount's great interest as a child was engineering and his most vivid memories were of helping his father design and build flowerbeds and outbuildings in the garden. He was fascinated by everything electrical which was then an energy source that had yet to be exploited in most spheres. Under the Darwinian tutelage of Spalding he had become interested in animal behaviour and watched with fascination the living hearts of salmon cut out to lie beating on a saucer for some hours, and he and Spalding tore the wings off flies and cut the heads off chickens in their search for enlightenment. Francis's personal experiments carried out on the household cats sometimes resulted in their untimely deaths. These interests were not catered for at Pembroke Lodge. Once he attempted to run away, but was caught after spending the night in the railway station waiting for the milk train, and was locked in the butler's pantry. He escaped again through the window while awaiting punishment and in answer to his grandparents' plea, when he was recaptured, that he should promise never to do such a thing again he merely assured them that next time he would inform them first.

Naturally it was soon decided that Francis should go to boarding school. He was sent to Cheam Preparatory School and was indignant to be referred to there as Viscount Amberley, for that was his father's name. When he went back to Pembroke Lodge for the holidays he was kept away from Bertrand 'the angel child', as much as possible as he was assumed to be a bad influence. He did attempt to teach his brother Euclid and was impressed by Bertrand's brilliance in geometry. When the younger boy complained to Francis that the axioms were, to his mind, anything but proved, Francis informed him that they *had* to be taken for granted, that they weren't designed to be true, merely essential for the comprehension of Euclid. 'At these words my hopes crumbled,'[20] remembered Bertrand. His doubt about them was, however, to fuel his most important contribution to modern mathematical thinking, *Principia Mathematica*, which he later wrote in collaboration with A. N. Whitehead.

Francis went on to Winchester where he was extremely happy. Here a passion for justice and exactitude stood him in good stead and he learnt the important art of being able to focus his attention on his work whatever pandemonium was going on in his environment. He got on well with the masters and boys, but he did not like the girls he met at home. An approved-of neighbour in Richmond, Annabel Huth Jackson, remembered, 'Bertie and I were great allies and I had an immense and secret admiration for his beautiful and gifted elder brother Frank. Frank, I am sorry to say . . . used to tie me up to trees by my hair.'[21]

By then the second earl, Francis had developed a rigid, almost Arthurian, morality when it came to women, but he also formed a strong attachment to a younger boy at Winchester called Lionel Johnson. He was a 'small, thin, palefaced boy with dark hair and looked like some young saint in a stained glass window', wrote Francis in his memoirs:

> Although a year or two younger than me Lionel was about fifteen years older both in erudition and in thought. At the age of seventeen he had read practically all there was to read in English literature, and had formed critical judgements upon it. I sat at his feet as at the feet of Gamaliel. He beat down my philistinism which was strong, and gave me a wider outlook on men and things. Above all he taught me to read and love Browning, but he taught me more than that, a lesson I have never forgotten, and that is that physical things, the humours, the happenings, disgraces, successes, failures, are in themselves the merest phantoms and illusions, and that the only realities are within one's own mind and spirit.

Lionel Johnson went on to become a critic and a Catholic convert and never fulfilled the considerable promise of his youth. He was one of the first members of what was later to be referred to as the

Bloomsbury Group and wrote poetry that undoubtedly had a seminal influence. The friendship of the two young men was to have continual and disastrous repercussions. The first calamity was that Francis was taken away from Winchester for his last year by his grandparents and made to cram for his Oxford entrance examination with a tutor in Limpsfield, although Francis was convinced that it was because he had committed the, in their eyes, unpardonable sin of being happy.

At Oxford, under the wise and watchful eye of the great Doctor Jowett at Balliol, Francis was again happy. He worked hard and gathered around him a group of friends who included Ion Thynne who was sent down for attempting in his cups to kick down the gates of Christ Church, and Edgar Jepson, grandfather of the novelist Fay Weldon, who became a writer, editor and lifelong friend. Francis spent much of his spare time investigating alternative religions and finally became a vegetarian, teetotal Buddhist. Bertrand remembered, 'My brother, who was at Balliol, had become a Buddhist, and used to tell me that the soul could be contained in the smallest envelope that I had ever seen, and I imagined the soul beating against [it] like a heart.'[22]

Towards the end of Francis's second year he was sent for by Jowett and told he had been guilty of 'disgusting conduct'[23] relating to a letter. Francis never saw the letter, nor was he told what he was supposed to have written in it. It was clear to him that neither had Jowett. On being requested to leave Oxford for a month Francis protested that he was being treated autocratically and that Jowett was no gentleman. He demanded an investigation and when this was not forthcoming, refused to return to the university at all. Evidently Pembroke Lodge (Francis's generic name for the Russell family) was being blackmailed, although it is not now known by whom. The letter was to Lionel Johnson who was himself in the habit of addressing his letters to Francis 'darling'. An article that appeared in *Vanity Fair* after Francis's first matrimonial trial in 1891 referred to the 'precious Oxford incident': 'Only be one thing clearly understood. In all matters of life and conduct, Lord Russell was at Oxford moral even to the point of priggishness; except that he was too simple-minded ever to make a real prig.'

Whether or not Francis and Lionel Johnson had had a homosexual affair was a matter of overt speculation on a national scale for the whole of Francis's life, though whether he was aware of this is not clear. He had an ability to ignore the obvious until, for him, at least, it no longer existed. He took no trouble to clear the mystery up one way or the other and one of the last letters he wrote before he died was to his confidant, George Santayana, who had asked him what exactly the nature of his relationship with Johnson was. Francis's letter in reply was evasive to the point of incomprehensibility.

Francis's innocence hindered his judgement when it came to his own affairs, particularly with the women in his life, and he was a gull and a dupe to any confidence trickster or adventuress that came his way. After Oxford he lived in a cottage by the Thames and refused any discourse with Pembroke Lodge. When he was twenty-two a Lady Scott induced him, by devious strategies, to marry her beautiful daughter, Edith. The marriage lasted three months, when Edith ran home to her mother complaining that her husband swore at her and had flourished a revolver. The women sued him for legal separation on the grounds that a 'Mr X' (Lionel Johnson) came to stay at the Russell house, then in Eaton Square, on several occasions and that while he was there Francis vacated the matrimonial bed in the early hours of the morning in such a way as to alert Edith's suspicions that all was not healthy between the two men. She accused him of what was then considered the worst crime that a gentleman could commit—sodomy. They also cast doubt on Francis's relationship with the cabin boy on his yacht and cited as evidence of his sadistic personality two events concerning his cats. The first was that as an experiment to see what it would do, he left the ship's cat on the dock while his yacht, *Royal*, pulled away. The cat, in desperation, plunged into the water and swam after the boat. The second was a possibly apocryphal story that he had established an eight o'clock curfew at his cottage near the Thames which the cat ignored. It stayed out all night and as a punishment was locked in a cupboard for three days and nights without food and water. Francis was acquitted on the charge of sodomy* but Edith never returned to him nor, by that time, did he want her to although he had been very much in love with her. Later she sued him for restitution of conjugal rights but he won that case as well. He was in this ambiguous state of matrimony when he first met May, in London.

After Christmas 'the Teutons' as Henry dubbed May and her family, moved into a flat in Abingdon Mansions not far away from her parents. The baby was born under the tender ministrations of Sydney, and to everybody's huge disappointment was yet another girl, christened Beatrix Edith. May and Francis continued to see

*The crowd that had gathered outside Bow Street Magistrates' Court reached as far as the Strand. When he appeared outside after his acquittal a great cheer went up.

each other after she had recovered and she lingered in England until July. Their parting was painful, but then Francis took his aching heart to California and the arms of a young lady there called Veronica while May resolved to spend more time on writing stories and none at all on further reproduction. Since, as she afterwards used to shock people by remarking, she used to get pregnant if Henning so much as blew his nose while in the same room as herself, he was kept very much at arm's length and he did not like it. It was not patriotic, it was positively anti-German not to wish to provide him with an heir to such an august lineage, but May was firm. As Liebet deduced in her memoir of her mother written in the 1950s: 'She developed a firmness, a reasoned defence of the conclusions she had arrived at with regard to this subject and triumphed, for the time being, over the very different views held by her husband, generation and adopted country.'

Henning took a mistress and May resented it. However, although their life continued with frequent stormy scenes, there was no question that May would ever balk her duties socially, no matter how fraught the situation in the bedroom. Henning was the grand-son of Frederick the Great's nephew Prince August who had wanted to marry Madame Récamier, a close friend of Madame de Staël. Although Henning's descent was through Marie Arndt, the von Arnims were intimates of the circle immediately surrounding the Imperial family and Henning and his wife were expected to make and receive calls, to attend parties and give them, and to appear for receptions at embassies. May did not enjoy this way of life, and she never came to like the Germans. Nevertheless she persevered. Now that she was free of the emotional and physical encumbrances of pregnancy, she concentrated on learning what to do and say and wear, drawing on the same single-minded determination that she brought to bear on everything else she did. She spent days shopping for the right gloves, feathers and ribbons. She took instruction from ladies at court on etiquette, in *fin de siècle* Berlin a highly complex, intricate and ritualized form of behaviour that had behind it the ponderous force of tradition. She recalled that finally, once she had learnt her lessons, the 'mellifluousness' of her manners was impress-ive. As soon as she had mastered German she was able to wind her 'way in and out of the most lengthy and intricate politeness, and bring out my verb, all proper in its place, at the finish, with the best of them'.[24] Much later, after she had been widowed and was living back in England, she startled her friends with the exquisite polite-ness with which she invited them to sit down, even though they were already seated.

On 1 January 1896 May began a diary with the statement, 'Wrote F. W. a.m.'. This is the first documentary evidence of her literary aspirations. She was working on a novel. There is no surviving manuscript with F. W. as the initials of the title but it was evidently the first draft of *The Pastor's Wife*, which reveals a somewhat jaundiced view of her Beauchamp family life, her engagement, marriage and subsequent life in Germany. She dared not show it to any of the characters depicted, waiting to publish it, rewritten and with a new ending, in 1914, after her husband's death.

For a woman to busy herself in her spare time writing a novel in 1896 was not at all unusual. Novel-writing was reaching epidemic proportions among women by the end of the nineteenth century. G. H. Lewes, later George Eliot's husband, and very much opposed to women novelists, had complained as early as 1847 that 'the literary profession, which ought to be a Macedonian phalanx . . . chosen, compact, irresistible, is being infiltrated by children, women and ill-trained troops.' In 1859 a critic declared that 'the number of young lady novelists extant at this moment passes calculation and was unparalleled in any former epoch. Indeed the supply to the fiction market has fallen mainly into their hands.'

The lady novelist was a familiar figure of fun in *Punch*, stereotyped as a bluestocking or a creature with ink half-way up her fingers, dirty shawls and frowzy hair. It was assumed that she was childless, by implication neurotic and probably subject to the charisma of clergymen. It was generally understood then that happy women whose lives were satisfied and full had little need of utterance. G. H. Lewes wrote '. . . if her thwarted affections shut her somewhat from the sweet domestic and maternal sphere to which her whole being spontaneously moves, she turns to literature as to another sphere.' So rarely did women combine the two activities that as late as 1950 Nancy Mitford asked, 'Were there any women who married in their youth and bore children and continued to write?' May had five children and wrote over twenty books. While it is true that she suffered much misery in the face of dreadful duty her basic nature was sunny and she had a gift for gaiety. 'Directly you come home, the fun begins,' said Liebet when she was a child,[25] and this sentiment was echoed by all who knew her mother. She had certainly not turned to literature because she was unfulfilled in the 'sweet domestic and maternal sphere' but more likely as a way of reaching out to those she loved and who were far away; a whistling in the dark in the face of her own loneliness.

· 5 ·

How Does Your Garden Grow?

Because of the unexpected and rapid enlargement of the von Arnim family May found a larger apartment in the Bruckenallee early in 1896. She and Henning were living almost entirely separate lives by then, she with the children and he inspecting the estates which had been returned to him by the young Kaiser. May ran the household, played with her children and worked on her novel. Every evening she went to the opera house where her latest infatuation, Rosa Sucher, sang Brünnhilde and other Wagnerian soprano parts with a magic that held May spellbound. She besieged the 'divine Rosa' with notes and flowers, often going backstage to talk to her in her dressing room, but on further acquaintance found her 'more terrestrial' as she noted in her diary.

Henning was spending most of his time in Pomerania where an estate, Nassenheide, which had been bought by his father had recently been drained from the surrounding marshes. Henning had begun to take a personal interest in the agricultural possibilities of the property and May wondered whether they might turn the empty castle into a place where they could spend their summers. On 18 March they set out by train from Berlin to Stettin and from there by carriage to Nassenheide. It was a cold, grey day, and the place had been empty since Count Harry had bought it twenty-five years previously. They roamed about the house and then, as she wrote in her first novel *Elizabeth and her German Garden:*

> Wandering out . . . into the bare and desolate garden, I
> don't know what smell of wet earth or rotting leaves
> brought back my childhood with a rush and all the happy
> days I spent in a garden. Shall I ever forget that day? It
> was the beginning of my real life, my coming of age as it
> were, and entering into my kingdom.[1]

56

For the next few weeks May travelled to and fro between Nassen-heide and Berlin. She called in workmen and ordered the amazed decorators to whitewash the interior walls, this being customarily done only to pig-sties. By the middle of April she had decided to live there for a time herself. With a staff of one housekeeper and one maid she cleared and cleaned a bedroom upstairs, and there followed weeks of bliss during which she was entirely alone. She was supposed to be overseeing the painters and decorators, but she rarely went into the house until the workmen had left. She was utterly happy, as happy as she had been as a small child when she had been sent out with a piece of bread sprinkled with sugar at eleven o'clock onto a daisy- and dandelion-covered lawn. During those first weeks at Nassenheide she 'lived in a world of dandelions and delights'.

At least, that was how she remembered it. In fact it was less than a month before the real world erupted but during that brief spell she spent almost all of her time in the garden, even having her meals brought out to her on trays. She lived on salads, brown bread and the occasional roast pigeon, glorying in the freedom and time that this regime gave her—Teutonic mealtimes were long and wearisome institutions and she hated them. The housekeeper was as scandalized as the decorators by the Gräfin's unconventional behaviour. In the evenings when the workmen had gone,

> . . . and the old housekeeper had gathered up her rheu-matic limbs into her bed, and my little room in quite another part of the house had been set ready, how reluc-tantly I used to leave the friendly frogs and owls, and, with my heart somewhere down in my shoes, lock the door to the garden behind me and pass through a long series of echoing south rooms full of shadows and ladders and ghostly pails and painters' mess, and humming a tune make myself believe I liked it . . .[2]

May kept a large dinner bell on a chair by the bed so that if she were frightened in the night she could ring it. Although nobody would have heard, the sight of it reassured her. The house at night was filled with the sounds of timber settling and animals and birds rustling in the eaves. But she loved 'the beautiful purity of the house, empty of servants and upholstery'.

Then Henning arrived and accused his wife of deserting her family and of not even having the courtesy to write them a letter. He told her that it was the purest selfishness to enjoy herself when neither he nor her children were there, and that the lilacs wanted thoroughly pruning. She offered him her salad supper in appeasement but he maintained that his duty was to be with the neglected family and left for Berlin. Guiltily May supervised the decorators with renewed energy. She wrote regularly and sent her love, but she could not find it in her overflowing heart to fret and yearn for her family. 'What are you to do if your conscience is clear and your liver in order and the sun is shining?'[3] Just then the bird cherries were in blossom and the garden looked like a wedding. From the topmost windows of the house she could see green plains and the line of forest beyond.

The house itself was a place of great beauty and history, although May never described it in her books. It was built in the latter part of the sixteenth century in the middle of an estate of 60,000 acres. Gustavus Adolphus stayed there often during his campaigns in the Thirty Years War and later, for many decades, it was inhabited by a community of nuns. Towards the end of the eighteenth century it was owned by Graf Henckel von Donnersmarck, who brought seeds back from his travels and experimented with them in the sandy Pomeranian soil, and it was from his heirs that Count Harry von Arnim had bought it. It is still standing, the gabled roof covered in weathered tiles, the walls in grey stucco supporting green or flaming Virginia creeper. The west wing has set in it the massive front door made of studded oak.

In the north wall of the hall is a door to the dining-room, kitchen and offices. Steps on the opposite side ascend to different levels of the living quarters which May turned into drawing-rooms, library and schoolrooms, Henning's study and laboratories. Most of these are strung along the one-storeyed side of the building which faces south. In the centre is a veranda where a series of steps lead on to a once formal garden of 'whirligig'[4] flowerbeds, and a sundial. The bed-rooms are on the upstairs floor, some of them huge, others the original cells of the nuns. Endless draughty passages and occasional staircases connect the maze of apartments. The huge hall in earlier times had been used as a chapel. When May found it, the walls were hung with stuffed trophies of local game. To one side of the door there was inscribed in Greek:

VENUS, EROS, THE GRACES, THE MUSES, DIONYSOS, APOLLO SWORE TO EACH OTHER THAT THEY WOULD LIVE HERE

Considering the innocent pantheism that seeps from all the books May was to write there, it appears that they succeeded in doing so. The aid of the Muses was constantly invoked during the time that the von Arnims lived at Nassenheide, and not only by May. E. M.

Forster's first novel, *Where Angels Fear to Tread*, was finished there and Hugh Walpole's first novel, *Troy Hanneton*, was both started and finished at the castle.

May lamented that she had spent five years in Berlin being 'perfectly miserable . . . and while we were wasting our lives there, here was this dear place with dandelions up to the very door, all the paths grass-grown . . . peace and happiness and a reasonable life . . .'[5] In this far corner she was happy, and in a letter to her father the following year she wrote:

> . . . Yes, indeed I am blessed, for I have found the kingdom of heaven, found by so few and without which babies, birds, books and flowers don't make one happy. But then everybody's kingdom of heaven isn't the same, and nearly every one of my acquaintances would be miserable if forced to live in mine . . . I have found the Lord [but] instead of having found Him in a chapel I have found Him in my garden! Well, Pa, I always feel how much you can understand and sympathise with my blessedness for of course I have inherited it from you yourself.

For the rest of her solitary stay in the castle May's diaries are a catalogue of shrubs and roses she ordered, paid for out of her pin money. She bought ten pounds of morning glory seeds and spent a happy and hopeful day scattering them all over the garden. But she had not been initiated into the mysteries of seed trays, and the birds ate them all. Her disappointment was acute when they failed to appear and, convinced it was the poverty of the soil that was to blame, she sprinkled artificial manure liberally but to no avail. When the weather was fine and sunny she stayed out of doors to enjoy it, and when it rained she sat in front of a log fire with Goethe's autobiography, *Fiction and Truth*, where she read about his great passion for gardens, which echoed her own, and his friendship with Bettina. It was she who so accurately shared May's feelings when she wrote:

> My soul is a passionate dancer, she dances to hidden music which only I can hear. You may tell me to be calm and demure but my soul does not listen and goes on dancing; if the dance were to stop it would be the end of me. I trust this element in myself which wants to kick over the traces. People tell me that independence is a bad characteristic, but it is by independence that we live.[6]

On 10 May the countess set out for Berlin, determined to bring the rest of the family back to Nassenheide within the next few days. Instead she bought a hat and it wasn't till near the end of the month that she persuaded the family to return there with her. Henning complained of stomach cramps as soon as they arrived and went straight to bed. May rushed into the garden: 'Found lilac in all its glory, so heavenly. How full everything looks, the trees so thick with leaves ... felt very blest and thankful.'[7] The household was managed by a skeleton staff and it was left to May to minister to Henning, a difficult patient. She ran backwards and forwards from the kitchen to his bedroom through miles of corridors so that after three days even the glorious spring weather could not 'put life into tired legs'. But by the end of May Henning was well enough to join his wife in the garden to water the plants.

> ... and we were like Adam and Eve in our innocent enjoyment. This month has been a very blessed one in spite of H, and I can't express the love and grace and fellowship that is with me whenever I go into my garden (which has grown to be the presence of God to me). It is a benediction every time I go into it and there alone can I realise what is meant by the peace that passes all understanding.[8]

The household began to move along more orthodox lines, May was robbed of the simple life that she had so enjoyed and the dreadful pattern of mealtimes oppressed the prophetess of freedom. Her husband and the staff were all relentless in their attempts to harness her into the trap of domesticity. In a little basketwork carriage with scarlet wheels, drawn by two stout, rough-coated ponies and driven by a patient old coachman, she often escaped in the early mornings of bright days to meditate under the branches of huge fir trees in the forest. May had no instinct or inclination to become a *Hausfrau*. Her love of nature and of being alone appeared highly eccentric to her country neighbours, while her lack of interest in such activities as making sausages, cheese and butter, slaughtering pigs, caring for calves, spring cleaning and local gossip was entirely scandalous.

The estate manager Herr Schleck and his wife soon became May's fiercest opponents in her quest for a release from duty. They had been put in charge when Count Harry bought the place and in the intervening time had successfully but ruinously salvaged most of the land from the swamps. May dubbed them the Pope and Popess because of their huge pomposity, and avoided them whenever she could. Fortunately they did not live in the house but inhabited a small lodge outside the front gate known as the Vatican. It became clear that the Popess, encouraged no doubt by Henning, intended to visit the countess every morning to go through the accounts and discuss the ever-present servant problem. May felt like a rabbit who had been successfully mesmerized by a stoat as hour after hour she was obliged to sit in the gloomy estate office with Frau Schleck. Etiquette did not permit her to terminate the session until the Popess had finished what she had to say. Meanwhile outside the sun was shining and many other more enjoyable things waited to be done.

The estate was almost completely self-sufficient as long as their eminences were in control. Henning, who could have relieved May of much of the burden of the household at Nassenheide, had refused to give up the apartment in Berlin and spent as much time there now as he had spent away on his estates before May and the children moved to Pomerania. On his visits he upbraided her for having offended somebody, usually the Popess, 'always mysteriously, always without the least notion of why or how'.[9] She dreamt more and more of escaping back to England, even if it were only for a holiday.

That June events conspired to make it perfectly reasonable that she should ask Henning for permission to go there. Her brother Harry was to be married, and Charlotte's son Sydney Waterlow, then at Eton, had won a poetry prize and was to declaim in front of the school and the Duke of York. Various family celebrations had been planned to mark these events, though May feared that they would appear too frivolous for Henning to approve of, but then she heard that a great friend had been taken seriously ill. She wrote to her husband who was in Berlin but received no reply. Ten days later he arrived by train and May eagerly awaited him on Stettin platform. As soon as she saw him she reiterated her request. Henning refused point blank to give her permission to go and there followed 'disgraceful scenes'. Tension mounted between them for several weeks. May had never been unreasonably thwarted in her desires before she had been married, she saw absolutely no reason why she should not go and insisted that she was held prisoner against her will. To make things worse the cook handed in her notice, the Popess informed on the nocturnal behaviour of one of the maids who had to be sacked, and Henning's cousin Bernd and his wife came to stay. May had to do all the cooking herself until a new cook could be found. On the day of Harry's wedding she packed her bags and ordered the carriage. Henning sent the carriage away again, but if he thought that he had succeeded in preventing his wife's departure he was wrong. That night she slipped out of the house when everyone was asleep, walked to the station, a distance of ten miles or so, and a few days later turned up in England in good spirits. Her diary simply records the word 'happy' for each day that she was there.

This daring escapade bore unexpected fruit. Six weeks later Henning himself arrived, 'cool and crabby'.[10] There had been no exchange of letters between them in the meantime. The family made a great fuss of him, however, even if his wife did not and it was not long before he mellowed and began to enjoy the Beauchamp method of spending the summer. They visited Kew Gardens, Cowes Regatta and other resorts of the prosperous. A reasonable harmony was established between the von Arnims, and Henning bought May's consent to return by promising to give up the Berlin apartment as well as his other amusements in the city. They left England in the middle of September, May tearful but resigned, and arrived back at Nassenheide to find the place swarming with workmen. Henning had decided that the house should be finished as soon as possible.

After two weeks of 'uproar and bewilderment' the family 'dined in the dining room for the first time'.[11] May's taste in decoration, white paint wherever possible and sprigged wallpaper, had transformed the place gradually into a castle fit for princesses—which her daughters in any case very nearly were. The library was to become May's special domain. It looked out on to the old, formal part of the garden with its low privet-hedged flowerbeds surrounding the mossy sundial. With its cheerful yellow and white colour scheme, big fireplace and four windows facing south it had 'anything but a sober air'.[12]

May 'slaved'[13] from morning to night until mid-October. Then the builders left and life began to move along conventional lines. A large and sometimes efficient staff heaved great baskets of peat through the maze of passages. Each room had a big old-fashioned stove which was kept alight throughout most of the year. The only source of water was a pump in the garden, but nevertheless cans of hot and cold water were brought to the bedrooms two or three times a day. Each room was supplied with oil lamps in the evenings which were removed in the morning for cleaning and filling. During the night an aged crone with wrinkled face, bent back and frizzy grey hair escaping from a grimy shawl crept along the corridors emptying the earth closets which were placed strategically throughout the house and smelt of whitewash and disinfectant. She was known as *die Hexe* because she looked so like a witch in one of Grimm's fairy tales and the children lived in mortal terror of her.

In shining contrast May rose every morning, fairy-like in the children's eyes. She carried around with her a great bunch of keys and her first task was to descend to the kitchen and discuss the menu with the cook, unlock the larders and begin the day with sausages— 'For the short time I am in the midst of their shining rows, I am practically dead to every other consideration in heaven and earth.'[14] The kitchen remained a hotbed of sin and constant intrigue but May wisely turned a blind eye and only took action when the Popess insisted that something had to be done.

That Christmas was to be the first in Pomerania. In Berlin it had been the fashion to regard it as 'a bore of rather a gross description and as a time when you are invited to overeat yourself and pretend to be merry without just cause'.[15] May thought, in contrast, that it was one of the prettiest and most poetic institutions possible if observed in the proper manner. Since she felt she had been more or less unpleasant to everybody for a year, it was a blessing to be forced, on that one day, to be amiable.

Generous by nature and finding it delightful to be able to give presents to her children without fear of spoiling them, May made several trips to Berlin to do her Christmas shopping. Advised by the Popess, she also bought presents for the staff and all the farm hands. Everything had to be prepared beforehand with the greatest secrecy as the little girls were convinced that the Christ Child himself brought them their presents. While their mother worked at wrapping parcels and decorating the trees in the library (which had been placed out of bounds several days before Christmas Eve) the children searched the garden for signs that He had been there. May set up a line of Christmas trees decked in silver. Opposite each were tables, one for each person in the house, piled with gifts. When the candles were lit, and she saw the circle of happy faces round the trees, she forgot all the effort, and the number of times she had had to run up and down stairs, and enjoyed it all as much as everyone else.

After Christmas the Kelly sisters, Annie and Posy, and Laura (Mouse) came to stay for a few weeks. Laura's husband was ill but raised no objection to being abandoned for a few weeks to the ministrations of a ferocious nurse. On New Year's Eve they drove in sledges three miles to the little church on the estate. It was lit by guttering candles and the wind howled around outside in the dark. Sitting there May 'felt very small and solitary and defenceless in the great black world'.[16] They came home and drank *Glühwein* to toast in the New Year. Annie became extremely bumptious and flirtatious with Henning, who merely removed himself to his study. The next day, far from being contrite, Annie found fault with everything. Bewildered by her mysterious behaviour, May spent the day in her room weeping while the young women moped around the house more or less dejected. Prevented by status and good manners from asking them to leave, May was forced to find entertainment for them, but the New Year commenced with the kind of weather that would have made a saint downcast and grumpy. On the first Sunday the sun came out at last and the four women drove for a picnic to the shores of the Baltic. Henning had no eye for wintry landscapes or frozen seas and was bored by the long drive through a forest that did not belong to him. 'A single turnip on his place is more admirable in his eyes than the tallest, pinkest, straightest pine that ever reared its snow-covered head against the setting sunlight,'[17] considered his wife who was continually astonished by his imperviousness to the great beauty of the surrounding landscape.

After that the weather held and they skated every day along the grid of canals that had been dug to drain the land. The water was frozen black and hard and it was possible to glide for miles. In some places the banks of the canals were so high that only their heads appeared, level with the fields. Two weeks later Annie and Posy left: 'Thank Heavens, Mouse and I are overjoyed.' May and her friend were able to spend the next few days solely in each other's company and were 'cosy and happy without those dreadful girls'.[18] May was desolate when it was time for Mouse to leave and her only consolation was the companionship of a huge great dane called Caesar and, as ever, a book. This time it was a recently published account of finding and renewing an estate in England called *The Garden That I Love* by Alfred Austen, the incumbent Poet Laureate, which had been given to her by Mouse.

Alfred Austen's book was to have far-reaching effects on May's own work. It is not a novel at first glance, but a fanciful and erratic diary going through one year and describing the agonies and pleasures of creating the perfect garden. The author, or 'I', in the book has a mild flirtation with a young woman called Lamia who enjoys teasing him and whose personality is remarkably similar to May's. Lamia calls the author 'Sage' in tender moments. May, whose name for Henning in her early books was 'The Man of Wrath', also called him 'Sage', not because he was wise, but because it went with onions and onions was assonant with husband, or so she goes to some length to explain. Towards the end of *The Garden That I Love*, Alfred Austen exclaims, 'Were it always April, May and June, one would discharge one's gardener and throw oneself on the gratuitous bounty of nature,' thereby proving that he knew, like May, practically nothing about gardening. But ignorance of horticulture was not, fortunately, in the 1890s any reason for not writing a popular book on the subject. Austen's was to trigger May's imagination in a way that Goethe and Bettina von Arnim had not, for in it she found a possible form that would suit her own way of writing. However it was to be five months and several false starts before the influence of the poet was to bear fruit.

In the meantime May was brought low by the dreary Pomeranian weather. At the end of one peaceful day walking with Henning, playful teasing quickly turned into something more serious. Henning fell upon his wife 'with fists and much thumping'. May confided to her diary that she was 'much grieved and shocked'. A few days later the maids became hysterical about a sudden infestation of ghosts in the upper portion of the house for which the doctor had to be called: the ghosts were laid low and so were the maids by liberal dosings of castor oil. May worked on a novel called *Amelia's Husbands* about which nothing more was recorded. She then turned her attention to a novelette called *The Tea Rose*, but not with any great spirit or energy. She was lonely and, after the amusing companionship of Mouse, craved company.

But she had her books. 'What a blessing it is to love books,' she wrote. 'Everybody must love something, and I know of no objects of love that give such substantial and unfailing returns as books and a garden. And how easy it would have been to come into the world without this, and possess instead an all consuming passion, say, for hats, perpetually raging round my empty soul.'[19] Her best and most lasting friendships with the immortals were made during those bleak days. The great beauty of her new pantheon of friends was that she could choose which one she wanted to commune with according to her mood without offending any of the others (this being the basis of her problems with the Kelly sisters). 'I read and laugh over my Boswell in the library when the lamps are lit, buried in cushions and surrounded by every sign of civilisation, with the drawn curtains shutting out the garden and the country solitude so much disliked by both sage and disciple.'[20] In the afternoons she pottered round the garden with Goethe although it was May's opinion that he had only pretended to like flowers and gardens because it was the poetic thing to do. In the evenings she would read Walt Whitman 'and listen to what that lonely and beautiful spirit has to tell me of night, sleep, death and the stars'. Keats she took into the forest and Spenser to the

Baltic.

Her most exciting discovery was Thoreau, who was sent to her by her father. Inevitably she took this liberated spirit to read beside the pond: 'He is a person who loves the open air, and will refuse to give you much pleasure if you try to read him amid the pomp and circumstance of upholstery.'[21] Of all the philosophers May had so far encountered only Thoreau was able to make her feel inferior. Her philosophy had not yet reached the acute stage, she concluded, which enabled her to see a door mat in its true character as a 'hinderer of souls', and besides, she liked to wipe her boots. To her father she wrote,

> I don't object to the number of wood-chucks in it, but I think there are too many ponds—about two-thirds is ponds . . . and as to dogginess [a Beauchamp word for scruff] I think it all must have been beautifully clean, for he went without nearly everything, so there was no place for dirt . . . He must have been a complete and perfect Pa-man.

May's gloom and feelings of isolation lifted, as always, with the weather. By the end of April it was warm enough to take her notepad out of doors and continue with her work. On 7 May her diary records: 'Began to write *In a German Garden* sitting among the raindrops and owls.' The book itself begins: 'May 7th—I love my garden. I am writing in it now in the late afternoon loveliness, much interrupted by the mosquitoes and the temptation to look at all the glories of the new green leaves washed half an hour ago in a cold shower.'

It was difficult for her to write that summer for there were many guests to stay at the castle and the rumbling differences between May and Henning were beginning to erupt to the surface. This made creative concentration difficult. Nor was May in the best of moods when she discovered that she was getting fat. Her remedy was to order her bicycle and pedal furiously round the garden for an hour and a half on end every day. Her resultant mood was chastened but not friendly. The children, too, were showing signs of chubbiness as well as growing increasingly quarrelsome, and they were ordered by their mother to run vigorously three miles every day. The route led through a pleasant wood, past an ice house and back through the park to the castle. This had to be done ten times and came to be called 'Ten Times Round'. Trix, in particular, developed an alarming increase in girth and was often put outside the carriage if the family were going for a picnic in the forest, and made to run along behind. She was hauled in, red-faced, breathless and tearful, only when the general cries of pity reached a crescendo. In May's eyes to be fat was close to being damned. Her other sovereign remedy for crossness or any sign of disease was castor oil or, as Carlyle called it, 'the oil of sorrow'. The children were given it in beer, coffee and milk at the slightest signs of irritability or sneezing.

In July May and Henning quarrelled openly, 'he wanting a baby and I not seeing it'. After four days of rows Henning left for Berlin— 'Great relief and blessing'.[22] When he came back the situation worsened steadily, and in the middle of September May wrote to her sister begging sanctuary. She was preparing, yet again, to flee. Charlotte wired back for May to go to her, but within a few days Henry Beauchamp arrived at Nassenheide. With his help a truce was arrived at for the time being and Henning left for Criewen, a von Arnim estate inhabited by his cousin Bernd. In October he proceeded to Berlin for an indefinite period.

When her father left May alone again with her thoughts and with time to return to her writing, she abandoned *In a German Garden* in favour of a return to *The Tea Rose*, which was completed and preserved. It is a turgid story of possessiveness and rage and ends with the wholesale destruction of a treasured rose garden. At the beginning of November she read the finished manuscript and 'found it very crude'.[23] She locked it away and began to copy what she had written of *In a German Garden*, which struck her as much better. She worked hard at this new book, interrupted only by Christmas, when Henning came back, and chronic cook troubles. Henning became 'easily tragic over his victuals'[24] and cooks rarely lasted long when he was displeased in any other department of his life, for it was at the table that he showed his feelings.

By the New Year 1898 May was typing out the finished manuscript of what had become *Elizabeth and her German Garden*. When and why May decided to call the heroine in the book 'Elizabeth' is not recorded, although it was her mother's name and that of her second child. Most likely it was the strong influence of Bettina (Elizabeth) von Arnim that was the deciding factor.

When she had nearly completed the book at the beginning of February she showed bits to Henning and he said, 'They must come out.' There was no fight recorded in her diary about this gross piece of censorship but Henning evidently had his way. He no doubt recognized it as highly publishable and his irritation at having a writer for a wife expressed itself in criticism. May was awake the whole night in a rage that she would have to rewrite and the next day she felt 'intensely irritable and desperate about it'.[25] When she had finally put together the version that Henning approved she retyped it, took it herself to Grambow and posted it off 'prayerfully' to Macmillan in London.

· 6 ·

Intimations of Immortality

May had nothing to do but wait for the publisher's reaction and she fell into a deep depression which was not helped by the equally dull weather—she never could be gloomy when the sun was out whatever reverses of fortune had befallen her. Such phrases as 'wondered why I was born', 'horridly depressed' and 'vain efforts to be sensible' appear in her diaries until 30 March, when 'Cloudy, windy and warm. Got answer re G. G. accepting it,' was the only entry for the day. Thirty-nine years later Elizabeth (as May will from now on be called), re-reading the diaries, wrote in the rest of the space available:

> I note I make no comment on this, to me great news, but I vividly remember my heavenly happiness that day at the family luncheon, hugging my secret. I think this was perhaps the most purely happy moment of my life and I make no comment. Oh little grumbler, always saying I'm lonely and depressed and not a word about this happy event.

During April Elizabeth corrected the proofs. In spite of it having been a record month for cold grey days—'indeed the gloom has been almost uninterrupted'[1]—she was not in the least lowered by the weather this time. She enjoyed the business of re-sculpting the book first in galley proofs which she sent back to the typesetter five times, and then in page proofs. As she did not have to pay the publisher for this massive amount of correction it is clear that Macmillan, like Henning, saw a potential winner on their list. They indulged the writer in her indecisiveness, guessing that they would be amply rewarded after it was published. This endless correcting was how Elizabeth liked to work, and in later years her secretaries were forced to wrench a manuscript away from her and post it off to the publishers if the book was ever going to get there at all, or so they thought.

With the first fine day in May, Elizabeth went into the garden and declaimed Keats's *Ode to Immortality* to the dandelions and 'was happy'.[2] A week or so later she read a book by a Professor Nettleship called *A Treasury of Human Inheritance*. In it she came across a remark that pleased her because it expressed conclusions that she herself was coming to at that time:

> Interest at its highest power is love, and if we could take an interest in all things we should be on the way to love all things and this means to be in all things or make all things our own, which is God.

Elizabeth commented in her diary:

> I get more and more to feel that there is absolutely no difference in principle between what is called physical and what is called spiritual and that if one understands a triangle one can understand oneself. If we knew all about anything, we should know everything.

Later that month she and Mouse went for a holiday to the nearby island of Rügen, the holiday island of the Baltic. When they returned Elizabeth found Henning had decked her desk out with flowers and particularly roses from the garden. It was 'like a rose show'[3] and she was delighted, for it indicated a change of attitude towards her writing which before Henning had resented. Soon she began work on a sequel to her first book called *The Solitary Summer*, although Henning held out little hope that they would remain unmolested by guests for the whole season.

Elizabeth also decided that something serious had to be done about the garden, for it was not the place she had described so lovingly in her book: her imagination had been more fertile than her flower-beds. Henning complained that there were few flowers, no fruit and that the vegetables were inedible. The last gardener had started to walk about with a spade in one hand and a revolver in the other, muttering oaths, and eventually they were forced to commit him to the local asylum. This was the third consecutive gardener to have gone mad and it had become one of Henning's jokes that all his wife's gardeners were driven insane. It was true that she used to read gardening books to them while they were working in a vain attempt to educate them up to modern standards, but she protested that she did not send them mad, she simply chose the type of men that were likely to go so, men of low expectations who would, she thought, believe that she knew as much as they did about gardening. She had had three such gardeners in succession and during that time learned what she ought to have realised from the first, that the less a person knows the more stubborn he becomes that he is right and that 'no weapons yet invented are of any use in the struggle with stupidity.'[4]

In spite of all her dreams, very little had been accomplished in the garden during the first two years at Nassenheide. Elizabeth despaired. She believed that she was a normally intelligent person, and that if such a person gave her whole time to a subject it was very likely that she would be successful. But at the end of two years, both regarded with philosophy, she used to go into her garden sometimes and cry. It was the weeds, and the way they flourished that finally persuaded her to engage an experienced gardener and give him reasonable help, for she found that much as she enjoyed a garden unencumbered with ubiquitous gardeners, yet she 'detested nettles more'.[5]

She complained to her husband: 'Nearly all the bulbs and seeds and plants I have squandered my money and my hopes on have turned out to be nettles, and I don't like them. I have had a wretched summer and I never want to see a meek gardener again.'[6] They advertised and subsequently interviewed 'shoals' of applicants. So many answered that it seemed half the population must have been gardeners out of a situation. Finally Elizabeth settled on a man called Leinau, an experienced worker who was to stay with her for years. He was very deaf and if any of his employer's ideas appeared to him too outrageous, he would grow deafer. He had strikingly intelligent eyes and quick movements and had shown himself less concerned with the state of chaos existing than with considerations of what might eventually be made of the place. Elizabeth found him filled with the humility and eagerness to learn which she considered were only found in those who have already learned more than their neighbours. He entered into her plans with enthusiasm and made suggestions of his own and they busied themselves altering the beds and laying down natural manure and compost when the due season arrived.

Another focus of the countess's attention was the plight of the villagers, those peasants who lived on the estate and whose welfare was, by English though not German tradition, her domain. She quickly discovered that superstition and ignorance were almost insuperable obstacles to persuading them to better themselves. One woman, whose child was wasting away from having spent the whole of its short life surrounded by stale air, refused to follow the doctor's instructions to wash, air and feed it at regular intervals. Elizabeth tried to reason with her: 'I wonder what would happen to my children if I kept them in one hot room day and night for six months. You see how they are . . . out all day and how well they are?' 'They are so strong,' said the peasant woman with a doleful sniff, 'that they can stand it.' Her child's first outing was to a cemetery two months later. Elizabeth concluded:

> If one could only get hold of the children! . . . Catch them young and put them in a garden, with no other people of their own class forever teaching them by example what is ugly, and unworthy and gross.[7]

Her own children *were*, by comparison, brought up in a garden, shielded from the world, apart from their father frequently calling them *'Esel'* or *'Dummkopf'*. The shock of the real world, when it came with its callousness and vulgarity, was to be a rude awakening for all of them.

Always meteorological in her explanations of moods and enthusiasms, Elizabeth attributed her interest in do-goodery to the bad weather, of which they had had more than their fair share that summer. Philanthropy was intermittent with her and seized her 'like a cold in the head'[8] whenever the weather was bad. On warm days her benevolence melted away, though it might increase again as the thermometer descended.

Elizabeth and her German Garden appeared in the English bookshops on 20 September 1898 and was an instant best-seller. It is not really a novel in any tradition then understood by practitioners of the form; there is no story line or plot and nothing of any significance happens in it. It is a description of the author's life written in a loose, discursive style reminiscent of a long and entertaining letter home for the whole family to read. She describes finding the house and her struggles with the garden and her pleasure in it with a charm and freshness that she was never again quite to achieve in her later books. Two women come to stay over Christmas and it is tempting to assume they are portraits of the dreadful Kelly sisters—who did assume this was so—but on closer inspection reveal themselves to be two facets of Elizabeth's own complicated personality. Irais is a sophisticated and witty courtier whose life is sybaritic and viewpoint ironic. Minora is the earnest English writer whose determination to find copy and 'jot' it down ready to 'throw together' into a book makes her the baffled butt of Irais' leg-pulling sense of humour.

Almost imperceptibly Elizabeth presents her personal manifesto which is sparked off by a discussion between the three women and Henning, 'The Man of Wrath', as to the justice of German women being classified legally with idiots and children:

> If your lot makes you cry and be wretched, get rid of it and take another; strike out for yourself; don't listen to the shrieks of your relations, to their gibes or their entreaties; don't let your own microscopic set prescribe your goings out and comings in; don't be afraid of public opinion in the shape of the neighbour in the next house, when all the world is before you new and shining, and everything is possible, if you will only be energetic and independent and seize opportunity by the scruff of the neck.[9]

The book was reprinted eleven times before the end of that year, by May the following year there had been twenty-one reprints, and it was still reprinting several times a year in 1914. Most reviewers were delighted with the discovery of such a fresh new talent though many people mistook the levity of the book for a sign that it was light-weight. Elizabeth's irreverent, light and witty style contrasted pleasingly with the intense and gloomy works that had been on offer, influenced by Darwin's pessimistic conclusions, the Gothic romances of Marie Corelli, Oscar Wilde's decadent movement and H. G. Wells's science fiction. There was an immediate response from the growing band of gardeners who, in the wake of Alfred Austen, were scandalizing their gardeners by getting their own fingers dirty with the soil. Gertrude Jekyll was inspired to write her first book, *Wood and Garden*, which appeared the following year. She joined Elizabeth in disliking the tight regimentation of flowers and flowerbeds and praising the charm of clambering roses, wild flowers and natural landscaping.

Curiously, the publication coincided with the first printed writing of Katherine Mansfield, then called Kathleen Beauchamp. Elizabeth's ten-year-old cousin had written a story called *A Happy Christmas Eve* for her high school magazine. Katherine's parents had visited England, spending some time with Henry (now affectionately known as Deepa to the family) and Louey. They took back with them a copy of *Elizabeth and her German Garden* to New Zealand and Katherine read and re-read it. After this, whenever she was asked what she was going to be when she grew up, she promptly replied, 'A writer'.

The book was published anonymously with not even a

pseudonym, and Elizabeth avoided the attention of her readers, at least for a short time. Only her intimates were aware that it was her book that was streaking across the skies of literary London like a small comet, and they were careful to remain silent. She had been ordered by her husband to remain anonymous, for the Prussian *Junker* class thought it disgraceful to write books for money. It would have identified them with the effete whom they had, for so many years, moved themselves as a warrior nation to suppress. There was no disgrace, however, for a woman of Elizabeth's own English class and taste to write a book. She had cleverly outmanoeuvred her husband's restrictions, for if she had signed the book with a pseudonym, it would have been accepted in literary London that the author wished to remain unknown. Declining the use of one made it quite certain that the literate would go to great pains to find out who she was. Elizabeth enjoyed anonymity, but only up to a point. On her travels and hikes she often dressed in the simple clothes of a governess or a dusty hiker and slept in inferior accommodation rather than reveal that she was a countess and endure the grovelling with which Germans treated their high-born. She enjoyed the innocent deception but relished her status and a flourish of her signature usually solved any tiresome problems.

At a conservative estimate Elizabeth made over £10,000 in the book's first year—over a quarter of a million in today's money. By any standards she was now very well off. Such was the law in those days (prior to the Married Woman's Property Act in Germany or *Gesetz über die gleichbane Scheidung von Mann und Frau*, 1957) that all of the money belonged, legally, to Henning. If Elizabeth wished to keep it for her own uses she would have had to seek a special marriage contract for separation of goods. This she did not do. The diary records serious ructions with Henning 'of a fairly disgraceful nature' concerning money as well as the vexing problem of the non-existent heir. Days went past and they did not speak to each other. A few months before her death Elizabeth meditated deeply on those early days of endless fights with Henning. She remembered:

> . . . it was very hot at Nassenheide, and for some reason,
> no doubt good, I had quarrelled with H. I was sitting in a
> trousseau chemise, locked into the little pink room . . . and
> H. tried to get in. I was working on *The Solitary Summer*.
> When he found the door locked, and me as silent as a fish,
> he went round into the next room which had a communi-
> cating door, and tried that and burst it open. I was sitting

at the writing table facing it. He picked up one of those big pencils they call a Bismarck Stift and hurled it at me. It missed me. I sat frozen with fury and didn't move, didn't speak and inscribed the date in the Nuttall dictionary open before me, so as never to forget. When he died eleven years later I cut this vengeful inscription out. Funny all this.[10]

Their new and lavish lifestyle attracted the attention of Henning's creditors, and duns arrived at the door. Among the hopeful were members of the family. Elizabeth realized that it might be as well to settle these debts in the interests of peace, and in any case she had little choice. With the release of Henning from his debts, which cost at least as much as his wife had earned in the first year, they were free to enjoy their good fortune. They employed liveried footmen and carriage drivers. All the servants wore the von Arnim scarlet and black with white gloves and many buttons. The entire family had beautiful clothes, all made for them in London, and for many years it was rare to see Elizabeth in the same fabulous evening gown more than once, or so it seemed to her children. Elizabeth soon realized that in repaying the debts she had bought power in the family, and she bargained to be allowed more freedom in her movements as well as complete authority over the children's education, on which she had definite views.

Meanwhile in the outside world the buzz of interest as to who she might be rose to a dull roar as her book continued to out-sell any other. Newspapers and magazines published regular articles of speculation during the first year. The *Daily Mail* produced a full-page inquiry weighing the pros and cons of three women who were likely candidates, of whom Elizabeth was one. The other two were Queen Victoria's granddaughter, Princess Henry of Prussia, and Daisy, Princess Pless. Unnamed, Elizabeth was, for a short time, the most famous woman in the English-speaking world.

The summer of the publication Elizabeth's work was continuously interrupted by rows with Henning about further offspring. This time her husband was clearly not going to tolerate her denial. One row towards the end of September 1898 went on for four days. Finally Elizabeth fled rather than be forced to submit to Henning's demands, and sought refuge at her sister's house in Fernhurst, Sussex. There the two commiserated about husbands, for Charlotte's had recently tip-toed into her room while she was sleeping and cut off all of her beautiful red-golden hair, and she was beginning to suspect that he was not merely eccentric but possibly a little deranged. Elizabeth's sister's problems paled by comparison to her own, however. The Beauchamps soon learned the reason Elizabeth preferred not to be in the same country as her husband, and parties of the family came down to Fernhurst to persuade her that it was her duty, even if not her pleasure, to bear a son for the preservation of such an august lineage. 'Relatives are like drugs,' she wrote, 'useful sometimes, and even pleasant if taken in small quantities and seldom, but dreadfully pernicious on the whole and the truly wise avoid them.'[11] Finally the two sisters left for Germany and after a few days Charlotte returned to England, content that her wilful sibling had finally resigned herself. By the end of November Elizabeth knew that she was pregnant again.

The reason Elizabeth gives to her public for this lamentable situation is characteristically removed to a degree from reality—she ascribes most of her husband's bullying to her own foolishness in the early books. She explains the lowering of her guard as being due to the shock of the sudden and violent death of her great dane, Caesar. Henning, seeing her grief, comforted her and, as she comments in her memoirs, 'one thing led to another in the way things do', and almost immediately she was caught once again in the burdens of pregnancy. A strange comfort, she thought, as she tried to deal with the 'aches and pains, the dark forebodings and tendency to make wills which always went with that condition'[12] in her case, although there was no doubt that it had, for a time, made her forget the dog.

Elizabeth's diary does not mention once, nor does it give any indication, that anything momentous has happened in her life that year. On the contrary the tone of her entries and her letters is exactly the same as before the book was published. No doubt she was heeding her own advice to her daughters: 'Never get excited about anything.'[13] At the end of December 1898 she sums up the year laconically: 'This a year of bad weather and kept it up till the last. Chief thing that happened as far as I'm concerned, appearance of "Elizabeth" with fair success—more a good deal, than it deserved. All well.'[14]

In spite of her condition she managed to finish *The Solitary Summer* by January the following year. She marks the event in her diary: 'Read it through—mixed feelings—chiefly disgust. Futility that cannot be uttered. Am, after all, a poor fool.' Her attention had been caught, as had everyone else's, by the Boer War. The Germans sympathized with the Boers and the local pastor had begun to lecture Elizabeth personally from the pulpit on the evils of war, so that she was forced to put up her lorgnette and glare back at him, feeling even more alienated from the race of which she was now a member.

Elizabeth derived much comfort from the company of her niece when Charlotte's beautiful daughter Margery came to stay at the castle to learn German and also to be with her aunt during the waiting months. Elizabeth had insisted that the baby should be born in England and it was planned that Margery, or Drish as she was known, should accompany her there when her time was near. The von Arnims enjoyed the companionship of such a pretty and accomplished young girl and she was taught to shoot and provided with a horse and a German tutor. Naturally Elizabeth was astonished when Charlotte sent her a telegram in the middle of April insisting that her daughter return home immediately. The reason afterwards given was that she was to greet her brother, Johnnie, who was expected back from a cruise, but Elizabeth could not believe this and suspected that the girl had been unhappy with them and had petitioned her mother to release her. Her diary records that she was 'surprised and puzzled so wept in secret'. Charlotte was notorious in the family for changing her mind and doting on her children excessively. Henning commented, 'If you were a squib, Charlotte would let you off to please her children.'

The following month *The Solitary Summer* was in the bookshops. Elizabeth had sent her father an advance copy with a letter which almost begged him to like it:

> What you say and think of *Elizabeth* is more to me than any other criticism and if the next one gives *you* pleasure then all my torments in writing it will be made up for—for it is poor stuff, I fancy, but I hope I may be wrong.

She received back a letter in which criticism went hand in hand with approbation. Elizabeth was crushed by this and wrote in her diary, 'Got a letter from Pa from which I gather he does not care for it— spent day in tears consequently, for I had been so sure that just Pa would like it.' She would have been less cast down had she known that in his journal he had commented on the day the book appeared, '. . . [It] should help to open our eyes to the beauties God so bountifully scatters abroad for all.' She wrote back to him, 'Please don't think I'm so silly as to mind any criticism so loving and appreciative as yours . . .' The only mitigating circumstance that can possibly be put forward for this display of gratuitous paternal cruelty is that Henry himself wished to be remembered as a literary man and no doubt cursed his luck to discover he was sandwiched between a father who was a locally renowned poet and a daughter who was being mistaken, in some reviews, for the Poet Laureate himself. He was not a man who enjoyed taking the back seat.

Charlotte arrived in Germany with Margery and Johnnie and they took Elizabeth back with them to England at the beginning of July to prepare for the birth at her parents' house in Addison Road. Henry wrote in his journal:

> Darling May with us, exceedingly bulbous—choked almost by incense elicited by her new book—well, she won't burn in the next world for anything she has yet published in this. Rather may have reward as having 'taught the blind to see' and 'look through Nature up to Nature's God'.

Henning arrived shortly afterwards 'beaming and jolly', planning to go to an agricultural show at Maidstone to buy English pigs to breed with and improve his own stock. English pigs as well as English wives were clearly highly thought of in Prussia as breeding stock. A week later he left with 'a whole herd of swine'[15] and Elizabeth moved into a house in Sheffield Terrace, Campden Hill. The weather was unbearably hot even for those not expecting babies, and she 'sweltered'[16] until the 29th when she produced daughter number four, Felicitas Joyce. Henning did not arrive for a month and when he did their meeting was tearful—daughters number five and six seemed an inevitability. Elizabeth guessed what can now be proved beyond doubt, that some men are only able to reproduce girls. That Henning had by then fathered five daughters seemed conclusive. She contemplated drastic and unconventional action to put an end to his fruitless quest for an heir.

The family returned to Nassenheide at the end of September to find it decked out with flowers and wreaths. The babies were ecstatic to have their mother home although puzzled by the existence of a new sister in their midst. The enigma was soon cleared up for them, however, when it was explained that she had been dug up in a parsley bed in England. Their mother went round the garden with Leinau and was very pleased with the progress of the summer and the promise of good fruit, for once, that season.

Three days later Henning was arrested for embezzlement.

The moment she heard the news was seared into Elizabeth's memory for the rest of her life. She never spoke about the shock of the event until years after her husband had died. It was a windy, sunny day and all the marigolds were in flower. After lunch she went into the drawing-room to read. She wore a stiff shirt and a long blue neck tie. Horne (the Pope's successor) came in and said, clicking his heels together, 'Countess, they want to arrest the count!' and his mistress, astonished, said 'Why?' After that,

> . . . everywhere was dismay and desolation . . . All that had gone before [had been] part of a long sleep—a sleep disturbed by troubling and foolish dreams, but still only a sleep and only dreams. She woke up . . . and remained wide awake after that for the rest of her life.

So wrote Elizabeth when describing the event in *The Benefactress*.

Henning had been taken away and thrown into prison in Stettin where he was remanded in custody. The managers of a bank of which he was a director had brought the charges. According to Henning they had conspired to get rid of him, for his abrupt manner with colleagues and subordinates had not endeared him to the staff. Someone had embezzled money, one of the clerks as it turned out, and Henning appeared to be a convenient scapegoat. Fortunately, and with the help of expensive lawyers, he was able to prove his innocence and was acquitted.

The children were told nothing of this at the time. They only saw that their father was not there and that their mother was distraught, her happiness completely shattered. Elizabeth had great difficulty in seeing her husband in prison, and when she did found him in a tiny airless cell:

> The few hours he had thought to stay in that place were lengthening out into days . . . a profound gloom was settling down on him. If no one helped him from outside, his case was indeed desperate . . . Where were they all, those jovial companions who shot over his estate so often? The hours dragged by, each one a lifetime, each one so packed with opportunities for going mad, he thought, as he counted how many of them separated him already from his free, honourable past life.[17]

Even Cousin Bernd, their staunch friend, stayed away. Neither Charlotte nor her father wrote. In a letter to his father-in-law written after the event Henning explained in struggling English some of the circumstances of the affair:

> The last two weeks I had a great fight, not as is generally the case with my wife, but with the managers of a bank of

which I am a chief director. I wanted to dismiss two of them because of their want of wisdom, their great stupidity and inclination to cheating, they wanted to hold their position and expulse me. At last they began to attack me in the newspapers and appealed to shareholders, who are, like all aggregate people, very inclined to follow the advice of the man who makes the most noise. The fight made me unable the last two weeks to think about all I love most in this world. I forgot my wife, my children, you, myself and many other things till the battle was over and I've returned home with the scalps of my enemies [sic].

Elizabeth wrote to her father:

Do you know Spenser's 'Sleep after toil, porte after stormie seas, rest after war, death after life doth greatly please'? H. and I have just got into port after stormy seas, and the lines won't go out of my head. I don't doubt that had things gone wrong with us, we still should have been happy—all the lovely things in life still would have been there, and as you so beautifully say, darling Pa, we would have looked more up at the stars. Well, we look at them now and, if with less philosophy, yet with more thankfulness.

Three years later, after the case had been heard at great length, Henning wrote again to his father-in-law:

It is very good that you did not know particulars of my trouble, as it would have been quite impossible to tell you details of an act of accusation of such size as this one. It formed a thick volume printed in small type of many hundred pages, each page containing at least one big crime, and crimes of such select quality that it is rather a pity they have never been commited [sic]. It was a museum of crimes and many of them were so complicated, that nobody, not even the public prosecutor who wrote the act of accusation, could understand them. He did his best and was extremely qualified to understand them as he had an uncommon amount of imbecility at his command— but he didn't succeed. An instance will show you the system of accusation. One point was the accusation of falsification of a public document. By the trial it was proved and the public prosecutor acknowledged, first that the act in question was not a public document, secondly that its content was true and quite correct, thirdly, that I had nothing to do with it. You will easily perceive how difficult it is to avoid such crimes. The key to all the extraordinary proceedings was that I offended very much an official of the government at Stettin, who wanted to play dirty tricks to the bank whose interest I as the chief director thought my duty to defend. It was he, I think, who suggested the idea to put me in prison to prevent my running away.

As you know the trial ended with a brilliant victory on my side, and I hope to have the pleasure to see the official in question punished as he deserves it. As I am a fighting cock I will probably not swallow all the injustice I had to suffer without kicking; you know perhaps Henning is the name of the cock in German nursery tales and so I can't behave like a hen.

Liebet remembered her father as being a kind, but short-tempered man with a tendency to call people *'Esel'*, *'Quatschkopf'* or *'Duselfritz'* and to mock and expose the dishonest or merely stupid and incompetent. It was clear that he had unnecessarily alienated many who might have helped him then, and later, when financial disaster loomed. Indeed, in spite of his wife's earnings, Henning was never very far from ruin. Although his land debts were paid off, the legal fees of this new court case and those his father incurred to clear *his* name were still outstanding. His farming activities were more in the way of experimentation than a serious attempt to make money. The land on the estate, so recently claimed from the marshes, was anything but fertile while the expense of digging manure into it was huge. Henning hoped that he might develop a strain of lupin, then grown as cattle fodder and in some places eaten by humans, that would flourish in Pomerania. He was also experimenting in an attempt to grow the perfect Pomeranian potato. His efforts failed to attract fellow owners of arid land, and even if he had been successful his profits would have been small. His daughters were often presen- ted, at mealtimes, with several small dishes of potatoes on which their father wished them to give an opinion. Beatrix remembered that they all tasted exactly the same, but they happily enthused over some and rejected others, as this pleased their father. She was delighted when Henning named a strain after her. In later years, whenever Beatrix put on weight, which was more often than she liked, her mother reminded her of this signal honour.

Throughout the dreadful times that surrounded Henning's imprisonment Elizabeth managed to continue working on the most lighthearted of all her publications, *The April Baby's Book of Tunes*. In it she describes how she and the children amuse themselves through the composition of musical settings for six popular nursery rhymes and for *Gentle Jesus Meek and Mild*. The April, May and June babies (Evi, Liebet and Trix), up till then only having made rare appearances in the novels, here take the stage. Their solemn conversations with their mother are full of the special brand of innocent surrealism for which their mother had already made them famous:

> Then the mother began to tell them about Miss Muffet, and of course the first question the babies asked was, 'What is a tuffet?' To which, equally of course, the mother replied, 'A thing you sit on.'
>
> 'But you sits on such a many things,' objected the astute June, 'and they still isn't tuffets.'
>
> 'I think it must have been a three-legged stool,' said the mother, who had gone to the length of examining the pages of *Nuttall's Pronouncing and Defining Dictionary* in search of enlightenment, and found that tuffets were left severely alone.
>
> 'I thinks it must have been one sofa,' said June.
>
> 'A sofa?'
>
> 'Yes, else two people can't sit together on anything other than one sofa.'
>
> 'But there weren't two people.'
>
> 'Yes, the spider did sit down beside her.'
>
> 'But a spider isn't people,' said April, looking puzzled.
>
> 'Yes, she is,' said June.
>
> 'No, she isn't,' said April, and then added, as though the truth had just dawned on her, 'She's an animal, and animals aren't people; they've got too many legs.'

The tunes sound like a nursery flirtation between *Hymns Ancient and Modern* and *Mad Carew*. The illustrations are by Kate Greenaway and they perfectly match the good humour and charm of the book. *The April Baby's Book of Tunes* was the first commission that she had worked on for three years, and the drawings were the first to be printed directly rather than be laboriously translated into etchings by a Mr Evans. Indeed, it was the only piece of work offered to her at that time, for although George Routledge was republishing her selected works, her style had gone out of fashion. She had even found it impossible to sell her own ideas for books to any publisher, though the *Athenaeum* was commenting with distaste on the 'stupidity and gaudiness' of most new children's books. It was Elizabeth who suggested to Macmillan that Kate Greenaway would be appropriate, and the illustrator accepted gladly, for Elizabeth was one of her favourite authors—she had even recommended her to Ruskin. Although the artist often apologized for producing the work late because of her bad health, she managed to finish three weeks before the deadline. When the book appeared for Christmas in 1900 reviewers hailed the drawings as 'Greenaway at her best' and Elizabeth's friends were astonished at the likeness she had caught to the three children of whom she had not even seen a photograph. Sadly, it was to be her swan-song for she died the following year.

Little Maids all in a Row

Elizabeth's diary falls silent on the day Henning was arrested and does not resume until January 1901. During that time she wrote, as well as the nursery rhyme book, a double-decker romantic novel called *The Benefactress*. This is the first work that Elizabeth published where the heroine is not in the first person singular although she is still, quite obviously, based on herself. Anna Estcourt is the unmarried sister of a poor philosopher of noble birth who 'had read a great deal of Schopenhauer and was uneasily conscious that it had not been good for him'. He restores the family fortunes by marrying the extremely rich Susie Dobbs, daughter of a Birmingham grocer. Anna, though pretty, has a tendency to waste her time 'in that foolish pondering over the puzzle of existence, over those unanswerable whys and wherefores, which are as a rule restricted, among women, to the elderly and plain'. Consequently, nobody will marry her. A German uncle dies, leaving her an estate in Pomerania, and Anna decides that from the revenue of the estate she will invite distressed gentlewomen to share her new-found freedom, for she is unable to bestow her love on anyone who is not deserving or blighted in some way (Elizabeth herself had a penchant for lame ducks). Anna's neighbour, a tall, handsome minor noble, falls hopelessly in love with her but this only irritates. It is not until he is arrested and sent to gaol for something he did not do that she realizes her love for him.

The most astonishing character in the book from the point of view of historical foresight is a German pastor called Adolf. He has a tendency, encouraged by his wife, to preach on weekdays. One of his favourite subjects is the thieving ways of the Jews.

> 'The Jews?' [Anna] echoed. One of her greatest friends at home was a Jew, a delightful person, the mere recollection of whom made her smile, so witty and charming and kind

was he. And of Jews in general she could not remember to have heard anything at all. 'They steal not only the money from our pockets and bread from our mouths,' continued the pastor leaning forward, his light grey eyes opened to their widest extent, and speaking in a whisper that made her scalp begin the process known as creeping, 'but blood—blood from our veins.'

. . . His wife, hearing the well-known rapid speech of his inspired moments, glowed with pride. 'My Adolf surpasses himself,' she thought.

The story had a happy ending although Elizabeth did not like such unrealistic things. She was still struggling with the love scenes while correcting the proofs and claimed to 'dislike love and loathe scenes'.

On her by then yearly visits to England Elizabeth was invited to attend the salon of Maude Stanley in Smith Square, and eventually became so intimate with this formidable and fascinating older woman that she habitually stayed in her house for the first week of every homecoming. Miss Stanley was a feminist who concentrated her energies in reforming the street-walkers of London. She formed a club for them and held classes on needlework and deportment. One day, in an attempt to get them to wear less make-up she plastered her own face with lipstick and rouge and stood up in front of the women saying, 'Girls, you see how lovely I look tonight; it is all due to artificial methods.'[1] Miss Stanley was a powerful and dedicated woman and had a strong influence on the upbringing of the two future Earls Russell, Francis and his younger brother Bertrand. Her salon was said to embody the virtue of the Stanleys' enlightened thinking but with little of the arrogance that was generated by some other members of the family. The Stanley milieu was as interesting as any that could, at that period, be found in England. Its atmosphere was liberal; discussion was carried on with total freedom in an adventurous and exciting search for the truth and, though often impassioned, was animated by a large tolerance. Here Elizabeth met Francis Russell's friend from America, George Santayana,* as well as Bertrand Russell. Francis himself was often there as well.

Naturally much of the old infatuation flared to life when they re-met. They were two of a kind, and both disregarded conventional

*Francis met George Santayana when he visited Harvard in 1894. Santayana had been a student there then and later he became a philosophy don at the same place. Over the years he became Francis's most faithful friend and adviser and their correspondence continued for the whole of Francis's life.

standards enough for their liaison to be relatively guilt-free. Francis had been entangled in lawsuits of one kind or another during the 1890s. His wife Edith and her mother had sued him unsuccessfully for restitution of conjugal rights. It was clear to the judge as to everyone else that they only wanted to have a lever to get more money out of him. They then printed 'libels of a most obscene and degrading character' purporting to be in the form of statutory declarations. Francis was forced to sue for criminal libel. It turned out on investigation that the pamphlets had been printed by a purveyor of pornography and rubber goods who lived in the same house as Lady Scott's sister, who in turn ran a massage parlour. During the proceedings Francis's cottage, which contained many documents for his defence, burned down and the chief witness for the defence died mysteriously in prison before he could be cross-examined by the prosecution. Nevertheless, Lady Scott was found guilty and sentenced to eight months' hard labour. At Francis's intercession she was made a first-class misdemeanant, but the sentence broke her and he had no more trouble from her or her daughter. Unfortunately, in spite of all the legal actions, he was still married to Edith. A divorce was a possibility, for when Lady Scott came out of prison she and her daughter set up house and lived on immoral earnings—men paid them money for the pleasure of their company and sometimes more—but the two women were careful and Francis could get no proof.

He spent much time on the Continent sailing in his yacht *Royal* and interesting himself in local politics.* He met through this a widowed colleague in the London County Council called Marion Somerville. She was a 'fat, florid, coarse Irish woman of forty, with black curls, friendly manners and emotional opinions',[2] according to Bertrand. She was also a well-known member of the Pioneer Club and an active supporter of women's suffrage. She and Francis 'seemed to take to each other at first sight'.[3] Soon they were living together but it was not long, however, before Mollie, as she was called, began to petition for marriage and she eventually agreed to an American one even though it would not be binding in England. The two of them set off for the States and lived for six months in Nevada to qualify for residence. Francis first procured a divorce from Edith under American law and then married Mollie. In 1900

*He was also a member of the Fabian Society and is referred to in G. B. Shaw's correspondence as 'John' Russell. As Francis makes no allusion to this in his memoirs it must be assumed that he soon became disenchanted.

they returned to England and set up an establishment in the Gray's Inn Road. A year later Francis was arrested for bigamy.

His divorce from Edith was found to be invalid in English law and in spite of Francis's protestations that in that case so was his marriage to Mollie, he was tried in the House of Lords, found guilty and imprisoned for six months. Naturally the salon at Smith Square was fascinated by the trial and Elizabeth was astonished to find that both her husband and her lover were going through the same ordeal.

One day Miss Stanley announced her intention of coming to stay at Nassenheide. The household was thrown into a great bustle before her arrival and the children were lectured severely on their manners. Elizabeth was uncharacteristically in complete thrall to this severe woman and heeded her advice as if it were Holy Writ. It was vital that her guest should be impressed, and Elizabeth had, perhaps, claimed some things about her garden, husband and children that might not be so obvious to the casual observer. Maude Stanley was anything but a casual observer. When she arrived she insisted on being shown everything and everybody that her protégée had talked of or written about, especially the children. She stared at them silently through her lorgnette, and they thought her an old and terrifying lady. Not until just before she left did she give her verdict: the children should make their own beds, darn their own clothes and carry out specific duties every day concerned with the welfare of another, if not a human then a rabbit or a cat. They should never be allowed to eat between meals unless it be protein biscuits which she pronounced to be a sovereign remedy second only to castor oil. Fruit and water should be struck entirely from their diet and they should see as little of their parents as possible. (The thirsty children were thereafter forced to drink from flower pots or dog bowls when they thought they were unobserved.) Finally Elizabeth was told that her floors should be thoroughly doused with petroleum once a month to keep down the vermin, and a vegetarian diet was strongly recommended.

The main reason for Miss Stanley's visit was to see for herself how Elizabeth's money was spent. The enlightened view of the salon had, naturally, deplored that the revenue from those delightful books was seeping into the sandy and arid Pomeranian soil or, worse, into the bottomless pit of the von Arnim exchequer. Henning was tackled by both women and made to agree to a contract separating the estates of the marriage. How this was achieved remains a mystery, but from then on Elizabeth's money was her own. The children's education was also exhaustively discussed. No matter that they were only girls.

Maude Stanley agreed with Elizabeth that they should be educated like boys, as if there was no difference at all.

Elizabeth greeted 1901 in her diary with the words:

> Ye dragons, whose sulphurous breath
> Lighten the dark abodes of death,
> Change your fierce hissing into joyful songs,
> and praise your maker with your forked tongues.

Even so she was happy for the first time since her marriage to Henning. He ascribed it to a sound digestion but his wife disagreed, for had she not always had a sound stomach and had she always been happy? Most certainly not. She had at last accepted her role as wife and mother and Henning had agreed to allow her to visit England once a year. She was finally free of the intermittent depression that had dogged her for the past ten years: at the age of thirty-four she was beginning to enjoy herself thoroughly and at all times. When she went to England in April her father commented:

> Our darling May spent a few days with us here yesterday, surprising us all by her brightness and seventeen-year-old appearance and simplicity—[She is] a rare and fascinating combination of dove and serpent . . . she is delightfully alive and full of work—therefore contented and happy— whilst apparently ten years younger than when [she] married ten years ago . . .[4]

As soon as Elizabeth returned to Pomerania she started to cast about for ideas for her next book. *The Benefactress* had not yet come out, and she thought it safest to return to her original, autobiographical form until she found out how the critics thought she could handle a straightforward novel. She turned an old orangery in the park into a writing retreat and called it her *Treibhaus*. No one was allowed to disturb her there: not the children, not the servants and especially not Henning. Above the door she had written up PROCUL EST PROFANI. She had had several fracas with Henning when she wrote in a room on the first floor of the castle, and this orangery or greenhouse appeared to be the solution to her constantly ignored requests for privacy. It was far enough away from the house for her husband to have very pressing news indeed to go all that way to disturb her. It was a calm retreat, rather like a grave, she thought, mouldy and 'smelling of the past'.[5] Complete silence reigned and she was able to write there undisturbed. Nobody could see her from the outside because the windows were so grimy, and no servants could succeed in rousing her. When they came she sat still and pretended to be elsewhere and very soon they went away. One gardener was allowed in every day at a fixed hour when his mistress was unlikely to be there. His job was to fill the numerous vases with fresh flowers and the fireplace with wood. If anything needed dusting or tidying Elizabeth did it herself. A maid was allowed to take out the rug and beat it once every six months. Its one large room contained a big desk, a day-bed and a comfortable easy chair, and bookshelves lined the walls.

Elizabeth was not yet in the habit of writing for regular hours and allowing her life to revolve around this discipline. She still put her household duties first and thought about what she was going to write while she was attending to them. She would usually rush over to the *Treibhaus* in the evening for a few hours and quickly write down what she had been meditating upon. This habit soon changed to irregular bouts of work alternating with walks in the park with her two great danes. If anybody were to see her walking with the dogs, they were instructed to flee from her. When mealtimes seriously interrupted her writing or thinking she would sit throughout silent and thoughtful. Because nobody was allowed to speak before she had, many meals were eaten in complete silence.

After several false starts it occurred to Elizabeth at the end of June that there was no reason why she should not drive through Rügen and write a book of her adventures. Filled with this idea, she wrote to an English friend called Oona and asked her to accompany her, and then ordered the ordinance maps and studied the guide books. In the middle of July she and Oona set out, travelling in a light, hooded carriage drawn by four horses. This was followed by a cart loaded with their luggage and their maids. Turning their backs on duty (Elizabeth believed that 'there is nothing so absolutely bracing for the soul as frequently doing so'[6]), they travelled to the island that had inspired the Romantic poets, where Titans had once lived and where to this day can be seen ancient altars dedicated to gods of long ago whose names have been forgotten but whose presences still linger. Elizabeth had been there often before with the children and had sat in a hooded basket chair on the beach while they played in the sand. Crowds had gathered to watch them, so different were they from other German children in their lively inventiveness. This time Elizabeth and her friend set out hoping for adventures while Henning stayed at home, uneasy but resigned. The result of this was *The Adventures of Elizabeth in Rügen*, an autobiographical account with some fictional elements which has some of the most sustained and timelessly comic passages Elizabeth ever wrote. There is included a superb portrait of a dotty militant feminist who is also the mouth-piece for some of the author's own ideas.

In October *The Benefactress* came out in America and in England. She feared it would fall very flat because she thought it was bad, and was astonished when the reviews were as good as any she had had. The *Daily Mail* said that the book 'has the same distinctive charm as its predecessors, the same unforced wit, the same wholesomeness that made Elizabeth's *Garden* so successful a tonic for the dreary minded'. *The Examiner* spoke of her as 'The Unknown Genius' and several critics saw affinities with Jane Austen. A week later the unknown genius commented in her diary:

> Got a bad review of *The Benefactress* in the *Athenaeum*—quite a just one but the flesh shrinks before justice of the sort however much one tries to persuade it not to. And however much one may protest one is always really conceited down at one's dregs, so the better part of me is gloomily rejoiced at seeing the viler part of me curling up.

To her father she wrote:

> Your appreciative letter on reaching p.197 of my book was as burning incense to my nostrils. I only hope that by the time you have reached p.297 and 397 your opinion won't have changed too much. Meanwhile I keep getting reviews that talk about froth and trifles and quite complete the chastening of my already drooping soul. If ever I write a second novel, which won't be ever, it shall be steeped to the top of its pages in blood. I might kill H. in it and give a detailed account of how he looked disembowelled and call it *The Murder of the Man of Wrath*.

At the beginning of March 1902 Elizabeth was 'full of forebodings of a horrible kind'.[7] She feared, correctly, that she was pregnant. She took a hot foot-bath to bring on her 'season' as she referred to her menstrual periods, but to no avail. The next day she spent in deep despair and the day after that she went to Stettin to see their doctor, Haeckel, about her plight. She tried to persuade him to terminate the pregnancy but he would not listen. The point was clearly something other than her conviction that she would simply produce another girl. This reason for a termination would hardly carry any weight nowadays, and at the turn of the century abortion was not only illegal but, in such circumstances, unthinkable. She was a supremely healthy woman who produced strapping children so that the argument of physical peril was also out of the question.

Elizabeth's reaction to this pregnancy gives rise to interesting speculation, the answer to which is unlikely ever to emerge. She had, by then, demonstrated that she thought little of the conventions of the day and may have felt that she could, after so many years of marriage to Henning, allow herself to be attracted to Francis. It was her custom to go to London early in the year and it is therefore possible that Francis was the father of her child and not Henning.

The 'wind was taken out of [her] sails'[8] and she wrote no more in her diaries except to say that she 'wrote a little, very little'[9] of the Rügen book. She sent her daughter Felicitas (now called by everyone Quiqui), who had become difficult, to her parents for an indefinite spell, glad to have at least one less child to worry about, and in early September left Nassenheide for England to take up residence in a flat in Whitehall Court. The other children meanwhile mooned about the castle, gazing out of the windows wondering when their 'darling Mummylet'[10] would be home. Evi described the garden as it was by that time:

> Those many acres with their lawns, flowers, beautiful beeches, chestnut trees, piney woods, the little stream with the irises, or flags as we called them then, growing beside it . . . The gardener's boy raking the paths . . . the horse, shod in leather, pulling the mower across the vast lawns . . . After rain there might be a stork wandering across those lawns looking for food, a much venerated bird, for of course it was he who so generously provided us with sisters. Well, everybody thought, he'd finally been generous enough, providing so many girls, it was time for a change. *Storch, Storch, du guter*, bring us *einen Bruder*, we implored him as he flew overhead towards his nest on the chimneytop, the other side of the lilac hedge.[11]

Elizabeth was seven months pregnant and the only person let in on the secret apart from Henning was her brother Sydney who was to attend the birth. None of the rest of her clan were contacted; her own children had only noticed that she was getting fat. Liebet confessed after the event to having guessed that a baby was on the way but did not share her insight with Evi or Trix. At Whitehall Court their mother waited for her baby in some perturbation. It is possible that she was in contact with Maude Stanley who lived a few streets away, and kept up with her friends from the salon, particularly Francis, but there are no records of what she did or who she saw at that point in her life. Francis had moved into a new town house in Gordon Square and spent much of his time in Sussex where he had bought a cottage on Telegraph Hill which he was busy converting into a large house with a tower.

The baby arrived on 27 October 1902 and was a boy. Still none of the family were told, even the fond grandparents, until mid-December. They were astonished when their daughter arrived 'imperturbable, calm and childish as ever' with the baby. There was 'much flutter among the feminines'[12] and Henry wrote a congratulatory letter to Henning, who in spite of the welcome tidings that the family now had a much longed-for heir, had not bothered to come to England to view the child. He somewhat lamely attributed his wife's tardiness in bringing back her latest triumph to the dismalness of the weather: 'I hope Dolly [his name for Elizabeth] will soon be able to return home; till now we had such a dreadful cold weather that I didn't want her to come.' His wife no doubt interpreted the letter as a signal of peace and forgiveness and a summons home.

Henning Bernd von Arnim (or H.B. as he was always thereafter referred to) appeared under the Christmas tree at Nassenheide that year. Evi and Trix were astonished. They had been expectantly gazing at the storks that flew through the Baltic skies crying 'ŏmtū ŏmtū',* to no avail, for they were told that their brother had been dug up in the same parsley bed in England that Quiqui had come from. This child had recently returned from England herself. While she was there she had been spoiled and dressed up and generally so doted on that she was more badly behaved than before she left. But she was radiantly cheerful and was the first to produce a smile from the generally ill-tempered baby, though when her mother asked her whether she loved him she replied with great promptness, 'I simply hate him.' 'So she soon took his measure,' Elizabeth wrote to her father, 'I thought she will be the making of him.' Quiqui entirely stole the new baby's thunder that winter. The other girls couldn't keep away from her—she talked without stopping, and sent them 'into fits'.[13] H.B. was king of the nursery and had several members of staff to cater for his needs. His mother was never to forgive him for intruding into her life and showed him little mercy, decreeing that he should be whacked with the back of a hairbrush if he chose to ignore his early pot training. Trix remembered that he was beaten every day 'because he was not wanted',[14] and that the girls, who had not

---

*'ŏmtū' is E. M. Forster's attempt to render phonetically the sound made by storks.

escaped their own share of beatings, were horrified.

That summer Elizabeth decided that a trip to England with some of the children would make a good holiday. Afterwards they planned to stay on an estate that had been willed by Henning's mother to his children called Schlagenthin which was also in Pomerania. Charlotte and Drish, who had been staying at Nassenheide since before Christmas, were to travel back to England with them and then on to a tour of the Lake District to worship at the shrine of the Wordsworths who were then occupying a high position in Elizabeth's pantheon. It was decided that Trix should stay behind and keep her father company, and H.B. could have a rest from being treated as a new animated toy by his sisters. Evi and Liebet were the elect and Quiqui was to go straight to her grandmother's in Kent. They left for 'paradise'[15] while Beatrice stood weeping at the door waving her pocket handkerchief as the carriage disappeared down the drive. Evi had been given a book with blank pages and told to write an account of the holiday in English.

When the train arrived in London Elizabeth disembarked at Holborn to arrange booking for the night at the Imperial Hotel in Russell Square which was then one of the most flamboyant and interesting buildings in London. It was also three minutes' walk from Francis's house in Gordon Square. The others went to Victoria to sort out the luggage. As soon as they arrived Louey appeared on the platform and without a word advanced on Drish, who was holding Quiqui, and grabbed the infant. There was a wordless struggle between the two women while Quiqui screeched, 'Drish, Drish, don't leave me'. But the older woman won, jumped into a waiting brougham with her grandchild and said to the cabbie, 'Drive on.' These were the only words she was heard to utter during the kidnapping scene. The girls, of course, were delighted with the drama they had witnessed. Drish was tearful, but fortunately Elizabeth thought it funny when she heard.[16]

They travelled down to Uplands near Fareham in Hampshire where the Waterlows had by then moved. Evi described it:

> . . . a large house surrounded by a park, in which the sheep graze. The dining-room at Uplands is much bigger than the dining-room at Nassenheide, it is simply enormous. The walls are filled with arms, and tin plates and heads of deers. An organ is at the end of the room, a very little one indeed. I think it must be very odd to dine at such a long table excepting [when] there are guests. We at

Nassenheide have a little dining-room but just big enough for us to dine at, when we have guests the table is made bigger but the room stays just the same.

The house also had a large walled kitchen garden and a big playroom which was full of the toys belonging to Charlotte's youngest son Cecil, or Puddle as he was always called. He had a whole set of electric tracks and trains set out and many pets in cages.

Two days later they set out for the Lake District. Elizabeth had a book of Wordsworth's poems and read it aloud to her sister whenever she could. Evi recorded:

> At last we arrived at Grasmere. We put our things in a hotel and marched straight off to 'Dove Cottage'. This is the chief thing why Mummy came to Grasmere, just to look at 'Dove Cottage'.

At the end of the holiday they all went to stay for a few days with Elizabeth's brother, 'Uncle Sydney'. Here 'we crabsen* enjoyed ourselves from heart to feet'. Sydney had recently built for his family two buildings in Penn, Buckinghamshire, 'one to live in and one for the horses'. He and his wife had three children, two girls and a boy, of four, five and six, Molly, Condle and Dickey. 'Dickey is a very sweet boy I think, Condle too, but Molly is too fat I think,' wrote their cousin.

When they arrived back in Pomerania they found Trix playing the *grande dame* of the castle and not at all pleased to see them. The need to think seriously about the girls' education was an urgent matter and Elizabeth was determined that the schooling of her daughters was to be as much of a feminist statement as anything in her life and work. Her humiliation at the hands of Prussian male dominance determined her to ensure that her daughters would be able to fight with as effective weapons as she herself had had at her disposal, if not better. They were not gifted and none of them yet had any musical ability—so overawed were they by their parents' combined gifts. Henning was so sensitive to music that no one unaccomplished could play any of the grand pianos in the house without wrath descending upon them. Elizabeth could not comprehend why her children were not able to tell what note a bird outside was singing; it was so easy for

---

*Elizabeth always referred to her children as 'crabs' and 'spawn'. 'Crabsen' is Evi's own word.

her that she did not understand that perfect pitch was neither common nor inherited. Only Quiqui learnt the piano during the time she spent with her grandparents, and she was eventually to become a gifted musician.

The school teacher was Herr Braun (Herr Schenk in *The German Garden*), a tall, pleasant young man with red hair and an easy nature. He was the local schoolmaster and found the girls so refreshing after his class of grey-faced infants in the village that he could not resist allowing them their freedom. The children spent far too much of their lesson-time trying to comb his stubborn hair into place and engage him with their antics. He had relatives in America who sent him candy which he took out of his pockets, all stuck together, and offered to the appreciative girls, and once he produced a sheep's eye, wrapped in newspaper, and explained its structure to them.

Trix, then aged seven, had had him in the schoolroom to herself the whole summer, and problems arose because she had fallen in love with him. She flared up at her mother one morning after they got back, and announced that she did not like being at Nassenheide and intended instead to keep house for Herr Braun instead. Her mother inquired how she was going to manage this and Trix calmly told her that she was just going to pack a few things and drive down to his house in the village. Mother and daughter went to the nursery and packed Trix's play clothes and a toothbrush into a little bag. The carriage was ordered and Elizabeth vigorously waved her daughter off at the door. The young adventuress was met at the gate by the governess who had been posted there by the countess and Trix was escorted back in rage and humiliation. She remembered the incident with pain in her eighties.

Herr Braun then 'suddenly gave way to a governess'[17] called Fräulein Beckmann. She was a sad-faced, ugly but precise woman, whom E. M. Forster described as:

> An awful old termagant to look at. But her nutcracker face, specs, grey locks and rounded shoulders accompanied a childlike soul. She was always busy making—I can't remember what: paper boxes inside which you found filigree rabbits. All animals loved her and so did the Count and Countess but she was not very happy.[18]

An instant and mutual antipathy sprang up between her and the children and they were sent to their father to be disciplined almost every day. But she did have a salutary effect on their manners.

A tutor was found for them from Cambridge called Mr Stuart. He was an undergraduate reading classics at King's and had been appointed on the recommendation of Sydney Waterlow, Elizabeth's nephew who was up at Cambridge himself. Charles Erskine Stuart very quickly fell in love with Elizabeth and interested her in the classics so much that she decided to take up learning them in the schoolroom with her children, thereby greatly enlivening the lessons.

The children were extremely difficult to teach, or as their mother put it, 'they resisted the acquisition of facts, and were entirely indifferent to the shame of not passing exams'.[19] Their tutors were later to complain that they lacked motivation in the schoolroom. For the three elder girls their mother was the 'beginning and end of all existence'.[20] They even called her *'Lieber Gott'* for no other earthly person could possibly come nearer to perfection in their eyes. Their studies suffered because every other consideration in their lives was dwarfed by the uncertainty about where their mother might be. When she went away, which was often and almost always at short notice, the family was stricken and the girls would wander around listlessly, become quarrelsome on the slightest provocation and show their abysmal contempt for all those in charge of them. Only gradually, and from sheer boredom, would they begin to take notice of what went on around them and possibly absorb a little learning. When she came home the children would arrange a welcome, standing in a beaming row, each clutching an elegant bouquet. The translation of their lives from dull and dour to adventurous and cheerful was remarkable and the children entered a state of blissful anticipation. At any moment during their highly regulated lives in the schoolroom she might suddenly snatch them away to pull on their boots and gaiters and go out. If it was winter they would help their mother to 'spoil the beautiful snow'.[21] If it was a lovely spring or summer day they might jump into the little open basketwork carriage with red wheels and drive off into the forest with a picnic basket and spend the day exploring. Elizabeth brought gaiety with her wherever she went. She had 'the gift of laughter'[22] and had tapped the source of fun, which made her books sell and her husband be prepared, in the end, to forgive her anything.

All of this adoration was accorded to Elizabeth by her children in spite of her lapses into strict disciplinarianism. This was necessary as Henning did not have the temperament to mete out the sort of punishment considered necessary in those days. He saw his role more as a comforter of his children's distress, helped in this by a large bar of chocolate he kept in his study. It was useless to threaten them with impending paternal ire, as had been the only method necessary in Elizabeth's own upbringing. From a very early age the children were soundly thwacked by their mother. She usually employed the back of a hairbrush and the punishment was a short and sharp one and used on occasions of disobedience, dishonesty, insubordination or generally bad or noisy behaviour. Evi remembered one day being whipped so hard with a dog whip that the governess whose duty it was to hold her down wept. Then Evi knew that she was being 'cruelly treated',[23] though she did not recall the sin that led to this punishment. Elizabeth was not always so harsh, however. On one occasion Trix refused to let the governess take off her vest before getting into the bath. Her mother was called in and her serious threats were to no avail, even with the brush in her hand. Beatrix cried out, 'Don't touch me, Mummikins, don't touch me,' hugging her mother round the knees. Elizabeth tore off the vest to give scope for the brush and was surprised to see Trix's waist wrapped around with a bandage. As Elizabeth and the governess worriedly unwound the dressing a sticky mess dripped out and they feared the worst. Finally they unwrapped three broken chicken eggs that the child had intended to incubate with her body heat. This changed the whack-ings into kisses.

As the girls grew older their mother resorted to a more sophisti-cated method of punishment. The erring child was temporarily shut out from her affections and was known to be 'under a cloud'. This was a fearful condition for the malefactor, Evi remembered. 'The rest of us were rather smug about it, thinking ourselves among the elect of the world and forgetting, so happy were we to be out for the moment in the sunshine of her approval, that our turn in obscurity would inevitably come.'

Elizabeth's goal for her daughters was not easy to achieve, but the children's lack of interest did not deter the parents from providing them with as good an education as money could buy. By 1901 there were usually two governesses and two tutors in residence. Elizabeth remembered that her daughters, in this most intensive period of their education, were most of the time pinned down by their tutors and governesses in a tightly organized timetable. All morning they sat in the schoolroom under stern pedagogic eyes. In the afternoons ponies were brought round from the stables and the children were taught to ride or they were taught to play tennis. At other times they were escorted to the pond and taught to swim or for walks when they learnt to botanize. They were in fact educated according to a scheme Henning had drawn up before they were born for the education of the sons he had hoped for.

All the English tutors were either Cambridge undergraduates who had been recommended by Sydney Waterlow or they had recently come down and were looking for an opportunity to acquire some German. Mr Stuart was replaced by Mr Gaunt who was, in due course, to go out and rule the natives in India. Mr Wilson endeared himself to the children by catching fish in the local ponds for their cats. Mr Stokoe was a very definite personality and considered he was a writer. He was encouraged in this belief, so he told Elizabeth, because when he lay in bed the shadow cast by his profile on the ceiling resembled that of Shakespeare, and he thought that this probably meant something. Anyway, it encouraged him to write long novels while the children sat round him doing their lessons. No one ever heard that they were published. He had replaced his sister who had come as a governess for a brief time. The children thought her old-maidish, pinched and inefficient. The second afternoon of her stay they went for a drive and it began to rain. The children had to wrap her up in blankets and they arrived home soaked to the skin while Miss Stokoe was warm and dry. Elizabeth dismissed her on the spot. Mr Gibb, 'he climbed trees',[24] was the son of the director of the North Eastern Railways, a great favourite with the girls and was one of the few tutors who took an interest in them. He deplored the way they were so regimented in their lives and was proud of the fact that by the time he left he had 'taught the girls to play'.[25] Herr Steinweg was the German tutor and he stayed with the family for many years until he had passed his exams for the ministry and become a Lutheran pastor in Berlin. One tutor was engaged by post and then Elizabeth heard something about him that she did not like and told him not to write to her again as she would be travelling. She then wrote to him saying that as she had not heard from him she assumed he was no longer interested in the post. Another arrived at the station, was met by her and took her to be one of the governesses. She could not resist the jape and told him stories of the countess's strictness and fury and the goings-on among the staff that made his hair stand on end. The next morning at breakfast the truth was revealed and he packed his bags and left.

· 8 ·

The Archangel and the Tutor

It was in the spring of 1904 when Fräulein Teppi Backe stepped off the narrow-gauge railway train at Nassenheide station. She had been recommended as a governess by a mutual friend and was greeted by a 'very small, delicate, friendly lady'[1] who stood in a muddy field surrounded by a quantity of little grunting pigs—it was their sty which marked the station. It was only by the lady's foreign accent that Fräulein Backe could tell that she was being 'personally greeted by the Countess'. Otherwise she never would have guessed that this simply-dressed, middle-aged woman, who so unaffectedly and heartily greeted her as if they were old school friends, was the mother of her pupils. They travelled back by carriage through a village and then through a 'never ending and well cared for park' while Elizabeth told the new governess that she was very happy living a simple country life and that she hoped Fräulein Backe would be happy too. 'My daughters are easy to raise when one knows how to handle them with love and cleverness, but they can be really unbearable if this is not the case,' she said. 'They have already scared away a whole series of governesses who failed in their eyes.' The new governess quailed at such a promise of *enfants terribles* but the little woman continued,

> They will apply every trick they know to get rid of you as quickly as possible. They only want to obey me. I am like God to them but I am too busy to see to their upbringing myself. I need someone to support me. Don't imagine it will be easy. You will be surprised at their inventiveness—they will lay rocks in your way. Be brave and just. This is the most important thing for my very critical children.

Fräulein Backe was delighted by the honesty of the mother and

deciding not to put her light 'under a bushel barrel', had already
formulated a teaching method when the countess said, as though she
were reading her mind, 'You yourself will have little to do with my
daughters' education. Your job is to influence them morally. You
will win them most easily if you don't try to take their love away from
me but stand behind me like an archangel.'

They stepped into the hall, which was empty of furniture except
for the stuffed animal heads and a beautifully carved oakwood
cabinet and some matching chairs. They sat down, with ceremony,
in front of three children who stood before them 'like organ pipes'.
The smallest jumped on to her mother's lap and pressed a posy to her
chin. She was introduced to the new teacher: 'This is Trixi, our little
tomboy—actually christened Beatrix. The name didn't fit her at all
so we shortened it to make it fit her round little person.' The second
had curly blonde hair: 'Here you have my oldest—we call her Evi—
who will have her future Adam dance to her pipe, because she is the
living spit of righteousness and goodness.' The tallest child was so
beautiful that Fräulein Backe could not take her eyes away from the
slim upright figure in front of her. She was drawn forward and her
mother stroked her dark brown hair: 'Here is my second born—she
is taller than Evi and my quietest child and the one who bears my
name. We call her Liebet for short.'

The children dragged the new governess up to the schoolroom and
such a good impression did she make on them by her frankness, open
manner and good humour that their laughter attracted the attention
of the parents. The girls took her to see their brother in the nursery.
'If he wets his pants Mummy hits his backside with a brush,' she was
told by way of introduction. 'Then he screams like on a spit. He's not
a very friendly baby, anyhow. We have another sister but she is still
in England with Granny and gets very spoiled and has only silk
dresses. Just let her be here again. We're going to pull the polish off
her.' Fräulein Backe tried to talk to the nurse in French but soon
gave up and encouraged the gloomy, elderly maiden to teach her
some songs. The girls meanwhile tried to make the baby do a
handstand at which he broke into a murderous howl. The noise was
earsplitting. The countess burst in and pulled the baby away from
the children, smacked him with the hairbrush as he had also wet
himself and, like a fury, swore in three languages at all of them. She
then vanished as quickly as she had arrived. That evening when the
children were dressed like 'snowflakes' and Fräulein Backe herself in
her best wool dress, Elizabeth appeared like a sweetly smiling fairy,
as though she was a different person altogether from the virago of the

nursery. 'A cream coloured lace gown wrapped her small body and a pearl necklace hung round her beautiful neck and was woven through the high piled brown hair. Beneath the flowing gown could be seen gold shoes which would probably fit Cinderella.'

Dinner was the most formal meal of the day and it had a set pattern which was the rule. There was a gong to warn everybody to go and change. Evening dress was *de rigueur* and the children were taken out of their everyday dark blue serge and dressed in fluffy white dresses, their hair flowing loose down their backs. The company congregated in the library, this room being the central point of the castle. It was filled with beautiful, white-painted furniture and only the black grand piano in the corner deviated from the general theme of airy light colours in the room. Upholstered chairs clustered round the huge fireplace and 'expensive vases, statues and oil paintings gave the room a look of highest culture'.

Elizabeth usually arrived just as the second gong was sounded and looked like 'a figure floated out of a fairy tale'. She would then take her husband's arm and lead the way through two more big rooms also containing white furniture and decorated with light flowery chintzes. In the last very long and narrow room stood another grand piano. From there a few steps led down into the hall and from there the company filed into the dining-room. This room was filled with beautiful carved oak furniture and the walls were lined with hand-painted porcelain plates, Henning's inheritance from his illustrious ancestor, Frederick the Great. Everyone stood behind their chairs while one of the hungry children rushed through the grace. Then the countess was seated by a footman, and the others all sat down in the places allocated to them. Each one of the tutors was ordered by Elizabeth to talk on a certain theme and the rest would discuss this afterwards, usually with great animation. The children were not included and were only allowed to answer questions.

Usually the conversation broke up into three languages and newcomers were unfailingly astonished at the wit and many-sided intellect of their hostess who could answer all questions with assurance in each language. After the meal had finished they all went back into the library where there was a choice of activities from chess to dancing or riotous games such as 'Tummy Aches and Castor Oil', the Nassenheide version of 'Oranges and Lemons'. Occasionally Fräulein Backe sang songs written by her great hero Goethe. She was accompanied by Elizabeth, but this was not popular as the governess sent the children into fits of giggles by her grotesque facial expressions, and besides she sang dreadfully out of tune.

The von Arnims found this 'frog-faced maiden'[2] engaging and extremely touching. She was tall and always overworked. Very soon 'dumb devotion bound her to the Countess'. It was her ambition to 'live in Art'. One morning when Elizabeth asked her how she liked her egg boiled she turned crimson and said, 'Oh no, this is too much,' overcome with the idea of having an egg at all. 'So completely did she shy away from the idea,' wrote her mistress to a friend, 'that it was like the behaviour of a modest and well brought up virgin when first a man tries to make love to her.'[3] Teppi, as she was to become, had huge resources of energy for whatever task she was given and soon she appeared to be in charge of everything. The children, of course, laughed at her because of the wholehearted way that she tackled everything that she did, and it was many years before they saw the value of this way of doing things. Presently she took on the duties of housekeeper, thus relieving Elizabeth of much of the burden of running the house, and finally she became only that, while remaining on the same level as the tutors in the hierarchy of the castle. Her intelligence was the most remarkable thing about her and soon, as another of the tutors, E. M. Forster, was to notice, the castle was full of people calling for her, 'Teppi this and Teppi that.'[4]

The Adventures of Elizabeth in Rügen, delayed by H.B.'s birth, was published early in 1904. The reviews were unanimously in praise, though none of them saw that it was one of the funniest books to be published for years. The *Spectator* called it a 'series of watercolour sketches in words, sketches so original, delicate and beautiful, so instinct with artistic feeling and bright with the atmosphere of happiness, as to give the author a high place among the word painters of today'. Katherine Mansfield, then at school in London at Queen's College, was inspired by it to write a story called *Die Einsame*, which was about love and death, two subjects which her much older cousin steered well clear of if she could. Prophetically, for Katherine was to die of tuberculosis, *Die Einsame* is a watering-place in Rügen which, because of its ozone and pine forest air, worked wonders for people who had anything wrong with their lungs.

Katherine had, that summer, been to stay with Henry and Louey and had met Quiqui. She described her in a letter to a friend:

> One Easter I was staying with Grannie . . . down in Kent, her German grandchild of five was there, so we took her [to church]. I shall never forget how beautiful it was. She wore the shortest little white embroidered frock, and white stockings and red shoes, and under her little white

satin straw hat, with just a wreath of field daisies round it—her curls tinkled round her. There was a hymn—*All Things Bright and Beautiful*—when the children had to hold their offerings as they sang. We lifted the German baby right up on the cushion of the pew, and she sang very gravely, holding her white basket full of coloured Easter eggs, and flowers—and the sun streamed into the little old quaint church, and the children's voices, very thin and high—seemed to float into the air—above them all I heard the German baby—exultant, joyful—her cheeks all rosy.

Granny and I enjoyed ourselves so much that we both cried, to the baby's horror and astonishment. She pulled my sleeve—'Kassie, why are you looking so wistful?' I can hear her now with a violent German accent—she was so precious . . .[5]

Quiqui returned to Nassenheide within a few weeks of Teppi's arrival. The following Sunday the family attended, as usual, the Lutheran church at Blankensee, a simple edifice standing on a hill. The pastor, Jacobs, was as 'offensive as ever' and dilated on the English brutalities to the Boers although the war had been over for two years—'Two thirds of the Boer women violated and so on'.[6] Elizabeth, as was her custom, put up her lorgnette and gazed steadily back at him, with a gaze that should have chilled his eloquence, but still he went on. Quiqui became bored and uncomfortable. When she discovered that her leg was going to sleep she piped up in a loud voice, 'I only had a cold potato for breakfast.' The whole congregation fell into a deep shocked silence into which the same complaint was flung again. When the child opened her mouth for a third time, her mother tried to stifle the sound with her hand. Her father rose quickly to his feet, picked her up, and removed her to the churchyard outside.

'*Mein Kind,*' said her father, standing her upon a convenient tombstone so that her eyes were level with his, 'is it then true about the cold potato?'

'No,' said Joyce Felicitas, patting his face, pleased at what her legs were feeling like again.

'*Mein Kind,*' said her father, 'do you know it is wrong to tell a lie?'

'No,' said Joyce Felicitas placidly, the heavenly blue of her eyes, gazing straight into his, exactly like the mild sky above the trees.

'No?' echoed her father, staring at her. 'But, *mein Kind*, you know what a lie is?'

'No,' said Joyce Felicitas, gazing at him tenderly in her satisfaction at being restored to a decent pair of legs; and as he still stood staring at her she put her hands one on each of his cheeks and squeezed his face together and murmured, 'Oh, I do *love* you.'[7]

Life continued, and the bond between Elizabeth and Teppi strengthened every day. Far from taking the children's love from their mother, Teppi eventually came near to replacing the children in Elizabeth's affections. She and the countess formed a relationship based originally on the seed of their mutual admiration for Goethe but springing up quickly to become a canopy of dense foliage which was to protect them all, to some extent, from the peltings of fortune so soon to befall.

One of the Cambridge students who had been highly recommended by Sydney Waterlow was a shy young man called Edward Morgan Forster. Elizabeth approached him by letter asking him to come and teach her children, requiring that he should have some previous knowledge of German, teach mathematics and stay with the family at least six months. He replied that he felt that the requirements eliminated him as he could fulfil none of them. 'The more difficulties I raised, the warmer grew her letters,' Forster wrote in an account of his stay there. Finally, she 'begged me to come when and as I liked, she trusted I shouldn't find it dull'.[8]

E. M. Forster arrived in the spring of 1905. He was terrified of the Germans and even more frightened of his future employer, having gathered from her books that she was a Tartar who didn't particularly like people, at least the ones she found around her: 'The people I like are always somewhere else,' she had written in her first book,

> . . . and not able to come to me, while I can, at any time, fill the house with visitors about whom I know nothing and care less. Perhaps if I saw more of those absent ones, I would not love them so well. At least that is what I think on wet days when the wind is howling round the house and all nature is overcome with grief.[9]

All of nature was overcome with grief the night Forster arrived. His agitation was augmented as the train drew up at the station in the late evening gloom, with nothing but glistening dung hills to greet him. A farm labourer appeared and showed Forster to the *Schloss*. He wrote to his mother of his arrival:

> Shlosh, we trod in puddles, there was no road, and when we got to the farm there were the most appalling smells of pig and horse and cow and we waded in manure. Here we parted and he indicated to me a rough carriage drive which was better, being only sandy and full of holes: presently I hit a large building which had a light in the upper window. I found a bell in it and rang. A hound bayed inside. By this time I was weak with laughter. I rang again, and at last a dishevelled boy with no light appeared. Yes, it was the *Schloss*. What did I want? I said I wanted to live here. He replied that he would see and got a light, revealing a long low whitewashed barrel-vaulted hall hung with trophies of the chase and at the end the inscription I DICTO, INSULSUE, TURPIS TRISTIS ABESTO or something of the sort. *Turpis* I certainly was, for my boots oozed manure.

Forster was told somewhat severely the next day, at his interview with the chatelaine, that he had not been expected that evening:

> The discomforts of my arrival had lowered me in her opinion. Indeed I had lost all the ground I had gained. Glancing up at my tired and peaked face she said, 'How d'ye do, Mr Forster? We confused you with the housemaid . . . can you teach the children, do you think? They are very difficult . . . ah yes, Mr Forster, very difficult, they'll laugh at you, you know. You'll have to be stern or it will end as it did with Mr Stokoe.'[10]

She took him to her *Treibhaus* (a signal honour, though he did not know it) and showed him her new Remington typewriter on which she quickly typed a quatrain of Swinburne, 'I have looked into the hand of God'.

> And a hard, tight, indestructible little spirited existence seemed to bob up and down: hard, yet if ever I cracked it, I should expect to find a spot of chocolate cream at the core. To be really liked, to really be liked is probably her deepest aspiration, and when she brushes aside one's cleverness and exclaims 'But haven't you a heart?' it perhaps isn't tactics entirely. May this explain her extraordinary power? It does seem odd that one should be so

anxious to please such a person for she isn't distinguished and she's always ungrateful.[11]

What it was that Elizabeth was ungrateful about is not explained in this case. Not, clearly, the opportunity to converse with one of the artistic status of her new tutor. But though her respect for him was sincere, especially after he heard that his first novel had been accepted for publication by Blackwoods, she soon enlarged it into a 'new sort of bunkum'. '[She] presented me to myself as a dark horse who saw and could do anything. Not only was she clever, but she had the power of making one accept her categories, and I wasted much time wondering how dark I was.'[12] He got it into his head that Elizabeth thought he wrote better than she did and that she was distressed by it. 'Anyhow, contact with her makes me more self-conscious writhing round: Am I modest or no? I think I do think little of myself, but then I think a good deal about it!'[13] She suggested that they collaborate on a book together, which appalled the young man who did not wish to work with 'this particular older sister', as she noticed, and duly the project fell through.

When the proofs of *Where Angels Fear to Tread* began to arrive she read them and said she hated the book. It spoke of underdone meat and spittle: 'Pfui, Mr Forster.' She read Chapters One to Three and said it was very clever but most unattractive, and she felt as if she wanted a bath. Then she read Chapter Four and said it was really beautiful and wanted to retract her first opinion. When she read Chapter Six, Forster's mother's favourite, Elizabeth returned to her original position. She took away an article Forster had written on the Italian philosopher Cardan in the *Independent Review* one day, remarking as she did so that she was a very severe critic. She returned in a chastened mood saying, 'You've simply got to go on and win, I've no more to say.'[14]

In Dresden on his way to Nassenheide Forster had met Posy Kelly, by then married to a Mr Farmer. He mentioned this to his hostess. 'They don't like me,' she said. He replied, 'Yes, so I saw,' which startled Elizabeth, who had not yet encountered the new fashion for frankness just then emerging in intellectual circles in England. Forster wrote of the episode to his mother:

> Here is a bit of gossip. It is a real quarrel between E. and Mrs Farmer; I thought so at Dresden. Mrs F. and her sister stayed here, once, years ago, and when the *German Garden* came out, the sister thought she was Minora and made London ring with her wails. E. says she would never

be so beastly as to put a guest in, and that Minora has no original. Anyhow there was a row, of which I have, of course, only heard one side, from which Mrs F. or rather her sister sounds to have behaved very badly.

Later he learnt that Elizabeth had nearly sent him back to England on the first day because he had been wearing a particularly unpleasant tie, or that was what she would have him believe. Forster had not liked her any better. His opinion changed, however, as he saw more of his hostess, though that was little enough for she was busy all day in her *Treibhaus* writing another book, *Princess Priscilla's Fortnight.* When they did meet 'she was most pleasant and amusing; and I think I shall like her very much'. He wrote to his mother, 'She is, as I rather expected, rather nicer than her books.' In an article he wrote for *The Listener* called 'Recollections of Nassenheide' in 1959 he described her as 'small and graceful, vivid and vivacious. She was also capricious and a merciless tease.' As for the famous German Garden, Forster could not find it, it was nowhere to be seen. Nor did Elizabeth take any interest in flowers. The garden merged into the park which was sylvan in tendency. Later in the summer there were some flowers—mainly pansies, tulips and roses.

> There were endless lupins which the Count was drilling for agricultural purposes. But there was nothing of a show and Nassenheide appeared to be surrounded by paddocks and shrubberies. [There was] a field . . . over whose long grass at the end of July a canopy of butterflies kept waving.
>
> It was the country, the flat agricultural surround, that so ravished me. When I arrived in April the air was ugly and came from the east. A few kingcups were out along the edges of the dykes, also some willow-catkins, no leaves. The lanes and the paths were of black sand; the sky was lead. The Chaussée, white and embanked, divided the desolate fields, cranes flew overhead, crying 'ho hee toe, ho hee toe' as if they were declining the Greek definite article. Then they shrieked and ceased, as if it was too difficult. Storks followed the cranes. Over the immense dark plough galloped the deer to disappear into the cliffs of a forest. Presently the spring broke, slow, thematic, Teutonic, the birch trees forming the main melody.

Because of the beauty around him he found he could not write properly, learn grammar which he had set himself to do, translate

Virgil, which he eventually did do, or write much in his journal:

> ... Concerning beauty: clear evening; green wheat against the sun, purple shadows of the birch trees and the sand, deer bobbing away over ploughed fields as big as a county—these things, followed by Rhine Music have made me happy and useless.[15]

The Man of Wrath returned from a holiday in Bavaria with Liebet shortly after Forster arrived and cast a gloom over the household. He 'became easily tragic' over his victuals and was rather what Forster expected,

> ... grave, quiet, stoutish, elderly, with twinkly eyes. I dread the end of each meal for then he sucks in the water of his finger glass like Charybdis, and after an awful moment, spews it out again. I wince and giggle and fancy that either is detected by Elizabeth.[16]

Even so the young man found the older one kind and tolerant, as he would need to be, he being the only man in a household of women, children and servants. Liebet he found to be the nicest child, also beautiful if a little too plump. She was a trial in the schoolroom for she took charge of the scatterbrained Evi and the tubby little Trix, and was the intermediary between her sisters and the higher powers in the establishment as far as their behaviour was concerned. She had had to keep them in line when inadequate governesses and tutors fell down or lost the children's respect. Her manner was governessy and a little bossy and over-protective.

Forster made particular friends with Herr Steinweg, so much so that Elizabeth warned him at table one day that he had better be careful, for soon he would be unable to call his soul his own. Steinweg was shocked when Forster confessed that he believed that telephone wires were hollow and that one ought to shout if the person at the other end was very far away. One summer afternoon when the English and the German tutors had been drinking the strong Pomeranian ale at Blankensee they wandered out into the forest where Forster encountered a leaf suspended in mid-air, with nothing but the mellow rays of the sun filtering through the leafy branches to hold it up. Steinweg's strict Lutheran convictions could not let him come to terms with this.

Easter came and Forster was given five eggs planted on a mossy bank which graced his breakfast tray. Three were chocolate and two were hen's painted with virulent watercolours by the children. After lunch they all hunted for more eggs in the garden. Forster had found about thirty or forty which had been hidden in little nests not very cunningly concealed behind tufts of grass and tree trunks. Suddenly, there was the Easter Hare himself seated under a tree with even more eggs in a basket in his hand. It turned out to be Fräulein Backe dressed in a great washleather mask, a mob cap and a dun coloured shawl reaching down to her heels. She declaimed a long rhymed speech which she had written herself and gave each child an egg and then hopped valiantly all up and down the gravel paths. It was agreed that there never was such an Easter.

Forster's only real complaints were about the animals and insects. Mosquitoes, gnats, flies, ants, woodbugs and small snakes all combined to make him uneasy. Also the dog was sometimes smelly, but in the hearty German language he could tell him so without hurting the dog's feelings. All that was necessary to say was '*Ingulf! du stinkst*' and he would get up with a pained look and leave the room. 'He's a sweet boy, though—about the size of a piano.'[17]

Towards the end of his stay Forster and the countess engaged in such heated intellectual arguments about writing that Henning banned the subject at the table. He did not bore them with endless talk about pigs at dinner, he said, although he thought them ten times more interesting than books. It was considered bad form to discuss one's trade while at the table in the elevated circles he was accustomed to. 'You will never be able to talk of Beethoven to a crayfish. Even if he hears you, you will never know it, for his bones are on the outside, and this prevents any intelligent facial expression.' An excellent argument and Forster was certain that the count preferred crayfish to Beethoven and himself. 'He would rather be with animals and plants, whom he cannot see at all than with men, whom he sees through.'[18] Clearly Henning thought literary people and indeed most people rather absurd though he was far too polite to show it. But the two writers did find time to discuss their craft and Forster discovered that

> Elizabeth's attitude to literary and spiritual questions is that of ours to food which depends not on the food but the state of the stomach. I hope I shall never again be depressed when she thinks me rot—and more difficult— elated when she praises me. For example Keats: I poisoned her against him by praising his letters in which he rags Wordsworth and is vulgar! Through me accenting this she is getting to mistrust his poems: 'My dear fel-

low—I don't know whether you are so supremely great or whether you are exactly on my level (plane) and that is why you seem so marvellous. You are now . . . twenty-three and it is the first of many times I shall sit at the feet of my juniors!'[19]

In his diary he kept a resumé of their conversations such as:

Keats in the letters shows a perfect attitude towards his art: absolutely serious but genial. And his enormous elevation amongst other men only makes him wish they would quarrel less. 'The best of men have a portion of good in them—a sure way is first to know a man's faults and then be passive. I believe in two things: imagination and the holiness of the heart's affections.' He has seized upon the supreme fact of human nature: a very small amount of good in it and the supreme importance of that little. He is content with his stuffy set as he would have been contented with anyone whom he knew long enough.

And, basing his view of all women on Elizabeth:

Not to revel in ragging and some kinds of sadness would be absurd. Women are not, I think, sillier than men but more shameless: as each mood, most of them digestive, arrives, they base a view of life on it, and pour out opinions they must inevitably contradict.*

On the whole his teaching was a success, although his own feeling was that he bored and chilled the children. Evi remembered him as a tall, shy young man with a moustache which he pulled protectively. He was also very emotional when he read Wordsworth to them, seeming at any moment to be about to burst into tears, which made them all laugh. But he managed to teach them something and wrote the matter of their dictation himself which pleased them. His main distinction in their eyes was that he had once been observed to eat eight hard-boiled eggs at one sitting. He entered into their games with good humour but managed, at the same time, to keep a modicum of control and retain their respect. He even consented one day to bite a piece of what was obviously soap but which was presented to him as bread. It had the tooth marks of previous gullible tutors on it. 'All you tutors fall in,' cried the girls in triumph, and

---

*In 1924 Elizabeth read *A Passage to India* and thought it very good, but commented in her diary: '. . . and always, like a smear across his work, is his non-comprehension of the love of men and women.'

offered the same piece to Mademoiselle who politely refused.

> She preferred to distract herself on the zither . . . presently
> the pendant on Mlle's bracelet caught in the strings of the
> instrument. There she was fixed immovable, and for five
> minutes neither the April baby nor myself could release
> her. Meanwhile June had twisted the leg of Quiqui into
> the back of the chair and the kitten, who had recently
> taken some pink medicine, began to rock to and fro in the
> most alarming way. But I left them very cheerful, and
> Quiqui writing a letter to her doll. 'My dear Comtesse
> Jane, I am glad to tell you that it is your birthday. I shall
> see you in time. I hope you will not die between . . .'[20]

They also wrote essays. The June baby (Trix) was the most
entertaining. In her essay on 'If there was a war between England
and Germany, which would you want to win?', she wrote, 'If there is
a war between England and Germany I shouldn't care which won; I
should run away as fast as I could.' She showed this up with a
passionate cry: 'I know I shall get no marks because I have spoken
the truth!' In another essay about a character in a book they had
been reading she wrote:

> He knew the whole bible by heart, so pious he was. Each
> time his children were naughty his face glanced with
> words out of it; and immediately out came a quotation and
> it flowed like a river. Perhaps he may have been soaked in
> religion in his child days, and then very clear it appeared
> to me that when thinking too much of higher powers his
> mind became a little disordered, and never could get it
> right again. He is a good man, but I would warn him not
> to think too much or his end might be rather doubtful.[21]

Evi said one morning, 'I dreamed of the *Lieber Gott*. He was at
Nassenheide station: no more.' Beatrice chimed in, 'And I. He was
scolding two proud ladies while I looked on disgusted.'[22] Evi, who
was then thirteen, could also be quaint and charming when she
wished but, in common with her sisters, would often retreat into a
fierce hauteur of aristocratic disdain. Evi's lapses into friendliness
were more marked than the others' and for a short time Forster
became the object of one of her passions. She would grip his hand
hotly and gaze into his eyes with a fixed and maniacal expression.
Her feelings got the better of her in the dining-room one day. It was
the custom that when the footman handed round the coffee after

dinner it went only to those above the salt, the count, countess and the children. The tutors and governesses were obliged to wait while it was consumed and were never offered any themselves. This was the fixed rule and neither the children nor the count and countess had protested against it before. Just before Forster was due to leave the hostess awoke in Evi and she rushed at the footman and abused him violently for his impoliteness. She sent him out for more coffee cups and served the others herself.

Forster left Nassenheide at the end of July and had been probably the most successful and best liked of all the tutors that had gone there from Cambridge because he had proved able to stand up to Elizabeth's teasing. He returned to England after visiting Rügen and the Baltic in time for the publication of *Where Angels Fear to Tread*. In a later novel, *The Longest Journey*, it is clear that his character Mrs Failing was based on Elizabeth, although he, in the tradition of his erstwhile hostess, denied this and claimed the character was based on one of his uncles. Mrs Failing, Ricci's sister, had occasional moments of prophetic wisdom, was prone to occasional acts of spontaneous generosity as well as occasional moods of kindness, tolerance, whimsical cruelty, cold vindictiveness and heartless contempt.

Forster had not understood the reason behind the incident of Evi and the coffee cups, but her mother did. Evi had never recovered her equilibrium after being ousted from her intoxicating position as the only child and the centre of her mother's universe; the births of her sisters had profoundly disturbed her. She had behaved badly at first, but this only ended in her being banished further into the outer darkness of her mother's disapprobation. She had then attempted to please her parent by aping the childishness of her younger sisters, which seemed to Evi to have been successful for them. Although her emotional development was retarded, physically she came to full maturity at the alarmingly early age of ten. Her 'perambulator face'[23] (as one of her uncles called it, the Edwardian equivalent of bedroom eyes) and her intense and passionate nature which led her to fixate on any male, however unsuitable, made her mother's 'wigs stand on end'.[24] Clearly, for her own safety she would have to be put in something similar to a convent. Furthermore, she had become extremely stubborn and argumentative and none of the other girls could get on with her for very long. She was generally getting too big for her boots. When a new tutor from Cambridge, Arthur Wilson, arrived, Evi pursued him to such an extent that Elizabeth was kept busy trying to suppress or circumvent her.

Maude Stanley was consulted. She had a niece called Lady Maude Whyte, daughter of the Countess of Airlie, who had married beneath her, had three children, was widowed and fallen on hard times. She lived in a small terraced house in Auriol Road, Earls Court, and would be happy to take Evi as a paying guest while she attended St Paul's School for Girls. Henning regarded this idea with immense misgiving but his opinion was overruled in the face of the omnipotent Maude Stanley. From then on Evi was, in her own eyes, banished, though fortunately she was happy at St Paul's. Her sisters were horrified at this sudden and seemingly irrevocable invocation of the 'final punishment'[25] and imagined their sister chained up in a rat-infested cellar. They wrote secretly to Forster begging him to visit their poor sister and cheer her up. He wrote to Elizabeth for permission and she replied, 'I don't believe the sudden appearance of a young man in that decent widow's house, however long and much he had been the child's tutor, would commend itself to Lady Maude . . . I have handed Evi over utterly, body and soul, for the time being to Lady M.'

By every account Lady Maude was a cold, cruel woman with no time for sympathy, love or understanding. Evi was left alone most of the time, or at best barely tolerated on family outings to church and so on. Only occasionally would her mother turn up, always unexpectedly and much to the utter joy and excitement of the unfortunate daughter: 'And oh, it was like balm to my soul', wrote Evi in her memoirs.[26] They would sometimes go shopping in Selfridges (a shop for servants in those days), and then on to enjoy one of Hale's Tours. These were an early type of travel documentary and instead of sitting in an auditorium the participant climbed into a simulated train carriage which began to rock and shudder while the sound effects and panorama moving along outside the windows gave the illusion of travelling abroad.

Unfortunately, when her mother left, the dreariness of her days in Earls Court was grimmer and more lonely still by comparison. The poor child, who knew, even then, that what had happened to her was the worst possible solution for her problems, wept alone in a cold room, her only companion a small dormouse in a cage. She spent her time miserably speculating as to how she had arrived at her state of banishment. One day she found a letter from her mother to Charlotte on a writing desk in her aunt's bedroom when she stayed there over the Christmas holidays. It contained a list of her sins and expressed horror at the way she had made a 'set' at Mr Wilson. It spoke of her 'extremely scattered wits' and that 'life at home with her sisters always brought out the worst in her'. Evi was hurt and baffled. Not only had she not made a set for Mr Wilson, she didn't like him very much and thought him 'officious'.[27] She guessed that Lady Maude had received a similar letter, for the thin-souled widow never missed a chance of telling her that she was 'stupid, selfish and obstinate'. Evi felt that the only happiness she would ever know must come through herself, 'and I was too young for that kind of philosophy'.[28] Evi began to doubt her mother's love and to feel afraid of her, which she had never been before, but each time they met the child was again reduced to being her mother's willing slave.

· 9 ·

Temptations

Princess Priscilla's Fortnight was delivered to the publishers in the summer of 1905. It is a charming fairy story of a runaway princess or, as some reviewers pointed out, a thinly disguised Elizabeth, who seeks the simple life in a cottage in Devon and leaves behind her a trail of death and disaster. Finally she is rescued by a prince. The ironical moral of the story is:

> It is always better, I believe, to be cautious and careful, to husband your strength, to be deadly prudent and deadly dull. As you would poison, so you should avoid doing what the poet calls living too much in your large hours. The truly prudent never have large hours; nor should you, if you want to be comfortable. And you get your reward, I am told, in living longer; in having, that is, a few more of those years that cluster round the end, during which you are fed and carried and washed by persons who generally grumble.[1]

The *Spectator* placed it behind *Elizabeth in Rügen* as the second best work she had produced so far: 'The whole tale moves in the bright clean air of comedy . . . at the same time there is much shrewd understanding of life.' It was not, however, a worthy successor to any of her books and it led to nothing in her later ones. It was a tale spun entirely out of Elizabeth's imagination; a caution to herself as to what might happen if she gave way to her own Wordsworthian ethic and sought the simple life; a justification, in a sense, for not doing it. As a result of having written it she knew that her salvation as a novelist lay in research and in writing directly from her own experience. The dramatic rights were bought by an American producer who turned it into a play which flopped on Broadway.

Elizabeth determined that her next novel, *Fräulein Schmidt and Mr*

Anstruther, should be well researched and deal, as much as possible, with real events. The main love interest is based on her experience with Stuart—an upper-class young Englishman comes to stay with an impoverished professor to learn some German and ends by falling in love with his daughter. He goes home to England having confessed his love and the lovers exchange letters. It is her letters which form the body of the book.

To find out exactly what it was like to be the daughter of a professor in Jena, Elizabeth advertised herself as an English governess, a Miss Armstrong, who worked at Nassenheide and wished to improve her German during the Easter holidays of 1906. She offered to help the woman of the house in exchange for lessons from the professor. Just such a professor as she had envisaged answered the advertisement and, telling no one but her husband, Elizabeth had some suitable garments made up. Even Teppi was not let into the secret, but one morning in March she came across Elizabeth's maid who was packing her trunk for this escapade: 'Did you ever see such clothes as I have to pack for the countess?' said the maid showing Teppi some coarse dresses. 'Suitable for a woman going to market,' she added.[2] Teppi was scandalized by the rough clothes that her 'God-so-blessed' mistress was planning to take with her.

Miss Armstrong's duties in Jena turned out indeed to be little more than those of a servant. For weeks she was required to sleep in a cold and sparse attic bedroom through which the March winds blew. She had to rise at dawn and buy the day's necessities at the market, carry the heavy basket to the house, brush out the family's clothes and darn and mend their underwear and socks. As sewing was one of the few accomplishments the novelist had not mastered, the mistress of the house sat her down and patiently instructed her in this art. All would have gone well had not the son of the house, a young man of twenty, fallen in love with the spry little servant and asked her to marry him. Miss Armstrong immediately arranged for Henning to send a telegram saying, 'Children ill. Come at once.' Even so she had trouble convincing the love-sick young man not to follow her.

That summer there were many outings and amusements, Evi came home for the holidays and Elizabeth wrote a play for them all to perform. Each child was invited, in turn, to have supper with their mother in 'The Flower House', their name for her flower-filled *Treibhaus*. 'After Supper, which will be Bread and Milk, there will be a Rehearsal of the New Play. The Guests need not dress but must come in furs and Galoshes,' she wrote on the invitations.[3] When the time came to present the play they were undismayed to find their audience consisted of only Henning. All the marble busts were collected from every niche in the house and dressed up in furs and hats and placed on all the empty seats. The count sat among them and attempted to provide a whole audience-worth of applause. Trix was heard to say, in a stage whisper, while peering through the improvised curtain, 'Daddy, he's the only alive thing out there.'[4] Another time Elizabeth, Teppi and Mademoiselle dressed up in blue serge tunics and the three girls wore their mother's best dresses, jewels and high heels. For the whole day the girls were allowed to correct and chastise their elders and there was great hilarity for everyone except the count, who became uneasy about this flagrant undermining of discipline.

Fräulein Schmidt and Mr Anstruther was published in the autumn of 1907. It is a further and much more mature progression on the problem that obsessed Elizabeth for the whole of her life: how to achieve the simplicity of her heroes, Wordsworth and Thoreau, who were lucky enough to be able to live in small cottages, while continuing to be the 'frightful little *Junker*' she was obliged to be. She could only do it in her imagination and subsequently in her novels and knew herself to be no better than Marie Antoinette playing at poverty while her country starved. At least she could describe the poetic illumination which is achieved through simplicity at one remove, and she achieved a certain masculinity of thought while the heroine in the book, Rose-Marie, becomes irritatingly fatalistic about her situation in life:

> Of course I am full of contradictions. Did you expect me to be full of anything else? And I have no doubt whatever that in every letter I say exactly the opposite from what I said in the last one. But you must not mind this and make it an occasion for reproof. I do not pretend to think quite the same even two days running; if I did I would be stagnant, and the very essence of life is to be fluid, to pass perpetually on.[5]

'Presumably I agreed with her,' wrote Elizabeth in her memoirs, 'was she not my mouthpiece? The trumpet through which, morning after morning, I so busily blew . . . ?'[6]

She underlines the reasons for the privacy of her own life and the secrecy of her emotions by putting into Rose-Marie's hands a book on the private lives of the great. The young hero-worshipper learns that Coleridge was a drug addict; that Wordsworth's greeting was a languid handful of numb, unresponsive fingers; that Keats's Miss Brawne was unwilling and saw little of him; that Milton was rather less than a loving husband and father, and so on about all the gods in her literary heaven. The heroine flings the book to the other side of the room and hopes fervently that 'present and future poets should wrap themselves sternly in an impenetrable veil of anonymity'. Then the author reveals an insight into the true motive of authorship, particularly her own: 'They won't, because of the power of the passing moment, because of the pleasantness of praise, recognition, of personal influence, and, I suppose, but I'm not sure, of money.'[7] There is much in *Fräulein Schmidt and Mr Anstruther* that reaches far beyond anything Elizabeth had attempted in her previous novels. When it appeared in 1907 most reviewers failed to recognize that Elizabeth had attained a deeply felt and serious pitch in her writing and that this book was the first in which she sang with a firm and true voice. The *Evening News* was the only paper to appreciate its worth, saying it was 'written with a grace and humour, a mellow wisdom, a command of emotion, an insight into life which makes the author one of the finest, if not the finest of present day writers'. Her father thought it 'decidedly clever'.[8]

Charles Erskine Stuart read it and instantly recognized himself as the fatuous young man who dallied with Rose-Marie's emotions so unfeelingly. Naturally he fell back in love with Elizabeth as Mr Anstruther did with her mouthpiece. He arrived for Christmas and immediately the astute Teppi noticed that 'dumb devotion'[9] bound him also to the countess. He was by then a successful and well-liked don at King's in Cambridge. He was twenty-three years old and of reasonably noble birth, being of the cadet branch of the earls of Castle Stuart, County Tyrone, in Ireland (and baronets of Nova Scotia). He was also a top-class sportsman, and famous in Cambridge for his imaginative selection of passages in English for his pupils to translate into ancient languages. His tutor described him as unlike 'a typical Irishman; he was more like Plato's Spartan—somewhat slow to speak, but carrying weight with every word he said.'[10] When first he came to Nassenheide conversation between him and the countess was 'delightful and easy'.[11] The lonely and intellectually thirsty woman passed through and was duly consumed by every terror and delight that comes with a platonic, but none the less passionate affair with a much younger man. Her view was that if it hadn't been for his chin, which was not of the strongest, he looked exactly like Charles II. She was certain that he was descended from kings.

Evi went to the Waterlows' house Uplands, in Sussex for Christmas and heard that her family in Germany had had a more successful festival than ever before — there had been no snow but hard frosts and the children had skated every day. Mr Stuart dressed up as Father Christmas, which made Quiqui and H.B. squeal with delight and terror. He gave them gifts and a long sermon on good behaviour. That night Father Christmas appeared again when all the children of the farms on the estate were gathered together for a feast.

One of Quiqui's less sensational gifts, as far, at least, as she was concerned, was. a new name. Her father had recently read a book about Martin Luther and was so struck by the facial similarities between the great religious reformer and his youngest daughter, that from then on she was always known to the family as Martin.

When Stuart went back to Cambridge for the Hilary term he wrote Elizabeth the most charming and tender love letters which contained such passages as:

> Little star in the east. Little sweet hope and guide. The flickering, darting wit of yours, and all your living, lively wisdom beginning to shine again and stir again.

And:

> You're so sweet, so brave, so various and alive — your sweet little fancies, little swirls of mood, kind sweet things.[12]

Elizabeth also received many fan letters from people who had drawn strength and courage from her latest book. One of them, from a Cambridge undergraduate called Hugh Walpole, particularly intrigued her. She replied: 'I'm glad Frl. Schmidt was beneficial, and I should certainly, in your place, proceed to count my blessings instead of contemplating the size of my annoyances — it is a most profitable occupation.' She also asked him if he would like to come to Nassenheide and talk to her children, and asked about the seriousness with which he obviously took himself and his literary ambitions: 'What makes you so sure you are going to produce a masterpiece? There's no earthly reason why you shouldn't, but it is unusual to be so sure.' Thus the tone was set for their future relationship. She ended: 'If you want to pour out your woes to a person who thinks rather like Rose-Marie on the subject of young men's sorrows write me a line. Your obliged, amused and interested "Elizabeth".'[13]

They met for the first time at Elizabeth's club in London, the

Lyceum Club, 128, Piccadilly, in March 1907. The Lyceum was a new ladies' social club which she had been invited to join a few years earlier and which she found extremely useful for business meetings when she was in town. The International Association of Lyceum Clubs had been founded in 1904 by the Honourable Constance Smedley, a novelist and energetic feminist crusader who saw the need for an all-female club where the old-girl network could be as useful as their masculine counterparts. The aims of the clubs were 'to create an association of clubs grouping women of all nationalities who devoted themselves to, or who are interested in, the arts, sciences and public welfare for the purposes of fostering co-operation and friendship'. Constance Smedley had recently introduced Elizabeth to H. G. Wells. It had not been a successful meeting as far as Elizabeth was concerned for she had invited him to lunch and he had declined. He had done it politely, but he had, nevertheless, declined.

Hugh Walpole duly arrived at the club at the time requested, hat in hand, and encountered 'a small, rather pretty woman. Very outspoken and sharp. She asked me to teach her children. Took me to a queer tea-party. Funny old ladies and everything quaint.'[14] Elizabeth was enchanted by the young man's enthusiasm and desire to please, for he had a naïve, childish, excited manner which was immediately likeable. She arranged that he should report to the castle in a month or two, after he had spent time in France learning something of French culture and the language. At least, that had been his plan. It was his first trip abroad on his own and everything went dreadfully wrong, and he finally found himself held a prisoner in his room until he was able to locate funds to pay for his board and tuition. The poor young man was profoundly embarrassed, as he was destined to be on and off for the rest of his life. He had an uncontrollable, Pooter-like quality about him which made it inevitable that if there was a cat curled up in an armchair he would sit on it; if somebody left a banana skin on the ground, it would be he that slipped on it; trousers splitting and boiled shirt fronts popping out during dinner were everyday occurrences for the agonizingly shy young man. Once he managed to topple off a gang plank and plunge ignominiously into the strip of water between boat and dock.

He was delighted with the clean spaciousness of Nassenheide and his own room there which was 'charming—white walls with a green stove, looking straight out onto a mass of green trees'. He liked the girls 'enormously, most original and amusing. Also the Countess is every bit as good as her books—she knows everyone too.' Henning he found 'most pleasant and quietly humorous'.[15] Walpole's duties, as far as the children were concerned, were light; in fact he had so much time on his hands that he was able to concentrate on writing his 'masterpiece', *Troy Hanneton*. He made good friends with Herr Steinweg and learnt from him that none of the English tutors had ever stayed longer than six months as Elizabeth liked to amuse herself with teasing them 'for the good of their souls'.[16] As they found that having their souls improved was not only uncomfortable but often highly embarrassing, as well as undermining their authority with the girls, they soon left. Hugh Walpole was no exception. In fact Elizabeth was delighted to find in him an almost perfect victim for her occasionally sadistic sallies and jokes. He became flustered, miserable and at a loss for words, and the girls screamed with laughter at his scarlet-faced reaction when their mother told Walpole that he clearly had no experience of women and that she was going to teach him. At least he managed to extract a gloomy satisfaction out of his supposed progress in submitting gracefully to the ragging meted out to him by the countess, but occasionally allowed himself the luxury of weeping in the passages. She usually waited until the table was full of aristocratic friends and neighbours and would then say in a cool but penetrating voice something like, 'Oh, Mr Walpole. I've had such an interesting letter from your father. Do you really wear flannel next to your skin?'[17] To a friend he wrote:

> The Countess is a complete enigma. I don't see much of her but, when I do, she has three moods (1) Charming, like her books only more so (this does not appear often). (2) Ragging. Now she is unmerciful—attacks you on every side, goes at you until you are reduced to idiocy, and then drops you, limp. (3) Silence. This is the most terrible of all. She sits absolutely mute and if one tries to speak one gets snubbed. She was like that at lunch today, and we all made shots in turn and got 'settled'. You see she is not an easy person to live with, but I'm sure there's a key somewhere which I hope to find.[18]

One day, while playing tennis with Elizabeth, she asked him how he had liked *Madame Bovary*. He blushed scarlet, for they were in the full hearing of the three girls who were fielding the balls. His response to his hostess's question was maidenly and she, sensing fruitful ground, first offended him by telling him that she didn't think it was 'a good book for boys'[19] and then teased him about that book and French literature in general so that in a short while he was reduced to tears in the full sight of his pupils. Discipline in the school-room was subsequently hard to enforce.

Walpole found the quiet of the castle the most difficult thing to cope with and determined, unsuccessfully, never to use that word in his diary as it would have become repetitive. Stuart came back to stay for the holidays and blended in very well, Walpole considered, with the prevailing silence. Stuart's dumb devotion was indeed expressing itself as a prolonged and mute resignation to Elizabeth's refusal of his suit and irritation with his inability to overcome his sulky silence. Henning spent much time away looking at his pigs and potatoes, preferring the simplicity of these things to the complex emotions abounding at the castle. Stuart pined in a silent agony and the more he showed his unhappiness, the more his beloved was impatient with him. Teppi noticed that the doomed Englishman followed Elizabeth 'like a poodle', only to be teased and laughed at by her, 'and yet he was so much in love with her that he couldn't be rescued'.[20]

Towards the end of Walpole's stay at Nassenheide Elizabeth found his diary and asked if she could read it. To her astonishment he agreed enthusiastically. Her comments in the margin became yet another front in her war on his innocence. He wrote, for instance, 'Spent a pleasant but idle evening over *Serious Wooing* [a new novel]—"The tipsy cake of literature" someone says—very daintily done—but oh! this novel reading.' In Elizabeth's handwriting alongside is added, 'Must really give it up. My brain is mere whipped cream and jam.' Another is: 'Picked glorious blue corn-flowers—a feast for the eye', to which his hostess added, 'Wished for five whole minutes that I were dead– then had a splendid time telling the family, they enthralled.' Or: 'Mademoiselle's owl has been making a noise like a creaking door outside my room all day. Maddening!' and in Elizabeth's handwriting: 'I couldn't help wishing I were dead. What a place! Nothing but frying pans as alternative to fires. Or do I mean Charybdis and Scylla? But I don't know their plurals, so will stick to frying pans.'[21] In a letter to Evi, Elizabeth wrote, 'He keeps a diary and I said "Do show it to me," never dreaming he would, but he immediately did, and there in it are all of his criticisms of each of us, some pleasant and some anything but. I laughed till I cried, it was so funny.'

Walpole and Elizabeth remained friends for the rest of their lives, indeed Walpole insisted that they were cousins, in which delusion Elizabeth humoured him and treated him as a member of her family.

Clearly none of her teasing caused a serious or permanent breach in their undoubted fondness for each other. He learned from her something about women, at least enough to make them believable characters in his novels, and she, by giving him the space, time and encouragement, nursed his first novel into the light of day, setting him firmly upon the path to literary achievement.

It was at this time that Liebet and Trix decided that their lives were so intolerable that escape was the only way out. (They too had been reading novels, Edith Nesbit's *The Treasure Seekers* in particular.) They decided to 'finally make a break from it all'.[22] They were allowed to ride their ponies unaccompanied during the afternoons along the endless paths that wound their way through the parkland that surrounded the castle. For several weeks they hoarded food and pocket-money. One day, when they decided they had enough, they hid their stores in their clothes and went for a ride as usual. Making for the furthest gate on the estate, they simply opened it and rode away. They had no further plan than that. It was not long, naturally, before their absence was noticed. The police were called and a search was instigated. Two young girls on ponies were not difficult to find and they were fetched home before nightfall, crestfallen, and assuming they were in for serious punishment. When they were ushered into the library on their return they were astonished to find 'their darling mother weeping bitterly'.[23] Far from scolding them, she explained again and again that she had no idea they were so unhappy. The rest of the evening was spent in mutual consolation. The girls never did pluck up enough courage to confess to their mother that they weren't unhappy in the least, only looking for a lark. That way, they knew, punishment lay.

At the beginning of July 1907 H. G. Wells, the novelist and political thinker, received a card from Constance Smedley. It was somewhat garbled and couched in the kind of baby talk then favoured by some of his mistresses, to whose swelling ranks Miss Smedley was perhaps a recruit. The general drift was that Elizabeth would like to meet him again. Miss Smedley had told Elizabeth that Wells might let her go down to Sandgate and call on him, and was startled when Elizabeth replied that she was prepared to make a special journey to England for that. 'And you'd like her *heaps*—I know,' Miss Smedley wrote to the great man in a second letter, '. . . *and don't be angry*: because you're a socialist you ought to be kind to humans who feel like you do.' Crammed into the top is a PS bearing her real import: 'She says she's frightened of you 'cos she asked you to lunch and she says you snubbed her and she was very humble about it and I said I'm sure you didn't mean to: 'cos you were a socialist and *always* were friendly to humans.'

The same day, Hugh Walpole, still at the castle, wrote in his diary: '*On this day was* Troy Hanneton *finished*. Of course there is much thinking to be done but the main writing itself was completed. As to what it is like I haven't the least idea. Went out for a walk *à seul* and met the C. and girls whereat I hurried back with them and had a lovely time. Of course I am ragged about the diary. But she's –!' Elizabeth found the diary which had been left, as usual, in a prominent place in the library and added, 'Since she's seen the diary I feel I'd better just keep to dashes. I can always pretend I mean something nice, but of course I really mean quite bad and naughty things!' The next day he wrote, 'The C. in bed and I missed her extremely which shows how things are changed since a few months ago', to which Elizabeth added, 'Later, retract what I said three hours ago. Discovered on close scrutiny that there's a peace and lightness about the atmosphere when the C. (she doesn't deserve her other letters) is safely in bed which irresistibly reminds me of a fine morning after a thunderstorm. Think that's rather a good image by the way. Must remember to put it into "Troy".'

· 10 ·

The Fiery Sword

There had been many thunderstorms that summer, terrible cataclysms in that flat part of Germany, which arrived after a sultry spell of weather with a fearful display of angry electricity often ripping trees apart or setting hayricks on fire. Elizabeth had never conquered the fear of thunder and lightning which began when she was three, lying awake night after night waiting for the Crack of Doom. At the first distant rumble over the horizon she would have all the windows closed, the curtains drawn, and lighted lamps brought in. She huddled in the library, uncharacteristically afraid, communicating her fear to her daughters. Henning smoked his cigar and paced the veranda, enjoying the magnificent spectacle, regretting yet again that he had not fathered a 'reasonable son'[1] to join him in this pleasure. Only he knew at that point that thunder clouds of a different sort were gathering thickly on the horizon of their lives.

In the middle of July came a letter from Constance Smedley enclosing one written to Elizabeth by H. G. Wells. He was anxious about the snub he was supposed to have given Elizabeth, and extended an invitation for the authoress to visit himself and his wife at Sandgate in Kent. Elizabeth replied the same day:

> My dear Mr Wells,
>
> What in the world has Miss Smedley been writing to you? Imagine my amazement this morning, innocently having breakfast under a tree, when your letter to her, forwarded by her to me, came! It's too funny. I have often thought of the three minutes' talk with you with such unclouded satisfaction, and never has it entered my head that you were rude. You were perfectly delightful, and I, when you couldn't lunch with me, perfectly intelligent and placid. Of course I deplored, but I did understand.

The only thing I said to Miss Smedley, or ever thought, was that I feared it had been in the nature of hangers-on asking you to lunch with a practically strange woman and that it was conceivable you might think so too. There was sorrow in that, never anger. And that, positively, was all. But you know just exactly as well as I do, that you were absolutely kind and pleasant, so I needn't go on. How nice of you to suggest I should come and see you and Mrs Wells at Sandgate. I should very much like it. I am caravanning with my three children in Kent and Sussex in August so if one morning an eager and dusty person appears and you think it's a tramp, you'll know it isn't and let me in. If you are ever up this way and would come to us, we would be delighted . . .

Elizabeth had been hinting in her letters to Evi that something was being planned for that summer, but 'I can't tell you yet about what we're going to do . . . but pray for fine weather, my child, for if it is wet, heaven knows what will become of us.' Elizabeth had seen an advertisement for the hire of vans and horses in *The Times*. The idea of spending the month of August as gypsies in Kent and Sussex had come to her 'in a flash'[2] a day or so later while she was walking in the forest. It was unheard-of then if you had the price of a hotel to choose discomfort: nobody would ever fling themselves into such rigours unless they had no choice, and certainly not for pleasure. Elizabeth was only waiting until she heard whether it was possible to hire the vans and horses before she broke the news to the children. By the end of July all was set ready and she wrote to Evi, 'I think now that our plans are perfectly ripe like fruit on a sunny wall . . .'

Liebet, Trix, Teppi and her mother came to Evi's speech-day at St Paul's. Afterwards they went down to Bexley and took tea with Henry and Louey. Henry wrote in his journal that evening: 'Three charming young creatures delightfully natural; and May looked like their sister.' They went to Cot in Surrey where Charlotte had fled from her increasingly oddly behaved husband. She was in a small house and Evi surmised that in her separated condition Charlotte did not know how much money she would be able to draw on and had sensibly pulled in her horns. Her son Sydney had insisted that his parents separate, for his father was prone to fits of manic-depression. Then the von Arnims and Margery (Drish) travelled down to a soggy field at Nab's Corner, Crouch, in Surrey. There the two vast caravans, 'humble forerunners of the modern trailers and offspring of the gypsy wagons'[3] were waiting for them. They were called The Erda and The Elsa. Two huge dray horses called Diamond and Prince were also there to pull them.

'What a holiday it was!'[4] In retrospect Evi thought it the best she had ever spent in spite of the almost constant rain. Looking back from middle age she only wished that she had been more mature so that she could have enjoyed it more than she did. Besides the six women (Elizabeth, the three girls, Teppi and Drish), there were also several tutors: Mr Gaunt, Mr Forster, Mr Wilson and Mr Stuart (or Cousin William as he was by then known in the family; it was a Beauchamp custom to refer to special friends as 'cousin' rather than the more formal 'Mr'). Mr Gaunt is a mysterious figure about whom nobody comments. He was destined to be 'swallowed up'[5] by India, which Forster deplored as soon as he came to know him well on the tour. However, their friendship caused Forster to develop a special interest in India himself. An old man called George was provided to attend to the horses. The ladies slept in the vans and the young men in tents. Mr Gaunt had brought a bull-terrier called Billy and Mr Wilson a little fox-terrier called Puck. The dogs started to fight as soon as they were introduced, and Cousin William fainted on the spot for he couldn't stand the sight of blood. They travelled from Crouch to Borough Green, the next day to Chatham and then on to Leeds Castle where Lady Baillie allowed them to camp in the grounds. It was from there that Elizabeth and the girls hired a motor and drove down to Sandgate near Folkestone in Kent to have lunch with H. G. Wells and his family in their new home, Spade House. It was a pleasant building with a deep, red-tiled roof and spacious interior, but its great glory was the garden which was Jane Wells's domain, and the view out to the sea which lapped the chalk cliff a sheer ninety feet below. The garden had several lawns for croquet and tennis, a pergola, summerhouses and a rock garden. Across the bay was the smooth sweep of the coast from Dymchurch to Dungeness and on a clear day France hovered on the horizon.

Spade House was built as the triumphant outcome of Wells's struggle against poverty, illness and all the odds. He had been born to a disappointed and overly zealous mother and an easy-going father who preferred to play cricket, which he did well, than run his small china shop at a profit. Herbert George Wells was the third child, and family finances were so bad at the time of his birth that his parents thought of emigrating. His early education was for 'Bertie' a battle between the constraints of the schoolroom and the limitless expansion of his own imagination. He decided early in life that he was destined to save England if not the world. Possibly because of an exceptional capacity to work and survive the vicissitudes of his difficult childhood, which culminated in tuberculosis, he maintained this dream long enough to make considerable strides, if not to save the world at least to open people's minds. Jane was his second wife and they had two boys aged three and six when Elizabeth first met them. Wells, who was born on 21 September 1866, was therefore almost exactly the same age as Elizabeth.

The girls played croquet and after lunch they all went up to the nursery to watch the progress of one of Wells's favourite war games spread out on the floor. It was a panorama with rank upon rank of lead soldiers, barricades, prisons and a whole landscape of battle terrain. Elizabeth became friendly with Jane and the two women spent much time in the garden discussing flowers and compost. Afterwards Jane and the boys travelled back with the von Arnims to Leeds Castle to view the vans and the romantic discomfort endured by the caravaners.

E. M. Forster arrived a day or so later feeling a 'sense of flux'. He caught up with them in a field near Great Chart to find Evi prostrated with what turned out not to be mumps. He slept that night in a shed surrounded by baskets, and the next morning he shared in the breakfast that was the unvarying rule: 'Porridge with very much cream, eggs and tea.'[6] These things were cooked on a small primus stove in one of the vans and handed out to the damp young men through a hinged flap in the side. Each day the vans rumbled and lurched out of the fields into the lanes. Nobody was allowed to ride on them unless they were ill or crippled, to save the horses' strength. They had to walk 'as out of Noah's Ark', one man and one woman together, while Drish and her 'not-to-be-parted-from cousin'[7] Trix brought up the rear in a pony trap. It was their duty to buy or beg the food. Everything was paid for by Elizabeth, and money for the odd packet of sweets or fruit bought by the company was carefully refunded. Elizabeth walked up and down the entourage handing out biscuits and encouragement.

On Forster's second day they called at Swinford Manor near Ashford in Kent, which was the home of Alfred Austen, to ask if they could look over the garden that he loved, and were welcomed by the poet himself who told them to 'Walk where you will.' In the evenings a cooking pot was hung on a triangular stand above a camp-fire and the girls threw food into it and busily stirred so that whatever it was became unrecognizable. The pot was rarely emptied and was simply topped up the next evening. Nobody had heard of salmonella poisoning and consequently nobody suffered from it.

One evening when everybody had gone to bed Teppi and Elizabeth stole down to a local pub to get a decent meal. They sat in a private bar until a table should be ready for them and realized that the laughter and voices coming from the other side of the partition were familiar. They looked round and were not surprised to see the young men just finishing up their own second supper. Naturally the women joined them, but the meal was constrained after that and it wasn't until the end of the tour that they could laugh together about the incident.

The party draggled good-humouredly along a looping trail through Staplehurst, Sissinghurst, Bodiam, Salehurst, Burwash, Staplecross, Sedlescombe, Battle, Brede and Rye. It was here that Elizabeth went to visit her old friend and mentor, Henry James, who had influenced her first books with his penchant for long and complicated sentences. She asked him, coquettishly, whether he would mind her remaining with him always and being his female Boswell, to which he replied, 'It would be the long squeezing out of a completely dry sponge . . .' an image which delighted her.[8] At Peasmarsh Elizabeth saw a cottage by the church which seemed to her to be 'the real thing' and which was to make a setting for one of her later novels, *Father*. She made an offer to buy it, as was her habit every time she saw something she liked, but it was not for sale, nor could the owner be budged with bribes. They trundled on through Wittersham, High Halden and Bethersden, planning to join the Pilgrims' Way to Canterbury. When they reached the turning-point which revealed Canterbury and its magnificent cathedral below them, they all knelt down and gave thanks for their safe deliverance, just as many pilgrims had done before them.

The main event of the trip was the rain. It was the wettest August on record, not only in England but in the whole of Europe. It rained every day and sometimes all day. Often it was impossible to sleep in the vans because of the thunderous noise of the raindrops hitting the roof. Much of the time was wasted struggling with the horses as they heaved the vans out of the mud. Liebet remembered:

> In the almost constant downpour, the wretched caravaners never dared to stray far from the main roads and missed many of the lovelier parts [of the countryside]. The physical difficulties of just moving along, of keeping dry and of getting fed were immense, and Elizabeth, to whom the simplicities had seemed so alluring while she

was lapped in the elaborate comforts of her home, felt that she had perhaps plunged into too many of them too thoroughly.[9]

They did manage to stay in the dry from time to time by the simple expedient of choosing to camp in a field belonging to a fine stately home. One of the tutors would go to the door and announce, 'The Countess von Arnim is at the lodge gates in her caravan, and asks whether she may put up in your park.' Most of the inhabitants recognized the name and were delightedly forthcoming with invitations for the whole party to stay in the house. Lady Maude Warrender was one such and described the visit in her memoirs: ' "Do you mean 'Elizabeth' of the German Garden? Of course . . . delighted." . . . It was my first meeting with this enchanting writer; together with countless others I always look forward greedily to each new book of hers, and her friendship is one that I sincerely value.'[10] Her children were thrilled at having a real caravan close by and at meeting the April, May and June babies. The next day the Warrenders accompanied the caravans and led them to a field belonging to friends. Lawrence Alma Tadema, the novelist daughter of the painter Sir Lawrence Alma Tadema, lived close by and was persuaded by the Warrenders to pretend to be the Queen of the Gypsies. Elizabeth was 'excited to a frenzy' by this manifestation.

> One could not help noticing Countess von Arnim's extra-ordinary powers of observation. Nothing, even the smal-lest detail, escaped her. She took in everything. This faculty no doubt accounts for the wealth of delightful characterisation and touches of humorous understanding in her books.[11]

Henning had promised to come over to England during August to watch the family being uncomfortable. (This penchant for living like peasants for fun, or even in the pursuit of the Wordsworthian ideal, was a trait of his wife's which no number of years of living with her could bring Henning to understand.) Unfortunately it had been an equally sodden month in Pomerania and his potato crops were ruined. He had also been ill, suffering from diabetes and recently a severe attack of boils. He had been diagnosed as having a heart murmur and his doctor had told him to take things easily if he could. The estate was again close to ruin and his anxieties about the future of Nassenheide had given him little rest. He stood at his tall desk night after night, burning the midnight oil in his attempts to produce a strain of potato on his farm that would make money in his doomed quest to salvage the estate.

In the last week, when the whole party was at its most bedraggled and dusty, they camped at Aylesford. Some of them attended the local church and the vicar was so interested in them that he cut the whole service short, including the sermon, which lasted for only seven minutes, in his impatience to find out who these people were. When they arrived back at the site, there he was talking to Teppi. He invited them all to the parsonage that evening and they had a gay time dancing reels accompanied by the vicar's wife on the piano. The sight of Elizabeth dancing the Highland fling with the vicar in his cassock engraved itself forever on the memory of Forster.

They had spent much of their time exploring the churches along the route. Evi recalled that it was not piety that directed them but simply love of the beauty of the buildings and their simple Episcopalian services. Billy, the dog, became a symbol, in Forster's eyes, of the whole thing: 'Nature with dignity!' He found the children nicer than ever with the exception of Liebet who had grown too silent and sharp. He left the company early from Borough Green station and found that London 'hummed strangely', for he had 'heard a new song'.[12] Indeed he had even tried his hand at poetry during the trip:

> Ten shadows flecked the sunlit road,
> Ten shadows passed, yet we remain
> Still marching to the Dorian mode
> Still summoning the Gods to reign.
> Gods of the country! Still in Kent
> The music of the pipe rings plain.
> Through places where ten shadows went
> The shadows passed but we remain![13]

The tutors left the ranks one by one and Elizabeth, Teppi and the girls spent a few days in Canterbury in a hotel having baths, regular meals and exploring the cathedral. The holiday in England for the von Arnims was by no means over. Elizabeth's imagination had been fired by the cottage she had failed to buy and she determined to spend more time with the girls searching the length and breadth of England for the perfect place, for Kent and Sussex had not yielded one up to her. All her life she had longed for that cottage with a cow and a vegetable patch which she had worried her parents with before she met Henning. At Nassenheide she had built a tiny little Thoreau-like hut near the pond and entertained the children in it for tea parties. She talked often to them of the joys of the simple life. 'The ideal cottage' became close to the Holy Grail in Elizabeth's mythology, its chief virtue, in those days, being no servants.

The family travelled back by train to London and booked into the Grosvenor Hotel to await the belated arrival of Henning, 'enjoying a great many baths and getting rid of the last of the dirt.'[14] At the beginning of September Evi and Trix accompanied their mother northwards on a 'luxury tour' where they enjoyed every comfort along the way. Evi gave squeals of delight over the little tea baskets for one that could be bought on railway platforms in those days. Liebet had been left behind weeping to have her teeth seen to and to start a course of Swedish exercises because she was, in the opinion of her mother, growing too fast. She was also 'under a cloud' for sulking at the reinstatement of Evi among them. The lucky ones spent their first night up north at the Peacock Hotel in Rowlsey, Derbyshire. They saw all the sights in the area such as the model village at Edensor and they visited the Devonshires at Chatsworth House who were new friends of Elizabeth. She found and made offers for several cottages but they were all either taken or unsuitable in some way. Then they travelled south. Evi was sent out early on the morning of their departure for a bottle of castor oil for her sister who was dosed without mercy from Chester to Land's End. Still they did not find 'the real thing' as far as a cottage was concerned but they enjoyed themselves tremendously. They planned further adventures, but a telegram arrived saying that Henning was waiting for them in London and would Elizabeth bring the children to see him as soon as possible—it was the voice of Authority, and they rushed back in the Cornish Riviera Express. They dined on the train and took a 'growler' to the Grosvenor where Henning was in bed asleep having ordered the staff not to disturb him. It was difficult to convince the man at the desk that Elizabeth was Count von Arnim's wife, she seemed so young, and there was much discussion before she was let into her husband's room.

The next morning the children were shocked to see their father looking so ill, and not only ill but profoundly depressed for reasons which they could not guess. That evening they went to Hatchett's for supper where Liebet joined them, no shorter in height but with some grisly dentist stories to tell them all. From there they went on to the Playhouse to see *French as He is Spoke*, the curtain-raiser, followed by *The Earl of Pawtucket*. The children were uneasily aware that all was not well with their parents and the atmosphere was filled with sadness and anxiety.

That night Elizabeth and Henning sat up till dawn discussing the future of the family. Henning revealed that the financial situation was parlous and far, far worse than he had allowed his wife to understand until then. A potato disease that broke out in 1904 had continued to blight his crops so that that year he had searched the fields in vain for three months for a single healthy tuber. All his careful breeding would have to be started again. It was a final straw when the crop failed as well because of the rain in August. In short he was on the edge of ruin and, unless Elizabeth bailed him out again, nothing could save Nassenheide from falling into the hands of the receivers.

In spite of Miss Stanley's arrangements, Elizabeth had been giving her husband large sums of money over the years when he had asked her for it, hoping vainly that soon his farming would begin to make a profit. They had also both spent money freely, for economy did not come naturally to either of them except, maddeningly, in small things. Standards had to be kept up. Elizabeth was desolated by the idea of having to leave Nassenheide, but fear of war between England and Germany, which she clearly saw coming, and anxiety on her own account as to how she would be able to support the five children after her husband had gone into a sanatorium as his doctor urged, brought her close to despair. She had no money of her own except what she earned and why everybody simply assumed she would go on producing popular books year after year she could not imagine. They had no inkling of the fear she lived under, in common with all creative people, that her gift might leave her.

Henning's main idea was for the family to move to Schlagenthin which housed the family mausoleum and was itself as dismal as one. Elizabeth was entirely opposed to such an arrangement. This would mean that in the event of a war she would be caught in Germany, as well as no doubt being expected to pay for the upkeep and repairs of such an unwieldy estate. No, she would come to England, find a cottage and keep a cow, rather than that. Schlagenthin, which had been wisely entailed to his unborn children by Henning's mother, would have to be sold for their upkeep.

The next morning Evi noticed that her mother's eyes were reddened with much weeping, but also large and frightened as though she had been looking into the future and had seen terrifying things there. 'She told us to prevent my father from buying her any gift for her birthday' (which had been at the end of August) 'as she would sent it straight back,' Evi recalled in her memoirs. Of course Henning was continuing to spend money like the prince that he very nearly was and intended to worry about the cost when the duns arrived at the door—and the duns were expected to arrive at

Nassenheide any time after 1 January 1909. They had until then to decide on a plan for the future.

Evi was tearfully deposited with Lady Maude Whyte: 'You are infected with my presence among you,' she flung at her sisters as she said goodbye.[15] Liebet and Trix went back to Nassenheide at the end of September with their parents. Only a few days after they had arrived Elizabeth received a telegram with the news that her father had died, and she immediately repacked her bags and set off again for England. She stayed with her mother in Bexley to comfort her and wrote to Evi:

> You did not know Deepa, but I can't tell you how proud I am I had such a dear father. So honourable, so straight, so sincere, and kind and philosophical—and *so* witty—and he hated lies and everything not quite plainly honest. Well, I am going to try to be more like him—Tit [Charlotte] and I both mean to try so hard, and we both bless him for having been such a beautiful example to us, and for having left nothing but happy memories behind . . .

Henning came over to England to collect his wife again and while he was waiting for her went to visit Evi at Lady Maude's. Unfortunately the confused child had gained the impression that Henning was 'under a cloud' and out of loyalty to her mother was short with him and sent him away sooner than she should have done. Lady Maude gave her a terrible scolding for the way she behaved towards him. When, a few days later, Elizabeth came to visit her eldest daughter it was with the hard news that Evi must stay in England for Christmas. Her mother looked sad, Evi noticed, and her eyes seemed larger in her face. She did not ask why this had been decided, and she guessed it was because that summer had proved that Liebet and Trix resented her being in the family with them, for they made no secret of their feelings.

That Christmas at Nassenheide was a gloomy affair, for nobody, not even the enthusiastic Teppi, could simulate cheerfulness or gratitude and everyone felt let down. The end of an era was fast approaching and what lay ahead nobody could guess.

As soon after Christmas as she could Elizabeth set herself to begin work on *The Caravaners*. Evi was to collaborate on it but in the event her mother included only a few morsels of her contribution. The novel is a strong warning to the British that war between England

and Germany was practically inevitable, judging by Elizabeth's reading of the Prussian character. It was extremely unfortunate that she was feeling less than friendly towards her husband at the time: the dreadful Prussian officer who is the narrator could conceivably have been taken to be a caricature of him. Baron Otto von Ottringe is entirely self-centred, a snob and the original male chauvinist pig, a superb caricature of the typical Prussian bourgeois. The other male members of the party are inclined towards Socialism, as were Mr Wilson and Cousin William. This scandalizes the baron almost as much as their habit of walking along in floppy shirts with their hands in their pockets. The friendliness shown by the others in their efforts to assimilate this monstrous German into their company is seen by the baron as overfamiliarity and he continually snubs them. He is constitutionally unable to appreciate the good and the beautiful. It is a fierce book which clearly indicates that the author's choice of company was not German officers. The baron spends much of his time licking his lips over England, 'that plump little island' which in his eyes was simply waiting to be gobbled up by the German Empire. He muses:

> It was not likely that I could be mistaken for I suppose that of all people in the world a Prussian officer is least likely to be that. He is too shrewd, too quick, of too disciplined an intelligence. It is these qualities that keep him at the top of the European tree, combined, indeed, with his power of concentrating his entire being into one noble determination to stay on it. Again, descending to allegory, I can see . . . all the other slow-spoken and slow-thoughted Englishmen flapping ineffectually among the lower and more comfortable branches of the tree of nations. Yes, they are more sheltered there; and they have roomier nests; less wind and sun; less distance to fly in order to fetch the waiting grub from the moss beneath; but what about the Prussian Eagle sitting at the top, his beak flashing in the light, his watchful eye never off them? Some day he will swoop down on them when they are, as usual, asleep, clear out their similar well-lined nests, and have the place to himself—becoming, as the well known picture has it (for I too can allude to pictures), in all his glory *Enfin seul.*

Clearly this was not a book designed to promote peace in the von

Arnim household.* Elizabeth's new enthusiasm for Fabian Socialism further exacerbated the domestic disharmony, for while Henning's original political allegiance had been to the Liberal Party, he
had, like many others, become a conservative in his later years. At
the base of all the 'sulphur' and disagreements was his wife's
determination that the family should move, as soon as possible, to
England, and Henning's equal determination that they should
inhabit Schlagenthin. The eighteen-year-old Evi, retrieved from
England for the New Year, opened her diary with the comment:

> There is really a very small amount of happiness on this
> earth and what is so bad, it is easily dispelled. By no
> means is happiness so quickly dispersed as by disagree-
> ment between husband and wife. Now here are Mummy
> and Papa, for example, each taken alone a very jewel, but
> together! I suppose all the sulphur there is always about
> now is mostly due to the different nationalities: England =
> M. German = P. Dear P. on one side brought up to
> despise all females and regarding them as if they belonged
> to a class entirely inferior in every way. Dear M. on the
> other side, witty, clever and altogether contrary to the
> accustomed German female, gifted indeed as the best of
> men. How sad that such a thing should be and it produces
> such lots of sulphur . . . poor lady; yet it is the natural
> German thing; but how dreadful; the man is all, the
> woman nothing. How everlastingly thankful I am that our
> household is not like that. How glad I am that in spite of
> the sulphur, Mummy has the will to bring us up as
> independent women. Ah, for this indeed I do thank God.

Evi went to stay at Charlotte's new house, Ropes, near Fernhurst in
Sussex for her half holiday in her spring term. Her aunt was living in
a much larger house, her financial status having been improved as a
result of her son Sydney's petitions on her behalf to her husband,
who was by then living openly with another, and not very nice,
woman. This house was to play a large part in the lives of the von
Arnims in the near future. It is set back a long way from the lane that
leads up to it and the drive lined with sweet-briar sweeps up to the
porticoed front door. Near the front gate, in those days, were the

*Henning had progressed from sucking the water from his finger bowl into his mouth to rinse
his false teeth, and now insisted in keeping the company waiting at the end of every meal while
he removed his teeth and washed them out in the finger bowl. Elizabeth confessed to Wells a
few years later that this had been 'the last straw'.[16]

stables, the coachman's house and a gardener's cottage. Behind
were tennis courts and a summer house. The house, built of mellow,
honey-coloured stone, is on different levels. It was, Evi remembered,
always filled with flowers and smelt dimly of these and her aunt's
lavender scent. Jack Waterlow, Charlotte's second son, had brought
a fellow naval officer to stay, and Jack's friend promptly decided that
he wanted to marry Evi. Nothing came of it but Elizabeth, when she
heard, said 'that it would have been such a good idea to have been
married to him, because he would be away half the time at sea'.
Wrote Evi: 'She seemed to think that a husband so much away was
worth snatching at!'[17]

Evi's mind was in a whirl of confusion, for all the old values
appeared to have been torn apart in tandem with her own family.
She had also seen much of the activities of the feminists in London,
who were making speeches, demonstrating and getting arrested. She
had no inclination to join them, for she followed her mother in
everything and the clear-sighted novelist was not a women's rights
fighter of this kind; everything obvious was repulsive to her, and she
believed that fair-minded conviction, clarity and purity of an idea
were more successful than a spectacle of mass gatherings. A clear
idea stated simply and read by many was her preferred method of
fighting injustice. Naturally she was in favour of women's rights, and
the whole body of her work as well as her own life and the way she
had brought up her daughters underlined her convictions, but she
had never heard a woman speak convincingly on politics and poked
fun continuously at the militant feminists who only succeeded, in her
view, in making fools of themselves and harming their cause. She
consciously wrote for the masses and often she was accused by her
literary friends of producing pot-boilers and making money instead
of producing art. Her answer was that she was able to write for
intellectuals as well as common people and that 'to give the simple
people a happy hour is worth more than to brag about great works of
art'.[18] Evi enthusiastically underwrote all of her mother's opinions.

The family went to Schlagenthin once or twice during 1908 to look
it over as a future home, but Elizabeth could not bring herself to like
the huge, ornate and deathly place. She toyed with the idea of
building a house for the family in the glorious park surrounding the
castle, but this idea was quashed by Henning as ridiculous when
there was a perfectly good castle to live in. Finally, with much soul-
searching, Elizabeth determined to buy a house in England, prefer-
ably in Devon and with a single pear tree—she was sure that she
would eventually find happiness beneath a single pear tree for no

reason that she ever explains. She set off to look for a small house in some peaceful place near a school where they would have 'few menials, tamed surroundings and a climate as different from that of Pomerania as possible'.[19] Almost immediately she found it, a modest but charming Georgian house called Blue Hayes at Broadclyst, near Exeter. It was surrounded by lovely countryside and there was a good high school for girls in Exeter. She returned to Pomerania and announced that she had bought the house. Evi, in England, received the news with a cry of despair that she would not be able to take with her all the animals at Nassenheide that she had grown so fond of. Her mother replied, careful to preserve the fiction that there was some choice about the selling of Nassenheide:

> I wish too I could take the ponies and Coco [the dog] and a stork or two and all the forests. It is very dreadful leaving [Nassenheide] and my dear garden where I have had so many years of happy meditation—the days rush by so, and every evening in the library with the lovely fire roaring in the chimney I groan a little—but what is to be done? The children must be educated, Papa can't go on slaving like this forever, and if he gets rid of it will still have plenty of work at Schlagenthin—it is true he loves to work but he doesn't love anxiety and slavery and bad harvests. Do you know what it did on Easter Monday, and yesterday—it snowed. A cheerful climate, isn't it?

It was while the unseasonable Easter snow still lay on the ground in the spring of 1909 that the removal vans silently lined up in front of the castle. It was already dark and the work was carried out as quietly as possible, for although Elizabeth had, some time before, bought the furniture that she was taking to England and had a bill of sale to prove it, she was, nevertheless, apprehensive that creditors might appear at the last moment and try to stop the removal of the goods. A few days later she herself left with many tears and accompanied by Liebet who would follow her 'Most Beloved'[20] to the gates of hell if need be, the tearful Trix, Martin, the unconcerned, and H.B. who thought it all, as usual, great fun. Henning stayed behind in the denuded house to negotiate its sale. He was to be looked after by his valet and a single servant, the ever faithful and valiant Teppi.

· 11 ·

Entangled in Tea Parties

The freezing April weather did nothing to raise the spirits of the
sorry little band of German refugees as it made its way across the
Channel to England. The children were quarrelsome and difficult to
control. Their mother had only her maid, the devoted Elise, to stand
by her in the teeth of what often took on the proportions of open
rebellion. Naturally they had all wanted to go with their mother to
England when the plan was first put to them. Had not this been the
highest honour they could aspire to during their childhood? Had not
the gloom of Nassenheide been almost unmitigated of late? Would
not this be the beginning of a new life where they could have their
mother always to themselves, untrammelled by the dreadful contemplation of her leaving them for her native land? But Liebet and
Trix had guessed that this journey would put the final seal on the
split between their parents. It was no use pretending their father
would join them when the castle was sold as was the current fiction.
He was far too proud and detested England and its soft ways too
much for that ever to be a remote possibility. Trix in particular
grieved; she, of all the children, was closest to Henning. The image of
her father ill, sad, broken and alone in that beloved but now desolate
house was often too much for her to bear. She flared up at her mother
and could not be quelled even by a threat of the castor oil bottle.
Only Liebet knew how much her mother had always longed to live in
England and at the same time how much she had loved her life in the
slow grandeur of the Pomeranian landscape; how betrayed she felt
by her husband's fecklessness and how much responsibility she had
taken on her frail shoulders. This small middle-aged woman was
now the sole provider for six people besides herself, and the only one
to whom any of them could turn for strength and advice.

Teppi had voiced her opinion of the family split in very plain
language to her mistress. She could not find it in her conscience to

condone this latest move and refused to accompany her beloved. No, her duty was plain—and in the matter of duty Teppi more than made up for her mistress's reluctant response to its demands. Teppi pledged to stay behind with Henning and do everything in her power to ameliorate the situation. She even submitted herself to cooking lessons from Frau Horne and personally braved Henning's periodic rages over the inferior quality of his food which had caused many a cook in the past to hand in her notice. And besides, she was in love with the local Inspector of Forests, a large, taciturn, handsome and married man about whom she had often become lyrical concerning the beauty and stillness of his life in the woods. The gallant Teppi had decided on her first meeting with the countess not to put her 'light under a bushel barrel but to draw the fiery sword of the archangel if it should be necessary'.[1] If ever there was a time when this should be done it was during this woeful period in the family fortunes. She had explained to the girls that they must obey their mother and be good; war between Germany and England was a very real possibility and Elizabeth was not able, given her temperament, to choose to be German. On the plus side, their education in England would be far better than any they could get in Germany as mere females. No doubt the two oldest girls would soon be going to Cambridge, for they were both studying for their entrance examination. But Teppi's justifications sounded hollow. It was also evident to the children that the parting of their mother and the housekeeper was on a far more emotional level than anything that at that time transpired between their parents.

The bedraggled von Arnims were met at the port by Cousin William, but his chinless and indecisive features were no substitute in the children's eyes for their abandoned father. Nor did their vulnerable plight prevent Elizabeth heaping coals on the young man's misery by ragging him whenever his dumb devotion got on her nerves, which was most of the time. If to be liked, to really be liked, was Elizabeth's deepest inspiration then in this, at the age of forty-two, she had signally failed. She was loved by almost everyone who knew her, adored by some and even worshipped by her children. She was certainly hated on occasion by some of those near to her for, though she was unfailingly just in her dealings with people and particularly scrupulous about behaviour, her friends and family were never in the same position for half an hour at a time. In temperament she was very like the English weather: she was unpleasant or uncomfortable for part of the time, but when the sun came out it was worth having waited for. Nor was she generally 'liked': she was too powerful a person and stirred up too many feelings of a disturbing nature to be associated with such a tepid emotion. But those who adored her—and she was adorable—roused her deepest ire, for in this spineless condition they were lost, not only to her but to themselves.

Elizabeth herself was far from happy at this time, though she would have been the first to decry considerations based on anything so insubstantial as mere feelings. Her own brand of faith in freedom and her work were the two poles of her existence; those she loved were often subordinate to their demands. She sensed an inevitability about her plight which appealed to the poetic side of her nature if to nothing else: she had found her Garden of Eden at Nassenheide during that first spring and summer of her arrival. When she lived there with her family she had tasted of the fruit of the tree of knowledge—this much is evident in her books. Now circumstances conspired to expel her from it. She was to be a woman alone and a woman who must bring up her children with as much pain and travail as she had suffered at their birth. She did not lack courage and she made no concessions to her vulnerability. Hard work, as always, was her avenue of survival and escape.

When, over twenty years later, Elizabeth came across her diaries and papers of the Nassenheide period while she was packing up to leave her house in Switzerland, she paused for a day or so and read them through. Her verdict on the person revealed to her in them was 'rather sweet'.[2] Throughout all the loneliness, frustration, pain, disappointment, struggle and sheer joy of those years the robust, wilful and, yes, rather sweet personality of the little English Miss Beauchamp shone through. But the sweetness of her nature was not to survive for long her return to England and the adversity that awaited her there. All who knew her were shocked at the change that was to be wrought in her over the next few years.

The lovely white Georgian house with beautiful views, walled kitchen garden, tennis court and orchard was not ready when the family arrived from Germany four days after the furniture. They were obliged to take lodgings in Exeter until the workmen finished the job at their own gentle English pace. The dog Prince, a mournful beast with 'malignant red eyes' who came with the house, saw no cause to rejoice and exhibited no pleasure when five women and two children moved in at the end of April (for Evi had by then joined them).[3] Elizabeth was unhappy and lonely. Her props, which she had for so long and with such conviction urged others to do without, had disappeared and instead she found herself submerged by responsibilities. Life in Devonshire after the more bracing climate of Pomerania seemed sleepy and lax, and she was shocked when the English gardener simply leaned on his spade when she spoke to him instead of springing to attention and clicking his heels together as she had been used to in Pomerania. Nevertheless she managed, with the fortitude of much practice, to turn the garden at Blue Hayes into something quite spectacular which is still appreciated by the residents to this day.

The girls remained quarrelsome, especially when Evi set herself apart from the others as someone who knew about the English and the nobler emotions honed by suffering. She declared that one day she was going to be a writer. Liebet had grown accustomed to being the oldest and still resented her sister's intrusion, while Evi herself harboured deep suspicions about Liebet only 'pretending to be good at tennis'[4] and of not liking her at all. Though Evi was affectionate and fond at times, she aped her mother's fickleness and could not be trusted to have the same response to a person or situation twice in a row. She became easily tragic, like her father, over the slightest of imagined insults and on the whole was an even greater worry to her mother than ever. Elizabeth urged Liebet to partner Evi at tennis, otherwise she would have been completely rejected by the rest of the children who felt more than ever that she was not one of them. The girl's conversation was the main stumbling block to arousing the interest of her brother and sisters, for it mostly concerned speculation about whichever mistress or older girl for whom Evi was currently suffering a *Schwärmerei*. She wrote in her diary, 'I'm afraid Liebet and I dislike each other very much and I only hope we will not get to hate each other.'

Their mother was practically invisible most of the time, busy in her cottage studio in the centre courtyard. Evi noticed that Liebet was the favourite, and of all of them she alone had her mother's ear. The good manners, charm and originality that Elizabeth wished on her daughters, and strove to achieve in them, was by no means the whole story. They all became 'exceedingly skilful in deceit . . . Pushing each other under the dreaded shadow [of their mother's disapproval], the ever tempting climax to private hostilities.'[5] Telling tales and character assassination were definitely judged unfair practice; nevertheless, according to Evi's diaries, Liebet was unable to resist abusing her privileged position and kept the others almost permanently under clouds.

A strange lassitude affected the family which could not be explained entirely by the unhappiness and bereavement they were all, naturally, feeling. The pragmatic Elizabeth, who had resolutely, on arriving in England, put German sentimentality and superstition behind her, was loath to admit that there was 'something'[6] in the atmosphere of the house that transmitted itself to the inhabitants, but she vowed, from then on, only to live in houses that she had built herself and in which nobody had ever lived before.

The children could not resist the delicious Devonshire cream and junkets made for them in quantities by the cook and they began to get fat. Ten Times Round was now a dreary journey up the drive to the gate and back ten times which had to be done every morning, but was of no avail in the struggle against their ever-increasing sizes. H.B. did not speak English and was bullied at school for being German. Trix was miserable away from her beloved father. Only the nine-year-old Martin, who was concentrating on perfecting Rachmaninov's first piano concerto night and day, appeared unperturbed by the move.

As soon as they were settled in, Elizabeth began to receive calls from the local gentry. 'They came in shoals, by the score'. The news that 'Elizabeth' was living in their midst spread amongst them like wildfire. She was obliged to return up to twelve calls a day, and defaulted on none of them, even when it meant a long drive over the moors in a pony trap, and she did less work than she hoped. 'After years of practically complete freedom from invitations owing to lack of *Hochgeboren* neighbours, I found myself entangled in tea parties,' she wrote.[7]

Four weeks after the completion of the move Elizabeth went to stay for a few days with Francis and Mollie Russell. He and Elizabeth had seen each other sporadically over the years, during which he had gradually lost his good looks but had gained weight as a debater in the House of Lords. He busied himself with various companies, of which he was a director, which manufactured arms; tinkered with his electrical gadgets and motor cars and continually planned and carried out improvements to Telegraph House his, by now, substantial property in Sussex. His wife pottered round the garden there in her knickerbockers with her Maltese terriers tumbling round her feet, or did a little writing or simply slept, and was never very far away from her glass of whisky and water. Bertrand Russell, Francis's brother commented:

> The view of her from behind [wearing green corduroy knickerbockers] as she was bending over a flower bed at Telegraph House, used to make one wonder that he

thought her worth what he had gone through for her sake.[8]

When Elizabeth returned from the visit she collapsed with a stiffness in her whole body that lasted for over a week. She would not eat and her worried daughters crept up to her room after their supper every night and talked to her about the news of the day. England and her allies had opposed German naval expansion in the Mediterranean and were intervening to prevent a Serbo-Austrian war. There was a silence about the political situation that worried the four women. Evi was so excited that she looked under her bed every night to see if 'the enemy'[9] were there, never dreaming that soon she herself would be considered the enemy. They also discussed the feminist movement, which had become increasingly militant in its quest for votes. Bleriot was making plans to cross the Channel in his flying machine and it seemed to them that the world had shifted on its axis as had they, and that all was strange and rather frightening.

Soon thereafter Elizabeth received a copy of Francis Russell's *Lay Sermons*. It was a revolutionary little book which says, in lucid prose and high sounding sentiments, that the Christianity of the Church as we know it is not where to look for the religious experience. His descriptions of his own quest for the phenomena of conversion and his finding of 'the path' sound convincing, even inspiring, but he doggedly persists in his view that the Church has misunderstood Christ's message. He accompanied the book with a note saying:

> . . . I cannot tell you with what reluctance I send this book, because in it I have said what I thought, and in a cynical world one dreads that . . . I cannot tell you how much we both enjoyed your visit—it was a rare and exquisite pleasure. A good cure for feeling 'head and shoulders above' may be found in press cuttings—I have just received one which calls us 'an uninteresting, heavy-looking middle-aged couple'!

Evidently there was much else that he could not tell Elizabeth. She, who considered him, as did his fellow Fabian H. G. Wells, a 'gentle and affable man'[10] replied that she was delighted with his book and that 'in and out and round about and over and under everything trails beauty—your love and perception of beautiful things, tangible and intangible. I miss you, dear boy . . .'

Henning was also writing a book, called *Pure Agriculture Cultivation Practices*. Teppi, who was still caring for him (her cooking had evinced few complaints from Henning so far), saw from Elizabeth's letters that 'inner harmony was totally lacking' in her beloved. They were short, and in her opinion 'indicated a torn, unpeaceful soul'.[11] In fact the terror Elizabeth felt at being the only breadwinner among the lot of them gave her little time for her soul and the girls hardly ever saw her. There seemed to be no happiness anywhere in the family and every member felt 'betrayed in their hopes and expectations'.[12] Henning's letters were filled with gloom. To Evi he wrote:

> You can imagine that the lonely life I lead here with Teppi isn't very gay, the impossibility to talk sensibly to anyone, the everlasting being alone and the perpetual remembrance of the absence of those I love and for whom I live— each corner of the house where everything is more or less the same, each plant in the garden which is maintained as though you would one day return . . .

He was obliged to stay at Nassenheide until it attracted a buyer, and as no buyer was in sight he was likely to remain indefinitely in the denuded house, like a guest at his own funeral. It was a curious reversal of circumstances that forced him to live there alone, he who had been so reluctant to move there in the beginning. The positions were not entirely reversed, however, for he still complained that his wife answered his letters inadequately.

What little time Elizabeth had for work was occupied in finishing *The Caravaners*; then she turned her attention to the adaptation of *Princess Priscilla's Fortnight*. The dramatic rights had been bought by Herbert Trench, the playwright, who wished to produce it at the Haymarket Theatre. Elizabeth protested that she had no understanding of the craft, but an introduction to J. M. Barrie solved the problem. Every day she worked in her studio and left the running of the household increasingly to Elise. When she went to London, which was necessarily often, she stayed at a tiny flat she had rented in Grosvenor Court, Davies Street. 'The flat is too sweet,' wrote Evi after seeing it for the first time. It consisted of 'the smallest, fuggiest, comfortablest little sitting-room' and two bedrooms leading off it on either side with folding baths in a cupboard, 'taps and all'.[13] Cousin William, a donnish Dante, stood by to escort his Beatrice if ever the need arose, while Evi, Liebet and Trix played tennis or wandered about aimlessly in the grounds of Blue Hayes during the school holidays. It was planned that they should 'come out' and do the English season, but they resented being taught to dance and talk to their English contemporaries at parties. Evi wrote:

> I can't in the least see what all these parties are for, just to

go and talk to each other about one's cooks and house-
maids and German stoves. I don't see the fun of that. Why
can't people be sensible, surely they have all of them got
some brains. Why on earth use it for something like that?
Oh, for a bit of wisdom, just one little bit.[14]

The rigidly orthodox young lady was shocked when she discovered
one summer evening that her mother was toying with some new and,
to her mind, dangerous heresies. They were sitting on the veranda
and the conversation drifted to the subject of God. Elizabeth calmly
explained the possibility that God was dead. He had lived once,
perhaps, and created the world. Having done that he had died and
the world survived 'just as works of art and cathedrals survive their
makers'. Evi went to bed that night 'perturbed, doubting, miserable'[15] and pondered the strange ways of the English people her
mother mixed with who speculated about the nature of the Deity as
coolly as they might comment on the weather.

Henning's letters became 'sulphurous' after the rest of the family
had been settled into Blue Hayes for only three months. He wanted
some, if not all, of the children back. Elizabeth read them with a
sinking heart, for even when they were there he never saw them all
day and had time only for a game of draughts in the evening. She
knew that she would never go and live in Germany again herself, but
she was aware that the resentment her children felt towards her for
forcing them to be English when they knew perfectly well they were
German, and furthermore had no desire to be English, was reaching
a climax. More problems arose because Martin had been discovered
in such a flagrant and creative deception that the other children were
aghast. Evi wrote:

Found out today that Quiqui is the most atrocious liar and
invents stories too clever for words. Last Friday she had
come down from her morning lesson telling us that after
dinner Miss Andrews [one of their teachers at the High
School] was going to tell her what class she was. And sure
enough, after dinner she disappeared and after a while
came back again and told us very radiantly that she was in
the first class. We, poor guinea-fowls, believed the
varmint. But today, meeting Miss Andrews on our way to
school, it occurred to me to ask if it was indeed true.
Would you believe it? Not one tiny word of it . . . Well, I
must say my dear sister is a very clever inventor and I only
hope and pray that when she grows up she will use her

cleverness to some better purpose.[16]

Their father came in the wake of his letters, looking older and more ill than ever. 'Never was a man so changed, so ancient, so bent down.' There were many days of 'sulphur and brimstone, dust and ashes'[17] before it was agreed that Martin and H.B. should go back with him to Nassenheide. Trix clamoured daily to be allowed to go too and she got her way. Evi wrote stiffly in her diary: 'She is evidently very differently made from me, for if I went to Nassenheide it would only make me long for it all the more afterwards which would, of course, be awful . . .'

Early in the summer of 1909 all of the children fell ill with influenza. Evi was not able to throw off a bad cough that was the legacy of the illness and when the weather became warm her mother decided to send her to the seaside to convalesce. Elizabeth had just read in the *English Review* the serialization of a book not yet out, *The Holy Mountain* by a young man named Stephen Reynolds. He was a friend of Leonard and Virginia Woolf's and later they published his collected letters at their press. He had already published *The Little Red House* which had attracted Elizabeth's attention, but *The Holy Mountain* she considered a work of genius and she very much wanted to meet the author. She heard that he lived in Sidmouth in Devon and survived financially by fishing and taking trippers out in his boat in the summer months. It seemed a good idea to take Evi down there and let the sea air help her lungs. Liebet joined them for some of the time and Cousin William, as always, came too.

On the first day Elizabeth located the fishing boat and went out to sea. Stephen Reynolds was not there but he heard all about it from his partner, Bob, and wrote an account of it to a friend: 'Countess von Arnim (Eliz. of the G. G.) came down here; heard I was in town; went out by chance to sea with Bob; found I was his mate, and has been to sea with us every, and pretty well all day since, to the considerable profit of our boats.' He was a charming, extremely good-looking young man of upper-middle-class origins. As a boy he had been sent down to Sidmouth for the sake of his lungs, but when his condition grew critical and his governess wired his father for instructions (his mother was dead), she received no answer. His father couldn't be bothered with him. Stephen Reynolds had not been an easy child to rear, the last straw, in his father's eyes, being apparently that he appeared late for breakfast. The headmistress of the local school in Sidmouth, out of compassion, took him in and nursed him and when he recovered she employed him as a teacher.

However, he did not stay long in the school for he had a consuming ambition to be a writer. He turned his back on the middle classes, whose values he loathed, and became a fisherman. His attitudes were so close to those of Elizabeth's when she had determined to earn her living as a crossing sweeper that an immediate friendship sprang up between them. Evi remembered that:

> In the morning he was a fisherman, and in the day he accompanied 'frights' about the town. He had wonderful blue eyes, a glorious deep blue colour and in them lay all of his character, his love, his soul, his everything. There was no false shame in him, he was truth itself. The worst fault was his doggedness [a Beauchamp word for worrying at a subject far beyond the interest of the audience], and his unswerving temper. But then again he would cast care aside and be so jolly that it made one laugh in spite of oneself.[18]

Twice he dined with the von Arnims at the Victoria Hotel in Sidmouth. He became 'beautifully cheerful'[19] and laughed and talked and Elizabeth enjoyed him hugely. Her verdict on him was that 'He's like a Christ with a great deal of the devil thrown upon him'.[20] He visited her often after that at Blue Hayes.

Cecil Waterlow (or Puddle), Charlotte's youngest son, came down one day to take Evi to see her grandmother, who had moved to a house near Ipswich. Evi had once described him as being 'exactly like a great, unfortunate, ill fitting tabby'. He was also more than a little eccentric. The nearer they came to Ipswich, the more cheerful Puddle became until at the entry to the town he was singing sailor songs and urging Evi to say 'Boo' to a lady alone in the next compartment. A few days later the Russells came to tea and stayed to supper. Evi considered Lady Russell 'awful to look at, like some ungainly monster, and she drinks (and is sometimes drunk) and smokes just like a man. Lord Russell is full of his lordliness though quite clever.'[21]

In November *The Caravaners* was published. Its theme aroused enough interest for it to be fully reviewed. Not since Shaw's *Broadbent* had a national type been depicted with such wit and devastating insight, and the 'witty genius' of the author saved the book from being bitter. *Country Life* thought it the most amusing book it had ever read, while *Punch* thought it 'one of the cleverest and most amusing stories of the year'. Fortunately the sales were high, for the family were in need of money that year as never before. Henning was, it appeared, constitutionally unable to sell Nassenheide and his wife, who had counted on the money from the sale to solve some of their problems, now found she was paying for the upkeep of two establishments. Henning was being stubborn because he was angry with her and had characteristically forgotten that the family were in this fix because of his own financial ineptitude. He played on the loyalties of the children mercilessly, and when the book came out and he perhaps suspected that Baron von Ottringe had been based on himself, was more entrenched in his position as the wronged party than ever.

Caravanning in England became, in the wake of the novel, a vogue activity for feminists. For several years landowners had to cope with a small army of literary females and their friends who were determined to find copy by the wayside and filled in dull moments by haranguing those who passed on the virtue of giving them the vote. They quickly became exceedingly unpopular with everybody, from the *bona fide* gipsy who found it more difficult to find a berth to the postmistress general who was besieged by scruffy women demanding to know the whereabouts of their letters. Several more books were published imitating Elizabeth's and a new brand of homespun philosophy sprang up called 'Wayside Wisdom'. In 1911 none other than Mollie Russell, produced a book from her experiences on the road called *Five Women and a Caravan*. In it she acknowledges her debt to Elizabeth, but does not forget to tell her readers that she is a friend. As the main character in her novel Mollie emerges as a female Baron von Ottringe, although it is more tragic than amusing since she is unaware of how unpopular she is with the other campers. She adheres carefully to the truth of events and even records an argument she has with one of the women who is shocked by the countess's drinking habits. Francis is seen as a mild version of The Man of Wrath and she refers to him as her 'owner'. When the action flags the reader is treated to a version of her adventures in Ireland, where she was born, and America, where she and Francis lived together before their marriage. She is always the heroine of these exploits and they reveal a woman who is entirely self-centred and self-satisfied. It is a sad book in every sense of the word.

Whatever they did that first year Elizabeth and the two older girls felt as if they were somehow floundering around under water. Obviously the vaunted Devonshire climate was having a deleterious effect on hardy Pomeranian constitutions. She put Blue Hayes on the market and almost immediately a man came forward to buy it. During negotiations she made arrangements for the girls to attend a

boarding house run by teachers at St Paul's School for Girls so that
pupils from abroad or the country could attend the school. H.B. was
to go to a small boarding school and then on to Summer Fields in
Oxford. Elizabeth took a flat in Whitehall Court with magnificent
views of the Thames which she had Harrods carpet wall to wall and
then filled with the best of the furniture she had brought from
Germany. There was not enough room there for all the children to
cram in on their half term so she started looking for something in the
country they could go to during the holidays. When she saw it, Teppi
was very impressed by the flat for every morning a menu was posted
under the door and it was possible to order the whole day's food as if
it was a hotel.

Nassenheide was still not sold and Henning wrote the girls long
and vague letters telling them of the alterations he was making to
Schlagenthin and how wonderful it was going to be when they were
all together again and living in the castle, although the doctor had
told Elizabeth that Henning must soon enter a sanatorium and that
there was little hope of him coming out of it alive. When the move
had been accomplished the children travelled to Nassenheide to
await Christmas and Elizabeth went to Switzerland with Cousin
William in a vain attempt to finish her play which she then called
Priscilla. They stayed during December at the Palace Hotel in
Montreux 'really slaving away and I expect all in vain. Well, that
can't be helped,' she wrote to Liebet.

Elizabeth arrived at Nassenheide two days before Christmas,
having at last finished the play. She was planning to build a new
house for all of them in Switzerland if it made money, as she hoped it
would. It was impossible for her to inject any jollity into the
assembled company that year for the place itself was too sad and
decayed to allow them to enjoy themselves. They all knew it was to
be the last Christmas there, and that nothing was ever going to be the
same again. Teppi was not present for she had taken a post as a
teacher in a German boarding school. Elizabeth stayed on in
Germany with H.B. after the girls had returned to school for the
spring term, for Henning was very ill and, besides, she intended to
employ her time with some long overdue meditation. She wrote to
Liebet:

> Here the sky is grey, the wind is loud and the snow—
> though you might not think it—is white. H.B. is
> extremely genial and bold and does all sorts of things he
> never dared do when you were all here . . . Papa is

invisible except at meals and in the evening we play draughts. I spend rather exciting days in my *Treibhaus* tidying and cleaning up my soul which has got into a great confusion and muddle lately. When I've finished that I'm going to England.

While she was there a buyer showed a real interest in Nassenheide. Henning reluctantly entered into negotiations and stalled the buyer for, to Elizabeth, unimpressive reasons. She left him in the hands of Teppi who was holidaying, and returned to England in February 1910 with the place still not sold. She was eager to get *Priscilla* into production as soon as possible. Her new flat in Whitehall Court was by then ready and the children came to stay with her at weekends.

In spite of Henning's prevarications, Nassenheide was at last sold. A portion of the price was paid and the rest was due in instalments, but because of the war this was never paid in full. The remaining furniture was sent over to Schlagenthin and Henning was ordered by his doctor to a sanatorium at Meran in the Tyrol. Evi wrote in her diary of the year past that she had woken up to many new ideas and also many surprises, shocks and wonders. She wondered what life held in store for her. Would it be a path 'covered with sulphur or with roses?' She saw difficulties ahead chiefly owing to her unconquerable inclinations to follow Descartes and sit and stare and 'shake all the vanity of the world' from her.[22]

That Easter all of the children except Evi went to stay by themselves at Schlagenthin. It was what they had always wanted, and apart from the servants, there were no grown-ups at all on hand to make them behave and send them for runs. They played violently at being grown-up themselves which mostly consisted in ordering the servants about with abandon, eating far too much and paying no heed to the conventions of table manners. Elizabeth was far more anxious that they would continue to get fat than that they were in any moral jeopardy from this situation. The only advice she wrote to Liebet was, 'Don't all eat too many *Streuselküchen* and other things of that attractive but insidious sort.'

In their absence Elizabeth decided to take Evi under her wing and introduce her to suitable rich young men while Stuart at the same time crammed her for her university entrance examination. They went to stay with the Redesdales, whose children were familiar to Evi as relations of Lady Maude's. Evi was overcome with shyness and was more or less dumb during mealtimes, which Elizabeth found so irritating that during the course of dinner on the first evening she ordered her daughter out to do Ten Times Round, hoping that this would loosen her tongue. Evi retired behind the summer house and wept for hours. The rest of the visit for her was a disaster, and she only made one friend, Nellie, one of the daughters of Lady Hozier, whose sister Clemmie was very beautiful and married Winston Churchill.

When the others arrived back from Germany, no thinner but happy and ready for another term's work, Elizabeth settled them at their schools and hurried out to see her husband. According to the doctors at Meran it seemed unlikely that his heart would hold out much longer. Teppi returned to teach at her boarding school in Marburg and Elizabeth was to be alone with her husband for the last time in her life.

The sanatorium grounds were full of lizards by day and glow-worms by night, and she and Henning spent solemn afternoons under the shade of the big pine trees in the garden. His nurse, Babette, was a charming woman with only one eye, though he did not like her because she was neither young nor pretty. Life would have been nearly tolerable for Elizabeth if it were not for Henning's attacks of nervous irritability which made him almost impossible to cope with and which were, she felt, catching. She was depressed at the prospect of becoming more and more ill-tempered herself until she reached the calm of the oyster state when she no longer cared about anything, and the children heard from their father that she never laughed.

She was anxiously wondering what was happening at the rehearsals of her play which were then at an intense stage. It was due to 'burst on an astonished world' on 29 June. When the doctor pronounced that Henning had improved, Elizabeth sped back to London in time for the opening. The first news to greet her was that both Liebet and Evi had gained places at Cambridge for the following year. 'Lovingest congratulations and sincere rejoicings over your passing,' she wrote to them immediately, for they were staying with their aunt at Ropes. Elizabeth secured four seats for the opening night for the three oldest girls and her brother Rally who was to chaperone them. She herself was intending to remain invisible. She instructed her daughters to wear white muslin dresses, to do their hair extra nicely, to wear gloves and on no account were they to shout 'Author'. 'That's the last thing you, my own spawn, must do—don't you see, apart from the fact that females don't shout, it is as bad as if I myself shouted for myself? For you three *are* me.' The girls did exactly as they were told and sat in a row, excited, delighted and dressed in white. They were instantly recognized by the audience, who were, naturally, all 'Elizabeth' fans, as the April, May and June babies.

The play was hilariously received and tumultuously applauded. Those unrelated to the author shouted for her to appear again and again but she refused, remaining as always true to her anonymity. The blushing girls received the bouquets on her behalf. It was a night for them all to remember; they dined afterwards at the Ivy and were assured by the attentions of everybody that they were stars. The play was a hit and was expected to run and run.

Two weeks later Elizabeth, glutted with praise and wholly restored by being yet again the talk of the town, returned to a sanatorium in Kissingen where her husband had been moved and where he greeted her from his bed with a laurel wreath he had contrived for her. He was much worse and Elizabeth immediately wired for the children to come. She had resumed the habit of making notes and comments in her diary recently, and for the 18th of August, after their arrival, she wrote that Henning seemed much better and happy to be with his children. The next day she and the girls went for the day to Bocklet and when they got back they heard he was not so well and that he had been sick all day. After supper the girls went up to his room and 'kissed his dear face for the last time'.[23] He scolded Evi because she touched something, and then regretted it and kissed her again. He had 'a strange sweet look in his eyes and breath coming in short little puffs', Evi wrote in her diary. The next day he died at 9.25 a.m. Elizabeth had just gone up to him from her own breakfast and found the nurse and the doctor with him. He was frantically excited, giving orders to everybody, wanting to be sick and not being able to. Five minutes later he suddenly died with a little groan. To her mother a few days later Elizabeth wrote:

> It is very dreadful to see somebody die . . . I can't tell what I feel like—utterly heartbroken—I know poor H. couldn't ever get well and would only have gone on being miserable, but being with him when he died and knowing how desperately he wanted to live, at any cost, even tormented, makes one feel such unutterable sympathy with him, longing to keep him and yet he looked so happy and peaceful after he was dead—a little contented smile on his poor thin face . . .

A few days later Cousin Bernd von Arnim-Criewen arrived and a funeral service was held in the cemetery mortuary chapel at Kissingen. The next day they accompanied the coffin to Schlagenthin. Teppi and Charlotte were there to meet them at the station and soon Henning lay with his ancestors in the little mausoleum on the hill. Winding up his affairs was a tedious and complicated business which Elizabeth tackled with characteristic energy. Liebet stayed to help and Evi took the younger ones back to England. It was a sad time for all of them but Elizabeth experienced her grief internally and deeply. 'How silly is the person who knows not what he possesses until it is lost,' she remarked to Teppi. 'How very much I miss the father of my children.'[24]

Teppi knew something of what was going on in her heart, but the children were not so lucky. When they had come through their own grief they discovered that their mother had changed towards them. She was, as usual, working hard and much of her spare time was taken up with the London season for the girls, as well as with her own now remarkably full social life. She was also, naturally, in the marriage market herself along with her daughters. She looked at least twenty years younger than her age and the presence of the three grown-up daughters belied her apparent youth. She unconsciously resented their rivalry as well as their economic and emotional dependence on her.

Teppi gave up her job and came back into their lives as governess to all the children, spending much of her time watching over her mistress with concern. She saw what the others did not, that Elizabeth was fighting off a crisis of nerves, an emotional collapse from having taken on too much responsibility for too long. Evi behaved strangely and was not easy to manage. She became convinced that she in particular had been singled out for her mother's dislike. 'I believe nobody loves me, that Mummy is thoroughly sick of me. It breaks my heart to think of it.'[25] But their mother's distraction was not an emotion directed simply at her. The other girls felt it too and nothing could heal the rift that sprang up: Teppi had her time cut out smoothing over the differences between Elizabeth and her children that bedevilled their lives at this time. It seemed to her that Elizabeth no longer wanted them to be with her, and as if she didn't want to understand their difficulties. But Elizabeth had realized that her children were over-dependent on her and still worshipped her as if she were a god. She saw no decent emotional life in the future for them unless this spell were broken and the once beautiful relationship was replaced by mistrust and bad humour.

When they were all exhausted by the Season they went down to

Ropes in Sussex where Charlotte had offered them the use of her guest house. Elizabeth decided that she should have a little house of her own and converted the coachman's cottage into a place where they could all stay. It is miniscule, perfect but nearly on a dolls'-house scale. It has two bedrooms and a living- and work-room for Elizabeth and a kitchen and family room where Teppi spent much of her time. A white sheet-metal cabin was built a few yards from it where the children slept when they came down, feeling like giants in a Lilliputian house.

Evi and Liebet went to Cambridge to read modern languages at Girton, and Trix, very much against her will, was sent to learn domestic science in Berlin. Elizabeth had, some months before, conceived a plan to build a large and beautiful chalet somewhere in Switzerland where she could retire from her social life and work for long periods undisturbed, and where the children could stay in the holidays. This dream could not be realized unless she had more money than was available to her, and yet it seemed the only solution to the rift caused by their differing national loyalties and their increasingly nomadic life as a family. She then discovered that she was legally entitled to sell Schlagenthin as long as the money went towards providing the children with another place to live. They were furious at the suggestion; had they not been told it belonged to them? It was useless to explain to them that a place in Switzerland would provide them all with neutral territory in which to live when war came, and that owning property in Germany if you lived in England was the best way to lose it in the event of war.

The relationship between mother and children went from bad to worse as the sale of Schlagenthin went through. But the real reason for Elizabeth's determined and strange behaviour was that she had, she thought, found the man she wished to spend the rest of her life with. Her problem was that he was already married. His name was Herbert George Wells.

· 12 ·

New Horizons

When H. G. Wells's novel *The New Machiavelli* came out in the autumn of 1910, Elizabeth bought a copy immediately for she had been in the habit of reading everything Wells wrote as soon as she could come by it. She thought him by far the most interesting writer at that time, and she was rapidly coming round to the views of the Fabian Socialists, to which Wells had made an active contribution.

The novel masquerades as the autobiography of a misunderstood genius who has become fatally entangled with political humbugs and it was written in the wake of Wells's disastrous entanglement with the sweet and coaxing young graduate, Amber Reeves, whose parents were fellow members of the Fabian Society. Carried away by the spirit of freedom her elders were continually discussing and the 'genius' of her lover, the eighteen-year-old girl had insisted on giving birth to the child she had conceived during her political discussions with the author. Wells's social circle consisted mostly, then, of the people who surrounded Sidney and Beatrice Webb. They included George Bernard Shaw, Frank Harris, E. Nesbit and her husband Hubert Bland, and many other politically orientated, creative and intelligent people. Amber Reeves's parents were among their number. They were already in a ferment about Wells's championship of free love and birth control and feared his courage in these matters. When his affair with Amber Reeves came to light they hounded him out of their drawing-rooms and Wells, already dissatisfied with them because he felt their ideas lacked breadth, accused his detractors of humbug. He presented himself in *The New Machiavelli* as an innocent outcast whose wife was about to divorce him.

Elizabeth, who was incapable of dissimulation to such an extent in her own books, believed this version. She was not aware that Wells had given himself a spurious middle-class background, making his father a property owner, or that his loving descriptions of Cambridge undergraduate life were entirely fictitious. She saw herself as the intelligent older woman he had clearly needed during the five hundred and twenty-eight pages of the novel. He had compared himself to Machiavelli as the inventor of a new state; at the same time he saw himself as the state's prince: a new kind of prince, a democratic prince, but none the less a prince. Was not Elizabeth, so newly widowed and almost exactly his own age as well as also being a best-selling novelist, a fitting princess to be his partner? What was more interesting to Elizabeth, he was a man who clearly loved women, had no false shame about his private lusts and also held the opposite sex in high regard. In *The New Machiavelli* he even asserted that women were probably better than men:

> I began life ignoring women, they came to me at first perplexing and dishonouring; only very slowly and very late in my life and after misadventures, did I gauge the power and the beauty of the love of men and women and learn how it must needs frame a justifiable vision of the ordered world. Love has brought me to disaster, because my career had been planned regardless of its possibility and value. But Machiavelli, it seems to me, when he went up to his study, left not only the earth of life outside, but its unsuspected soul . . .

A few weeks later Elizabeth turned up on the doorstep at his new house in Church Row, Hampstead, which Wells had bought for his wife and sons when the family was close to dissolution earlier that year, though now they were still living at Spade House. Elizabeth's praise and obvious admiration of his genius were a much-needed balm to his troubled and dented ego. 'Much work, and the gravity of life much alleviated, yesterday, by the sudden interruption of the bright little Countess von Arnim,' he wrote the next day to his wife. Elizabeth cheerfully proposed to have lunch with him and then that they should go for a walk together on the Heath. Wells thought she talked very well, was impressed that she appeared to know *The New Machiavelli* by heart, and was flattered when she teasingly called him the 'Great Man'. He thought she was 'a nice friend to have'.[1] She told him all about her plans to find a site in the Jura in Switzerland where she intended to build a chalet, and invited the whole Wells family to stay. He liked the *risqué* nature of her conversation, and the fact that she was a countess flattered his self-esteem. She on her side was enough enamoured by the small man's genius (she had a high respect for excellence) to overlook his common accent and bad table manners—at least for the time being.

Wells took lodgings at a farm near Haslemere shortly after Elizabeth came to call on him in Hampstead. This was, by arrangement, very near Ropes. They went for walks together on the downs and 'came to an easy understanding'.[2] They soon became lovers and spent many months, as he was to reveal in his posthumously published autobiography, *H. G. Wells in Love*, enjoying each other's company on the Continent without anyone being any the wiser. He described her as a 'very shrewd, wise and witty little woman. She mingled adventurousness with extreme conventionality in a very piquant manner and I attracted her.' Somehow he had got hold of the idea that she was Irish, no doubt a piece of enlarged bunkum and a private joke of her own. She claimed to have found love-making with her husband a 'serious and disagreeable business' and Wells was only too happy to teach her the modern lore of birth control and some of the pleasures of the boudoir that she claimed were entirely new experiences for her.

The two of them soon fell into the habit of meeting regularly when they were in London. Wells also had a small flat in Cardover Street where he had amused himself with various ladies who called there to see him. Elizabeth soon became his only visitor and eventually insisted he give the place up. They then each took a flat in St James's Court and were seen together in London, causing well-deserved gossip which they ignored. Jane Wells, a much steadier and more powerful rival than Elizabeth had imagined, refused to consider a divorce.

In the following spring Wells and Elizabeth went to stay for the weekend at Telegraph House with Francis and Mollie Russell. Wells's bedroom was situated some distance from Elizabeth's down an unlighted passage and he was obliged to feel his way along and had difficulty with a 're-entrant angle' that puzzled him. Mollie slept across the landing with her door wide open, fortunately very heavily. 'Little e,* even then found Russell an attractive, misunderstood man who needed only an able wife to be reinstated socially.' Mollie was not a social success.

At the top of Elizabeth's agenda was the finding of a suitable site for the chalet, and she and Wells and Teppi often went for walking tours of the Jura mountains with this in mind. They stayed in various little chalet-inns and twice Wells and Elizabeth broke the bed. 'It

---

*Wells always referred to Elizabeth as 'little e' and during the time that she was his mistress she began to sign her letters to him with a lower case e. When she was feeling particularly low the e dropped to the bottom right-hand corner of the page as though sitting on the sea bed.

was a cheerful thing to hear little e—I doubt if she weighed six stone—explaining in pretty but perfect German why her bed had gone to pieces under her in the night.' Elizabeth often thought she had found the perfect site. Once when she was out walking she found a green ledge with a solitary but meaningful pear tree on it in full bloom. Recklessly she bought the land, but the architect refused to build because there was neither water nor access. There followed a few weeks of bitterness during which Elizabeth grew reasonable, and she was eventually obliged to sell it back to the people she had bought it from for half the price.

She finally found another site near Randogne-sur-Sierre. There, she strongly felt, the family could be happy together, skiing in the winter and walking in the summer while living in her 'house of God at the Gates of Heaven'.[3] The site lay just below the health and winter-sports resorts of Montana and Vermala, the sunniest and least rained upon part of the Swiss Alps, or so the brochures claimed. The view over the Rhône Valley was breathtaking and included in one sweep the Pennine Alps, the Weisshorn, Rothorn and the Mont Blanc range, and to the east the Simplon. If ever the weather became too bad it was easy to drop down into Italy and wait for it to improve. She engaged a new architect who had been recommended to her by a postman she met walking in the lane, and continued to behave, as she recorded in her memoirs, 'altogether as persons behave who have lately, for the first time in their lives, become completely free, and responsible to no authority of any kind'.[4]

When she was outlining her plans for the building she insisted that the visitor's room next to her own should have a secret door that slid open on well-oiled castors and was hidden by a wardrobe with a false back on each side. There were to be sixteen bedrooms and a small chalet nearby for her to work in. Elizabeth's intention was for the house to be 'a little Nassenheide with many added advantages and beauties'.[5] She strove to create a place as near as possible to paradise and the children were to invite their friends whenever they liked.

However, in spite of promises to the contrary, the house was not to be finished until the spring of 1913. In the meantime Elizabeth and Wells continued to travel abroad at regular intervals and together visited Amsterdam, Bruges, Ypres, Arras, Paris, Locarno, Orta and Florence while Teppi spent this time visiting relatives in Germany. Their irreverence for the normal code of behaviour extended into every area of their lives, and even God they uncharacteristically anthropomorphized: Wells couldn't believe in a deity that 'had no thighs'[6] and Elizabeth remarked about the Victorian habit of printing 'G*d': 'How unkind to deprive God of his middle.'[7]

Teppi and Charlotte were worried that Elizabeth had given up writing. She had plunged headlong into the London social whirl and the building of the chalet, and for the time being her entire emotional horizon appeared to be dominated by Wells. There were occasional arguments between the women on the subject but Elizabeth always retorted, 'Why write books if one wants to live?'[8] Of course there was no possible answer to that.

The two older girls went to stay at Ropes if ever they had time off and their mother was not available for whatever reason. Evi became seriously entangled with two young men, one of them the son of her mother's solicitor and the other the son of a collier from Yorkshire, a fellow undergraduate called Minor, his older brother being called Major. She was the more popular of the two girls with her pretty little face framed in blonde hair, while Liebet, though more beautiful, was a serious girl.

Just at this time the young Rebecca West had been astonishing Wells, Elizabeth and the general public by her powerful articles in the *Clarion*. They lacked the personal stamp of pieces she had previously written in the *Freewoman* but they were inspired by an energy which originated in passions aroused to particular violence: her feelings for H. G. Wells. They had met and were attracted to one another during a weekend at Wells's house, but he refused to succumb to her demands that they become lovers. He was on his 'good behaviour' because of 'little e' as he referred to Elizabeth. Later Rebecca visited him at his house in Hampstead and when, 'face to face with my book-shelves, in the midst of a conversation about style or some such topic, apropos of nothing, we paused and suddenly kissed each other . . . Then Rebecca flamed up into open and declared passion.'[9] Elizabeth was naturally jealous when he told her about the incident. Instancing the fiasco caused in his life by Amber Reeves, she was utterly against his having anything to do with Miss West and took her lover on a prolonged tour of Italy to get the girl out of his system.

They visited Milan, Pavia, Bologna and Florence, and Wells was tiresome and dejected. They called on friends and saw sights and Elizabeth was particularly pleased to make the acquaintance of Vernon Lee the travel writer. The two women enjoyed each other's company and conversation and Elizabeth invited her to come to the chalet on her way back to England some day. When they left, Vernon Lee confided to a friend that she thought Elizabeth like a 'china faced Hampton Court doll'. 'Why Hampton Court?'

Elizabeth asked when she was told.[10]

When they arrived back in England in the spring of 1912, she could tell that Wells was not cured. They found an invitation for both of them to have lunch with Asquith at 10 Downing Street. Elizabeth's opinion of the Prime Minister was that 'he was like a cushion. He bears the imprint of the last person who sat on him,'[11] a comment she might have written, with some truth, about her lover.

Meanwhile Rebecca West had followed them on their tour in a parallel journey down the peninsula of Spain and attempted suicide twice while doing so, once with a bullet through her chest and another time by taking an overdose of veronal. The bullet missed her heart and the veronal simply caused her to spend the night wandering the streets of Malaga in a confused state. Elizabeth was triumphant when she heard, for it underlined her own opinion that the girl was unstable and that the best thing Wells could do would be to keep as far away from her as possible. After the news reached Wells he was of the same opinion, and he wrote to Rebecca telling her that there was no future in their relationship. She fired back that he had kissed her and therefore he must fulfil the promise of that kiss. He wrote again, tired of the whole thing, and she was baffled and humiliated by the cant phrases with which he put an end to it all.

The young journalist interpreted his lack of sympathy as aggression and wrote him letters saying, 'I am always at a loss when I meet hostility, because I can love and I can do practically nothing else,' and 'I would give my whole life to feel your arms around me again.'[12] Naturally Jane and Elizabeth diagnosed youthful hysteria and continued to advise Wells to steer well clear, and he continued to take their advice. His replies to Rebecca's letters were brief and cool: 'How can I be your friend to this accompaniment? I don't see that I can be of any use or help to you at all. You have my entire sympathy—but until we can meet on a reasonable basis, goodbye.'

Rebecca was, however, a determined woman, and she set herself to impress Wells and win him finally by her brilliant journalism. She threw her emotions, in common with many other frustrated women at the time, into the fight for the vote. The Women's Suffrage amendment to the Franchise Bill was in the process of being defeated. Exacerbated by the repressive actions of constituted authority, Rebecca gradually threw aside all restraints in her writing, and this revulsion reached its climax in a tirade in the *Clarion* called *The Sex War*, most of the paragraphs in which end with the refrain, 'Oh, men are miserably poor stuff.'

That summer Elizabeth took Wells to Switzerland to watch the chalet take shape, and they stayed in one nearby called Jenny Lind. Perhaps Wells actually needed to be at least mentally unfaithful to the woman in his life to be happy with her, for ironically it was the tangled and unsatisfactory state of affairs that afforded them both an experience of real happiness and harmony, a broadening of the horizons, something far more deeply interfused, as if the threat from outside had jolted them into a closer alliance. One day they went on a hike in the mountains. They had taken a copy of *The Times* to read and in it was a letter from Mrs Humphry Ward denouncing the solemn and moral tone of the younger generation, with particular reference to Rebecca West. This mention of her rival in *The Times*, albeit a dubious one, bothered Elizabeth. There was very little that could be said after the initial argument which the letter produced between them had died down. A gesture was needed. Elizabeth hit on the idea of making love on the newspaper and then setting fire to it.

> So we stripped ourselves under the trees as though there was no one in the world but ourselves, and made love all over Mrs Humphry Ward. And when we had dressed again we lit a match and burnt her. *The Times* flared indignantly and subsided and wriggled burning and went black and brittle and broke into little fragments and flew away.[13]

The lovers returned in high good humour and declared to the shocked and disapproving Teppi as they came through the door that they were 'kindred spirits'.[14]

Another time, while sitting on the slopes above the chalet in the sun, Wells read out to Elizabeth parts of his book *The World Set Free*. She started to scold him and bang him with her furry mittens declaring that he '*liked* smashing up the world':

> If little e had been God the Creator, there would have been no earthquakes, no tigers and no wars, but endless breezes and quite unexpected showers; the flora would not have been without its surprises, a trifle burlesque, but very delicate and variously scented. And there would have been endless furry little animals popping about in the sweet herbage.[15]

At least, that was what Wells thought of her then. It is curious he did not revise his opinion in the light of later events. That summer of 1912 Elizabeth vented her irritation about Rebecca by teasing Wells with Stuart. 'He was faithful and tender and true,' Wells wrote in *Mr Britling Sees it Through*. 'He asked nothing but to love. He offered honourable marriage; and when one's heart was swelling unendurably one could weep in safety on his patient shoulder.' This patient shoulder ultimately became Wells's most exasperating rival.

In the autumn the lovers travelled back to London, exhausted with emotion and a little with each other. Elizabeth began to spend more time with her friends, some new who were to remain with her for life: Maud Ritchie and her father Lord Ritchie of Dundee, the Strutts, Stanley Owen Buckmaster, who was destined to become Lord Chancellor for eighteen months in 1915, the Bristows, the Birrells and a particular favourite, Francis Russell's one-time guardian, 'Cobbie' or Cobden-Sanderson the bookbinder. Wells, somewhat disillusioned with Elizabeth, began seeing something of Rebecca.

The Christmas of 1912 was scheduled to be spent at the newly finished chalet. As could have been predicted, it was not ready, and instead they all gathered at Ropes. Cousin William was there and irritated Elizabeth by demanding to know if she were serious about Wells. Was he going to divorce his wife and marry her and should he, Stuart, step down from his suit for her hand? She could not answer him on any of these points except the last. She was not in the best of humours, for her lover was enjoying a family Christmas at his new large house in the country, Easton Glebe, which seemed to indicate that he had no intention of leaving his wife. She was a little short-tempered with William on that account.

Teppi took over the organizing of the festivities at Ropes and with her usual enthusiasm, attempted to recreate a typical German Christmas as they had known them at Nassenheide. She became, in her own words 'Christmas happy'.[16] But it was not a success and she was deeply disillusioned about the British attitude towards the celebration of the birth of Christ, being forced to conclude that mistletoe meant more to them than the manger. Charlotte did not run a particularly Lutheran household, and the Beauchamps tended to become bawdy when celebrating, relaxed rather than devout. On 1 January 1913 Elizabeth went back to Sierre to make the final arrangements for the furniture at the chalet. To Liebet she wrote a postcard:

> . . . if you ever have the luck to live here you may thank
> your lucky stars or whatever else one thanks that you
> happened to have a mummy so energetic as to build a

chalet. Life is too lovely here, because it is so invigorating and serene and pure that one doesn't mind what happens but lives just like I suppose a happy animal lives. The *Lieber Gott* abounds up around my terrace. You and Teppi will get a much clearer view of him up here because he's so close.

Underneath it all, though, Elizabeth was dissatisfied. It had been common gossip for some time among the smart *literati* that Wells was making an exhibition of himself with the recently widowed 'Elizabeth', and she seemed, on the evidence of those who witnessed his discomfiture on occasions, to enjoy displaying her command over him—or at least this was how Mrs Belloc Lowndes described it. As an example of Elizabeth's taunts the following story became a much-relished piece of literary gossip about town. At a dinner party which included George Bernard Shaw and Somerset Maugham, the talk turned to Wells's recent visit to Up Park, a famous Elizabethan stately home where his mother had held the post of housekeeper towards the end of her life. Wells himself had lived there, below stairs, from time to time during periods of ill health or unemployment. He described the place wittily, comparing his impressions with those of his first visits. Elizabeth asked, with wide-eyed ingenuousness, whether Wells had entered the house on this recent occasion by the front door or by the servants' entrance at the back. Some years later Frank Swinnerton asked her why she had done this. 'Because I wanted to know,' she replied without shame.[17]

Wells was no longer as unpopular as he had been after the Amber Reeves episode, and there were many who were genuinely fond of him. They did not like to see him treated badly by Elizabeth. Wells himself wrote:

> She had a teasing disposition and liked to vex me by sudden, inconvenient changes of plan and by attacking things that might move me to anger. She wanted to get more out of me than the fun and fellowship I gave her. She wanted us to feel the keen edge of life together—in spite of the fact that we both resolved it should never cut us.[18]

She developed an unreasonable resentment towards Jane Wells and was jealous of the daily letters that passed between the couple: if Wells ever laughed over any of his wife's replies there would be sulphur for some hours. She wanted the easy, happy-go-lucky tenor of their affair to intensify into something she better understood. She resented being taken so easily, wanted a grand passion and insisted that he was only trifling with her affections if he did not weep or tremble when he came near her, or so he maintained in *H. G. Wells in Love*, which appeared in 1984 but was written during the 1940s. His son, Anthony West, many years later, arrived at a different interpretation: 'My impression is that his inability to deliver a major emotional response in a love affair was looked on as a positive asset by [Elizabeth], and that his quickness and lightness were just what she wanted.'[19] The truth, no doubt, lies somewhere in between.

Elizabeth did not necessarily want a major emotional response, but she did want marriage, which some might consider the same thing. It was beginning to dawn on her that there was never, at any time, the slightest question of Wells and Jane separating for good. Jane was far too important to him as a stabilizing influence, a home to come back to, the mother of his sons and his business manager. It also did not escape Elizabeth's notice that Wells enjoyed being with Jane and the boys. It was true that Jane was not an enthusiastic partner in her husband's quest for the recreational aspects of sex but she was wise enough to tolerate his philanderings and there was plainly a tacit understanding that his wanderings in this respect were not going to rock the boat. It was she that bought Amber Reeves's layette and found, later, a nurse for Rebecca West's child. Having understood this at last Elizabeth spent much time pondering her own role in this triangle, which gave her little pleasure, no pride and a great deal of uneasiness—for if anyone were dispensable it was she.

In October Elizabeth fled both her swains to join Teppi and Trix on the slopes of the mountain for the last effort to make the chalet habitable. Wells saw her off at Victoria and she asked him to go with her. 'But he didn't want to enough.'[20] She must have sensed the presence of another woman in the background for when she arrived at the chalet she wrote to him, bowing herself out of the relationship, and concentrated all of her energy on the task in hand. To Liebet she wrote:

> We're in the fearfulest dirt, confusion and general beastliness but the air is such and the snow is such, the beauty is such that we *don't care!* We laugh over the fearfulest catastrophes, so huge is the joy of just being alive up here. Trix is the greatest dear—and so busy and happy and so intelligent and a *real help*. We're buried in snow . . . Yesterday I saw Evi's wardrobe she had at Nassenheide

standing all alone at the wayside station being snowed on. The mountain side is strewn with furniture which can't get further because of the snow.

The three women were camping out under the fatherly protection of the gardener from Nassenheide, whom Elizabeth had asked to landscape the terrace and the garden slopes, when the snow came unexpectedly early. Gradually the chaos cleared and they moved into the house with great ceremony. With that, the life of travel for the time being had finished and a tedious period of work had begun. But the vision of the beautifully decorated new home sped their enterprise and the name Chalet Soleil led Teppi to hope that at all times 'the sun would be a radiant power to the mistress who would go in and out there'.[21] Teppi sent up thanks for the time of travel that had just been and for the opportunity of seeing other facets of Elizabeth's personality which had hitherto been invisible to her. She hoped that the new mountain home would bring her mistress poetry.

Now it was completed the chalet could be seen from the valley below standing low and ornate and proud among the green foothills. On the north and west sides were two long, adjoining verandas. Over the porch was written: ON THE HEIGHTS LOVE LIVES WITH JOY MAGNIFICENT AND BEAUTIFUL AND GAY, and over the front door: ONLY HAPPINESS HERE. It was reached by an alpine railway which stopped short of the chalet by a little over a mile. The furniture had to be dragged up the remaining meadows by a team of oxen with melancholy tolling bells round their necks as, later, was the luggage while *châtelaine* and guests toiled up behind on foot.

The front hall was panelled in oak and had a huge sofa, book shelves and a wide fireplace in which a roaring fire was kept going almost all the year round. For sentimental reasons Elizabeth kept hanging there a coat that had belonged to Henning. She had never had it cleaned, for then it would no longer have smelt of him, she said, and he had never had it cleaned either for there was a thick collar of grease round the neck band. Beyond the hall were two living-rooms and a connecting dining-room. A stairway swept up to the two floors above, where each of the sixteen bedrooms was decorated in a different colour. There were four bathrooms and altogether seven lavatories—whenever Elizabeth felt depressed she claimed, she thought of her lavatories and was comforted. Under the roof there were rooms for servants, while the back stairway led to the apartment of the caretaker. A little front garden framed the chalet from where the whole amazing range of mountains was visible. In all there were twelve acres. About twenty yards down the slope from the front door she had built a small working cottage called the Little Chalet. Above the door she wrote: I HATE THE COMMON HERD AND KEEP THEM OUT.

The abandoned Wells sent Elizabeth a stream of reproachful letters, wanting to know what she was thinking of by ending the relationship on a whim. They contained such phrases as, 'My wife has every virtue, every charm, *only* she's as dead as a herring . . .', and 'You are the eyes of the whole universe to me. If it wasn't for you the whole thing would be an eyeless monster, a mask, a hood. You spirit of the inmost. You response . . .' and 'I'd love you if I was being dropped out of a tenth-floor window . . .'[22]

The letters soon turned into telegrams which in turn gave way to Wells himself. His appearance initiated 'horrid talks'.[23] He annoyed Elizabeth by inquiring, on the second day, who helped her with her stories. She had begun work on revising *The Pastor's Wife* and was writing a new second half. When she told him it was about adultery (and indeed it was about his own), he rubbed his hands together and exclaimed, 'The best sport in the world',[24] further alienating his hostess. They tried, lamely, to patch things up. The chalet had in fact become for Elizabeth much that her lover was not: a centre and a sure fortress against the vicissitudes of life, and he was angry and jealous to be in competition with an inanimate object. Elizabeth recorded in her diary: 'A devil in G. of cruelty and horridness'. She began, in her annoyance, to invent cruel nicknames for Jane, parodying her way of talking and devising preposterous fantasies about her. 'She was comic and malicious and unendurable,' wrote Wells,[25] and to Frank Swinnerton he later confessed, 'When you've had her for five days you want to bang her head through the wall.'[26] All this led Elizabeth to realize that because of the house, the surroundings and the strong air, 'Somebody was always having emotions . . . violent ones because everything in that place was exaggerated.'[27] There would be an argument between the two lovers, words flung with the highest literary skill, and an abrupt and stormy exit from the room. Wells would sit by the fire and meditate on the 'extreme unsatisfactoriness of life'.[28] Presently Elizabeth would appear, calm and resolute, with the castor oil bottle and a large spoon.

It was Wells, with his passion to confess to the wrong person— that is whoever would be most wounded by his revelations—who precipitated the end of his relationship with Elizabeth. Rebecca West had come to visit him in his flat in St James's Court one afternoon recently and they had made love hurriedly for fear of Wells's valet returning and finding them. It was only the second time that they had done such a thing and she became pregnant. Since Wells was the experienced party he, of course, took the blame. No doubt expecting the forgiveness he had always had from Jane, he now told Elizabeth that Rebecca West was to have a child by him. Suddenly she stopped teasing him about Jane. They began, very politely, to discuss the weather. The castors on the secret door remained silent; Wells lay awake for hours expecting Elizabeth to come through in a state of surrender. He left after a week on 2 December, meekly. At the door he flung at her, 'It's because I'm common, isn't it?'[29] which naturally startled Elizabeth. It was as if he entirely discounted his infidelity and the child conceived as reasons for their parting.

The child himself, Anthony West, many years later arrived at his own, probably correct, conclusions about what went on between his father and Elizabeth towards the end. 'I think he saw himself through her eyes . . . and read a judgement on him that he couldn't take there: "You're perfect in broad comedy, but for gahds sake don't ever try to play Strindberg, you haven't the figure for it." '[30] 'The lovely morning he went away,' Elizabeth wrote in her memoirs, 'unverrichteterdinge [unfinished business] as the expressive German phrase has it. There I stood on the terrace, having duly waved goodbye and I felt like a convalescent, like one whose fever had left him and who is filled instead by a great peace.'[31]

She asked Teppi what she had thought of Wells. The faithful housekeeper had noticed that he was glad to come to the chalet, stepping into the guest room like a butterfly; and also he was glad to leave; that he was continuously in a good humour and ready for pleasure. Everything about him was in marked contrast to Stuart— Cousin William—who was 'not able to give any sunshine from within'; who was like a moth that always flew, again and again, into the flame to burn his wings on it. Teppi was unable to prevent Stuart from tormenting himself with his unhappy love, but she had made friends with Wells, and his ingenuous, kind nature charmed and impressed her. 'But how do you actually find H.G.?' the countess asked her friend again.

'Very clever, very amusing, very egotistic,' was Teppi's reply.

'You have forgotten something in your short characterization. He is creative like God and cruel like the devil. He deserves contempt, but a genius must certainly be compared by other measures.'

'A genius is unfortunately mostly an egoist; one ought to admire him, but not love him,' responded the wise Teppi, who was contemplating the parallels between the private lives of Wells and Goethe.[32]

When Wells had left, Coco, a splendid dog Elizabeth had recently bought from a passing peasant, was her only consolation. He had been their companion on outings, and became mournful and spent much time sniffing outside Wells's door, coming away from it only reluctantly. His mistress, always alert to signals given by dogs ('they say dogs always know'[33]), wondered if there had not been something 'outstandingly admirable' about the man.

She wept much after Wells's departure, upsetting Teppi, who had never witnessed such a reaction in her God-so-blessed friend. She met Wells again a few weeks later when he appeared in her drawing-room in St James's Court, for he still had a key to her flat. 'It was your fault,' she said. 'You were only half a lover,' meaning by this that he was not only married but had become entangled with other women when they were together.

'It was your fault,' Wells replied. 'You didn't really love.'[34] If she had really loved him, he meant, she would have put up with any amount of bad behaviour. In spite of being, as Wells claimed he was, a strong feminist, he had the cad's attitude to women: if they did not let him do what he wanted to do then this was not 'real love'.

'You don't know how much I loved you,' she protested. Nor did he, though he claimed that he did. He thought her 'one of the most uncertain, intricate and entrancing of feminine personalities'.[35]

The match point was played out in their novels. Elizabeth's prototype, representing aristocratic disdain, is even discernible in the novels written by Wells before he met her: Beatrice in *Tono-Bungay* and the girl on the wall who captivated Mr Polly. What fire when they were melted! Elizabeth appeared as Mrs Harrowdean in *Mr Britling Sees it Through*.

> . . . she seemed just exactly what was wanted to keep his imagination out of mischief. She came bearing flattery to the pitch of adoration. She was the brightest and cleverest thing of young widows . . . she had an intermittent vein of high spirits that was almost better than humour and made her quickly popular with most of the people she met. . . . There was something, she said, in his thought and work that was like walking in mountains. She came to him because she wanted to clamber about the peaks and glens of his mind . . . Pleasantly and trippingly she led him along the primrose path of an intellectual liaison. She

came first to [Church Row] where she was sweet and bright and vividly interested and a great contrast to [his wife], and then he took some work with him to her house and stayed there.

She went away to [Germany] for a time and he wanted her again tremendously and clamoured for her eloquently, and then it was apparent and admitted between them that they were admirably in love. Oh, immensely in love.

The transitions from emotional mountaineering to ardent intimacies were so rapid and impulsive that each phase obliterated its predecessor, and it was only with vague perplexity that [Mr Wells] found himself transferred from the role of a mountainous object for pretty little pilgrims to that of a sedulous lover in pursuit of happiness.

Elizabeth put Wells into the second half of *The Pastor's Wife*, the part that had to do with adultery where he runs away with the heroine to Italy. As a character, he sticks out from the others like the proverbial sore thumb. Never before had she written about a masculine character who had such a breezy indifference to the conventions and never again was she to write about one who was entirely likeable and admirable, even though immoral. She saw in him 'a light and a warmth, however fitful, and a greatness'.

This ending to their passionate entanglement was sad but inevitable, and the cause lay in the roots of their personalities. Wells, with his essentially working-class background, had no innate understanding of the subtleties of Edwardian infidelity; in his determination to blurt out a confession for immediate tactical gain and to relieve his own conscience he ignored the long-term implications and so made a fatal error. Even had Elizabeth already known about Rebecca's child, which was probable for very little escaped her, that Wells used it as a weapon on their personal battlefield meant Elizabeth was forced to play by the rules and, for the sake of her pride, disengage. He recklessly ignored the conventions of upper-class courtship and in the face of this there could be for her no redress and for him no reprieve.

· 13 ·

The Crack of Doom

Elizabeth's 'imagination turned to Earl Russell'[1] after the final
scenes were enacted with Wells. She invited the earl to spend that
Christmas of 1913 with her and the family at the chalet. She did not
include Mollie in the invitation and she knew that it would cause
gossip if he accepted, which he did. Evi thought him 'a perfect dear –
so large and simple and truly great'.[2] He made himself useful and
soon became a favourite with Teppi also. When he left, after the New
Year, they were all sorry to see him go, particularly his hostess who
had, over the holiday, resumed her status as his mistress. Francis
had made no commitments about marriage, nor had he spoken of
divorcing his wife over Christmas, and Elizabeth was merely content
to have a man who could smooth the plumage ruffled by her final
skirmishes with Wells.

On his return to England Francis sent her a copy of his latest
publication, *Divorce*. Elizabeth wrote thanking him fulsomely and
added, 'I miss you, dear boy – I knew I would, and I shall go on
missing you till you come back again. Your affectionate cousin
Elizabeth. (Widowed, lopped, deserted.)' The parenthesis referred
respectively to the fate Elizabeth had suffered from Henning, Wells
and Francis himself, leaving no doubt in his mind, if he thought
about it at all, as to the direction her imaginings had by that time led
her.

A week later she received 'a wonderful letter' from him. She
'wondered if it wouldn't shine through [her] and give [her] away'.[3] 'I
love you,' he wrote, 'and it's not with the greed of possessive love I've
had for women before but as if the feeling one has for lights on
crystals and clean water, the feeling of beauty in deep delicate things,
has become personified and exalted. You are my star, my miracle,
the bath of my soul. I put my heart between your cool little
hands . . .'[4] She could not work 'but thought of Frank and happi-

171

ness instead'.[5] Her happiness and her admiration of him were evident to all at the chalet. Hugh Walpole, who was there early in 1914, saw one of the girls and a friend on the ski slopes near Montana and overheard one of them say, 'Elizabeth does know how to enjoy herself, doesn't she!' Elizabeth wrote to him in London, 'I won't even begin to tell you how happy I am – I seethe and sizzle . . . '

Elizabeth and Teppi were alone together for several weeks at the end of January. They worked in the mornings, met for lunch, and worked, for a space, in the afternoons: 'But underneath what surgings and rollings and reverberations and cataclysms and convulsions and heaven and earth and God and eternity and all the mightiness of living souls', wrote Elizabeth to Liebet. Trix had decided that she wanted to study the piano at Speyer and in February Teppi escorted her there from Munich. Elizabeth spent 'four mortal nights alone' at the chalet and 'quaked at the thought' for it was the first time she had been there entirely on her own. Meanwhile Mollie's wails made London shake with scandal. She confided in Francis's friend, George Santayana, that her husband had come back from the chalet and simply told her that he was in love with someone else.

Elizabeth was sitting alone in the blue drawing-room one Friday morning in February doing the accounts. She was contemplating nothing more serious than the expensiveness of guests when she became aware of one who climbed slowly up the ice-covered path to her front door. She wrote later and with hindsight that he wasn't so much another guest as Doom, 'and from Doom there is no escape'.[6] Francis Russell had come to propose, but first he told her to get her path covered in cinders and feed the dog on fresh chopped beef. Elizabeth was delighted with his 'rocklike' calm and thought him a 'reliable, kind, simple, restful man, and so sensible'.[7] Twenty-five years later she was to remember that day from a different perspective and with regret. She wrote in her diary then:

> F. arrived at the chalet early a.m. where Teppi and I were alone . . . My doubts and misgivings. His overwhelmingness. Teppi's enthusiasm – Ah, if only I had steered clear of that devil then . . .

Elizabeth trusted Teppi's instincts about people and even more did she trust Coco's. There was no reserve in Coco's welcome to Francis when he opened the front door and walked in, nor, Elizabeth was forced to admit, was there any in hers. Certainly she had a feeling, 'unusual so soon after breakfast', that she was in the hands of God, a feeling she had not had since she was dressing to go to the party where she met her first husband. It was a 'sinking feeling', she recorded in her memoirs, 'Perhaps husbands never agreed with me.'[8]

Francis immediately contracted flu and was put to bed, but the three of them managed to be very happy for a few weeks. After he returned to London he sent Elizabeth 'depressed' letters, for he was being tormented by talk and the advice of well-meaning friends which mostly consisted of three words, 'Don't do it'.[9] In one of them he wrote.

> One gets into a sort of well at times, out of sight of faith and kindliness ... Silent, pathetic wives. They never speak unless they're spoken to or seem to care anything except to get about in clothes or be in the way and watch her man, of course. Why don't women *contribute?* They are female bum-bailiffs, legalised extinguishers. Each bagged her man in the early twenties of her life, and then *went out.* How much better me the bad! There's a gambling ruffian here, but the difference is animation![10]

Elizabeth decided to spend a few weeks in Italy with Teppi, and they took Martin, then at finishing school in Lausanne, with them. Elizabeth found her youngest daughter 'too sweet and clever for anything – so extremely and delightfully, intelligently interesting ... such a blessed relief, such water in the wilderness to be with an interested crab ... '[11] But there were other aspects of Martin's character that made Teppi anxious. She prophesied that Martin would have difficulties in later life, for the child was still not able to distinguish between her own wistful version of events and the truth.

H.B., by then at Summer Fields in Oxford, a small but strict prep school, was not endearing himself to his mother. She refused to write to him until he wrote her letters 'less horrible in handwriting and shocking in spelling'. She was offended by his 'dull, sleepy indifference ... a most dreadful thing because it is so near to not being living at all'. The previous autumn she had visited him at his school and remarked to Dr Williams, the headmaster, that she was sure her son was not beaten enough. H.B. understood it as a joke but he was, as a result, 'in for a really bad time with frequent trips for the black book, getting three on the hand, having my knuckles rapped with Miss Penny's hexagonal blue pencil and making a trip through the green baize door to kneel with my head bowed to the floor to receive three or six', as he recalled in *A Century of Summer Fields*, an anthology of reminiscences by old boys.

Liebet had been proposed to by a young man called Colin Norbert and had refused him for she considered him an inept lover and, worse, he wanted to settle in the colonies. Her mother was disappointed: 'I think you would have been extremely happy with Colin N. leading exactly the sort of free, outdoors life you love . . . He is a person one would love very much as a husband. Good and kind and practical . . .'[12] Evi and Liebet had both gained first-class honours degrees in modern languages, to their mother's great pride, and had become medical students in London. But Elizabeth had little inclination to think much about her children just then for her own life was absorbing all her attention.

Francis returned to the chalet a few weeks later and there was 'perfect sunshine inside as well as out'.[13] He and Elizabeth had decided that they were destined for each other. She accompanied him down to the station when he left and bade him farewell saying, 'God keep you, my heavenly love.' By the end of the month he wrote that he was getting a divorce from Mollie and two days later that he had left her.

Elizabeth thought she was in love. To Teppi, much later, she confessed that perhaps she had not been but that for the first time in her life she had *believed* in it and not known the difference. All of her friends, many of them also Francis's, were astonished at the transformation in her and concluded that she was, indeed, experiencing a powerful and uplifting emotion.

'She wants to be his wife; she wants me to divorce him,' complained Mollie to her only confidant.

'Why, does the silly woman want to be a countess?' Santayana inquired.

'No, she isn't silly and is a countess already. She is the Countess von Arnim, author of *Elizabeth and her German Garden*. Russell is very much in love with her,' replied the grief-stricken woman.[14]

The account that Elizabeth presented to Francis's brother Bertrand was at variance with Mollie's version. Bertrand wrote about it to Lady Ottoline Morrell:

> She says – and I believe her – that she was unguarded with my brother at first, because she looked upon him as safely married, and therefore suitable as a lover. Suddenly, without consulting her, he wrote and said he was getting divorced. It took her breath away, and rather flattered her; she drifted, said nothing definite, but

THE CRACK OF DOOM

allowed him tacitly to assume everything. Now she is feeling very worried because the inexorable moment is coming when his divorce will be absolute and she will have to decide. Her objections to him are the following: a) he sleeps with seven dogs on his bed. She couldn't sleep a wink under such circumstances. (I told her about Josephine's dog biting Napoleon.* What emperors have borne she may); b) he reads Kipling aloud; c) he loves Telegraph House which is hideous.

I dare say other objections might be found if one searched long enough; they are all three well chosen to appeal to me. She is a flatterer, and had evidently set herself the task of getting me to be not against her if she breaks with him. But it is an impossible task. I am too fond of my brother, and shall mind his suffering too much, to forgive her inwardly even if she has a perfectly good case. She says she is still in great uncertainty, but I don't think she will marry him. She would be *delighted* to go on having him for a lover, but I feel sure he will never agree to that.

Francis Russell was violently, possessively and overbearingly in love with Elizabeth. His moral code did not allow him to make love to a member of his own class without offering marriage if they were single, although the lower and servant classes were fair game. He wrote passionate and eloquent love letters to her which, of all the ones she had received in her life, she kept. Liebet destroyed all compromising letters and documents after her mother died but Elizabeth copied fragments of the best love letters on to the manuscript of a play she wrote of *The Pastor's Wife*. They are headed: 'Saved from the holocaust'. In all probability Liebet did not find them for they were well hidden. He wrote:

> You delicate and worshipful soul, you strong sturdy friend of my heart, my sister, my mother, my lover, my undeserved, unmerited mate, my pride, my salvation, treasure of life, thing like a little flame in the heart. And though I am warped and encrusted and blundering, I'm of your stuff.[15]

When they had first met in 1894 they were young and both married to other people, Now, at the age of forty-eight, Elizabeth was free and Francis, at forty-nine, could easily, it appeared, become so. He was

*Josephine's dog bit Napoleon in the calf on their wedding night.

no longer the handsome, slim young man in an excellent but shabby tweed suit that Elizabeth had first known. He was a 'blustering, pink-cheeked, elderly schoolboy entangled in motor cars and electrical gadgets', as one of his brother's later mistresses, Lady Constance Malleson, described him. Frank Swinnerton, a fellow member of the Reform Club, remembered him as a big burly man with a rosy face, longish white hair, his own teeth, and smiling, pouting lips. His eyes were blue, but there was a hardness there which robbed them of geniality. He moved slowly and carefully. He was not a sensitive man and was often obtuse, but on certain subjects such as Canon Law he was learned – he had been called to the Bar when he was thirty-six. His judgements of men were often harsh and contemptuous and he was not liked by his fellow members either of the Reform or of the House of Lords where his reputation as a speaker was high. An unpopular Cabinet minister and fellow member of the Reform once asked Francis if he could take the vacant chair next to him. He replied, 'Yes, if you take it away.'[16] He was invariably disagreeable to servants, who could not retaliate, and it was this that offended his companions most.

'I should think that the servants in this club must curse like devils when they see you come in, Russell,' said a fellow member.

Francis, who was sitting near the novelist Arnold Bennett, laughed and said, 'Nonsense, he's talking nonsense, isn't he, Bennett?'

'All that he says is true,' replied the writer, gloomily sticking out his chin, 'and more . . . '[17]

Elizabeth had long ago ceased to be 'rather sweet' and resonated with power like a small, unexploded powder keg. Many people, at this time, apprehended her to be almost witchlike, and she inspired fear in most of the people she met then. In contrast, Liebet noticed that 'never before had she been so anxiously, so meekly acquiescent to another's wishes'[18] as she now was to those of her lover.

In 1913 Telegraph House had been all but finished and Francis was assailed by a 'sadness of spirit'. He had done all the building he could afford; made all the roads that were necessary; and perhaps was merely sighing, like Alexander, for fresh worlds to conquer. He ought to have sat down and 'basked and purred'[19] in the midst of his possessions, but instead his mind was obsessed with the words of St Luke:

> . . . a man's life consisteth not in the abundance of the things which he possesseth . . . I will pull down my barns,

and build greater . . . and I will say unto my soul, Soul,
thou hast much goods laid up for many years; take thine
ease, eat, drink and be merry. But God said unto him:
'Thou fool, this night thy soul shall be required of thee.'

Nor was Elizabeth inclined towards the sybaritic life. She remained
entranced while in Francis's company, but as soon as he left she
began to have misgivings. She perceived the inconstancy with which
she had behaved and doubted that marriage to him was what she
really wanted. She had accepted her merry widowhood, and enjoyed
herself during her years of freedom. She contemplated re-entering
the constraints of married life with some reluctance. In the spring of
1914 she wrote Francis a well-reasoned letter stating politely 'that
once a widow always a widow' ought to be her motto, suspecting as
she did that she had no real gift for the married state, and that 'I did
think it generally best, after a certain age, to leave well alone'. By
return of post she received a postcard from Francis asking her to
define the word 'well'.[20]

Further discussions along these lines were precluded in mid-July
by a letter from Martin's headmistress, Mlle Bollinger, asking
Elizabeth to remove the child from school. She had pilfered money
'again', the princely sum of two shillings and sixpence. Francis
arrived at the chalet as soon as he could (bringing with him, as
presents, a small dog and a cat), and went with Elizabeth to
Lausanne. Martin's rebellious behaviour had caused her to be put in
a sanitorium above Montreux and for two days her mother and
Francis sought, vainly, another school in the town where the girl
could be placed. Francis was 'very supportive, kind and dear' [21] but
departed for England three days later with a promise from Elizabeth
to lend him money. Teppi was sent to fetch Martin and there ensued,
on the day of her arrival, 'horrid and degrading scenes'[22] between
mother and daughter. Elizabeth did not believe Martin's denials, for
the child had never set any store by the truth, and was bitterly
disappointed and anxious. She was particularly fond of this
daughter who was pretty, charming, talented and 'irrepressibly
gay'.[23] Confession and remorse on the part of the criminal were
clearly the first steps and Martin was confined to her bedroom until
these were forthcoming. She remained there for twenty-four hours
when only the maid could step inside to clean and bring her food.
Finally Teppi escorted the weeping child to the school in Marburg,
Germany, where she had once taught. It was renowned for its
strictness and the exact opposite of the lighthearted one that Martin

had left. Elizabeth did not bid her daughter farewell, refused to see her off and gave instructions that she was forbidden to play the piano, the one activity from which Martin drew any real peace of mind and where her true talents lay.

Liebet arrived at the chalet a few hours after her sister's departure. She was surprised, under the circumstances, to find her mother in an unusually placid mood. Vernon Lee came to stay, and there was no mention of the recent 'passionate and painful scenes'. When the travel writer departed Elizabeth and Liebet went for a hiking tour in Italy and Elizabeth did not refer to the fate of her youngest daughter at all. Liebet hoped it was because her mother wished to spare her anxiety when she fobbed off any inquiries with 'vague assurances that all things were done for the best'.[24] Elizabeth's only comment in her diary was that the weather was 'hot and heavenly'. After two days they encountered a peasant on the shores of Lake Orta who told them 'of a blown up Archduke'.[25]

As soon as they returned the chalet rapidly filled with the summer guests, most of them friends of the children. Evi arrived to find her mother ill in bed, and Cousin William was ensconced 'as lame and unmanly as ever'.[26] Rumours of war were spreading rapidly. Austria and Hungary officially declared war on Serbia and, while William scoffed, Elizabeth told Liebet to go to Sierre and get in supplies of food while they still lasted. Amused at the prevalent hysteria, Cousin William left for England. The guests bickered gently among themselves, feeling vaguely dissatisfied as they sat, well fed and aimless, in the hot sun. There was, occasionally, a slow game of badminton, but the fierce heat drained all energy from them; somebody picked out bits of Handel on the piano; and they waited for news of the war. Francis wrote from London:

> The state of things is awful tonight; people failing left and right. New anxieties and terrors every hour – Russia mobilizing, Germany on martial law etc. Closing the Stock Exchange at the eight per cent bank rate will help to steady things . . . Never in our lifetime has there been anything like this crisis – people are actually buying flour tonight – it all seems quite without reason – unworthy of any civilization – I am as much amazed as horrified.

On 29 July Elizabeth and Liebet went down to Sierre to remove as much cash as possible from the local bank, and not before time. On the second of August Teppi arrived back from Berlin, where she had visited her family and Trix after depositing Martin in Marburg. She

had had great difficulties in getting about because of the mobilization and had sprained her ankle, so that she arrived in Basel in a
wheelbarrow flanked by two policemen. Her news that the Deutsche
Bank, where Elizabeth and the children kept their capital, had shut,
increased the sense of foreboding and panic at the chalet, as did her
account of what she had seen in Berlin which Elizabeth later
incorporated into her novel *Christine*:

> The weather is fiercely hot. There's a brassy sky without a
> cloud, and all the leaves of the trees in the Tiergarten are
> shiny and motionless as if they were cut out of metal. A
> little haze of dust hangs perpetually along the Lindens
> and the road to Charlottenburg – not much of it, because
> the roads are too well kept, but enough to show that the
> troops never lay off tramping. And all down where they
> pass, on each side, are the perspiring crowds of people, red
> and apoplectic with excitement and heat, women and
> children and babies mixed up in one heaving, frantic
> mass. The windows of the houses on each side of the
> Brandenburger Thor are packed with people all day long,
> and the noise of patriotism doesn't leave off for an instant
> . . . The drunken crowds – that's the word that most
> exactly describes them – yelling, swaying, cursing
> . . . Somehow a spectacled professor with a golden chain
> across his blackwaistcoated and impressive front, just
> roaring incoherently, just opening his mouth and hurling
> any sort of noise out of it till the veins on his head and neck
> and forehead look as though they would burst, is the
> strangest sight in the world to me . . .

Provisions in the shops at Sierre and Montana rapidly dwindled to
nothing, and Sierre was filled with Swiss troops who seized everything from the trains. At the chalet there were only potatoes and a
little cheese that had been given to them by nearby priests in
exchange for flowers. All of the chalet guests left and the four women
were alone and unprotected waiting for news of Trix and Martin and
living in momentary fear of being raped and pillaged by soldiers.
The local peasants were already suffering from hunger. Elizabeth
had been told that unless she left immediately it would be her last
chance, but the two girls wanted to stay on at the chalet: as German
citizens they preferred to be on neutral territory. Besides, their
sisters might have escaped from Germany and be making their way
to Sierre, and they wanted to be there to meet them. The faithful

Teppi was to stand guard over them and Elizabeth had full confidence in her astonishing powers.

On the evening of 4 August, after giving Teppi and the girls many instructions and a loaded revolver, she set off for England. The others barricaded themselves in as Elizabeth had instructed and sat down to an exiguous supper. A few hours later they were terrified to hear a loud rat-tat on the door and when they could pluck up enough courage to find out who it was, discovered their mother back again having failed to get a train. 'That evening . . . there was pure joy in my heart,' wrote Evi, 'especially when I had to give up the pistol. I don't mind shooting, but I couldn't shoot anybody.'[27]

The next morning Elizabeth telegraphed to her brother Sydney for passports, for without them there would have been no hope of any of them getting into England with their German nationality. As their few hours with their mother away had been so nerve-racking, Evi and Liebet decided to accompany her to England. Fortunately one of Sydney's patients, by the name of Arnold, volunteered his family's passports, and they were smuggled out of England by a Dutchman and brought to Switzerland. Meanwhile two young Englishmen in Montana offered their assistance and protection. While the women waited for their passports to arrive Elizabeth sorted her papers, destroyed many and buried the rest in a tin box in the garden.

One of the Englishmen, Mr Fletcher, was 'wonderful, kind and clever'. Elizabeth enjoyed his company so much that she urged her daughers to flirt with him to 'keep him amused'.[28] Evi was her mother's choice for the task because of the 'come hither' look in her eyes, but Minor, her boyfriend from Cambridge, indicated by post to Evi that they should go their separate ways, and she was brokenhearted and so of no avail. The other Englishman, when asked if he would accompany the three women to England, turned pale and 'trembled in every limb' showing such fears of the risks to be encountered that they could not but call him a 'perfect coward'.[29] To cover his shame he abused them as frightened women and added much vehement language which greatly amused the von Arnims.

On 7 August the violation of Belgian neutrality caused great consternation at the chalet. Teppi was 'worrying herself sick'[30] about her family, and they decided that she should go by Berne and Zurich to Germany. She managed to get back to her village, finding there a state of anarchy and chaos, and she showed great courage by leading the village women out into the fields to gather in the harvest which had been forgotten in the general panic. The von Arnims read with alarm reports of ships being sunk in the North Sea, but were generally baffled about the progress of the war as all the newspapers contradicted each other. Evi heard she had failed 'thoroughly and completely in everything'[31] in her first-year medical exams. Although it did not matter in the long run as she would never go back to her studies, she was profoundly cast down. Liège fell to the Germans and had to pay ten million francs. Brussels had to pay fifty million, but the Russians seemed to be making good headway on their march to Berlin. Violent thunderstorms rumbled around the mountains and Evi regretted her fear of them as they were spectacular to watch.

The new passports arrived and Mr Fletcher, already 'Cousin John', arranged that they should leave for Montreux and England on the 28th. On that date 'Mrs Arnold' and her two daughters took with them only a knapsack and a handbag each and abandoned the chalet to looters or worse. Coco was the last member of the household that they saw. He had carried his mistress's bag in his mouth by its strap to the point across the field where the fly was waiting to take them down to the valley. When the parting came he tried to hold onto her bag, imagining, no doubt, that she couldn't possibly go if she didn't have it. But he was too polite to try very hard, and allowed her to take it from him and stood looking after her sadly.

They set off for Paris via Geneva by the ordinary train. At Amberlieu they coincided with a trainload of wounded French soldiers. The passenger train was shunted into a siding and those aboard watched the stretchers being lined up on the platform to await further transport to the hospital. The soldiers were fed and then taken away again, but one man was left writhing and noisily dying on the platform for he had had his stomach shot away and, it appeared, was not worth wasting time on.

The 'Arnolds' eventually arrived at the Gare de Lyon and dashed over to the Gare du Nord where they just managed to catch the train to Le Havre. It was packed, for the victorious Germans were approaching the city and the frightened Parisians stormed every outgoing train. Men, women and children, clutching their valued possessions, clung to any foot- and hand-hold they could find. The refugees spent the night flopped on to coils of rope on the deck of a steamer in an exhausted and fitful sleep, particularly the girls, for they had had to be careful not to be overheard talking. Their still violent accents would have given away their nationality and there was no telling what might happen to them then. Fortunately it was a fine night. The next day they arrived in England.

'Lovely day, fearfully happy,' Elizabeth wrote in her scantily kept diary. Of course she flew into Francis's arms as soon as she arrived. She took a flat in Albemarle Court and she and Francis spent much of their time together and were 'intensely happy'. She met Wells and 'thought him dreadful'. Cousin William's sulks irritated her beyond endurance. 'Finally sick of him and sent him away,'[32] she wrote.

On 20 September, with the help of Maude Stanley who swore on oath that she considered Elizabeth worthy to be a British citizen, Elizabeth was accepted for naturalization and after twenty-three years she was once more an Englishwoman. News of her heroic escape buzzed around London and she was besieged, as usual, with invitations. Her telephone hardly ever stopped ringing, and her friends were delighted to see her safe, avid to hear her tale and happy to have her once more in their midst.

Evi and Liebet did not have such a pleasant time. They had been saved from the possibility of deportation or internment by their mother's naturalization, but their accents gave away their nationality and they were treated with profound suspicion by the people they met, so hysterically anti-German was the feeling in London by then. Their Uncle Sydney managed to get them both jobs as probationers in two of London's largest hospitals, and Evi was quartered at Bedford College and Liebet in York Street, but they were forced to report at the local police station every day and forbidden to travel further than a short distance without special permission. At weekends they went, if they could, to join their mother at Hatch, Kingsley Green, near Haslemere where Charlotte had recently moved her family. Elizabeth went to Summer Fields and told her son that he was at least half English now. He expressed pleasure that he was 'at least something'.[33]

H.B. had been delighted when the war came because the von had been dropped from his name and at roll-call he suddenly found he was one of the first instead of being, rather muddily, always at the other end of the alphabet. He was ragged a reasonable amount by the other boys for being a German but he stoutly maintained that he might be a German but he was also a gentleman, and his mother had told him that the people who had started the war certainly were not gentlemen.

Martin wrote a letter to her mother in which she hoped never to have to see her again and wished she had been a boy so that she could join the army and 'kill as many Englishmen as possible'.[34] Trix, who had given up her piano studies and was working as a nurse in Berlin, wrote that she was sick to death of the war and shocked beyond

'A pert, unlovable child. . .'
as May (Elizabeth) was described by her great aunts.

Henry and Louey Beauchamp after 'boots had given way to bulbs', in the 1890s.

The beautiful Charlotte
with the red gold hair in
her late teens.

The April, May and June babies with their mother
the year she discovered her German garden.

Henning as a young man in the 1870s.

Francis, Earl Russell as a young man at about the time he first met Elizabeth.

Bertrand Russell as a 'Woman's Suffrage' candidate in the Wimbledon division in 1907.

Above Elizabeth in her thirties.
Right Henning on a snowy morning at
Nassenheide *circa* 1901. Elizabeth always
kept the coat with her after he died for
sentimental reasons.

Nassenheide in summer with the April, May and June babies.

Henning and his longed-for son and heir in front of the lilacs at Nassenheide.

Elizabeth and H.B. standing on the sundial at Nassenheide.

Right Four little maids. From left to right: Trix, Evi, Elizabeth and Liebet.

Below E.M. Forster, H.B. and Felicitas by the 'whirligig' flowerbeds on the south side of the castle.

Felicitas with her grandfather, Deepa (Henry Herron Beauchamp) at the Retreat in Bexley, Kent.

The basketwork carriage outside the front door at Nassenheide. Evi in the driving seat, Liebet and Trix behind.

Teppi spinning on the porch at Nassenheide in spring sunshine.

Hugh Walpole as a young man.

Herr Steinweg and E.M. Forster at Nassenheide having thrown their hats to the wind.

The caravan tour. Billy the dog became their symbol: 'Nature with dignity.'

Liebet and Evi at Blue Hayes in the summer.

Above Passport photograph
of Elizabeth aged forty.
Above right Elizabeth at fifty-
seven.

H.G. Wells.

Above Frere at about the time of his first meeting with Elizabeth.
Left Wells and Elizabeth at the chalet, answering to 'no authority of any kind'.
Below The chalet Soleil and Little Chalet.

The chalet from the iris walk.
Frere is standing in the porch.

The chalet taken in 1922 by
Thelma Cazalet from the
opposite mountain.

Francis, Earl Russell in middle age on his yacht *Royal* soon after his marriage to Elizabeth.

From left to right: Bertrand Russell, Elizabeth and Frere on the terrace to the chalet.

Katherine Mansfield at the period when a 'thousand devils' sent Elizabeth without her German Garden to tea with her in Hampstead.

Left to right: Victor Cazalet, Hugh Walpole, Elizabeth, Rudyard Kipling and Mrs Cazalet at the Cazalets' house, Fairlawn in Kent, 1928.

Elizabeth and her son-in-law Tony von Hirschberg.

Le Mas des Roses from the back in 1932. Unfortunately there is no hint in this photograph of the spectacular view down the valley to the sea beyond.

Elizabeth on the roof of Le Mas des Roses with her puppies in 1932. Her family referred to her at that stage as being 'all dog'.

Elizabeth at the Golden Eagle Hotel in Beaufort, South Carolina, 1940. 'I'm going to stay here till driven away by agile alligators and snakes' she wrote to Liebet.

Elizabeth in the early 1920s.

measure at such behaviour on the part of 'God's children',[35] all at each other's throats. She was worried about what German newspapers swore was true about the English and was beginning, greatly against her will, to believe they really were the wicked people they were made out to be. Teppi did what she could to soothe the two girls and was always there if they needed her. She was again teaching in a German school and took on the duty of proxy motherhood with good will. During their holidays Trix and Martin went to stay with Cousin Bernd and Tante Lotte at Criewen.

There was a plan for Elizabeth and Liebet and Evi to go to Carolina to stay with the Doubledays, Elizabeth's American publishers, but eventually she decided, 'I can't turn my back on my dear country just at this crisis.'[36]

In October *The Pastor's Wife* was published and acclaimed as the most serious and finished piece of work she had produced so far. The *Spectator* thought the book:

> . . . brilliantly faultless in literary detail and execution. There is a touch of virile originality in 'Elizabeth's' style which is often amazing. One wonders where she acquired this clarity, this power of subtle suggestion which yet never makes for obscurity, this intellectual detachment which is never a non-conductor . . . What a rare and delightful gift.

Elizabeth's daughters were interested to observe that their mother appeared to be, for the first time, more or less indifferent to the reviews of her book. They correctly assumed it was because she was totally bound up in what Francis thought about her and gave little heed to anybody else's comments. The days when she did not manage to see him were written off by her as days lost, but at the same time she was beginning to see the first glimpses of the real personality behind the mask.

Francis Russell was a man who was capable of enormous charm when the occasion demanded, but he was not able to maintain it for ever, relapsing, as his worried mother had seen when he was child, into an almost maniacal tyranny as soon as he was with people who didn't matter, that is, his nearest and dearest. With Elizabeth, now that he was seeing so much of her, he was sometimes moody, changeable and stubborn. There was tension between them because the money she had promised him with which to fund his divorce from Mollie was lying uselessly in the Deutsche Bank. He began to be 'tiresome, tyrannical and dreadful'.[37]

He received a letter from George Santayana containing truths that were impossible to ignore, begging him not to leave Mollie whom he saw as humble and resigned and possibly the perfect wife for such as himself. Santayana argued that Russell was like Henry VIII in that he desired to marry his lady-loves; but that only made him wish, later, to cut their heads off to make room for the next. Goethe, 'less bigoted and morally calmer', had finally married only one, the humblest of his women, who had been his mistress and housekeeper for years. Mollie was used to all Francis's ways and kept his house economically and in good order. 'What a mistake to send her away and insist on marrying Frau von Stein.'[38] When Elizabeth saw the letter she could not but understand the profound truth of the philosopher's perceptions and there was a coolness between Francis and herself which lasted several weeks. She was not to know, and possibly never did know, that Francis was already having an affair with his housekeeper at Telegraph House, Miss Young, for whom a change of countess would make very little difference, or so he imagined. She was passionately fond of the animals there, healed sick or broken creatures and wrote him regular and engaging letters every week telling him of the progress of whatever plan of his was afoot on the estate. He had never considered marrying her because she was not of his social class.

Things improved, however, when Elizabeth's money at last came through from Germany – Mollie, after all, had no money of her own. But then Francis confessed to having been unlucky at the bridge table (it had been Elizabeth's money which he had lost). She managed to extract a promise from him that he would not play for money again, but he was unable to keep to this and from time to time boyishly confessed that he had fallen into error. Elizabeth began to write and talk about 'the hopelessness of marriage,'[39] though Francis followed her sedulously wherever she went. When she was in London he stayed in his house in Gordon Square. When she was staying with Charlotte at Hatch he went to Telegraph House which was within easy motoring distance. He taught her chemistry and the natural sciences and she found them fascinating, not least because he was a superb teacher. Finally Elizabeth felt 'disinclined to face a future of separation and loneliness'.[40]

The couple spent the Christmas of 1914 at Telegraph House and managed to remain 'glowingly in love'[41] throughout. Although T.H. (as it was always called) was an ungainly, ugly house in itself, comfortable and with no pretensions, it was in a magnificent position, centred on top of the downs in a wild and varied park of 230 acres of downland. To its other virtues was added the charm of complete solitude. Like the chalet, it had to be approached from the station by cart which cut deep ruts in the grassy hillside as it wound and tilted, like a boat over the waves, up to the house. There were enormous views to east, south and west. In one direction there was visible the Sussex Weald to Burgess Hill; to the other, the Isle of Wight and the liners approaching Southampton.

Telegraph House owed its name to having been a semaphore station at the time of George III, one of a string of such stations by which messages flashed between Portsmouth and London – probably the news of Trafalgar reached London by that route. In *Vera*, a novel Elizabeth was to write about the house, she describes it briefly: 'Grey sky, grey water, green fields – it was all grey and green except the house which was red brick with handsome stone facings and made, in its position, unhidden by any trees, a great splotch of vivid red in the landscape.'

Bertrand was to take the house over from his brother in the Twenties when he started his, at the time, shockingly progressive school, Beacon Hill. The children were allowed, even encouraged, to do more or less what they wanted. When a prospective parent came to the door one day and was startled when it was opened by a naked child, he exclaimed, 'Good God!' to which the child replied calmly that there was no God.[42]

On 1 January 1915 Elizabeth, with ever buoyant optimism, wrote in her diary at Telegraph House, 'Loved F very much – what happiness I've had this whole year because of him . . . Saw the new year in under the happiest of conditions. So ends 1914 – it has been the happiest year of my life, now let's see what this one's got in it.'

During the first part of 1915 Francis and Elizabeth did quite a lot of motoring, a sport that Francis took very seriously. He was the first person in England to receive a driving licence and was very proud of his A1 number plates. He was a founder member of the Royal Automobile Club and took a great interest in the club's magazine, for which he procured his friend Edgar Jepson as editor. Santayana used to enjoy his drives with Francis:

> Sitting by him as he drove was an unmixed pleasure; he did it perfectly, with sureness and ease, and his casual observations as the road opened up before [us] and various little scenes appeared, belonged to the original sphere of our friendship. This sphere was play of mind, intellectual, light; not philosophy, not theory, but quick

intelligence turned upon common things, enquiringly,
fearlessly, and universally. Theory and philosophy would
have crept in had [we] pursued any subject very far; but
[we] never did . . . [Ours] were flying comments made for
the pleasure of making them. [We] never laughed much,
but [we] were always laughing a little . . . [43]

Bertrand had a different experience, and avoided driving with his
brother if he could, for Francis perpetually ordered the chauffeur to
go faster or slower or cursed road hogs with abandoned fury.
Elizabeth's feelings were mixed for she enjoyed the tours as long as
all went well, but on 9 June for instance: 'Discovered a tyre
punctured. Much fuss and severity in consequence – was ordered
about and scolded as though were a chauffeur in the course of
putting on the spare wheel. Felt greatly unnerved in consequence.'[44]

In July Francis left for South Africa on business for a mining
company. *'Vive, Valeque! Quid desiderior sit pudor aut modus?'* his mistress
wrote in her diary, or 'Why should there be shame or stint in regret
for the loss of one so dear?'[45] Stuart, who had joined the army early in
the war, came to spend his leave at Hatch with Elizabeth and
Charlotte, arriving the day after Francis had departed. He was very
poor company and gales whipped the cold and relentless rain blindly
against the window panes. All of nature was overcome with grief and
so was Cousin William. In the morning he did not speak at all and in
the afternoon they struggled out for a walk in the wet woods near
Marley where he was 'too boring for words and gloomy and
difficult'.[46] He loved Elizabeth hopelessly, irrevocably and for ever.
He spoke laconically of death and that he hoped to come to grief in
the trenches. He then announced, to her surprise, that he was
thinking of getting married, but would not say to whom. He left after
tea on his motor cycle to the great relief of the sisters.

That evening Elizabeth drove up to town to attend a dinner party
which included Beverley Nichols. The talk naturally turned to the
war and one of the guests told of a young soldier they knew who had
been wounded in eleven different places. Elizabeth, thinking of
Stuart, remarked that she didn't know that a man had eleven
different places.

In October Francis returned and there was much 'bliss and
perfect joy' at being with him again. But the rest of that year was an
anxious one for Elizabeth for she worried about her children constantly. Evi was sacked from every job that was found for her and
eventually obtained a post as an apprentice midwife, again through

the influence of her patient Uncle Sydney. She was unreliable, took nothing seriously, and her mother found it extraordinary that she did not appear to grasp the gravity of the war nor the deadly seriousness of her own situation. Evi claimed that she was discriminated against because she was a German, but the matron she worked for considered she was scatterbrained and irresponsible and that they could never be sure that she would carry out orders. Trix had been transferred to a German hospital at Lille in France and complained that instead of nursing the wounded she was put in charge of 'horrible men with venereal diseases'.[47] The French there glared at the German nurses with hatred and called out dreadful names at them, and Elizabeth was afraid that if the French army got back to Lille, they would make short work of a German woman. Her heart was leaden at these complications. Martin's letters were so persistently abusive that Elizabeth forbade her to write again until further notice. Liebet was mostly weepy and feeling sorry for herself and considered taking up an invitation meant for Evi from an old Berlin acquaintance called Poultney Bigelow to stay with his family just outside New York. H.B. wrote that he had been moved up to the 'top form', to his mother's great pride and joy, until she turned over the page and the letter continued 'but two'. She considered that a really modest boy would have said, with equal truth, that he was in the bottom form but two.

Francis and Elizabeth quarrelled more often and, on one occasion, he simply walked out of her cottage and did not contact her for nearly two weeks, during which time she suffered agonies. Then he turned up for lunch and she was amazed to find he hadn't been particularly aware of anything out of the ordinary all those days. The servants at Telegraph House and at Gordon Square caused trouble because Elizabeth was not married to Francis while behaving as though she were. Once, when she was out walking near Telegraph House, two children saw her peer at a cottage through her eyeglasses and chanted out that she was a spy. 'So have the disgusting ways of the Germans dragged us down to all sorts of ugly behaviour.'[48]

On an impulse Elizabeth telephoned Wells, thirsting to hear his views on the war. Jane answered and invited her round to tea. Elizabeth found him 'much moth-eaten and run to seed'[49] but was greatly amused by his talk. However, the greatest pleasure of her existence that year was the opportunity of long conversations with Bertrand Russell, who reminded her of Wells and whom she found fascinating and amusing. So animated were their talks that Francis often protested and became angry, but most of the time the three of them spent many happy days together at Telegraph House. The news was depressing and worrying. Elizabeth thought the war an unforgivable crime against the intelligence of humanity, 'the monstrous interference with the only things that matter and one's mind's life and activity'.[50] She told Bertrand that it was her belief that the war had brought to her generation 'a tragic knowledge. I mean by this knowledge . . . deserts of vast eternity. But the difference is . . . I couldn't tell anybody *bang out* about those deserts: they are my secret.'[51] Liebet left for the States in January of 1916 and Evi followed her a few weeks later, 'not caring half of twopence for any of us',[52] her mother noticed.

In spite of the rows, unhappiness, and often the cruelty now of Francis, who berated her in public and, worse, in front of the servants, Elizabeth approached the inevitable outcome with baffling serenity. The closer to marriage they came, the less she was in any conflict about it. It was as though she had been truly mesmerized by her Doom and somewhere knew that she could not reverse her position. The divorce from Mollie came through at the beginning of February 1916 and Francis and Elizabeth went to St Paul's Cathedral to render thanks for their 'great happiness',[53] a little solemn and quaking at the possibilities ahead of them. Mollie had gone to live in Brighton, taking with her her pack of white Maltese terriers, and spent much time playing bridge and quite happily spending the £400 a year she had gained for life as alimony. If she was pleased to be away from the tyranny of her ex-husband she did not say so to Santayana who once met her there, and her replacement chose not to think of it.

It was unfortunate that Elizabeth's need for an English name – without, of course, having to give up being a countess which she enjoyed – led her at this time only to remember and act upon the positive aspects of the involvement. Her friend Mrs Belloc Lowndes opined that her passion for Francis was evidence of a dual personality, and indeed there was a fundamental inconsistency in her highly complex personality. She could never enjoy the purely frivolous, gay and apparently superficial life she always lived when she was in London without hankering for a lonely cottage somewhere where she would be able to work in solitude and meditate. But once in the solitary reality of that state she yearned for stimulating company and the flattering attention of her friends. The grass was invariably emerald green on the other side of the fence. *Procul est profani* or 'Proximity is the first and only deadly sin,' she had written above her work-house doors while paradoxically spending much time yearning for her loved ones there. She sought an elusive golden mean which was, as Liebet understood, 'the very essence of her personality',[54] and caused more than one critic to describe her as 'Greek' in her outlook. It was a platonic quest for a joining together of disparate elements in her personality, and naturally, by extension, in her life. In Francis she thought she had found the key. He, in turn, thought her 'the finest, most wonderful and loving woman in the world who also has the courage to marry me'.[55]

The wedding day, 12 February 1916, dawned through a thick yellow fog. Charlotte came and collected Elizabeth and they made their way to the office of the Russell solicitor, Mr Dobson, for will-signing and the marriage contract. Francis and Bertrand were waiting for them in high good humour, Francis even wearing a wedding buttonhole. On impulse as much as on the advice of Charlotte, Elizabeth conceded Francis no rights over her income or possessions and left everything to her children. This did not please the earl, in fact it cast rather a shadow over the proceedings which, for some reason, escaped Elizabeth's attention.[56] Then they travelled to the registrar's in Henrietta Street. There were no guests, for they wanted to keep the wedding as secret as possible: if the news leaked to Germany, it might have been dangerous for Trix and Martin. After the ceremony they called, on impulse, to see Elizabeth's mother to surprise her with the news. She was 'immensely horrified'[57] and could hardly speak to the happy couple, let alone bless her daughter as she ought to have done. Then Elizabeth and Francis went on alone to Telegraph House, presenting themselves to the housekeeper, Miss Young, to announce that they were indeed and at last married and were staying for the weekend. Miss Young, who had earlier complained of the irregularities of their relationship, refused to believe it and went about muttering under her breath and shaking her head.

It was a beautiful, sunny, clear day in Sussex. Elizabeth walked by herself on the downs in the afternoon, and lay in the sun 'so warm and happy'. After tea she stood alone in the twilight listening to the birds and gazing at the rising moon, 'completely and perfectly happy'.[58] This was to be the beginning of years of acute misery, but she was blissfully unaware of it at the time.

· 14 ·

The Dregs of Misery

On their return to London the following Monday, a cold and wintry day, Francis announced that he was going to have tea at his club. His wife, naturally, felt surprised and deserted and 'dreadfully hurt'.[1] Never before they had married would he have left her completely at a loose end in a strange hotel – they were not able to live at Gordon Square for a time because Elizabeth was having the house redecorated. She tried to get into a concert at the Queen's Hall, but there wasn't one on and so she called on a friend. That evening she dined with Francis who appeared to be entirely unaware that anything untoward had happened.

Two nights later they quarrelled in bed because the dogs kept Elizabeth awake. Harsh words were flung on both sides and she felt like a 'very wretched, horrid pig' and was profoundly dejected. The next day, exhausted after her sleepless night, she found Francis 'adamant and as hard and unyielding as rocks of steel'. They travelled down to Telegraph House and Elizabeth went straight to bed, having developed flu. She discovered while she lay there that Francis bullied and shouted at the servants in an alarming and, to her, novel access of rage. He left the house and she crept downstairs and sat in his office which at least was warm. When he came back he accused her of meddling with his papers, though she had touched nothing. She was entirely 'put off Frank and marriage'[2] and greatly surprised.

From her account of events, Elizabeth obviously never guessed that Francis was probably still angry at not being conceded any rights over her money when they married.[3] It is even possible that this was the reason he married her in the first place, for she would have been delighted to go on being his mistress, as she told Bertrand. In addition, Miss Young had withdrawn her favours to him after the wedding and Francis fell into and persisted in 'cross, grim, silent moods'[4] that were becoming familiar to his wife, and which she found 'impossible to believe'. On several nights she was 'awake all night wretchedly contemplating the future'. Whenever they went down to Telegraph House Francis became tyrannical: Elizabeth was shocked to watch him deliberately drop a table napkin on the floor and then call the servants and berate them for it. The huge scenes between Francis and Miss Young terrified her: ' . . . usual horrid scolding of Miss Young. Really quite intolerable. I feel hot shame when I'm obliged to be present at this baiting of a quite decent and good human being.'[5] Even so, when they were away Miss Young continued to send her employer a weekly newsletter which contained no rancour:

> Today I walked [the dogs] all round by Kill Devil Copse and had many interesting incidents on the way. At the rough boundary plantation a pheasant and about half a dozen chicks met us, and just beyond a Jay was teaching a family to fly, the smallest was rather 'wobbly' and came to the ground. I picked it up, but until I managed to settle it on a tree, it opened its beak and nearly howled all the owls from their nests. In a big beech tree near the tank there are two such pretty squirrels living, so possibly there is a nest there also. How odd the Dell Bridge Plantation looks at the corner where the lightning has blighted it. I wonder if the trees will grow. Hundreds of big and small rabbits about, especially in the main dell. I never get one for the doggies now, although I know C. shoots them for himself. The old cat is so good to the kitten, and occasionally brings in a half-eaten small rabbit and lays it down in front of the kitten and then makes such a fuss so that I shall see what he has done.
>
> Just by the clothes green a partridge is sitting on sixteen eggs. I hope she will not be disturbed away then we shall see how many will hatch.
>
> The ferrets have a litter, how many nobody knows, they are invisible.[6]

Elizabeth made up her mind not to take anything her husband did or said to heart but sedulously to cultivate not caring, even if it meant letting her great love for Francis go. It was a terrible decision to arrive at and she felt that she was living in a nightmare. She wrote, 'Shall I ever forget these T.H. days in later life? I hope some day to see them from their humorous side . . . I can't go on every day recording F's bad tempers.'[7]

Evi wrote her mother a 'feather-brained, irrepressible, long letter of wild excitement'[8] from the Bigelows who, taken in by her manic cheerfulness, had invited her to stay with them. Elizabeth had feared that the Bigelows were misled, and that they would be disillusioned the first time she became bored or cross. She could only hope that Evi would steady down to a persistent amiability, and that if she practised long enough it would become a habit. Liebet was also in America and had been living with some Vassar graduates and rapidly developed an enthusiasm for the feminist life. Her mother disillusioned her by pointing out that a spinster, unlike a widow, was 'only half a woman'. Later Liebet was invited to stay with some millionaires and at this news her mother was delighted as 'millionaires attract other millionaires'.[9]

At Easter Elizabeth had a letter from Liebet telling her that Evi had quarrelled with the Bigelows, as had been feared, and moved into a cottage, living the simple life she had so often heard her mother extol, digging in the garden and 'wreaking her discipline on bees'.[10] Her mother hated the thought of it and began to toy with the idea of wintering in California with the two of them. At the same time all the American newspapers published the news of her marriage and the English ones soon picked it up. Elizabeth was sick with anxiety about Trix and Martin, for news of her activities was dangerous for her daughters in Germany and this particular item might inflame the German authorities. She hoped it had not been Evi who had leaked the news but feared it might have been.

Elizabeth and Francis were forced to flee from the attentions of reporters down to Cornwall. H.B. spent the Easter holidays with a friend's family in Scotland, and the Russells had a difficult time together. Elizabeth could not conceive why her husband had wooed her as he had, and was bitterly tired of the 'reckless waste of opportunity and happiness'. When they went back to Sussex she spent much of her time in a little tin shed in the grounds, as Mollie had done before her, which she called her 'hutch', and meditated on 'the complete incompatibility of us two wretched mortals'.[11]

Things could not have been more black, or so she thought, until she read in *The Times* that her nephew Jack Waterlow's ship, the *Black Prince*, was lost in the North Sea. Elizabeth hurried over to her sister's house and was met by Margery and her brother Sydney at the door with the news that Jack had been killed. But worse was to follow. A telegram had come to Hatch for Elizabeth.

It was from Teppi and brought the news that Martin was also

dead.

Elizabeth lunched at Hatch and then drove back through the rain and gales tasting the depth of desolation. When she told Francis he was 'very kind and dear' and that night they reached a communion which they had not had since they were married. To Liebet she wrote:

> . . . my poor little Martin – it's too dreadful – I can't bear it – and yet I am going to bear it, and you dear other crabs are going to help by being absolutely quietly courageous over it. What I find most awful is the realization of what my poor Trix is suffering . . . She has been so heroic so long, and so dear and resourceful and dutiful – oh I long to take her on my lap and comfort her. Martin's death is just as directly the result of the war as Johnnie's [Jack's] – it will be days before I get letters telling me why, and so I sit and conjecture and all wrongly, I'm sure.

The seventeeen-year-old Martin had changed schools once again and had been attending Frau Zockder's school in Berlin at the outbreak of the war. Because her money had been frozen in the banks she was not able to pay the fees, and Frau Zockder, naturally, told her that she must leave. Trix went over to sort things out and found her sister's bills 'terrific'.[12] Teppi then put Martin to work in a children's hospital near Bremen and was preparing a 'sweet little room'[13] for her in a cottage she had rented when she had a telephone call that Martin had been taken to hospital. Later it was discovered that the child had been playing the violin in front of an open window wearing damp clothing and had collapsed with double pneumonia. Teppi hurried to the hospital and found her speechless but smiling and she held Teppi's hand very tightly. An important engagement required Teppi to leave that evening and she asked the doctor if she should go to it. He replied that, although it was a serious case, Martin was strong and healthy and he was sure that she would pull through.

Martin died in the night towards dawn. While going through her pitifully few belongings Teppi found a diary which reiterated that she had not stolen the half-crown she had been punished for. Teppi wrote to Elizabeth with the details who telegraphed that her daughter should be buried at Schlagenthin 'near her father who loved her so'. To Liebet she wrote:

> It is the realization of what my poor Trix is enduring [that is the most difficult to bear]. You remember how she broke

down over Papa's death – conceive her situation now. I got a telegram from her saying she was starting for Bremen when Martin died, and had telegraphed to Uncle Bernd. Just before I got a letter from her written on March 20th not mentioning Martin at all, but full of intensest longing and beseeching to let her come to me at the chalet. My instinct was to rush to the chalet and have her there – but I'm told this would be very dangerous for her.

Liebet darling, don't fret – try not to – if you crabs will only hold out and set your teeth and look forward to the happy times that certainly will come, then so can I. But if you aren't able to then I feel that neither shall I be able to. So remember that, won't you, my little blessed crab.

Elizabeth tried to arrange for Trix to escape to California. Trix, however, wrote to say that she wanted to stay in Europe, and then no more letters came from her at all on the subject. Those few that did get through the censors were crazily optimistic about the success of the Germans. Her mother realized that she had been somehow threatened to write in the way that she did, and this did nothing for her peace of mind. To Teppi she wrote:

No one knows better than you how shattered I must be . . . because of everything that preceded this, because of my thoughts of the last time I saw Martin, leaving for ever and ever, without a kiss, without love, after the sad scenes of the last days of the chalet. If only I had held her in my arms once again! To tell her how deeply I loved her, and that it was just because I loved her so that I suffered so greatly on account of what she had done. Teppi, how can anyone bear such things?

Cousin William, that patient shoulder on which Elizabeth had been used to lean in times of trouble, had married an eighteen-year-old girl, and immediately departed for the trenches, assuming never to see her or anyone else again. Elizabeth confided in her diary that life for her was then unbearable – 'no light anywhere'. She longed for Francis to understand what she was going through but he was unable, even for a day, not to go and play bridge at his club, leaving her to eat her heart out alone. She badly missed her children, but beyond that the difficulty she had in relinquishing her idealized love for Francis was her chief torment.

Nobody could understand why, throughout all the tragedies that befell Elizabeth at this time, for all her husband's appalling bullying and childish tantrums, she still appeared to love him. She had become his willing prisoner and was completely submissive to his demands. She never moved without asking permission and constantly begged his pardon if she had done anything contrary to his wishes. She appeared to have entirely forgotten the proud feminist of her youth who had so confidently advocated a shaking-off of all props and the necessity to go it alone. Her husband called her brutal, vicious and sulky (all adjectives, she was not slow to notice, that perfectly described himself) and she reached 'the very dregs of hopeless misery'.[13] Liebet wrote in her memoir of the summer of 1916:

> The sun shone or failed to shine, the English countryside displayed its beauties for all men to see or hid them in rain or mist, but though Elizabeth, as was her wont, made daily note of these phenomena, they could neither lighten, nor deepen her spiritual dependence. [She was] entirely at the mercy of whatever mood Frank chose to indulge in.

Elizabeth's endurance finally cracked when she discovered evidence of Francis's adultery. She interrupted him one day at Gordon Square in the arms of his secretary. Her written records are discreet about the details, but she now had proof of what she had suspected for some time. She could not understand why he needed to do these 'secret things'[14] when they were so happy with each other on the physical side of their marriage. She did not then have any understanding of the product of the pro-consular public school system who needed women for specific purposes: mistress, housekeeper, companion, wife and hostess, and to whom it was often of no consequence whether these functions were embodied in one woman or three. Towards the end of her life Elizabeth wrote to Bertrand asking him to elucidate for her the word 'ambivalence', which he had used in his book *Marriage and Morals*. He replied instancing children's towards their parents, though he might just as well have cited his own and his brother's towards wives.

· 15 ·

Escape

Elizabeth wrote to Liebet at the beginning of August that she was
planning to go to the United States for the winter as soon as she had
seen H.B. safely installed for his first half at Eton. 'I would far rather
die,' she wrote, 'than go on living as I am.' Her departure had,
necessarily, to be by stealth for at Telegraph House she was virtually
incarcerated within the limits of the high wire fencing that surrounded the property. She was able to get out of the house and walk
in the grounds only if she asked permission first, but to go outside the
limits almost always meant bad blood between the couple and days
of temper and fury. In her reduced state Elizabeth felt that it was
easier, for the time being, to submit.

In early September Elizabeth was shocked to discover that her
husband was in the habit of inhaling cocaine. She had found some
in his study and asked him about it and he had boyishly confessed
to it, although afterwards he made her pay for his confession with
free-ranging fury. Fortunately he was due to be away on business to
do with an arms-manufacturing plant of which he was a director,
and for a short time there was peace at Telegraph House. Early on
the day following his return Francis 'made a scene in bed early,
quite suddenly',[1] asking Elizabeth why she had not written to him
while he was away. He insisted on an answer so she had, very
gingerly, to tell him she had not had the heart nor the inclination to
write because they had not parted friends. He appeared, or
pretended to appear, oblivious of this and denied he had been
unkind to her at all, asking for instances. Elizabeth mentioned his
rages over the discovery of the cocaine. He then denied that he had
ever had anything to do with drugs at all, told her she was suffering
from delusions and accused her of insolence, perpetual insolence,
not only to him but to everybody else. He raged and foamed. 'He is
really wonderful the way he accuses me of all the things he has been

doing to me. Well, well,' she confided to her diary.

Elizabeth escaped at the end of September while Francis was on another of his business trips. She left an explanatory note for him, saying his infidelity had 'finally finished'[2] her. She fled to Hatch where she spent the night in fear, and early the following morning she drove to Liverpool and boarded the *Adriatic* at six o'clock in the evening. Her sense of new-found freedom was clouded when the next day the ship was chased by a German submarine, but ten days later she landed safely at the dock in New York and was met by an ecstatic Liebet – Evi had not yet been told of her mother's imminence. Mother and daughter spent a pleasant week in a cottage in the Catskill Mountains outside New York which had been lent to them by friends and then Elizabeth went to see Evi in Connecticut where she was having a difficult time as a teacher in a girls' school. She was easily slighted and bitterly resented not having been told of her mother's arrival until then. They had a furious scene and Evi clearly did not intend to join her mother and sister on a trip to California. When Elizabeth returned to the Catskills she made immediate plans to depart for the West Coast and she and Liebet took a train to Chicago and from there they travelled to California on the Santa Fe line.

In *Christopher and Columbus*, the novel Elizabeth later wrote about this adventure, she describes the sensation of travelling by train from the wintry plains of the October Middle West to the warmth of the Pacific basin:

> Suddenly the door opened and in came summer, with a great warm breath of roses. In a moment the car was invaded by the scent of flowers and of fruit and of something else strange and new and very aromatic. The electric fans were set twirling, the black waiters began to perspire, the passengers called for cold things to eat . . . they could only conclude that they were in heaven. Of course there were orchards after orchards of orange trees covered with fruit, white houses smothered in flowers, gardens overrun with roses, tall groups of eucalyptus trees giving an impression of elegant nakedness, long lines of pepper trees with frail, fern-like branches, and these things continued for the rest of the way; but they would have been as nothing without that beautiful great bland light.

From Los Angeles they took the train to Santa Barbara and then a taxi to a poetic and isolated cottage hotel in San Ysidro where they arrived 'dead tired but very laughy'.[3] Elizabeth allowed the beauty and warmth of the place and the kindness of the people to lull her into a state of gentle euphoria. She procured a little cottage on the estate called Stone Cottage and disappeared into it every morning to work on turning her novel *The Benefactress* into a play, a project she had been working on since arriving in England in September 1914. After a few weeks in the atmosphere of San Ysidro she had finished it, changing the imprisonment for the hero into the outbreak of the First World War. It was called *Ellen in Germany*, and she proudly showed it to a theatrical agent she had been introduced to called Crownin-shield who enlightened her to the fact that no play where the heroine fell in love with a German could possibly be considered for the stage in any of the Allied countries. If she wanted to sell, she should write novels with an anti-German message as a contribution to the war effort. After much heart-searching and a false start on a novel called *Widows* (later to re-emerge as *Expiation*), Elizabeth decided to work on a book based on Martin's letters from Germany at the outbreak of the war and incorporate what she remembered of Teppi's experiences in Berlin. In this way she hoped to vent some of the anti-German spleen that had gathered in her since the death of her daughter and nephew and the virtual imprisonment of Trix. (She had once even expressed regret to Bertrand that her five German nephews were still alive. 'She is a true patriot,' he commented to Lady Ottoline Morrell. 'The Americans would like her.'[4])

Most of the propaganda being disseminated by Britain at that time was calculated to inflame the masses. It had only the half-hearted support of the educated to whom its simplistic sentiments did not appeal. Elizabeth decided to write for the more discriminating members of the British public. In the spoof preface to the book the authoress, Alice Cholmondeley, explains that she has decided to publish the letters of a young English girl to her adored mother at the outbreak of the war because she felt they might have a certain value in helping put together a small corner of a great picture of Germany 'which it will be necessary to keep clear . . . before us if the future of the world is to be saved'. The book is a long way from the truth of that sad correspondence with Martin. Naturally Elizabeth was alive to the possibility that Trix had been identified by the Germans as her daughter, and therefore fiercely repudiated the authorship of *Christine* when it came out, even to her closest friends.

Liebet noticed with surprise that her mother was now able completely to abstract herself from her work. She walked up, after a morning in Stone Cottage, through the sunlit, flower-filled garden where the humming-birds hovered over heliotrope and arum lilies and darted into the bright cones on their quest for nectar, and the turquoise-bellied lizards craned their wrinkled necks to watch her pass, arriving at the restaurant in the best of humours, always entirely her natural self. Their meals were in great contrast to those grim functions that Liebet had tensed herself to endure at Nassenheide when her mother usually arrived reluctantly at the lunch table with her thoughts still very much on the work in hand in her *Treibhaus*. The only cloud between the two was the struggle against Elizabeth's urge to get in touch with Francis. The younger woman was to intercept her mother if she got anywhere near a telephone, as had been agreed between them when Elizabeth was stronger-minded. She dubbed her daughter 'Frying pan' in which she must perforce sizzle rather than jump back into the 'Fire' that was Francis. Finally Liebet failed in her vigilance and Elizabeth cabled Francis their whereabouts at the beginning of November.

As usual she had made friends and adorers from among the guests at the hotel, and hardly an afternoon went by without their being offered a jaunt to see the sights or share hospitality. Christmas came and with it rain. There was no word from Francis. Liebet caught cold and spent Christmas Day in bed and she and her mother played chess all day 'very lonely and sad',[5] both of them thinking of other Christmases. Later Elizabeth wept with despair as she recorded in her diary that 1916 had been the most wretched year of her life and that she had never been so unhappy as from February to September.

Francis arrived, jauntily, unannounced, and quite sure of a welcome, on the fifth of January 1917. Elizabeth's diary from then on is silent and remains so for eighteen months. The other periods in her life when she neglected it are times of great personal conflict and unwilling submission to duty; evidently the reconciliation between the two was not as ecstatic as she had hoped. Liebet remembered that after he arrived in San Ysidro gaiety became sadly limited and 'all their comings and goings were now strictly ordered by a heavy hand, and there was instant retribution in the form of prolonged ill humour at the slightest, even accidental, deviation from the laws set down by the patriarch.'[6] She was also astonished to see that her mother did everything she could to please the dictator.

Liebet herself was happily engaged in a flirtation with a handsome East Coast Ivy Leaguer called Corwin Butterworth. After her stepfather arrived her time with Corwin was strictly chaperoned, but Francis was not to know that it was too late for this kind of supervision: Corwin had already secretly asked Liebet to marry him. The holiday continued for another six weeks and the weather was dull and rainy as if to reflect their mood. In March Elizabeth travelled with her husband as far as New York and saw him off to England on the *Adriatic*. 'It was dreadful being torn away from you, my own sweet little Cortez, my faithful companion for four happy months . . . ' she wrote on the train to Liebet who had decided to stay on.

Elizabeth settled herself into a hotel in Virginia to recover from a face-lift which she had undergone in New York at the end of March. She also managed to finish *Christine*. At the end of April she received a belated letter from Stuart's sister telling her that he had died of wounds on 15 March. He had been shot two days before while serving at the front and Elizabeth could only pray that what he went through before he died was not too agonizing. She regretted all of the times she had laughed at him and his dog-like devotion, and remembered how she had always felt his 'immense affection' for her. He had written her a letter only a few days before his death in which he told her he probably would not come back. He wanted her to know that he felt it was best for his wife that he die as he only wanted her to remember the two happy weeks they had had together. Unfortunately he never knew that he had fathered a daughter. Elizabeth wrote to Liebet:

> . . . well, he's dead and life is getting very much whittled away of all one has had . . . But thank heavens Francis is still in the world – the first one of him is gone, but the second and revised version is still here. Lieb darling, death is the most dreadful thing – it behoves one to live in the utmost peace and love with each other while we've got each other – however tiresome and difficult we are sometimes, we're still alive – that awful, cold, endless death, that wiping out for ever of love and dearness is intolerable to think of . . .

Liebet's personal code was rigidly Christian, and such embracing of despair and nothingness as her mother evinced was highly shocking to the girl.

Having posted this doleful letter off to Liebet, Elizabeth found in her post-box one from her daughter announcing that she intended to marry Corwin. Because of the war and the uncertainty of Liebet's future, they wanted the wedding to take place as soon as possible. Although Elizabeth was sad, for Liebet would be living so far from

England, she was also glad. She pleaded for a little time so that things could be arranged 'straight and proper', writing:

> I'm so very happy that you are happy – and of course I approve. It's true I've exhorted you to think twice before committing yourself to marriage, as well I might, for it is a tremendous adventure, but I've also told you there was nothing in the world like one's own lover and husband – that all other happinesses pale compared to that as sleep is pale and unreal compared to being awake.

Elizabeth returned to California and visited Corwin's small but extremely pretty ranch outside Paso Robles where the couple were going to live. Everyone was astonished at her incredibly rejuvenated appearance, for she looked younger, almost, than her own daughter. Corwin was twelve years older than his future bride; a laconic, impractical, vegetarian stockbroker. Most of the time he sat behind the *Wall Street Journal* watching his stocks and shares rise and fall. He was soon labouring under one of Elizabeth's nicknames, this time 'The Triple Dated Crow' (an inaccurate quotation from *The Tempest*, actually 'treble dated') the meaning of which she found obscure but felt it suited him, and, of course, it also annoyed him. She further alienated him by commenting on his Red Indian appearance and making jokes about squaws and papooses. Then she asked her daughter in a loud aside whether Corwin was a gentleman.

Elizabeth arrived back at Telegraph House to find H.B. ensconced, tall and slim with a perfect Etonian voice and manner and sporting a moustache. He was enjoying the company of his stepfather, who was teaching him Greek. Francis was delighted to find that he was now married to a woman who closely resembled a fourteen-year-old girl, and entirely enveloped her to the exclusion of the world so that Elizabeth considered she was in a 'bath of love'.[7] She regarded her escapade to America as one of the best things she had ever done in her career. Apart from several 'curdled' letters from Evi, who was farming in Oyster Bay, in which she clearly resented the whole world and in particular having to write to her mother and thank her for the money she was sent, the whole summer was an idyll.

In September Bertrand came to live with them in Gordon Square and the house became full of signs of intelligence which it had never had before. Bertrand was sent all the books and reviews that mattered and hung up pictures of Spinoza and Leibnitz. He was also delighted to have more occasion for being with Elizabeth whose mind he respected and whom he therefore treated, she was amused to notice, exactly as if she were a man. He had been latterly involving himself with a pacifist organization called the No Conscription Fellowship, a body opposed to compulsory National Service, and his zeal for the cause had resulted in him being evicted from his flat and forced to seek shelter with his brother. He confided in his sister-in-law that he was getting tired of his work with the fellowship and hoped to have withdrawn in November, for he was thirsting once more for philosophy. He and Francis were, in Elizabeth's view, the greatest contrast and she anticipated that her *ménage* would be one of volcanic interest. She thought Bertrand a 'most charming queer creature – elf-like, Punch-like, imp-like, a Christ and a devil, angelically saintly and thoroughly malignant – the weirdest of human beings . . . '[8] while her husband was solidly aristocratic, practical and reactionary.

One day a friend of Bertrand's, Frank Swinnerton, telephoned Gordon Square and was answered by a little drawling voice, the owner of which recognized his name as the author of *Nocturne* and invited him to tea. Thus the young man put his foot into a new world, formerly closed to him, in which lavender and furs were associated with sophistication, love affairs, pre-war Berlin, sentiment, shrewdness, cruelty and 'unflinching candour about husbands'.[9] He thought her, at first glance, to be no more than a child, but then he observed that the child was precocious and then terrifying. He had heard that she so frightened some men that they trembled under the gaze of her prominent light blue eyes which contained no mercy, and they were annihilated by the 'demurely drawling boldness of her tongue'. As she passed the young man his tea Elizabeth indulged herself in some indiscreet but witty comments about the people they knew in common. Frank Swinnerton interrupted her with the words 'I trust you.' 'Oh, you mustn't do that!' she replied, imagining that the young man in front of her had committed a *naïveté*. A moment later she understood his meaning: he would like to count on her discretion not to misinterpret what *he* said. She concluded that this novelist, who had trapped her into such a protest, must be more complex and less easily demoralized than she had thought. Thereafter she was a true and candid friend to him, while he quickly understood her to be an unusually kind woman, though unhampered by sentimentality so that her judgements often appeared to be cruel or destructive. Vestiges of the gentle and light-spirited woman who wrote *Elizabeth and her German Garden* still clearly lingered in the woman sitting in front of him, and the pleasure her readers took in the discomfort of such pompous and overbearing people as are depicted in the *Caravaners* was in line with the tenor of her personality:

> . . . we are, as it were, hand in glove with the author, who, perceiving our enjoyment, will playfully decorate her accurate observation with newly invented absurdities of the most scathing and, to the victim, infuriating order. Thus the lucid ridicule of dullness and brutality which quicken all her books was what produced for every hearer an awful delight in her more intimate conversation. I have never known any woman with the same *comic* detachment of mind.[10]

Swinnerton maintained that her style did not change, although in reality it did for every book she wrote, and shortly after their first meeting she was to explore, for her, entirely unknown territory. He described her as seen through her books where she unobtrusively depicted herself as she was or had been, surrounded by husbands or friends seen in what Jane Austen called 'open pleasantry', and he thought her unique. He was also sharp enough to see that her talents lay in fun, satirical portraiture, and farcical comedy, all qualities that were or would soon be scorned by the rising young writers of Swinnerton's generation who were obsessed by the modern dilemma – the grim, post-war search for a more direct method.

In February 1918 Liebet gave birth to a girl who was christened Clare Elizabeth. When the news arrived at Gordon Square Francis had no doubt that he was a grandfather. Bertrand attempted to explain to him that his wife's daughter's daughter was merely his step-granddaughter and no blood relation at all, but in vain. Elizabeth, bursting with pride, wrote to Liebet that she was going out to buy a grandmother's outfit complete with spectacles, mob cap, bath chair and snowy hair.

In May Bertrand wrote an article for the *Tribunal* about the probability of the American troops' imminent occupation of England or France. 'Whether or not they will prove efficient against the Germans [they] will no doubt be capable of intimidating the strikers, an occupation to which the American army is accustomed at home,' he wrote. In the dangerous career Bertrand had embarked upon when he loudly became a pacifist, this was the last straw as far as the authorities were concerned and he was committed to six months in Brixton Gaol. Fortunately Francis, having been there himself, knew everyone concerned, so that when the Home Secretary was disobliging about giving the prisoner aristocratic status, Francis remarked, 'Oh, you know, he was my fag at Winchester. He'll do it.'[11] And he did. Elizabeth was once again startled by this, by now, chain of convicts she seemed to husband in her life and meditated deeply on the subject.

Bertrand was allowed a special cell and, for 6d a day, the services of another prisoner to relieve him 'from unaccustomed tasks and offices'. He was allowed his own food and books and newspapers as long as they were not of a pacific nature, and also visits by three friends or relatives at a time. Bertrand had compiled a weekly list of who was to come with whom before he went into prison. Elizabeth was to come with Reginald Clifford Allen, later Lord Allen of Hurtwood, a Labour politician and author of *Conscription and Conscience* and himself recently gaoled for three months as a deserter. Francis was one of the first visitors and he went alone, thereby wasting two places that week, for Bertrand's friends were all clamouring to see him. The prisoner was, as ever, patient with his brother and explained later by letter, 'You seem to think I should grow indifferent on that point but I am certain you are wrong. Seeing the people I am fond of is not a thing I should grow indifferent to . . . ' Elizabeth helped to smuggle letters in and out of Brixton to ease the path of a new love affair between Bertrand and Lady Constance Malleson (more commonly known by her stage name, Colette) as well as to his current mistress, Lady Ottoline Morrell. Once Elizabeth and Ottoline went to visit him together, and they were an extraordinary sight to see, for Ottoline was nearly six feet tall and Elizabeth barely over five. Ottoline informed her on that occasion that the general view was that Elizabeth was without sufferance or enthusiasm, a piece of information that naturally rankled, though Elizabeth was wise enough to see that it was because the accusation was too near the truth, though she never would have suspected or believed it left to herself. 'But Bertie does inspire me to be better,' she wrote to her new tall friend, explaining how she would cope with the insight into her character that Ottoline had been kind enough to give her ' . . . he really is extraordinarily like Christ – a very intelligent Christ.'

That summer George Santayana was invited down for the weekend to Telegraph House. Arriving at Petersfield station, he looked around for Francis's car, and then he noticed Elizabeth sitting in a small grey motor. Although Santayana claimed in his memoirs that this was the first time they had met, they did in fact know each other very well. They had first met at the Smith Square salon and Elizabeth had often visited the philosopher in his rooms in Oxford while taking her son out from Summer Fields. They had spent many enjoyable afternoons and on some of them discussed topics that H.B. only understood as being well over the top of his head. Santayana was astonished to find Elizabeth, as she sat waiting for him in the car, looking hardly older than a child, and he had to remind himself that she had three grown-up daughters and a son at Eton. He was glad that his travels had trained him not to doubt anything because what he saw seemed odd. Even at close quarters and in the open air she seemed very young, 'A little thing with a little nose . . . and a little innocent mouth.'[12] He climbed into the seat next to her after slinging his luggage in the back, and she explained at once that she wanted to see him before he spoke to her husband because of the letter Santayana had written before the marriage likening Francis to Henry VIII and Goethe. She wanted to reconcile him to the marriage and convince him that she was indeed the providential Frau Stein 'destined to lift her happier Goethe into a great statesman and man of the world'. She wanted to demonstrate to him that she was the first *decent* woman to take Francis in hand. She instanced an occasion when she and Francis visited a friend of his just after the wedding who had assumed she must be 'improper' to have married Francis, a reflection, she thought, on the kind of women that got him in their power. She felt that she had the intelligence and character to hold him permanently and to make a new man of him, that he was basically good but that the people he had associated with in the past had degraded him and smothered his true and beautiful nature. She was so eloquent that Santayana could not help but see that there were elements of truth in her prognostication. After all, had he not seen that Russell had suffered when she left him to go to America? Had not the earl protested that he loved and worshipped her and that his life was blighted by her absence? Santayana understood Elizabeth to be anything but the savage and cruel woman of her reputation and found her cool but tender, with infinitely honed sensibilities and a determination to do good in the world which was as unusual as it was refreshing. He felt that she always saw the good side in people first, as a reflection, no doubt, of her own innocence, and was shocked and bitterly angry when their behaviour revealed them to be less than perfect.

Santayana marvelled that so many women in Francis's life had had the same determination to redeem him and 'anchor him in the safe haven of their arms': he supposed that their vanity conspired with Francis's persuasive charm to blind them in their infatuation.

Elizabeth told him, with another display of unflinching candour, that Francis was very different as a lover than he was as a husband. His ways of making love were capricious and exacting. Elizabeth said he was sadistic, that 'lovemaking was no laughing matter, no playfulness of a mad moment'.[13] It was a loving wife's sworn duty to be obedient; and if she rebelled and fled from her husband, he said she was cruel. She confided years later to the startled and embarrassed philosopher that Francis had used her as a sexual chamber pot, as had her first husband, and that the reason she married two such men would forever remain a mystery to her as well as to everyone else.

Edgar Jepson was also invited for a weekend and brought with him his sharp-eyed daughter, Margaret. (She was later to become the novelist Margaret Birkinshaw and the mother of Fay Weldon.) Unlike Santayana, who had thought Elizabeth beautiful, Margaret Jepson thought her hostess plain, with a face 'rather like a potato'.[14] She saw Francis as a big man dressed shabbily, but with a certain kind of expensive shabbiness that could only indicate that he was an earl. He was sometimes like Lord Emsworth and at others like a circus ring master, forever cracking his whip and demanding to be obeyed. She was not a member of the grown-up company, and was supposed by them to be a nice little friend for H.B. whom she thought unhappy and boorish. She spent much time wandering round the house and grounds alone. In the kitchen quarters lots of little white Maltese terriers leapt out at her, barking. Russell would take the dogs for walks, and it was strange, she remembered, to hear this large man call them 'Poppet, my love . . . Poppet, my lion!'

It was during that weekend that Elizabeth found Francis chasing Miss Young round the dining-room table shouting at her that she was 'a speckle-bellied, broken-legged old hen' and a 'speckle-bellied louse'. Anna Paues, a tall and clever don at Cambridge and a friend of Elizabeth's who was also there, was delayed returning from a walk on the downs. There was general speculation at lunch as to whether she might be stuck behind some new wire fences that Francis had recently erected around his land. 'Oh, no,' drawled Elizabeth, 'she would simply step over them.'[15] Miss Jepson found this extraordinarily funny because the timing and delivery had been perfect. Most of the witty things that her hostess entertained her friends with simply could not be retold successfully for that reason. Her comedy was of the moment.

Margaret Jepson also noticed that there was a young and attractive housemaid there called Elizabeth who regarded Russell and his wife and guests with a supercilious air. Possibly the earl's dalliance extended to her as well. The Countess Russell had very acute antennae about most things and she may have had an inkling or anyway suspicions about his behaviour. Certainly there was an element of revenge in some of her conduct towards him. For instance, one day Miss Young called her into the kitchen and showed her an egg which the chicken that was going to be served for dinner had laid *after* its neck had been wrung by the gardener. Elizabeth regarded it thoughtfully for a few moments and then told Miss Young to serve it to the earl the next morning for breakfast. After Francis had eaten the egg Elizabeth asked him how he had enjoyed it. He told her that he had enjoyed it neither more nor less than he usually did his breakfast egg. 'Good,' replied his wife, 'because that egg was laid by a dead hen.' Without a word Francis walked to the window, threw up the sash and vomited into the shrubbery.[16]

Elizabeth had nursed an ambition since she first encountered the genius of E. M. Forster to persuade some brilliant man to write a book with her in the form of an exchange of letters. They were to be between a literary gentleman called Mr Arbuthnot and a girl called Ellen Wemyss whom he had met on a train and lent a book. Bertrand seemed a perfect partner to the project and they began to write to each other in this manner. His first letter, written as from 200, St James's Square, commenced:

Dear Miss Wemyss,
I am glad you liked my book – I am half surprised to find myself answering your letter, which in another mood I should scarcely have done. But there is a peculiar satisfaction in discovering that others can still believe the exalted sentiments to which one has grown indifferent. One is led to suppose that you have never known an author, for, if you had, you would realize what disappointing folk we are. Did you ever hear of the free-thinking French Jesuit who spent his life converting the Chinese, saying that no pleasure is so exquisite as persuading others of what one does not believe oneself? Perhaps the poor devil envied his yellow catachumens. Let us hope he was too considerate to respond to their zeal as I have to yours. As I looked out upon the dripping trees of the Square, the gloom and grime of a winter morning in London brought into my mind a strong desire for the

clean-cut severity of the Yorkshire moors. Perhaps there
'visions' have a potency of which they are robbed, for me,
by the 'actualities' of a complex metropolitan existence.

After the first few exchanges Bertrand opined that Miss Wemyss was
a very silly girl whereupon Elizabeth became distant and the project
folded, leaving Bertrand to conclude that the character of the woman
was not as fictitious as he had imagined. Some months later
Elizabeth persuaded Hugh Walpole to take Bertrand's place. He
agreed and the first few exchanges went well. Then Hugh (as
Arbuthnot) wrote such a letter that Elizabeth gave a yelp:

> To be frank it *wasn't* a delightful letter, and in fact all page
> two would simply shut her up forever . . . she is your
> refuge and refreshment in a dusty and harassed life – she
> is your cup of cool water. But what could she say to your
> jeers except hurt things?

Hugh suggested changing parts, he taking on Ellen and she Mr
Arbuthnot, but Elizabeth protested that she didn't feel 'manly
enough' for the role. Yet again the project was abandoned.

At eleven o'clock in the morning of 11 November 1918 the war
officially ended. The King's guns which had previously sounded as
signals for air raids were fired all at once to mark the signing of the
Armistice. Elizabeth and Francis were at Gordon Square at the time
and in common with everyone else rushed out on to the streets in the
sure knowledge that this time it was exactly the opposite of a raid.
Everybody talked to whoever they met. Perfect strangers kissed each
other and, although Elizabeth managed to avoid being kissed by
anyone herself, she met an unknown Belgian officer and they
beamed at each other. Elizabeth said, *'Eh bien, c'est fini'*, and he
replied, *'Oui, c'est chic,'* which the countess thought 'a heavenly
comment'.[17]

London was mad with joy, but there was also a solemnity about it,
for every person had suffered from the war and some of them badly.
Elizabeth began to feel great anxiety about Trix when she heard
there was a general state of hunger in Germany which could quickly
lead to anarchy. She wrote telling her to write to the chalet and
hoping that soon it would be possible for both of them to get there.
Elizabeth sent her note to August, the caretaker, with instructions
for him to send it on to Teppi and for her to get it to Trix. In the end
Trix received it, and was relieved to be able to write her mother long
and detailed accounts of everything that had happened to her. She
posted them off, as her mother had instructed, to the chalet to wait

for her arrival there.

Two months after the signing of the Armistice Elizabeth wrote in her diary: 'Frank did something wrong.'

On the afternoon of 15 January 1919 Francis had gone, as usual, to play bridge at his club. A business associate had rung Gordon Square about his overdraft and given Elizabeth the impression that it was urgent. Francis had instructed her never to tell his business associates where he was in the afternoons so she rang the club herself to leave a message. The Reform told her that her husband was not there and that he hardly ever came in in the afternoons. Elizabeth was astounded, and when she inquired of her husband where he had been that afternoon he replied innocently that he had been playing bridge at his club as usual.

For four weeks she remained undecided, but as her suspicions had been aroused she noticed that he did too many 'secret things that are entirely incompatible with marriage'.[18] This, combined with his bad temper, which was again beginning to take over as his normal mood, was making her ill and decided her definitely to leave him. The difficulties were enormous. She thought of going to America for three months and taking their secretary, Miss King, with her, but Francis had sacked her and had employed another 'for carrying on purposes'. Francis's habit of a lifetime – dalliance with servants and secretaries – could not be broken by any amount of good intentions. He had secretly taken another office outside the house which was where he repaired in the afternoons, his wife never suspecting what was happening. The name of the new secretary was Miss Otter.

Elizabeth wrote to Liebet:

> You know what he was like at San Ysidro – well add to that and worse than that of tempers, rudeness, secret plottings, everlasting gambling for high stakes at bridge and adultery. I caught him at it that last spring and forgave it but said I wouldn't again forgive. Now I've discovered other times and I'm sick to death.

What she found most extraordinary about him was that in spite of his affairs with other women he appeared to be still fond of her.

On 18 February 1919 Louey, Elizabeth's mother, died of flu and pneumonia. She had a peaceful end and never knew that she was ill from first to last, which, considering what a hypochondriac she had always been, was ironic. Charlotte came to stay with her sister for the funeral and they discussed Francis, coming to the conclusion that there was nothing for it but for Elizabeth, or any decent woman, to leave him. Charlotte's own husband was living in open sin with a woman who was manifestly not his wife in an hotel in Brighton, so she had had some experience herself. Elizabeth wanted to go again to the States to see her daughters and new granddaughter. Evi had been ill but was recovered, and once again her mother was overcome with pity for her eldest daughter, at the loneliness of the life that she was living. She could not keep a job or make friends and was entirely dependent on the money that Elizabeth sent her. However, she felt that the chalet should be seen to first and, most important, some contact made with Trix who might be in all sorts of difficulties which Elizabeth could help her out of with money, a place to live or advice.

A few weeks later Elizabeth fled from her husband once again, this time to her beloved brother Sydney's house in Berkhamsted. She had left behind her a note for Francis telling him that she had found out what he was up to and, as she wrote to Liebet, 'that when I forgave him before I said it would settle me if it happened again and that it *had* settled me'. She imagined he was quite happy, having found and read the note, plotting how to punish her. She implored her children not to worry about her: her family were being supportive and she was feeling nothing like as wretched as she had done before she knew how bad he was. She had used to think of him as good and honest but cursed with an ungovernable temper, now she was in no dilemma. Indeed she was apprehended by her friends to be in great high spirits at that time and Hugh Walpole, who spent 'a gorgeous time' with her in March commented in his diary: 'I really like her far better than any other woman alive. She has everything – brains, heart, humour, pluck . . . !'

One bright event was the publication of her novel *Christopher and Columbus* which, despite its somewhat tepid reviews, was selling more successfully than any of the others since *Elizabeth and her German Garden,* no doubt because it hardly mentioned the war at all and concentrated relentlessly on the frivolities to be encountered on the West Coast of America. 'This cheers me up and makes me able to face life,' she wrote to Liebet.

Elizabeth's cousin, Katherine Mansfield, who was by then married to the editor of the *Athenaeum*, John Middleton Murry, reviewed the book in the magazine with tact and perception:

> She is, in the happiest way, conscious of her own particular vision, and wants no other . . . In a world where there are so many furies with warning fingers it is good to know of someone who goes her own way finding a gay garland,

and not forgetting to add a sharp-scented spray or two and
a bitter herb that its sweetness may not cloy.

Elizabeth was exhausted emotionally, mentally and physically by
the pain of her final disillusionment and by the effort of detaching
herself from her husband. Before she was free to go to the chalet she
was required to hold herself together for a few months while the
depressing and boring details of the separation were somehow gone
through. She rented an unfurnished flat in Whitehall Court and
realized that her furniture and books would have to be removed from
her husband's houses by stealth, for Francis refused to believe that
she had left him for good. She chose a time when she knew he would
be away and, with the enthusiastic connivance of the staff at both
Telegraph House and Gordon Square, she hired a firm called
Shoolbreds and removed everything that was hers. When Francis
discovered the deception, he was so enraged that he immediately
issued a writ against Elizabeth for theft, claiming that she had taken
some of his things as well. He met Bertrand in the street and foamed
and fulminated against his wife, vowing revenge in court. Bertrand
was alarmed, telephoned Elizabeth and the next day he wrote to his
brother:

> When I saw you yesterday your account of what you were
> doing as regards Elizabeth so surprised me that I hardly
> knew what to say. On thinking it over, however, I feel that
> I should not be acting kindly to you if I did not tell you
> that I think you are acting unwisely from the point of view
> of your reputation and your interests . . .

He went on to say that he thought Francis's grievance a small one,
that he did not gather that Elizabeth had removed anything that
Francis could prove to be his and that she had an undoubted right to
remove anything she wanted to if it was her own. As regards how she
did it, Bertrand suggested that Francis's tyrannical ways made any
other alternative unworkable. He warned his brother that if it came
to court Elizabeth might be forced to tell the judge that her husband
had been unfaithful to her, and Francis himself knew that she had
enough proof to convince a divorce court.

> I do not dwell on the fact that the spirit you are showing
> must strike everyone as cruel and vindictive; but for my
> own part, since you are my brother and I have affection for
> you, that is the one chief reason why I hope that you will
> reconsider the matter and agree to an amicable

settlement.

Francis wrote back by return of post and accused Bertrand of belittling his grievance and for not wholeheartedly attempting to persuade Elizabeth to go back to him. He also accused him of being on Elizabeth's side. Bertrand replied that Francis was like the people who thought he was on the side of the Germans in the war, that it was a pity to quarrel and that Elizabeth had as a result of his pleadings 'become exceedingly inclined to a reconciliation, but after your writ her mood changed'.

At this time Francis did not want a divorce for he was only too aware that Elizabeth had evidence of his infidelity that she would not hesitate to reveal if she was forced to. Neither did she, either then or later, for in those days divorce carried with it a severe stigma. Also, although she would have been allowed to retain her title, she would thereafter have had to call herself Elizabeth, Countess Russell, signalling to all her status. Worst of all, she would have had to renounce her seat in the gallery in the House of Lords which it was her right to occupy whenever she chose and where she often went in the afternoons to hear her husband speak both before and after their separation.

Finally Francis sued the removal firm. The case of Russell versus Shoolbred & Shoolbred naturally caused a stir in society circles and Francis found himself once more engaged in litigation concerning a wife. (In his life he spent £30,000 on it, the equivalent today of half a million pounds, not counting the £400 a year he was obliged to give Mollie as a settlement.) The case was a lengthy and expensive one for both of them. Elizabeth hired two counsel, and as the facts stood it looked black for Francis. Elizabeth had given him £600 for a wedding present and requested in return that he move the little tin house she called her hutch nearer to Telegraph House. She also contributed £100 to the redecoration of the Gordon Square house. Francis's argument rested solely on the verbal agreement he had had with Elizabeth when Telegraph House was being redecorated that she would pay for half of it and when the time came to do so she offered her furniture to be set against the £100. 9s. 7d of her share, although its value was far more than that. Some time in 1915 she had lent him £300 which had not been repaid and there was no mention of the money she gave him in 1914.

Elizabeth took enormous trouble before the case commenced to go to all the places she had bought things from for both houses and get receipts and invoices for them. She then rang Francis and told him what she herself had actually bought, which included most of the things he accused her of stealing. Realizing he was on soft ground, he agreed to whatever she wanted, but as soon as he had put the phone down he simply drew up another list of objects: some cushions, electric light fittings, tennis balls, a hammock and a tea table. Each item was the subject of lengthy cross-examination by Sir Edward Marshall Hall who was acting for Elizabeth. When she stood in the witness box she could hardly see over the top and a box had to be found for her to stand on as if she were a child.

Q: Now about the hammock. You bought the hammock on the 17th April 1916?
A: Yes.
Q: Is it a suitable hammock for Lord Russell?
A: No.
Q: Did you ever give it to him?
A: Never.
Q: You have more regard for life?
A: And for the hammock.

Mr Mould, acting for Francis:

Q: Now with regard for the hammock. Do you say you did not give that to Lord Russell?
A: Certainly not. It was entirely for me. It would not have held him.
Q: The hammock, I take it, was to be for general use at Telegraph House?
A: No, it was solely for me. I used to allow small visitors to sit in it.

The verdict was a foregone conclusion and the whole event looked upon by everyone as an expensive farce, but one that provided great entertainment for the spectators. Elizabeth was exonerated completely, and the cool manner with which she conducted herself in the witness box was in great contrast to the heated bluster of her husband.

When the proceedings were over, with what little energy she could summon, she sub-let her flat and 'crawled'[19] to the chalet.

· 16 ·

In the Mountains

Elizabeth had feared, during the war, that the chalet would be looted or occupied by starving peasants or careless soldiers, but August had fended off all invaders. The place 'reeked' of the alternately perturbed and placid summer of 1914 when she had been in love with Francis, exasperated with Martin and happy with Liebet and Vernon Lee. She continually 'saw' Cousin William leaning from the window of the room he used to occupy. 'It is full of ghosts, but I won't be German and sentimental, and I turn my back resolutely on them and my face to the future that is still left,' she wrote to Liebet.

Letters from Trix awaited her, some written in 1917, which contained pages of enthusiasm about a man called Melilfretter, a doctor whom Trix was going to marry. Elizabeth assumed that he must have been 'pretty awful' from her daughter's prolix explanations that she would not mind him really. Another more recent letter contained the news that she was about to be married to a forty-year-old German officer called Anton von Hirschberg, former adjutant during the war to Crown Prince Rupprecht of Bavaria, General Field Marshal of the Bavarian and Prussian armies and regarded by the Jacobites as the rightful King of England because of his direct descent from James 1. Hitler in time was to declare that he should be crowned king of Germany but was deterred by Prince Rupprecht's vocal abhorrence of himself.

'Tony' had no money and Elizabeth greatly feared that he thought he was going to live on hers. She had little faith in Trix's shrewdness in her choice of lovers, though it was clear that she was very much in love and wrote ecstatically that Tony was wonderful. Her mother was sad, for she knew that being married to a German would cut Trix off from the rest of her family – for years to come there would be mistrust and dislike between the Germans and the Allied countries. On the other hand she had known that Trix *would* one day marry a

German, ever since the time when, as a child, she had set off in the carriage to keep house for Herr Braun. It was beyond Elizabeth's strength to go to the wedding in Bamberg, although she was invited and it was not impossible to get there. The truth was that she could hardly bear to hear German spoken any more. Trix was personally insulted and never forgave her mother.

There were threatening letters from Francis's solicitors and a letter which gave Elizabeth unqualified happiness from his brother:

> It is quite hateful to think of you being so tormented and battered. I wish you were coming here [Dorset] to listen to the sea on the rocks and watch the gulls sailing through the sky. But the Chalet ought to be healing . . . Now I hope you have done with [Francis]. Remember how many gay and delicious things there are in the world – don't forget that you have won liberty, which is worth a price – and that you can build up friendships with people who will appreciate you without wanting to destroy you . . .

Elizabeth was revived and inspired by this and began work on her next novel, *In the Mountains*, taking the title from a passage in Nietzsche, 'In the mountains of truth you never climb in vain.' The novel describes a woman fleeing to her chalet from some dreadful event in England. She remains there alone contemplating the ruins of her life until two sisters – aspects of the authoress – pass by and ask if the chalet is a hotel, for they are exhausted and seeking shelter. The narrator takes them in, they stay and she finds herself drawn into their curious lives. Eventually her uncle, the Dean, appears 'and the rude wind . . . frisked . . . about his apron, twitching it up and bellying it out'. He falls in love with the younger of the two visitors and there is a happy ending. The book is not intended solely to afford pleasure to the reader, for in it Elizabeth sought to exorcize the 'dreadful betrayal of trust that is the blackest wretchedness of all' that she had experienced at the hands of her husband. She came to the conclusion that she would rather have loved thoroughly and been vulnerable and hurt than never to have felt anything, just to have been a sort of 'amiable amoeba'. She plumbed the depth of her worst fear:

> I'm afraid of loneliness; shiveringly, terribly afraid. I don't mean the ordinary, physical loneliness, for here I am deliberately travelled away from London to get to it, to its spacious healing. I mean the awful loneliness of spirit which is the ultimate tragedy of life . . . It is a comfort to

215

> write this. To write does make one in some strange way
> less lonely. Yet – having to look at oneself in the glass for
> companionship – isn't that to have reached the very
> bottom level of loneliness?[1]

Elizabeth spent much time meditating in a spot overlooking the most magnificent views of the mountains opposite. There she had dallied with Wells and later with Francis and she called it 'the poetry spot'. This time she took Coco and found great comfort in his presence, 'for he at least is simple and kind'.[2] Trix came to the chalet for a few weeks after her wedding and her mother, assuming that the war and marriage had matured her scatterbrained daughter, started by talking to her as she did to Liebet, with candour and humour. She very soon discovered that Trix never listened to her, never answered questions and was 'amazingly indiscreet',[3] repeating to others everything she was told. She had no curiosity about her brother and sisters, and her mother decided not to tell her about her separation from Francis, something Trix made easy by never inquiring. Search as she would, Elizabeth could find no common ground on which they could begin to build a new relationship.

She returned to England to spend Christmas with H.B. at the Waterlows. Only just beginning to recover from the breakdown of her marriage and much else, she was shocked to discover Francis was spreading slander amongst all her friends, while H.B. had reached his penultimate year at Eton and was distinguishing himself by having an affair with the forty-year-old wife of one of the tutors. The headmaster felt that under the circumstances, and taking into account that he was obviously not academically minded, it was probably better that he be removed from the school. He had not been very happy there, for although his German accent had disappeared his name caused animosity among his more patriotic schoolfellows. The activities of General Sixt von Arnim during the war had not escaped their attention.

There was no chance, because of this 'removal', that H.B. would be accepted at an English university. Elizabeth attempted to keep her son under close scrutiny after he had left school, but the tutor's wife followed him to London and made difficulties, persuading H.B. that he had a beautiful singing voice, and that his mother was overlooking a great talent if she ignored it. This only determined Elizabeth to send the boy away as soon as possible before the arrival of the woman's husband with a horse whip. She wrote to Liebet and suggested that H.B. stay with her on the ranch and help Corwin with the work. She felt that the independent atmosphere of America was exactly what was needed to make a man of him. 'He's very obedient and good and would give no trouble,' she explained, 'but at present he has no initiative. That I hope will change.' She offered to pay £250 a year for his board and lodging at Paso Robles and he would also have 1,000 marks* a year of his own, as did all the children, from the residue of the von Arnim estate. Corwin reluctantly agreed and H.B. was despatched to America 'full of beans and joy and looking forward and good resolutions'.[4]

In May Elizabeth met a woman, Mary Frere, who told her an intriguing story. Twenty-four years previously she had had a son by a sporting gentleman called Colonel Reeves. She put the child, christened Alexander Stuart Frere-Reeves, into an orphanage and completely ignored his existence, but she had recently heard that he had fought bravely in the war and had belatedly gone up to Cambridge as an undergraduate after he was demobbed, as many veterans over a certain rank were then able to do. His mother visited him there, to the huge embarrassment of the young man, and found him desperately poor, living on sandwiches and working during the vacation at any job he could get to pay for his tuition. Elizabeth met him by design at a party given by Arnold Bennett and they became 'tremendous friends'.[5] He told her that he had joined the army in August 1914, served in Egypt, Gallipoli and in the trenches in France, holding a commission in the East Kent Yeomanry, and was seconded to the RFC as flying officer in 1917. His best friend was J. B. Priestley, with whom he was now editing *Granta*, the Cambridge magazine. Elizabeth recognized a quality of brilliance in the young man which she found attractive and which would one day take him far, she thought, if he was given the chance. Although he was short, only a few inches taller than she was, he had dash, good looks, charm and a sense of humour. She offered to employ him during the summer vacation to catalogue her books at the chalet and followed the invitation up with a letter. He gratefully accepted.

It was Frank Swinnerton who told Elizabeth, a week before her return to the chalet in June, that the critic and short-story writer Katherine Mansfield, who had written such a favourable review of *Christopher and Columbus*, was her cousin from New Zealand, Kathleen Beauchamp. Elizabeth wrote to her and arranged to visit her at her house in Hampstead for tea. The two writers had met only occasionally over the years at Beauchamp blood-parties in Kent,

*£1,100 today.

and Elizabeth had not been popular with her New Zealand cousins ever since she had referred to one of Katherine's sisters, Jeanne, in a carrying voice as 'a little New Zealand frump'.[6]

> A thousand devils are sending Elizabeth without her
> German Garden to tea tomorrow – her last time before
> she goes abroad to her Swiss chalet. I expect she will stay
> at longest half an hour – she will be, oh such a bundle of
> artificialities – but I can't put her off . . .

Katherine wrote to her friend Violet Schiff. Possibly Katherine was more ashamed than scornful, for the last time she had seen Elizabeth was when introducing her to her first husband, the singer George Bowden, whom she had married because she was pregnant with another man's child. The marriage had not lasted much beyond the wedding day, Katherine lost the child and the whole episode was one of which she would rather not have been reminded.

The meeting was, contrary to her expectations, the beginning of a new and valuable friendship for both of them. They fell easily and immediately into the Beauchamp 'feminines' habit of discussing husbands and 'family love':[7] Elizabeth told Katherine that she had no use for a physical lover 'to go to bed with', that her very being, her gift, her vitality, depended on her not surrendering sexually to a man since her disastrous marriage. In retrospect the over-sensitive younger woman was shocked by their talk and considered her cousin had a 'vulgar little mind'.[8] They also talked about writing and Katherine's health, and Elizabeth urged her to come to the invigorating atmosphere of Montana in Switzerland, to be near her; to have somebody from the family near by; to continue their discourse which they had both found so enjoyable; to each write the novel they had yet to write; to bully and encourage each other – 'all that'.[9]

Elizabeth came away inspired to write something that was not filled with gay garlands tempered with a bitter herb. She wanted to write a novel about her marriage to Francis with no sham or pity, and within three days of her arrival at the chalet, galvanized by a 'horrible insulting letter'[10] she found waiting for her from her husband, she began *Vera*, which was to be the most highly acclaimed of all her novels. It was to be about a truly dreadful man and his second wife and victim. She had also planned a continually expanding and contracting house party to which she had invited people of whom she was particularly fond. First came Cobden-Sanderson and his wife, Ann, who was the daughter of Richard Cobden, the Whig politician and founder of the Anti-Corn-Law League. Maud Ritchie, the large and talented daughter of Lord Ritchie of Dundee was invited, as well as a young Russian diplomat and socialite, Gabrielle Wolkov, who was a friend of Diaghilev. Festing Jones, the biographer of Samuel Butler, came, and Augustine Birrell the biographer of Charlotte Brontë and Hazlitt. There was much talk of biography, and they spent happy hours thinking up and laying traps for their own biographers. Robert Trevelyan, great nephew of Macaulay and Cambridge undergraduate friend of Bertrand Russell, Margery Waterlow, Elizabeth's lovely niece who was married to John Norton, and other visitors all in their turn followed the ox cart up to the chalet. It was to be the first of many summers during which hospitality was generous, hearts were broken and eternal friendships were forged.

Frere-Reeves travelled to the chalet filled with misgivings. He had no idea what to expect and had no experience of the kind of people he had been told he would meet there. He knew such people existed but thought of them as being so rarefied in their way of life as hardly to be part of the human race. He was astonished to discover that they were the same as anybody else except that they were unfailingly amusing, not to say brilliantly witty, 'the most brilliant people from the most brilliant era',[11] and friendly. They pretended to be living the rugged and simple life and romantically saw themselves as coming back to nature while in reality they were surrounded by every conceivable luxury. If Frere had been losing his faith in goodness and beauty in common with his post-war generation, then this experience reorientated him as nothing else would have done. Although he was an employee he was meticulously included in the general gaiety: 'Bring your own salt,'[12] they joked, so that he could sit below it as he felt he should. In deep gratitude he efficiently catalogued all the books (persuading Wolkov to help him with the German ones) and did everything in his power to see to the smooth running of the house party. It was not long before his hard and conscientious work as a self-appointed major-domo led him to be nicknamed *Lieber Gott*. Elizabeth enjoyed his company and invited him regularly on her morning walks. She wrote to Liebet:

> We are very happy here just now and I only wish you and Corwin and the spawn were here too. I take no notice of my guests and work just the same, and I think they like this. I know I would if I stayed a long time in a house – heavenly never to see one's hostess . . .

Elizabeth's way of working had become much more ordered and

time-consuming over the years than the rapid jottings and snatched hours at Nassenheide. After she had decided on her subject she bought many little hard-backed exercise books and wrote the whole novel out in them first in her spidery handwriting. This she copied on to a battered Remington typewriter with a German keyboard, using two fingers and triple spacing on long foolscap paper. After this was blackened by corrections she typed it out again and corrected it again. Even when the house was full of guests she never varied her working day. She appeared in the dining-room where breakfast was served for guests at eight o'clock, chose a favoured guest and went for a walk while waiting for the post to come at nine-thirty. She worked and wrote letters, sometimes as many as sixty a day, in the Little Chalet for the whole morning, emerging for lunch and occasionally between times, appearing and disappearing like royalty. In the afternoon she played a little chess and then worked until tea which she took in front of the fire in the hall, after which she worked until eight. After dinner the guests played fiercely at intellectual games such as writing two lines of a sonnet or limerick each and then passing it on to the next person to write the following two lines and so on. Another was choosing the two people in history or fiction they would most like to have been their parents, with such pairings as Wordsworth and Cleopatra, or Keats and Mata Hari. Each guest would then have to give an account of what their childhood had been like with such parents. Elizabeth never joined in these games herself as she was too practised and too good at them.

If the weather was particularly lovely, she announced that the day was ideal for a picnic – she had a weakness for picnics. The guests put on walking clothes and tramped into some distant field with a beautiful view, where they ate bowls of hot stew carried up in a thermos flask as big as a bucket. They had no spoons or forks and scooped the delicious concoction up with hunks of fresh bread. Everyone was allowed to sit next to whoever they liked on these occasions, which was not the case at the chalet. The fierce making and breaking of alliances that was prompted by the altitude and fresh air necessitated something more formal there, and Cobden-Sanderson invented the 'planetary system': all the women sat with an empty seat on either side of them and the men rotated one seat at every meal. When 'Cobbie' had circled round the table once and was again seated next to his hostess he asked her if she did not think the plan had been a success. 'Ah yes,' she replied, 'but you have avoided me, and the movement was only an escape.' He protested that the movement was a generous one as it brought each man in turn to her side, first to her right and then to her left. 'As for avoidance, when the sun is at its highest I seek the shade,' which elegant gallantry amused and flattered his hostess.[13]

In the first week of August Frere fell ill with a chill and had to stay in bed. A few days later he was allowed up to dinner in his dressing gown and, to make him feel at home, the other guests all wore their dressing gowns too. Cobden-Sanderson's was the most imaginative costume and he came down the stairs, cheered by the other guests, wearing a sponge bag on his head, his fob watch as an order and a bunch of Dorothy Perkins roses behind his ear.

During the summer Elizabeth corresponded affectionately with Bertrand Russell, who had just returned from Russia where he and Clifford Allen had been as part of a Labour Party delegation. Clifford Allen fell ill with pneumonia and at one stage had been given only two days to live. Elizabeth, who had become fond of him, invited him to stay at the chalet to recover, and he remained there after she returned to London in October. She reported to Bertrand that she had left Allen 'high and dry as Noah's ark' on top of a mountain beyond the reach of microbes. She thought him an interesting man but was aware that he was 'certainly possessed of the devil', and while she liked devils, so that her affection for Allen was sincere, they always made her wistful. 'In the large flat respectability of my colourless character I look on and envy all those who have got any. You for instance.'[14]

During the summer she had received two letters of 'extremely wicked, lying abuse'[15] from Francis, copies of which he sent to all his friends and acquaintances. This Elizabeth could tolerate, but not the fact that they were dictated to Miss Otter. She answered the first one in a conciliatory tone, but the second was too much. When she arrived in London she found he had turned almost all her friends against her. The only ones who sought her out were those who had been with her at the chalet, had experienced a 'different reality'[16] there and knew what she had suffered from her husband's lies and vindictive revenge. However, George Bernard Shaw had moved into Whitehall Court and he often stepped in to have tea with her, for she amused him, and Frere, who had been teased about his youth at the chalet, threw a Coming Out party for her where she was to be the débutante.

In the Mountains appeared anonymously with no author's name on the cover as was usual for Elizabeth, but also no hint inside as to who the author might be. Of course it was an open secret that Elizabeth had written it but she vigorously and consistently denied authorship for fear of what Francis might devise in terms of libel suits – she took and acted upon her solicitor's advice at all times when it came to dealing with Francis, who was addicted to litigation. The book immediately became a cult, for there was so little plot and so much atmosphere that it was considered *avant garde* at the time. The critics called it 'poignant', 'humorous' and 'inspiring'. Francis, who was spending all of his time, as his wife had predicted, thinking up ways to annoy her, wrote a parody of it, and sent it around to all her friends. He also sent Elizabeth a copy of the Bible in which every familiar reference to faithless wives had been underlined. This made her laugh, for it was he who had been faithless to the point where she had had to leave him. Her reaction was simply, 'Poor Francis,'[17] and she said nothing of this to any but her most intimate friends. She was, as Frank Swinnerton understood, entirely free from the sly viciousness of female gossip.

Elizabeth was disappointed not to see Katherine Mansfield, who had been ordered abroad by her doctor, but through Frere, whose devotion she found flattering, she met many young people of his set. Wolkov introduced her to his friends, including Nijinsky, all of whom thought her witty and naughty and were instantly devoted to her. Elizabeth was being ostracized by most of her own so-called friends though she put a brave face on it, as she did with everything. While before her marriage to Francis she had been sought out and lionized by society, now they held back, for she had committed the worst social *faux pas* by becoming involved in a scandal that obliged people to take sides.

Beverley Nichols, who cultivated literary and society hostesses, saw her as dwelling in an early Victorian drawing-room and listening to passionate dialogues carried on outside her window:

> The voices rise and fall, the rain splashes against the bright window panes, the wind moans and whistles round the stoutly built walls. Then there is a lull and in the silence may be heard the scratching of her little quill pen . . . catching the thunder in a polished phrase. And when she has finished writing, there, on the paper, is a story full of tension, fierce and frightening as any that dwells in the broken, passionate sentences of Emily Brontë.[18]

Nichols was fascinated by Elizabeth's voice and felt there ought to be some musical notation for giving the exact timbre of it. He thought it delicious, 'like a dove that has become slightly demoralised by perching too long on a French hat'. Her 'U' sounded, he thought, French and she did not really talk but crooned aloud. 'No other woman could possibly deliver herself of such remarks in so utterly dulcet tones.'[19] He had first met her at a lunch party to which she arrived twenty minutes late. The door opened and 'a little figure with blue eyes floated across the floor saying, "Du forgive me, will yiu? I feel I must be late." ' He was enchanted and they became friends. Elizabeth commented of the socially assiduous young man that he 'climbed and climbed, like a convolvulus, and at the top he bloomed'.[20]

He challenged her about the authorship of *In the Mountains*. '*In the Mountains?*' she replied, 'it sounds like a Bliu Guide . . . Yiu may know I wrote it, I haven't even read it. But if yiu like it, it must be improper. So I shan't read it.' Her defence against any accusation of authorship of the book was that she had only just published one, and the truth was she wrote 'terribly slowly' scratching out all the time! Anyway she was working on a play. She often spoke of writing a play, as opposed to converting one of her novels, but she never set any of it down. It was to have many tiny scenes, none lasting longer than five minutes and with Bach fugues in between. It was to be exquisite and brittle and beautifully lit, tragedies and comedies like the things that happen in everyday life and some of them might even be silent, 'and then after each funny little emotion, one would always have the fugue to call one back to life'.[21] It was fashionable at that time and for years to come to apply the adjectives 'tiny', 'minute' and 'little' to any description of Elizabeth or anything to do with her.

A few weeks after the lunch party she was invited as a guest of some people called Johnson to their beautiful Elizabethan house, Poling. Frank Swinnerton was also there and was not in the least startled when Elizabeth said to him at breakfast on the first morning in her usual, drawling, nonsensical way, 'Mr Swinnerton, you'll have to sleep with me tonight, or we must exchange rooms.' She said she had been woken in the night and had had a strong sensation that a deep shaft of black space had opened beneath her leading directly to the nether regions. She had not been the first person to have experienced this, the Johnsons said, and there were further stories of a mysterious procession of monks across the lawn which threw the domestic dogs into a frenzy. Elizabeth, who had turned her back on superstition, affected to believe none of it. Lady Johnson, who did believe it, read her palm and told Swinnerton afterwards that she had not been able to tell Elizabeth that her success was at an end.[22] This was anything but true, for her best and most successful novels were still to come.

Almost every day of that winter, including Christmas, Boxing Day and the New Year, Elizabeth spent some time with Frere and Wolkov. They went dancing and to the theatre, out to lunch, tea and dinner and when there was nothing else to do she and Frere stayed at Whitehall Court and played chess. She had, because of the slander put about by Francis, few other claimants for her time and clearly Frere had rescued her socially as well as emotionally. However, although she was enjoying herself and the company of her young friends, she felt there was something possibly unbalanced about Frere's adoration and dependence on her.

She left England for Switzerland in the middle of January 1921. When she arrived the snow covered everything like a 'lovely pearl blanket'[23] and she was convinced, as she had often been before, that goodness and mercy had followed her all the days of her life. She intended to put herself through a 'strenuous course of self-examination'[24] about Frere. She had become for him an ideal and he wrote to her that winter:

> I find myself pinned down by dreams, dreams of the unattainable. Yet – 'thou art so true that thoughts of thee suffice to make dreams true and fables histories'. Aren't you glad to be idealised –even by such an insignificant being as myself?

She reasoned that she had arrived, after much struggle on her mountain eyrie, at a state of serenity and even happiness as a woman alone without a lover or a husband. But in the company of Frere she came very much alive, more alive than a separated widow of fifty-four ought to be, and she enjoyed it. In the end, she decided that he could not remain in ignorance of their age difference much longer, and continued to observe him with 'surprise, amused delight and only intermittent consternation'.[25] She wrote to him that *Vera* had disgusted her when she looked at her again after the Christmas interval, and that she thought of putting her on a shelf and 'going to the Argentine', a place she often mentioned her intention of visiting which was merely a ghastly alternative to something ghastlier in her vocabulary – in this case going on with her novel. He replied that if she did he would wait for her to come back; 'Poor Vera. She deserves something better than being shelved,' he wrote from Christ's College, Cambridge. Things seemed very different to him there that term and time dragged with footsteps of 'leaden eternity'. He felt that if it were not for Elizabeth's strong stabilizing influence, he would have packed up and left. He wrote to her:

> Now I understand the force and power of religion. It's
> very nice to have a religion – mine is vitally necessary and
> a religion implies a deity and in my case the deification of
> someone and you know who that someone is.

His letters brimmed with worship. She was delighted in some ways, although she did not tell him so, for here, at last, she felt, was a man with whom she could always feel comfortable. He was not a pa-man of the sort that Beauchamp women were enjoined to marry, and two of whom she *had* married, but a man with an understanding heart who was able to learn the great truths of life through his own experience. Ever since the success of *Elizabeth and her German Garden* she had become inclined to see her life as a gathering of literary experience. Less, as she grew older, was she able to resist a situation which she would later be able to turn into an episode in a novel, if not the entire subject matter. She was to do this in her next novel but one, *Love*, which was about Frere, and she wanted to subtitle it *I Never Should Have Done It*.

However, in the meantime she concluded that time would bring him to his senses and did nothing, concentrating her attention on the writing of the by then forgiven *Vera*. She finished it by the beginning of March, having 'tidied the poor dear up finally for sending her off to Macmillan'[26] (she had forsaken Macmillan for Smith and Elder when she published *Princess Priscilla's Fortnight* and returned to them with *Christine*). Elizabeth then wrote to Maud Ritchie inviting her to come and stay, telling her mendaciously that she hadn't finished the book and was planning to stay over until the summer instead of her usual visit to London in the less attractive in-between season of spring. She hoped that this message would filter through to Frere, which it did. She added that she and Clifford Allen, who was still at the chalet and naturally in love with Elizabeth, had had:

> . . . divine weeks of brilliant weather here. I'm so glad I
> didn't die on the various occasions I have earnestly
> wished I might, for if I had I would have missed a lot of
> lovely weather, wouldn't I . . . Poor L.G. [*Lieber Gott*, as
> Frere was still called] – I haven't heard from him lately
> and fear he is having a fit of the miserables . . .

Frere was indeed extremely depressed for he suspected that his passionate letters of the previous few months had shocked his idol and that he had jeopardized his chances of being invited back to the chalet for the summer. He had also heard rumours of Clifford Allen and felt foolish. Meanwhile Elizabeth and her guest went down to Lake Orta for a week and Allen found a house there.*

She searched impatiently for a place in Italy where she and Maud might stay for the few weeks of April that were impossible in Switzerland because of the melting snow. It had to be somewhere where she could work, for the glorious weather, the mimosas and flowering fruit trees were too beautiful not to be described in detail and at leisure. Then she heard that a picturesque *castello* near Rapallo (with the less picturesque name of Castello Brown) was to let for the whole of April and rented it from the owner, Frances Yeats Brown. A week later the two women were installed and were joined by a friend, Mary Mallet. They had come across her a few days previously, and she was an amusing if voluble *raconteuse* who had been a lady-in-waiting to Queen Victoria. By the 3 April Elizabeth had started to write *The Enchanted April* which was to be her most popular novel. Every page of it that has to do with the *castello* is haunted with the serenity and beauty of the place. The plot is touching, hilarious, romantic and farcical and in every way a complete contrast to *Vera*.

Four women decide to abandon their dreary lives and even drearier husbands or lovers and spend a month in a beautiful, medieval vine-draped castle in Italy called San Salvadore. It is not long before the abandoned males turn up and they become interchanged bewilderingly, all of them being transformed by the beauty of the place. When Lotte, the heroine arrives:

> All the radiance of April in Italy lay gathered at her feet. The sun poured in on her. The sea lay asleep in it, hardly stirring. Across the bay the lovely mountains, exquisitely different in colour, were asleep too in the light; and underneath her window, at the bottom of the flower-starred grass slope from where the wall of the castle rose up, was a great cypress cutting through the delicate blues and violets and rose colours of the mountains and the sea like a great black sword . . . Far out in the bay a cluster of almost motionless fishing boats hovered like a flock of white birds on the tranquil sea.[27]

*In 1938, after Allen had suffered a nervous breakdown, Elizabeth, who was by then living in France, offered him the chalet again to recuperate. He stayed for some months and then, it is thought, overcome by the gigantic solitude there, committed suicide.[28]

The coast soon came alive with old and new friends and they spent their month in a whirl of socializing. Elizabeth met Max Beerbohm and they became friends. She visited him once unexpectedly when she was walking in the hot sun one day above his house, descending on the unprepared genius who was alone, his wife having gone to Genoa for the day. Elizabeth sat on the terrace overlooking the sea and drank golden honey wine, delightedly listening to his talk. Later he showed her the drawings for his forthcoming exhibition in London. He also introduced his new friend to an old friend, Norman Douglas, author of the best-selling *South Wind*, but Elizabeth did not like him in spite of his brilliant talk and evident liking for her. When Douglas asked if he could come to the chalet, she became evasive.

At the end of April, Elizabeth decided to stay in Italy another month so as to avoid paying Swiss income tax. She arrived back on the first of June, '*fearfully* happy and excited at getting back to the adorable chalet'.[29] She did not write to Frere until the end of June. He was spending part of the long vacation at Loiret in France, and had been bombarding her with letters and postcards because 'the next best thing to hearing from you is writing to you'. She had written instead to Katherine who was staying nearby at the Hôtel Château Belle Vue in Sierre. Elizabeth invited her and John Middleton Murry to come and stay at the chalet, but when there was no reply she finally wrote to Frere, inviting him to stay and telling him that she was not going to have a house party that summer. He answered ecstatically that he would like to come in a fortnight's time.

On the 15th of June John Middleton Murry climbed to the chalet from the Palace Hotel where he and Katherine had moved, bearing a note from his wife begging forgiveness for what must have appeared to be 'just dreadful black heartedness'[30] for not having answered her cousin's first letter. She explained that she had been ill when Elizabeth's letter had arrived and put off answering it because she felt she was too much of an invalid to stay with other people and worried in case her hostess turned against her because of it. They came shortly to live 'a few alpine meadows away',[31] further up the mountain from the Chalet Soleil in a house belonging to her doctor's wife called the Chalet des Sapins.

The proximity of the Beauchamp writers was to facilitate the flowering of a friendship which was like the mountains amongst which they sat: always craggy and dangerous, sometimes bracing and healthily productive, and occasionally, when the mists cleared, revealing unscalable vistas. Katherine wrote to Lady Ottoline Morrell about their life there:

The only person whom we see is my cousin Elizabeth who lives half an hour's scramble away. We exchange Chateaubriand and baskets of apricots and have occasional lovely talks which are rather like what talks in the afterlife will be like, I imagine . . . ruminative and reminiscent . . . although dear knows what it is all about . . .

It was to be expected that the relationship would not be an easy one between the two writers, for Elizabeth's diffidence was nearly equal in quality to Katherine's huge reservations. That it was possible at all was because of the discovery they both made of the things they had in common: delicate personal fastidiousness, a love of order, the need to be much alone, and their shared, instinctive, familial, almost identical sensitivity to beauty. They also shared a love of the same poets and in particular Shakespeare, Wordsworth and Keats. But there was the problem of their widely different outlook on life as well as writing. Katherine wrote in her journal:

> . . . the late evening is the time – of times. Then with that unearthly beauty before one it is not hard to realise how far one has to go. To write something that will be worthy of that rising moon, that pale light. To be 'simple' enough as one would be simple before God.

No such prayer had ever occurred to Elizabeth for 'she hardly knew the want of it', and whose own constantly reiterated prayer just then was 'surely goodness and mercy have followed me all the days of my life'.[32] Life for her had reinforced that robust, extrovert quality that was the Beauchamp inheritance as it had all but cancelled the same thing in Katherine. Elizabeth's books were intended to convey her belief that happiness was attainable by all except the unworthy and deluded. The motto on her book plate was *Chanterai Ma Chanson*, but when talking to Katherine she preferred to conceal what must have appeared an inappropriately simple article of faith; in the presence of 'this spirit so tragically set apart' it seemed to shrink into merely a facile assumption.

Elizabeth was having difficulty with *The Enchanted April*, which now seemed to her a frothy thing compared to the intensity of the genius further up the hill. But it was finished in July, having taken only three months to write, 'and as I typed the last full stop after the words "The End" my typewriter broke! So kind of it to wait till then.'[33] She immediately packed up the manuscript, sent it to Macmillan and prepared herself for her guests. First came Frere and later Hugh Walpole, Maud Ritchie, Anna Paues, Festing Jones and Edward Strutt, who was the perfect guest, 'beaming all day long'.

That summer Hugh Walpole was suffering from the reviews of his latest novel *The Thirteen Travellers*, which had not been well received. His hostess, never merciful where writing was concerned, and not in the habit of being so with Hugh, told him that it had 'just missed' for her, 'like a telescope not being quite focused'.[34] She recommended that he read 'three simple and beautiful books: Hudson's *A Shepherd's Life*, Dorothy Wordsworth's *Journals* and Hardy's *Two in a Tower*'. The *Nation* published a review of his book by John Middleton Murry which, in the space of nearly three columns, ferociously attacked it and compared the author to female writers such as Ruby M. Ayres and Ethel M. Dell. Murry went further and threw doubt on Walpole as a writer, ridiculing his style, his romanticism and his very existence as an artist. Elizabeth could not resist inviting Murry to tea with his victim. Afterwards Walpole wrote in his diary: 'I can see that I must be everything he dislikes – but time will prove all.' He had been mild and patient with the reviewer and afterwards wrote to his friend Arnold Bennett:

> If I didn't sell and found life a horrible tragedy and wrote in the Tcekhov [*sic*] manner he'd find me a darling. He's a weird bird, his knowledge of life all from books and his solemnity amazing . . . Murry thinks it dreadful of me to be happy with the world as it is but how can I help it with so much that is lovely, so much that is exciting? It isn't my fault if my experience of people is that on the whole they are good sorts making the best of a difficult bargain.

Later Elizabeth, who never allowed complacency to pass unchecked, wrote to him, 'You know perfectly well that you yourself knew your *Thirteen Travellers* wasn't up to the mark, and knew it so well that you refused to give it to me on that ground. So why shouldn't Murry share your opinion?'

Frere was just as helpful in his capacity as *Lieber Gott* as he had been the year before except that he demanded all of Elizabeth's attention, sometimes to the exclusion of the other guests. They began to be known as 'Little E and Little Oui' or 'E and Oui',[35] because of Frere's willingness to help with everything and Strutt's difficulty in pronouncing his r's so that he called the young man 'Fwea-Weeves'. The couple often visited the ledge with the pear tree on it where Elizabeth had been courted by Stuart, Wells and Francis, and at some point during that summer they became lovers.

It was not long before Elizabeth began to discover that he was quite a different person behind his urbane and charming exterior. He was distressingly neurotic and maladjusted because of his loveless upbringing; pessimistic, fearful, hyper-sensitive and suspicious and had never before had a relationship worthy of the name with a woman.* He more or less demanded that his hostess should take him over and remake him, although he was not so precise in his request. The instincts he aroused in her were more maternal than otherwise, at least at the beginning. She became keenly aware of everything he said or did and began to hope he would make a good impression on others as anxiously as if he were her own son.

Almost every second day or so there was some sort of communication between Elizabeth and the Middleton Murrys. Katherine was still too ill to be able to walk any distance and had been forbidden to talk by her doctor. John often came down to the chalet to play chess or use the library or simply talk about the 'problem of Katherine'.[36] It was not just her frailty and tubercular condition that worried him, and it was not because of her art, he told Elizabeth, that he had decided not to send her to a sanatorium. Frere recalled hearing them discuss how in a fit of self-destruction, or madness even, Katherine had dressed herself up as a *poilu* or French soldier during the war as did the whores and camp followers. She went down into the trenches and, as a result of what happened there, contracted syphilis† In the light of this revelation Elizabeth revised much of her opinion of John's behaviour towards his wife, which had been poor. 'He did little to look after her; often left her alone for long periods; was mean with money and unfaithful.

Elizabeth visited Katherine often, usually with huge bunches of flowers, so that her cousin began to fear that the chalet garden was becoming completely denuded. 'If I could only sweep all my garden up the hill to your door,' was Elizabeth's response to this. 'Her perfect little gesture as she said this,' wrote Katherine.[37]

Frere did not like or approve of Katherine and related how once he had made a passing comment on the attractiveness of some begonias only to be given a lecture by her on how he could never imagine what it was like to see such flowers knowing he had not much longer to

---

*A wartime aeroplane crash had resulted in at least two years in various hospitals, during which time Frere was convinced that his sanity hung by a mere thread.

†Katherine visited Francis Carco in Gray near the trenches in February 1915, but this story does not fit with the tone of her letters written there nor her now known medical history. She was already by then suffering from untreated gonorrhoea which she called her 'arthritis' or 'rumatiz' and never contracted syphilis.

live. She complained constantly about everybody and everything and his opinion about Elizabeth's feeling for her cousin was that she was 'probably more embarrassed by her than anything else.'[38]

During September the guests began to disperse and only Frere stayed on. On the 16th *Vera* was published and Elizabeth sent Frere to the Chalet des Sapins with a copy and a bunch of flowers. A few days later John and Katherine rang up and told her 'wonderful things'[39] about *Vera* which enormously cheered Elizabeth. The first review, from the *Westminster Gazette*, was not good, however, and the author 'felt dejected for a bit but recovered'. Four days later there appeared a crushing review in the *Times Literary Supplement* and Elizabeth spent the rest of the day 'not minding but did'. It accused her of 'having laid aside all trammels of humour, pity and fastidiousness'. The next day Elizabeth and Frere went to Pepinet and arrived back in time for tea to find John on the veranda profoundly cast down by the *TLS* review. He said it was no good, these days, doing real, good work for only abuse was one's portion. 'Of course, my dear, when the critics are faced with *Wuthering Heights* by Jane Austen, they don't know what to say.'[40] The remark shot through Elizabeth with the 'warmth of a flame . . . it comforted me and raised me to my feet in a moment when I was beaten down on all fours . . . ' she wrote to him later.

There were one or two good reviews. The *Pall Mall Gazette* said it was 'altogether a most holding novel', and the *Daily Express* guessed correctly that it was 'this famous writer's masterpiece'. The *New Statesman*'s review was written by Rebecca West and was very fair and perceptive, much to Elizabeth's surprise, but she could not resist an opening broadside: 'The author of *Vera* has so little heart that when she writes of sentiment she often writes like a humbug.' Miss West was, however, too good a critic not to recognize good writing and gave the book its due. She continued:

> . . . but she has a clear and brilliant head that enables her to write a peculiar kind of witty, well constructed fiction, a sort of sparkling Euclid which nobody can touch. *Vera* is distinctly a triumph . . . The author has produced a remarkable little book because she has had the courage to override a tiresome literary convention. She has insisted that there is no real reason why a book should not be just as tragic as comic. Her book is primarily designed to exhibit a comic character, a husband who is a storm in a teacup, a rude but excessively domesticated Boreas. With

a perfection of malicious humour he is described as solemnly celebrating his own birthday, showing a patriarchal care for chastity of even inanimate possessions by keeping his books in locked cases and the piano in a red baize cover ('even its legs being buttoned round in what looked like Alpine sports gaiters'), and blustering round his composed and satiric servants. But the author goes on to perceive that what would have been fun for the parlour-maid would be death for a wife. She is brave enough to encumber this comic character with a dead wife whom he has driven to suicide by his futile tyrannies, and a living wife whose sensitive youth he is driving in the same direction by forcing her to live in the house where her predecessor killed herself and repeating the home-loving frightfulness which led to that tragedy. With enormous technical skill she recreates the soul of the dead wife out of trifles which the living wife finds in the house to which they had both in turn been brought after their honeymoons: 'The pencils whose end had been gnawed as the pencils of a child at its lessons are gnawed,' which lie on the writing-table that stands in Vera's room by the window from which she threw herself; her bookcase, stuffed with Baedekers and books 'describing remote, glowing places' which the poor soul had read in her increasing despair, dreaming dreams of solitary travel, until the fatal day when it occurred to her that there was one journey she could take without fear of being accompanied by her husband. By the unsentimental justice of its values, by its refusal to make Weymiss less of a comedian because he is murderous or less of a murderer because he is comic, *Vera* achieves a peculiar, poignant effect. It is without any question the most successful attempt at the macabre in English. The one flaw in the book is the delineation of the living wife. The author knows perfectly well that a young and innocent and fairy-hearted girl like Lucy could not have felt romantic love for this uxorious buffoon. There is just the least suspicion of insincerity in her choice of such an obvious heroine to play the part, instead of the not less genuinely sympathetic type of woman who might, for the sake of companionship or home, have attempted to tolerate bawling fatuity. One remembers with alarm the persistence with which she reminds us on her title pages of those not too creditable early successes which saw innumerable tiresome women all over England smirking coyly about their gardens as if they were having a remarkably satisfying affair with their delphiniums. It would almost seem as if she revised these achievements of her maturity by standards of that miniature work. If she would only forget the nice public that she gained with *Elizabeth and her German Garden* and give rise to the lower and priceless self which inspired her to the conception of Everard Weymiss, she might be a most admirable satirist.

The other novelist Rebecca West was obliged to review in the same issue was, curiously, also one of H. G. Wells's ex-mistresses, Dorothy Richardson, who did not come off at all well by comparison with Elizabeth.

Bertrand read *Vera* with mounting horror, so exact was the depiction of his brother. As soon as he had finished he resolved to advise his children never to marry a novelist. Sydney Waterlow wrote to say he considered the book a 'triumph' and admired 'the complete elimination of woolliness' that she had attained both in style and vision. It was the same quality, exactly, as the pleasure he took in Jane Austen. Sydney took literature extremely seriously, and would never have committed himself to an insincere compliment. Although flattered by the occasional comparison to Jane Austen, Elizabeth remarked to Frere that if, like the monkeys in the library, she wrote for a hundred years, she would never be able to write as well as Jane Austen. 'Why bring Jane Austen into it at all?'[41] She knew that *Vera* was her high watermark and that she would never write anything as good again, but she had no wish to do so for it was extracted from her by torment. A female friend of her husband rang her and asked her how she dared write a portrait of him that was so unflattering. 'He can't have been that bad,' to which Elizabeth replied, 'He was worse!'[42] Swinnerton considered that there was no exaggeration at all, but unerringly cruel moderation. Mrs Belloc Lowndes put it out that she thought Elizabeth was not very 'nice' to have written such a book about her husband, this being the general opinion, to which Elizabeth replied, wilfully misunderstanding the implied meaning of that word as used by her friend, 'I know myself far better than you can know me, and I think I am quite nice as are most women.'

Katherine had written to Dorothy Brett that she thought the book 'amazingly good'.

> I am sitting writing to you on the balcony among teacups, grapes, a brown loaf shaped like a bean, a plaited cake with almond paste inside and nuts out. M. had forsaken it to join our Cousin Elizabeth. She appeared today with a bouquet – never smaller woman carried bigger bouquets. She looked like a garden walking, of asters, late sweet peas, stocks and always petunias.
>
> She herself wore a frock like a spider web, a hat like a berry – and gloves that reminded me of thistles in seed. Oh, how I love the appearance of people – how I delight in it, if I love them. I have gathered Elizabeth's frocks to my bosom as if they were part of her flowers. And then when she smiles a ravishing wrinkle appears on her nose – and never have I seen more exquisite hands. Oh dear, I hope we shall manage to keep her in our life. It's terrible how one's friends disappear and how quickly one runs after to lock the door and close the shutters.
>
> But no doubt Elizabeth is far more important to me than I am to her. She's surrounded, lapped in lovely friends . . . Except for her we are lost in the forest.

The deaf painter replied that she thought the book 'drivel in cold blood'. Katherine replied:

> I'm very interested in what you say about *Vera*. Isn't the end extraordinarily good? It would have been so easy to miss it. She carried it right through. I admire the end most, I think. Have you never known a Weymiss? Oh, my dear, they are *very* plentiful! Few men are without a touch. And I certainly believe that husbands and wives talk like that. Lord, yes! . . . it is incredible the follies and foolishness we can bear if we think we are in love. Not that I can stand the Weymiss 'brand'. No. But I can perfectly comprehend Lucy standing it. I don't think I agree about Lucy either. She could not understand her father's '*intellect*' but she had a sense of humour (except where her beloved was concerned). She certainly had her own opinions and the aunt was very sodden at the funeral because of the *ghastly* effect of funerals! They make the hardest of us melt and gush. But all the same your criticism is awfully good . . . only one thing, my hand on my heart, I could swear to. Never *could* Elizabeth be

influenced by me. If you knew how she would scorn the notion, how impossible it would be for her. There is a kind of turn in our sentences which is alike but that is because we are worms of the same family. But that is all . . .

Francis was wild with fury when he read *Vera*, and carried a copy everywhere he went, accosting people in his club, pointing out passages and asking them if it was a true description of himself or Telegraph House. Wells agreed with the foaming earl that he did not have photographs of all his ancestors hung in the hall, 'But *is* it you?' he mildly inquired. 'Ugh,' Francis replied, realizing that his wife had her hook firmly fixed in his gills.[43] He threatened a libel action and Macmillan received writs from his solicitors. They were delighted by the prospect because *Vera* would have sold thousands as a result. Elizabeth laughed at the idea. Imperturbable, calm and innocently wide-eyed as ever, she said, 'If the cap fits . . . It's so silly of Francis! If he does sue me, I shall simply go into the witness box and say, "Of *course* it's not Francis!" '[44] 'Poor little thing, wouldn't I have been, with only my little eyes or the tip of my nose appearing over the top of the box!' she wrote later to Liebet.

Francis was persuaded by his lawyers to drop the case but he simply switched it to suing his wife for desertion. None of his frantic attempts to get her into the witness box once more succeeded, for she had no intention of paying him any more attention and saw no necessity for a divorce. However, the rumour got out to the general public, as inevitably it would, that the book was a portrait of the author's husband and as a result the sales of *Vera* rose dramatically.

The Shadow of the Valley

John and Katherine endured the descent into winter up in Montana with stoicism. 'If this is the between season then people are wise to avoid it,' Katherine wrote to her cousin who had avoided it. 'The worst of it is our brains are frozen too.' Elizabeth, who was once again surrounded by her friends in London, saw the two of them as if through the other end of a pair of opera glasses, 'the tiniest little remote figures',[1] a sort of awful innocence surrounding them like a halo, knitting, steeping themselves in Jane Austen (copies of whose novels they had borrowed from the chalet), and at intervals emitting wisdom. She wrote them long and amusing letters filled with descriptions of the gilded life she was leading and the shivering couple read them 'round eyed'. Katherine wrote back: 'I see you slipping into a carriage, driving to a play, dining among mirrors and branched candlesticks and far away sweet sounds . . . '

Elizabeth went to Stratford-upon-Avon in the company of Frere. It was her first visit, inspired by John Middleton Murry's interest in Shakespeare about whom he was writing a book. She and Frere saw *Hamlet*, read *Lear* in a punt on the river, stole some of Ann Hathaway's snapdragons and meditated for a long time in the graveyard. She wrote about it at length to her two friends in Switzerland and ended with a PS which is perhaps the only recorded comment she made about Francis's persecution. 'What I want to try very hard to do is not let anything F. may do or drag me into touch *me* – my *me* and not wound it, not wound that.'

H. G. Wells gave a party at the Thackeray Hotel in Bloomsbury for Charlie Chaplin and Chaliapin to which Elizabeth went in the company of Lady Ottoline Morrell and her party, which included Sydney Waterlow, Elizabeth's nephew, who was by then working for the Foreign Office, Mark Gertler, the young Jewish painter, and Dorothy Brett. Elizabeth met Samuel Koteliansky, Kot to his friends, the translator of Chekhov and friend of Gertler and Katherine. He had corresponded with Gorky and knew a great deal about Russian literature, which was then very much in vogue. He seemed so refreshing to Elizabeth in his calm and determined dislikes that she invited him to tea. He arrived early at Whitehall Court and waited for his hostess in the wrong reception room in that huge, complex building. Elizabeth waited for him in her flat, 'both thinking sorrowful things about the other'[2] and they never did meet.

She went off to see Bertrand and his extremely round wife Dora, who were snugly settled down in a little house in Chelsea. Dora was imminently expecting the child who was one day to be the fourth earl and the house was full of 'tiny jackets and nighties and powder puffs and cradles and Bertie looking perfectly blissful', Elizabeth wrote to Katherine. He told Elizabeth of a passage he had recently come across in a manuscript which was dated 1065 and which he translated into modern English as it exactly reflected his own feeling about any children he might have: 'When a child is born the parents want it to be intelligent. I, through intelligence having wrecked my life, I only hope that my children grow up being ignorant and stupid and thus crown a successful career by being a Cabinet minister.'[3]

Elizabeth dined with Arnold Bennett and they talked of Hugh Walpole. Murry's article about Walpole in the *Nation* had let loose the wrath of the literary set on the novelist's head: they had long been envious of his success and the fact that he never struggled over his books, and made no secret of it, that he never made corrections in his manuscripts and appeared to be entirely immune to the elation and gloom which his less successful colleagues understood as being an inevitable concomitant of the trade. And he was happy. Some of them regarded him as 'one of the larger devils',[4] while others, including Elizabeth and Bennett, were fond of him but unable to appreciate his writing.

Walpole was to give a party in honour of Melchior, the Wagnerian tenor and the love of his life, which unfortunately coincided with another in Devonshire House given by the duchess. Elizabeth asked Bennett if he was going to Walpole's party and he 'screamed out a negative'. She then asked E. V. Lucas whether *he* were going and he 'yelled' that he was not. Arnold Bennett told Walpole he would be abroad, but instead went to the Devonshires' party. When Walpole heard of this he was hurt but, in the generosity of his nature, forgave his friend and merely remonstrated with him mildly in a letter. Elizabeth, who had been invited to both, went to a dinner given by Sibyl Colefax and then on to Walpole's, considering that life was too short not to go to his parties (or to read Proust who had just published the last volume of *À la Recherche du Temps Perdu*). That evening she heard a young woman hissing at her husband, 'Don't you go Weymissing* me,' which delighted her.

She later wrote to John and Katherine:

> Here it is raw and dark and the wind is howling along the river. I ought to be depressed and I am happy. The very terrifyingness of life interests me so desperately that I tingle with the enjoyment of it. Things are so absurd, so fantastically horrible everywhere that they do not produce a reaction that glows. One defies and in defying shoots up to the stars. But I don't like to feel happy because it means there is no difference between my vision and Hugh's . . . but he is an engaging creature.

Perhaps she had tempted the gods too far with this statement for she was shortly to have cause to revise her attitude.

The Saturday after Walpole's party she went up to Cambridge to hear him in a lunchtime debate at the Union. She planned to have a late lunch there with Frere, who had passed his finals and landed a job on the *Evening News* but was reluctant to leave his cosy digs in Cambridge, commuting to and from London in the week. She asked Walpole if he would like to travel back to town with her in the evening but he was to open a bazaar in Ealing that afternoon which Elizabeth found immensely amusing and 'so like him somehow'.[5] She travelled up on the train, having missed the announcement in the newspapers that her brother Sydney had been run over by an omnibus in the Mall. As soon as Frere, who met her at the station, saw her stepping gaily off the train, he realized that she did not know and, reluctant to spoil her day, kept the news from her. When she arrived back in London she saw it in the evening newspapers and was shattered.

Of all the deaths of all the beloved people in her life this was the one that grieved her the most. For days she secluded herself in her flat, seeing nobody, not even writing in her diary. She mourned him deeply, intensely and privately and everyone who knew her remarked on the change in her when she appeared once more amongst them. She was more serious, less flirtatious, less inclined to banter and tease and, curiously, more intelligent in her conversation as if in letting go of her brother she had also let go of her childhood.

*Pronounced 'Weemsing'

Now she and Charlotte were truly alone in the world; for, having unanimously shed their husbands, it had been to Sydney that they had turned for help, advice and comfort. To John and Katherine Elizabeth wrote:

> I loved him so *very* much, I can't remember ever having been cross to him or he being cross to me, not ever, not right back to the very beginning . . . there has gone up the most dreadful wail from hundreds and hundreds of people I never heard of who all appeared to have felt as we do about him.

To Liebet she wrote:

> He was composed only of love – I can see no flaw at all in his character, and have never known him even impatient. He was a child of light, and had such a happy life – well, he is gone and it was glorious to have had him. I know no man so good, I don't believe there is one, for his goodness had such a quality of radiance. How he laughed!

An incident once took place which throws a curious light on the manner of Sydney's death. When Sir Harold Beauchamp, Katherine's father, first came to London in 1889 from New Zealand, it was the custom for gentlemen to wear top hats in the street. When Sydney met Sir Harold he was wearing a bowler or 'hard hitter'. Looking at him in dismay, Sydney exclaimed, 'Oh, for goodness sake, Harold, fall into line with us and get a topper, otherwise they will take you for a runner or a tout. As for myself, I pray that if I am accidentally killed in the street I shall have my tall hat firmly wedged on my head.'[6] Curiously enough, when he was picked up after his accident his silk hat was in the position he prayed for.

Sydney Beauchamp's career had been an unmitigated success. After he qualified at Cambridge he set up in a practice in Kensington where he specialized in obstetrics. After a few years he moved his practice to Harley Street and soon became the most fashionable doctor to consult. Elizabeth was always astonished at the number of people she met in the most unlikely places who had been brought into the world by her brother. Jeanne Beauchamp, Katherine's sister, once fell off a fence she was climbing in Hyde Park and hurt her arm. She was only a child and the arm was only bruised but Sydney Beauchamp paid her a visit and cheered her up. 'I've got a lovely crop of babies coming up this spring,' he told her, and she joined the ever-increasing ranks of people who thought the world of him.[7] He became gynaecologist to Queen Victoria herself and was loved by everyone in Buckingham Palace. He was appointed in a voluntary capacity as physician to the British delegation at the peace conference at Versailles in June 1919 and soon afterwards was awarded a knighthood.

Elizabeth passed a gloomy Christmas with Charlotte at Hatch and the two of them spent the New Year at Whitehall Court. Elizabeth planned to retreat to the chalet as soon as she could get her passport renewed, but as she was packing her bags Frere appeared looking deadly ill, weak and miserable. He was coughing and had come to her for a doctor's address. Elizabeth advised him to go home immediately (he had just moved to a flat in George Street), and then 'set a doctor and a nurse on him'.[8] It appeared he had caught a bad dose of flu and had weakened his constitution by overwork. Although she did not like to leave him, she decided not to alter her plans and left for Sierre two days later, having posted off a note to Walpole asking him to keep an eye on Frere. Hugh, who had shown a particular interest in the handsome young man, was only too happy to oblige. While Frere was flattered and was fond of Hugh, there was no basis for her original alarm over the relationship, and later she threw them together whenever she could and teased both of them about it.

At Sierre Elizabeth was met by August, but no Coco as she had expected. She quickly and apprehensively asked what had happened to the dog and was told, to her surprise, that he was not well. *'Vous avez fait venir le veterinaire?'*[9] But he hadn't, excusing himself by saying that he was waiting till she arrived to obtain her permission. He had said nothing to her in his last letter and protested that the dog had been well three days ago. Now it seemed that he was lying in his kennel unable to move. She struggled and stumbled on up to the chalet and on the slippery path up to the front door she fell, sprawling, twice. All the time she called out Coco's name and told him that she was coming to look after him. On the porch the dog was stretched out across the threshold of the door, blocking it so that she would not be able to go in without stepping over him – Coco had somehow struggled round the house from his kennel yard, knowing that she was coming home. She had him carried carefully into the warm and telephoned the vet, but it was too late. Coco had to be put down. That night she went to bed 'Extraordinarily tired. So queer to be back, all silent and empty, but very lovely . . .'[10]

Early in the morning of the next day, after unpacking, she pulled on nailed boots, leggings, breeches 'and all the tiresome snow paraphernalia' and went by train to Montana to surprise John and Katherine with a visit. 'She looked fascinating in her black suit,' Katherine wrote in her journal, 'something between a bishop and a fly.'

Elizabeth was not to know it but a fundamental change had taken place in her two friends at the Chalet des Sapins. John had been sent a book to review by the editor of the *New Age*, Orage, called *Cosmic Anatomy, or the Structure of the Ego* by a benefactor of the *New Age*, Dr Lewis Wallace. John rejected it immediately for it dealt with occult doctrines of which he did not approve, but Katherine snatched it up and became absorbed in it, to her husband's alarm. What she read concerning the mystic expansion of consciousness and the evolution of reality reinforced her own suspicions that the real cause of her illness was not her lungs but 'something else', her spirit, soul or her id (as Freud was then naming this invisible force which lives our lives for us). Whatever it was, it could only be cured by a 'conquest of the personal',[11] which could not happen by passively lying on a bed following doctors' orders.

She was also becoming obsessed with the possibility of a cure through expensive treatment with a radiological contraption being promoted by a Russian called Manoukhin in Paris. She had learnt about him through Koteliansky, a friend of the Russian writer Ouspenski who was also known to Orage, and all three of these men had become interested in the teachings of a psychologist and magus called Gurdjieff of whom Katherine was not to hear until later that year. Murry was absolutely against both of these ideas to which his wife seemed to be trusting the slender remains of her life. She had improved since she had been in Switzerland, she was writing well and he was happy enough with the way things were. He did not want change and she could think of little else. She became fiercely bound up in a dangerous desire to cure herself one way or another, and in her desperation turned in every direction at once. There is no doubt that she was undergoing a spiritual crisis which had been predicted for her by Sydney Beauchamp a few years previously.

When Elizabeth arrived that bright morning, the Chalet des Sapins was filled with dark but invisible forces, the manifestations of which took her entirely by surprise. She sat downstairs with John for an hour gossiping over cups of hot chocolate and then went up to see Katherine. Congratulating her on *At the Bay* which had appeared in the *London Mercury* the previous autumn, she thoughtlessly referred to it as a 'pretty little story'. Later Katherine wrote in her journal:

All the time she was here I was conscious of a falsity. We said things we meant; we were sincere, but at the back was nothing but falsity. It was very horrible. I do not want ever to see her or hear from her again. When she said she would come often, I wanted to cry *Finito!* No, she is not my friend.

Elizabeth sent August the next day with the gifts she had brought Katherine: a green and white knitted petticoat and some bath salts. Katherine wrote a charming note in thanks, having to some extent overcome her revulsion, but added, 'Ah Elizabeth, what can I do to know that my little figures projected on the bright screen of time make a "*pretty* little story"?' She also told her cousin that she had decided to go to Paris in a fortnight's time to see if Manoukhin would allow her to take his cure which cost £7 a session. Her assured income was £5 a week from her father.

Katherine had sunk to the 'bottom of the ocean'[12] after Elizabeth had gone the day before and stifled her rage by writing another story called *A Cup of Tea* which would never be called pretty, especially not by Elizabeth, for it contained a cruel portrait of her. Elizabeth is caricatured as a spoilt socialite who takes up young and promising artists and writers and patronizes them. One such near-starving young woman, clearly Katherine herself, is taken home out of the snow and given a cup of tea. The story reeks of the stifled falseness of that morning at the Chalet des Sapins. In the end the girl is ejected back into the snow because of a petty jealousy.

A few days later Elizabeth travelled up to Montana again to visit Katherine whom she found alone and pathetic. Elizabeth wore a little blue hood fastened under her chin by a diamond clasp and looked, Katherine thought, like 'a very ancient drawing'.[13] They talked of Katherine's planned visit to Paris and the cure, and Elizabeth put forward, with the brashness of a healthy person and with the best intentions, the thought that if Katherine became cured she might lose her extraordinary gift. She said this to comfort her cousin, for she was not convinced of the efficacy of Dr Manoukhin's machines and felt alarmed that Katherine was pinning her hopes on him, but it sent her cousin down once more to the bottom of the ocean, and this time she was not so reticent in her fury. When John next came to the Chalet Soleil he replied to Elizabeth's anxious inquiry about his wife by telling her somewhat vaguely that he thought she was 'under a cloud – something to do with a cloud',[14] with Katherine. Elizabeth immediately wrote a baffled letter of apology which melted Katherine.

> Thank you dear Elizabeth for your beautiful letter. It was
> happiness to receive it; I feel it has put a blessing on my
> journey . . . It is bitter to be ill, and the idea of being
> well – haunts me. Ever since I have realised this possi-
> bility I dream of it at night – dream I am alone – crossing
> streams or climbing hills or just walking. To be alone
> again. That is what health means to me; that is freedom.
> To be invisible, not to be offered chairs or given arms! I
> plan, I dream, yet hardly dare to give way to these
> delights . . . (though of course one does). But if I should
> become an odious bouncing female with a broad smile, *tell
> me at once*, Elizabeth, and I'll flee to some desert place and
> smile unseen.[15]

Katherine had been keeping to a strict regime for the past few
months and seemed better in herself, and her lungs were undoubtedly improved by the alpine air. The domestic peace of the Chalet
des Sapins and Elizabeth's encouragement had produced the most
fruitful phase in her writing career. If she stayed where she was she
might produce the novel of which *At the Bay* was a beginning. Both
Elizabeth and John were agreed that it would be a tragedy if this
progress were jeopardized by Katherine chasing after a dream. In
spite of her improvement she did not look strong enough to survive
the journey to Paris, let alone the rigours of the treatment. During
the time that was left, Elizabeth visited them every second day or so.
Katherine wrote to Dorothy Brett:

> Elizabeth was here yesterday and we lay in my room
> talking about flowers until we were really quite drunk, or I
> was. She – describing 'a certain very exquisite rose, sin-
> gle, pale yellow with coral tipped petals' and so on. I kept
> thinking of little curly blue hyacinths and *white* violets and
> the bird cherry . . .

Two days later Elizabeth visited her cousin for the last time to say
goodbye and found her looking 'frail and transparent'.[16] She was
lying on her big bed under the eiderdown. Elizabeth sat down beside
her, lay back on the pillows and talked about women and how fine
they were, but Katherine was 'bored and disgusted' by their talk.
When she had left, Katherine prepared for her journey as though
preparing for her death, tearing up and ruthlessly destroying much
she had written since she had been there. 'Should I never return all is

in order. That is what life has taught me.'[17] Elizabeth went down to the station to see them off but they missed each other – John and Katherine were engrossed in a passionate discussion as to whether or not John should go with his wife, and Elizabeth was wearing a veil 'like a pea-souper'.[18]

Elizabeth met John on skis on the way back, was astonished that he had not gone with Katherine on what must have been for her an exhausting journey and told him so. She learned later that Katherine was shattered when she realized she would have to go alone. She wrote from Paris:

> It served me right, poor John . . . he is like a fish off a line swimming in his own element again, and never dreaming, really, of living here. It made me feel like a very stuffy old Prospero who has been harbouring a piping wild Ariel. I hope he does stay where he is. Poor John! It's horrible to think how I've curtailed his freedom. In my silly innocence I felt certain he couldn't bear not to know what this Russian man said and so on. But not a bit of it. He is hand in hand with his new novel . . .

Elizabeth was soon able to shame Murry into joining his wife, and because he was in Paris he had a chance of meeting James Joyce whose novel *Ulysses* was about to be published by Sylvia Beach of Shakespeare & Company. Murry was given a copy to review and Violet Schiff, who was a friend of Miss Beach, arranged for the Murrys to meet the author in their hotel. Afterwards, it was Joyce's opinion that Katherine understood the book better than her husband. Elizabeth was sent a copy by Hugh Walpole, but although she saw it was 'a wonderful book', and understood its potential stature and importance in the development of the 'modern' novel, she claimed that nothing would induce her to finish a book, 'even God's first novel',[19] if it bored her. *Ulysses* made her feel as if she were shut up with a lunatic who was exposing himself. She had, she said, read as far as the detailed description of a man's morning visit to the lavatory, and then sleep overtook her.

That winter she was inundated with letters from Frere which arrived by every post, some of them pages long. They were filled with a yearning loneliness and it both pleased and disturbed her to realize that he was passionately, head over heels, in love with her.

When Elizabeth arrived back in London in March she was delighted to hear that Nelson Doubleday, her American publisher whom she adored, and his wife Ellen, whom she did not, were planning to come to England. They arrived at the same time as bitter weather which in turn coincided with a coal strike. The Doubledays brought her news of Evi which was not reassuring. The year before Evi had written her mother a stream of letters demanding her capital in the Deutsche Bank because she had met a man she wanted to marry. She was eager to have children as soon as possible and her 'man',[20] Eustace Graves, would not marry her until he could get enough money to put a down payment on a house on the outskirts of Los Angeles. He was out of work, and considered by those who had met him not at all the kind of man who would make Evi a good husband. She would never be able to get her share of the capital which came from the sale of Schlagenthin while her mother was able to prevent it, but Elizabeth reluctantly agreed to give her an increased allowance, for Evi had been ill and could not pay the doctor's bills.

To escape from the cold, for there was no coal to be had, the Doubledays easily persuaded Elizabeth to take them on a pilgrimage to Nassenheide. They went the first part of the journey by rail and then motored from Stettin. It was a difficult journey because Nelson was confined to a wheel chair, but the two women combined to manage him. The house was empty except for Hermann the gardener who was employed as a general factotum and was inhabiting the rooms where the tutors used to live. He had become very fat and so had his wife, which was astonishing considering the scarcity of food during the war, and their daughter was about to be married to a truculent Prussian officer who told Elizabeth that the Germans had not been defeated in the war. The house itself, however, had hardly changed on the outside except that weeds were gaining in the garden. They walked in the park and from some angles they might have been transported back to the nineteenth century. None of the trees in the huge forests had been cut down and all the peasants looked fat and prosperous. The fields were beautifully kept, much better than when Henning had been in charge, and altogether the place was flourishing. Elizabeth presented Hermann with a hundred-franc note when they left which was all she had on her, but he was not impressed.

Back in London Elizabeth saw Wells, who was busy writing prefaces to a complete edition of his novels. He told her that he had come to the conclusion that *Mr Polly* was the 'best of the lot' which pleased her for she had always been of that opinion. He was enormously rich, 'drowning in profits' from his books, especially from *The Outline of History* which alone gave him as much trouble with revisions and foreign editions as would managing a large estate. He complained that he could hardly find time to write novels, and Elizabeth remarked, 'It must be awful not to be able to prophesy *all* of the time.'[21]

Katherine Mansfield's *The Garden Party* had been published and become a bright literary event in a year of many which included T. S. Eliot's *The Wasteland* and James Joyce's *Ulysses*. 1922 was, in fact, an *annus mirabilis* of literature, a watershed after which 'modern' writing, painting and sculpture as well as music became the accepted form. Elizabeth, who contributed to much modernity in novel writing during her own life time, as well as to a great deal of modern thinking, although her efforts were not then recognized, published *The Enchanted April* in that year, which is the best loved of all her books after *Elizabeth and her German Garden*. It also contributed to the feminist cause for after it was published it was no longer considered outrageous for women to leave their husbands and go off on holiday on their own or with each other. She described the book as being like 'a thin flute playing in an empty afternoon'.[22]

She wrote Katherine a letter of sincere praise after she read *The Garden Party* which moved the younger woman to tears of gratitude. Katherine had, by then, undergone five doses of X-ray treatment in Paris and felt as though her bones were melting. 'I suppose this is the moment when real martyrs break into song, but I can think of nothing but fern grots, cucumbers and fans,' she wrote in reply. Elizabeth recommended Katherine's book wherever she went, and many years later Frere maintained that if it had not been for her support Katherine might have remained virtually unknown till after her death.

To him Elizabeth wrote of the book:

> . . . some of the things in it are marvellous – some less so, but still leave a queer, extraordinary impression on one – all are bleeding with reality . . . They are extraordinary little things. I'm fearfully proud of her – just as if I had hatched her.

Everyone noticed how well Elizabeth was looking and how rapidly she had recovered from her marriage. Indeed, she admitted that she found it hard to remember that she was still married to Francis at all. Those who knew her well were aware that her relaxed and carefree attitude sprang from Frere's presence. Liebet understood, however, it was not simply the pleasure of being, albeit unsuitably, the very centre, the guiding star, in the life of another person that made her mother so happy. He had also led her into the company of many clever, younger people with whom she spent much of her time and whose liveliness infused her with vitality. It invariably annoyed her, though, that the young men were hesitant to admit that they had read her books, but assured her enthusiastically that their mothers or aunts thought them simply topping.

However, a week after her return to England from Germany the shadow of the first cloud on the horizon of their relationship was to cast a gloom. Elizabeth spent Easter with friends at Lynton in Devonshire, and thought two days a long time to go without seeing him. She arranged with Frere to meet her at a pub in the village, for she felt she could not take him to the house for fear of scandal. The weather was vile and they quarrelled bitterly while struggling through the wind and freezing rain along the cliff tops on their way to visit a spot where Shelley had lived in 1812 after his marriage to Harriet Westbrook. They found the myrtle-twined cottage in Lynmouth, the twin village of Lynton below the cliffs, but Elizabeth thought 'L.G.'s views on pilgrimages to places great poets have lived is regrettable.'* They parted 'brass rags'.[23]

It took some time for the rift to heal, but heal it did, for their need for each other, though widely different in motive, was equally strong. She needed him as a bulwark against the inevitable descent into old age (she was fifty-six) and he needed her because she was his passport to luminaries of the literary world who helped him in his work and gave him standing among his contemporaries. Another reasonable cause for friction was the amount of time she spent with Bertrand Russell, with whom she dined almost every night when he was in London. She found him the most entertaining and amusing talker she had ever met, but Frere rightly suspected that their relationship did not stop at merely dining together, although it was Elizabeth's opinion that the philosopher 'smelt like a bear garden'.[24]

News of this reached Francis through his aunt, Lady Agatha, a pinched elderly spinster who took an inordinate interest in the carryings on of the younger set. He wrote to Bertrand, remonstrating, and his brother wrote back denying that there was anything between Elizabeth and himself. By the same post he sent a letter to her, warning her that if Francis should tackle her about it, to 'minimise' what had been going on between them.

By May Elizabeth heard from John that Katherine's treatment

---

*Elizabeth still referred to Frere as 'Lieber Gott' at that time or in her diary simply as L.G. Later he became 'Tuppence' or 'Tup' by which name she also called herself, names based on the saying about rubbing two pennies together.

had been a success and later received an enthusiastic letter from her to the same effect. She had gained weight and her chest was almost silent of tubercular wheeze. On 4 June Dorothy Brett saw John and Katherine off at the Gare de Lyon on their return to Switzerland and noticed Katherine had an understanding 'beyond all understanding – and she has won so complete a victory over herself that one could almost worship'. Murry lost the luggage ticket, couldn't find a porter and tipped with a five-hundred-franc note instead of a fifty. He later left his wife's favourite little clock on the train and her baggage was lost at Randogne. John hired an open cart to take her to the Hotel d'Angleterre and it poured with freezing rain on the way, soaking Katherine to the skin for he had also lost her coat. As soon as they arrived John discovered he had lost his fountain pen and then sprained his ankle. Perhaps his 'resistance', as it would now be called, was because the safe return of a cured wife was not what he really desired.

The next day pleurisy attacked Katherine and she was as ill as ever before. To Elizabeth she wrote in answer to an invitation to stay at the Chalet Soleil that summer:

> . . . Rather a disappointing thing has happened. I sup-
> pose my enthusiasm was too much for the furies. At any
> rate I wish I had waited before praising so loudly. For they
> have turned in their chariots and are here in full force
> again. I was 'silly' to be so happy and to say so much
> about it; I feel ashamed of my last letter . . . However
> perhaps the truth is some people live in cages and some
> are free. One had better accept one's cage and say no more
> about it. I *can*, I *will* . . .

She refused Elizabeth's offer, fearing she would be a nuisance, and signed the letter 'Your sister, Katherine'.

Elizabeth returned to Switzerland in June and visited her in the hotel. Katherine was established in a glass veranda all to herself, having successfully fended off the two elderly spinsters who ran the establishment and who were determined to wrap her in poultices of hot mashed potato and mustard. Elizabeth found her plump but coughing badly. L.M. (or Ida Baker), Katherine's friend from Queen's College who worshipped her to the point where Katherine lost all patience, but who had looked after her devotedly in the past, had returned to be of use. Katherine's energy, as a result, was liberated for such writing as she felt up to and was not expended on the tiresome business, for the sick, of keeping going. Elizabeth had reserved the month of July at the chalet for John and Katherine, and she was now forced to spend it alone feeling disappointed, lonely, dejected and uneasy. She busied herself on corrections of *The Enchanted April*, but was perturbed by a change of tone in Frere's letters. They were distant and somehow evasive, but how or why she could only conjecture.

For August she had invited, among others, both Frere and a new young friend called Betty Clifton who had an intense lesbian crush on Elizabeth. These emotions, as long as they came from intelligent young girls and not women of her own age, always elicited a warm response in Elizabeth, and she went out of her way to be friendly to the lovelorn young women. She was in fact, often much nicer to them than she was to her own daughters, which did not pass unnoticed by them and was fiercely resented. Betty Clifton was exquisitely beautiful, an heiress, Baroness Clifton in her own right (the daughter of the Earl of Darnley), and was the prototype for Lady Caroline Dexter in *The Enchanted April*. She was also remarkably intelligent and became a barrister, one of the first women to do so. But she was plagued by depressions, felt she could never marry for she might destroy her children, and committed suicide in her early thirties. After lunch on the first day of her visit Elizabeth was talking to her on the terrace about quite ordinary things when Betty suddenly said, 'I can't bear this,' and rushed indoors, leaving her hostess startled and perplexed. Frere's behaviour was equally unaccountable, for he refused to join in any games, succumbed to bouts of nervous irritability and broke out in blistering attacks on his hostess and everything else. At first Elizabeth thought that he was overworked and that the chalet air would soon calm him down, but when, a few days later, Betty suddenly jumped up from the bridge table, knocking her chair over with a crash, and rushed upstairs, Elizabeth's acute antennae picked up that there was something afoot between the two of them. She deduced, without much effort, that they were having an affair and became pensive. In her diary she merely noted, 'L.G. freezing his course between the devil and the deep blue sea with admirable and sweet skill.'[25] A week or so later Thelma Cazalet arrived 'very untired and frisky', and Elizabeth sent her and Frere off for a walk together, being sure that he would like her too. He arrived back 'furious', having guessed en route that Elizabeth had seen what was going on between him and Betty. In consequence there was much talk between him and Elizabeth of a 'bewildering and confusing nature'.[26] She pointed out that a young man of his age ought to get married to a nice young woman and that he was right to look around, while he hotly denied everything and at the same time accused *her* of infidelities. H. G. Wells came for a time and took a great liking for Thelma. He marched her up and down the terrace and demanded to know whether she had a lover, and if not, why not. She stood up to his onslaught and resisted his advances with spirit.

When it was time for Frere to leave, Elizabeth wickedly booked a double sleeper for him and Margery (Waterlow) Norton's daughter, who was leaving at the same time. When they discovered this the poor young man had to spend the night in the corridor, for had 'something happened' between the two travellers Elizabeth was bound somehow to get to know about it. 'She had very acute antennae for that sort of thing,' Frere remembered with a shudder nearly sixty years later. 'The last thing I wanted to do was cause waves with her – she was everything to me.' The next day he took the girl to lunch in Paris and they both drank 'quite a lot of gin' to break the ice between them. 'I discovered I needn't have bothered to spend such an uncomfortable night after all,' he recalled, for she became very friendly to her escort.[27] Nevertheless the spectre of Elizabeth fell like a pall between them.

Towards the end of the month Bertrand and Dora Russell arrived, and Dora quickly settled down to lecturing the others about Russia and Bolshevism. She and Bertrand had been to Russia and China the year before and had been impressed by what they had seen, although Bertrand had nearly died and Dora became pregnant. Elizabeth thanked God a) that she was uneducated, and was never taught anything as a child, and b) that everything her daughters were taught slid off them almost immediately. Thelma 'bearded old Bertie with a courage and persistence that convulsed [them]. He *is* a beaver inside. I'm sure his soul has an enormous wagging beard,' Elizabeth wrote to Frere.

John came over to tell her that he and Katherine were attempting a trial separation. His wife's huge disappointment at the failure of her treatment, combined with radiation sickness and the break-up of her marriage, compelled her towards even more extreme forms of therapy. She borrowed £100 from Elizabeth, calling herself a 'desperate character'[28], and confided to her sister Vera, 'I *can't* be ill any longer.'[29] She spoke of at least saving her soul if she was not able to save her body, to the alarm of Elizabeth, and was demanding that her disease *must* be annihilated, presenting Life or God with an ultimatum. In August she left Switzerland to continue her X-ray treatment. She cast about for a suitable gift for Elizabeth but could find nothing but a 'brand new little *Jaquette* the colour of zinnias . . . may it hang behind your door or where such things hang in well regulated households'.[30] Elizabeth, who always changed into a pretty coloured jacket for tea, usually Chinese silk ones, was delighted and had never seen 'anything so sweet'[31] and so like her cousin.

As if to put a seal on the unsatisfactory events of the summer, to her horror and fury Elizabeth heard that a parcel of land between the Chalet Soleil and the view of the mountains had been sold to an Englishman who intended to build on it. She immediately determined to sell the chalet and find somewhere else to live. It was an unavoidable tragedy and she quickly became philosophical, but the rest of the summer was blighted as a result. She christened the owner of the new chalet 'Winter' after the title of the best-selling novel *If Winter Comes* by A. S. M. Hutchinson. To Bertrand she confessed, in a letter, a more sinister objection:

> Winter has come, and his chalet is having its roof put on. I can see it and it can see me, from my flat path, but I'm going to buy a strip more of that and plant him out behind trees. I've not seen him yet, and don't want to. I've written to Rehder [her solicitor] to find out what he can about him, for he might be an emissary of F's . . . I don't even get angry, only fleetingly regretful that it should be so. It would indeed be idiotic, seeing that it is so, to make it worse by being infuriated. Winter may come to my gates (if I had any) but he shan't get into my thoughts.

Evi had married her 'Useless Eustace' and wrote ecstatic letters, though she remained mysterious about what he did for a living when he was employed. Her mother was forced to conclude that he was a plumber, for only a life spent among lavatories would account, she thought, for her daughter's extreme reluctance to tell *what* he did. The previous year H.B. had fallen for another older woman, although she was not as old as the tutor's wife, who, he assured his mother, was very nice, and they wanted to get married. Elizabeth thought it a very excellent thing for him to get engaged for it would keep him straight and make him work, but nothing could come of it until he was of age for he would have to have his mother's consent, and that she would not give. She wrote to Liebet:

> H.B. is so unbalanced – always wanting this, that or the other and quite oblivious to the hard facts of life. If only I had a clever, quick son! But he seems such a helpless little thing, full of good intentions and nice feelings, but so all

over the place, and so unripe.

H.B. got married anyway and Elizabeth became aware, from her children's letters, that, at least for the time being, all four of them were happy with their spouses. She thought it a pity she had not been so lucky as to have someone she could utterly trust and be happy with, too – just then she was alone after her guests had left and ashamed of herself for hating it. She had thought she would love the solitude and was strong enough and free enough in spirit to rejoice in it, but to her disgust and disappointment she found she was nothing of the sort, and realized that she still was not grown up in a lot of ways. 'There must be someone in the world who loves one more than anyone else, and the person who hasn't got that background is a forlorn thing . . . I know now why all the elderly go to so many parties and rush where there are crowds – they go to forget for a little while . . . '[32]

She was at last beginning to sink into what she would later call her real old age, and was no longer able to pass as twenty years younger than she actually was. For a woman who was flattered by the attentions of young men, and whose most recent young lover was showing signs of preferring the company of women of his own age, it was to be a truly difficult descent. Elderly men were often introduced to her by well-meaning friends as an ideal solution to her loneliness but she did not like them and thought, as she once shocked Katherine Mansfield by saying, that 'they *exude*'. The elderly men of her acquaintance who would have been only too pleased to come to some arrangement with her she called her 'old boys' and avoided.

In September 1922 Elizabeth attempted to struggle on with the proof corrections of *The Enchanted April,* the most high-spirited of her books, but her own spirits remained heavy and downcast. She travelled twice to Lausanne, where the happiest part of her childhood was spent, but could not shake off this new mood of doubt and fear. It seemed she had made a rapid change from the triumphant, admired, spoilt darling of London society to a small disconsolate figure alone in empty hotel lobbies, listening to meaningless string quartets and being attended by impersonal waiters. Occasionally she escaped on solitary walks, looking at shops and churches, but she never found the consolation that she sought. She was surrounded by great, enormous, empty days, full of nothing but sunshine which seemed to her to be 'too bad to be true'.[33] She wrote profoundly gloomy letters to Frere to which he replied that he did not understand what she was talking about.

News reached the chalet that Francis was working on his memoirs, which caused his wife some sleepless nights. It was altogether conceivable that he would publish an account of their life together which could be both upsetting and damaging to her. When *My Life and Adventures* was published she was relieved and also hurt to find that she had not been mentioned in it at all, and a sad photograph of Mollie bore the inscription of 'The Countess Russell'. Elizabeth was thrown into a panic by the last words in the book, '*Au revoir*', which indicated that he planned a further volume, supposing in it she might not come off so lightly. 'Does that mean, do you think, that he is going to write a sequel?' she anxiously asked her friend Mrs Belloc Lowndes. 'If he does it's bound to be all about me.'[34]

At the end of the month Frere and his friend Orlo Williams came to stay at the chalet. Orlo had distinguished himself in boxing at Eton and sabre fighting at Oxford, became a barrister, was elected a Chevalier of the Légion d'honneur and was then, in 1922, conveyancer to the Supreme Court. He also wrote articles for the *Times Literary Supplement* and other journals, and he and Frere spent much time together, when they were in London, drinking at the Café Royal and dancing at the Savoy. Their hostess was again 'completely happy'[35] in their company, in spite of Frere arriving almost entirely broken down from overwork and reverting to his tiresome and wrangling moods for much of the time. Orlo travelled on to Italy after a few days and Elizabeth and Frere back to London at the end of October in time for the publication of *The Enchanted April*. It was greeted with muted reviews. Rebecca West in the *New Statesman* declared that it was in the nature of a disaster:

> The author . . . has the most enviable talent, a penetrating and graceful intelligence, which might have belonged to the eighteenth century and which finds its natural form in wit, and a pretty style which paints a clear pastel of the world. She suffers however from a fatal tendency to humbug.

Earlier, when Elizabeth had been correcting the proofs, Frere had sent her a copy of *The Judge* by Rebecca West. He thought it 'full blooded' and wanted to know her opinion of it. (He and Miss West were seeing rather more of each other than Elizabeth would have liked, had she known, especially as the younger woman was attempting to reform Frere's taste away from 'froth' and towards serious novels, as she thought of them.) Elizabeth's reaction to *The Judge* was that it was 'quite strangely bad'. It had, she thought, among almost all of the bad qualities a novel can have, the supreme and final one of being uninteresting:

> I just can't wade through the thick black stuff . . . that made up diseased stuff . . . the effect of Rebecca's dark scowlings at life . . . If her book is full blooded, and all the blood in it is black, mine is too thin blooded, and its blood pale pink.[36]

Their dislike of each other's work was not because one writer was good and the other bad, but simply that Elizabeth attempted to write books which people would enjoy reading, to entertain them, and along the way uplift them with her unique brand of hopeful philosophy. Rebecca West, who was part of the nihilistic, post-war generation, had, in company with her contemporaries, pushed aside anything of the sort as being irrelevant and was attempting to get to the bowels of reality, as she saw it. Since Miss West had never been happy, by her own confession was not happy when she wrote *The Judge* and according to her son was never a particularly well-adjusted person in her lifetime, it is hardly surprising that her novels are rather gloomy. The difference between the two writers was that Elizabeth *knew* that her books sounded, then, like 'a thin flute playing in an empty afternoon, all alone,' and were not robust or particularly realistic although they were serious, while Rebecca West was grimly determined to capture the Real Thing, whatever that was, like spearing a butterfly. There was further enmity between them because of the lovers they had shared, of course, though each of them thought she was far too mature to allow personal jealousies to cloud her judgements on art. In fact, the situation between the two women was exactly the same as it had been between John Middleton Murry and Hugh Walpole, which was a symptom of the ferment in the art of the novel, and much else, which erupted in 1922. As Walpole remarked, time would tell.

Elizabeth was shocked to find that the usual junketing in which she was persuaded to join in celebration of her book and of herself being back in London seemed as hollow to her as the solitary silences which had echoed so deafeningly at the chalet that summer. Her sure, safe and well-tried methods of shaking off the attentions of what she called the 'black dog' of her lowest moods were no longer effective. In defying the things that were so 'fantastically horrible'[37] everywhere she no longer shot up to the stars, and even though she attempted to hold on to the notion that something good would always turn up in time – a sunny day, the love of a good man or the first primrose of spring – enormous vigilance was needed. It was also taking up far more of her energy than she had to spare to maintain the precariously poised relationship with Frere, whose moodiness was almost continuous. She was often unwell, with pains and nausea which were emotional in origin and kept her low in the daytime and prevented her from sleeping at night. When she consulted a doctor he diagnosed the menopause.

At Christmas she invited Frere down to the Isle of Wight where she had taken a cottage in Shanklin for the two weeks surrounding that – for the lonely – truly dreadful holiday. She told her friends that she was staying with the Waterlows and told the Waterlows that she wanted to be alone. He agreed to come down for Christmas and at the weekends, for he was working in the week. She travelled over by herself on 21 December to Ryde 'packed like herrings in a small cabin'[38] and decided immediately she saw the cottage that she liked it. As soon as she had settled in her pains vanished. Still anxious about the wiles of her husband, who was not above having her dogged by private detectives to gather evidence for adultery, she booked a room for Frere in a nearby lodging house. He arrived the next day and they had a very pleasant time: 'I like this Xmas better than any I've had for ages – so peaceful and simple and quiet.' The following weekend he arrived liverish and cross and became more and more so as the weekend progressed. They had 'rather a poor thing in days'. She said things too that she 'grieved to say',[39] though towards Sunday evening they were friends again. When she arrived back in London she told Charlotte that she had 'a wonderful Christmas of utter silence. I never spoke a word all day except to wish the servant a Merry Xmas in the morning and the hope that she'd had it in the evening.'[40] During this latest attempt to enjoy being with Frere as a couple she had had a blow which was to signal the end of their relationship as nothing else would have done. They had gone to lunch at a nearby pub and fallen into conversation with an elderly man and his daughter who innocently assumed that she was Frere's mother. She was to describe this episode with feeling in her novel *Love* which is about her affair with Frere.

When Elizabeth arrived back in London she found a letter from Katherine waiting for her. It contained a cheque in repayment for the £100, and was written from Gurdjieff's *château* in Fontainebleau which had been a Carmelite monastery and was called the Institute for the Harmonious Development of Man, or The Prieuré for short.

I wish I could explain why I have not written to you for so

long. It is not for lack of love. But such a black fit came on me in Paris when I realised that the X-ray treatment wasn't going to do any more than it had done beyond upsetting my heart more that I gave up everything and tried a new life altogether. But this decision was immensely complicated for 'personal' reasons too. When I came to London from Switzerland I did (Sydney was right so far) go through what books and undergraduates call a spiritual crisis, I suppose. For the first time in my life everything bored me. Everything, and worse, everybody seemed a compromise and so flat, so dull, so mechanical. If I had been well I should have rushed off to darkest Africa or the Andes or the Ganges or wherever one rushes to at those times, to try for a change of heart (one can't change one's heart in public) and to gain new impressions. For it seems to me we live on new impressions – really new ones.

But such grand flights being impossible I burned what boats I had and came here where I am living with about 50 or 60 people, mainly Russians. It is a fantastic existence, impossible to describe. One might be anywhere. In Bokhara or Tiflis or Afghanistan (except, alas, for the climate!). But even the climate does not seem to matter so much when one is whirling along at such a rate. For we do most decidedly whirl. But I can't tell you what a joy it is for me to be in contact with living people who are strange and quick and not at all ashamed to be themselves. It's a kind of supreme elation to be among them.

But what nonsense this all sounds. That is the worst of letters; they are fumbling things.

I haven't written a word since October and I don't mean to until the spring. I want so much material; I am tired of my little stories like birds bred in cages.

But enough, dear Elizabeth, I have not thanked you even for *The Enchanted April*. It is a delectable book; the only [other] person who could have written it is Mozart . . . How do you write like that? How? How?

Do you see John, I wonder? He sounds very happy and serene. Life is a mysterious affair!

Goodbye, my dearest cousin. I shall never know anyone like you. I shall remember every little thing about you for ever.

This was the last letter Katherine was to write to Elizabeth. Indeed, it was the last letter she was to post off to anybody.

While Katherine had been in London during August and September, she had had several conversations with Orage concerning the psychologist Gurdjieff. She learnt that this mysterious Russian who had been born in Alexandrapol, Georgia, in 1877, had done many extraordinary things in the intervening years, including leading his friends and pupils out of Russia over the Caucasus during the Russian Revolution. He had fed and found them shelter, presented with them a ballet called *Struggle of the Magicians* in Moscow at the height of the war and unfolded to his pupils secret doctrines which he had learnt on his travels as a young man in the East, contracting much accepted dogma and heretically explaining the workings of the universe. He so impressed Lady Rothermere that she gave him enough money, on behalf of the Theosophists, to set up his Institute and harmoniously develop those who came to it. It had been open only a few months when Katherine arrived. The people already there were working at a fever pitch to restore the *château*, and they became reasonably self-sufficient by cultivating the gardens and keeping animals. In the evening they all ate with their master who encouraged them to drink and eat exotic foods which he cooked himself, and teased them all in various ways to help them, he hoped, 'WAKE UP'. After supper he taught them the whirling dances which were based, it was said, on the dervish method, but were mostly his own creation. They were also reconstructing a hangar in the grounds inside which was created a huge rug-lined Moorish tent where the dances and lectures were to be performed and Gurdjieff's pupils gathered for celebrations.

Katherine had travelled over from England in the middle of October and spent three freezing months at the Prieuré. L.M. went with her, but had no time for Gurdjieff and found herself a job looking after chickens at Lisieux. Gurdjieff apprehended Katherine's quality and gave her comfortable rooms in the house, but a few weeks later moved her, as was his method, to extremely uncomfortable ones. She was put on a balcony above the cows in the cow byre during the day where she was supposed to inhale their breath.*

Katherine's interpretation of the philosophy she encountered

*Gurdjieff's medicine was based on the homeopathic method that like cures like. The sweet breath of the cows was supposed to mingle with Katherine's and encourage her lungs to cure themselves. He himself had lived in the byre before her and his pupils had lavishly and imaginatively decorated it.

there was: 'Risk! Risk! Anything! Care no more for the opinion of others, for those voices. Do the hardest thing on earth for you. Act for yourself. Face the truth'[41] – an uncanny echo of Elizabeth's youthful warnings against props – 'Shake them off . . . and go alone, crawl, stumble, stagger, but go alone.'

After Christmas Katherine invited John to visit her, but on the evening of his arrival she suffered a massive haemorrhage and died. Ida Baker was to see her once again. Her shade, or ghost, passed through a room in which Ida was working with John, and she 'seemed to smile'.[42] She had no stick or arm to lean on, so perhaps she had found the freedom that she had so earnestly sought.

In her will Katherine left Elizabeth her annotated Shakespeare and (a private Shakespearean joke) her second best walking stick, while a book of poems published posthumously was dedicated to Elizabeth. Love and respect had grown up between them equally, although Katherine was the only person Elizabeth was afraid of –she felt in her presence 'spiritually all thumbs'.[43] But their pride in each other was their most evident emotion – Elizabeth felt that she had hatched Katherine, which in a way she had, for it was Elizabeth's influence which started the younger woman on a writing career, while Katherine wrote to Dorothy Brett:

> The point about [Elizabeth] is that one loves her and is proud of her. Oh, that's so important! To be proud of the person one loves. It is essential. It's deep – deep. There's no wound more bitter to love than not to be able to be proud of the other. It's the unpardonable offence, I think.

· 18 ·

The Descent

In the spring of 1923 the musical drama *The Immortal Hour,* with music by Rutland Boughton and libretto by William Sharp, based on the novel by Fiona Macleod, was playing at the Regent Theatre in London. It is a Celtic phantasmagoria with music, chanting, declamation and singing that catches the atmosphere not only of the early Celts but also of London in the Twenties filtered through Celtic mysticism. It is intensely romantic, but takes place in a realm that has nothing whatever to do with marriage, which was a relief to many who had been battered by that institution. Elizabeth saw it and was not only uplifted by the experience but sustained by the hints of other realities with which it was infused. She went to it again and again until she became a member of a small band of people who went to it practically every day, whether to the matinée or to the evening performance. She wrote asking Maud Ritchie to accompany her in April, saying, 'It will be my eleventh time. It is the most wonderful thing – each time more exquisite than ever.' She even went to the stage door and made the acquaintance of the actor who played Etan, the hero, and invited him to tea with her on several occasions. In her next novel, *Love,* she attributed the birth of the passion of Christopher, the hero, for Catherine, the much older heroine, to the stirring effects of the production.

> The first time they met, though they didn't know it, for they were unconscious of each other, was at *The Immortal Hour,* then playing to almost empty houses away at King's Cross; but they both went so often, and the audience at that time was so conspicuous because there was so little of it and so much room to put it in, that quite soon people who went frequently came to know each other by sight, and felt friendly and inclined to nod and smile, and this

259

happened too to Christopher and Catherine.[1]

In *Love* Elizabeth described with relentless honesty her own doubts and reluctant submission to Frere's demands, the shocked reaction of her friends and the inevitable tipping of the scales as her dependence on him gradually outweighed his on her. It is a tragedy told with humour and insight and points up the inevitable outcome of such a relationship: she gets older, and under the strain begins to look her age in spite of every effort not to. She even submits to a course of treatment from a Manoukhin-like character to have herself bombarded with electricity, which episode is based on what Katherine had told her on that glassed-in veranda at the Hotel de l'Angleterre about her own ordeal. Christopher inevitably, and in spite of his best intentions, begins to prefer the company of his own age group to an increasingly anxious, elderly woman.

John Middleton Murry wrote to Elizabeth that spring about Ida Baker, Katherine's devoted friend, who was not sure, now that Katherine was no longer in need of her, what to do with herself. Elizabeth felt that the least she could do for her cousin's memory was to take on the responsibility of Ida's welfare. She employed her to help move her flat to a smaller one in Whitehall Court and left her there as housekeeper when she went back to the chalet. There she was to be utterly alone for two months to work hard on *Love*.

She advanced on the problem of her loneliness with courage, realizing that it was likely to be her lot for the rest of her life, but she soon became possessed with a 'cannibal urge'[2] to see some of her own flesh and blood and, conquering her distaste for the Fatherland, she paid a surprise visit to Trix. It was Elizabeth who was surprised, however. Trix had continually written to her complaining of dire poverty, but Elizabeth found her daughter living in a beautiful old house, surrounded by every sort of luxury, and her husband, Tony, a pleasant and charming man.* On her way back Elizabeth called to see Teppi at the school she had started up and 'loved her more than ever'. After an initial few confused hours of great joy and excitement and happiness, Teppi learnt of all that had happened to the family,

---

*In spite of appearances, apparently they were indeed as poor as they claimed to be. Their daughter Sybilla wrote to the author in 1986: 'My parents were bitterly poor, so poor that . . . they often went out for bread and butter picnics because they did not have enough money to buy meat for the servants and themselves (you may ask why servants? You had to have servants in those days, certainly in their social position). They did not own their house and E[lizabeth] must have known it as I know my parents asked her for a loan to enable them to buy the house on a mortgage.' This she gave them.

about Elizabeth's marriage to the 'once so gentle and affable lover who must have developed into a despot', and was pleased that the wings of her friend's soul had not been 'clipped by her dreadful experiences'.[3]

That summer of 1923 the chalet was again full of guests although more and more of them were women of a Sapphic orientation. Although Elizabeth's family were becoming anxious about the number of such women in her life, she, however, merely enjoyed their company and never would be one of them. She was very much the type of woman they adored, and of course she loved to be adored. Frere came in August and his 'gay, sweet, kind natural self' was more often than not eclipsed by his fault-finding and tiresomeness, so that Elizabeth's gaiety was 'smudged out'.[4]

After Frere had left to go back to England Elizabeth looked back on the time he had been there as having been

> 'like a dream, your visit . . . I felt too melancholy when the dusk engulfed you, and wandered round the empty house like a lost sheep, went into your room and shut the windows and drew the curtains – I don't know why . . . Don't think about differences and arguments – only think of resemblances and all the laughter and happiness . . . Hugh went off yesterday, beaming from ear to ear, after assuring me he was more devoted to me than to anyone in the world except Melchior! Never did anyone depart in such spirits from the object of his regard.[5]

She determined to stay on at the chalet after everyone's departure and after much tedious business to do with the children's German money she set herself to work on *Love*, which proved almost impossible at times and more often than not six pages were torn up for every one written. To Frere she wrote at the end of September, ' . . . writing isn't an easy job, and the easier it looks when it's finished the more soul sweat has really gone into it. But I wouldn't be without it for anything – to be happy one *must* create . . . '

H. G. Wells had recently advised her on how to conduct an affair with a much younger person, and the gist of it was that when the younger person's ardour began to flag, the older person must make haste to break off the relationship. Unfortunately, Elizabeth could not take his advice, although she tried. Back in England, she travelled around sightseeing to avoid pining for the young man, but wherever she went she wanted to be somewhere else and when she

ELIZABETH

got to the other place she wished she was back where she was before.

Over the Christmas holidays she was ordered by her doctor to take a trip to South Africa – she begged to go to America but he would not hear of it. She had a miserable time and wrote a stream of yearning letters to Frere while she was there. She struggled to do all the things the doctor ordered, for it was supposed to be a rest cure and she was not to talk or walk very much and to sleep as much as she could. She missed her brother Sydney dreadfully and 'the whole trip from start to finish was purgatory', although she made friends with Lord Lambourne who had also been ordered out there by his doctor and was also hating it. The ship heaved 'like a fat woman's emotional bosom', and Arthur Churchman sent her a container 'as big as a hip-bath'[6] full of pineapples before she departed so that in the Bay of Biscay they all rolled over her and she claimed to have decorative bruises in the shape of pineapples. When she got to Cape Town it was swept by a high wind from dawn to dusk and she felt it was an overrated spot. 'Nobody can be either dignified or happy in a high wind. With one hand I keep my hat on, with the other I keep my skirts down, and with my feet I carry my bag and hankerchief, etc. and brush the dirt out of my eyes,' she wrote to Frere. She was treated like royalty there.

The following summer, 1924, she went as usual to the chalet alone in June and felt 'like a sponge, full of holes absorbing any sort of liquid of life that came along'. She felt extraordinarily sensitive and responsive as if she had been turned inside out, and the least touch set her off quivering. It was an agreeable state, and everything seemed wonderful. She wrote to Frere:

> When I'm alone . . . every sense seems to grow incredibly more acute. I feel as if I were all over antennae, waving round and catching up every impression. Music is more wonderful, love and friendship, beauty – it all gets increased a thousand fold . . .

Almost immediately she went for a tour around the Lake of Geneva and Ida Baker joined her at Lausanne. She told Elizabeth that Katherine's last book of poems, which Elizabeth had been looking for everywhere and couldn't find, had been dedicated to her, and Elizabeth was amazed that John had not bothered to let her know. They visited the Château de Coppet where the Lassetters had lived so many years ago, and long before that, Madame de Staël had given refuge to her friend Madame Récamier, fleeing when her husband's reversals of fortune made it impossible to stay with him. There

Prince August, Elizabeth's children's great-grandfather, had fallen in love with her.

In July Liebet arrived at the chalet from California and she and her mother sat up far into the moonlit night joyfully talking about everything under the sun. Four days later Trix arrived. She did not know that Liebet was there so Liebet hid in the chalet and burst out at her. Trix was delighted for they hadn't seen each other for eleven years and Elizabeth felt it was like a dream listening to her own children talking about their babies to each other. After two weeks the girls went off to Germany together and Liebet returned in the first week of August. From then on the chalet guests started to arrive in a steady stream which included Maud Ritchie and Frere. Elizabeth was struggling with the end of *Love*, which she never did feel happy about. She read *Something Childish* by Katherine and appreciated the strides Katherine took in that book and felt sure that, had she lived, she would have done great things. She went to Paris to see Liebet off and arrived back at the chalet in the middle of September to be surrounded once more by her female friends, her 'feminines'.

In an attempt to find some mortar to bind herself and Frere, Elizabeth resuscitated the Mr Arbuthnot and Ellen Wemyss exchange of letters idea which had foundered with Walpole and Bertrand, suggesting to Frere that he might like to take the part of Mr Arbuthnot. He agreed to try, and wrote some perceptive, but black-blooded, nihilistic, and definitely 'modern' things about how the war had turned all his values upside down, and had nearly sent him mad; taught him nothing but the 'eternity possible in a moment',[7] and so on, which caused Elizabeth to withdraw tactfully. She became convinced that God wanted her to be a recluse, and paradoxically started to dream about buying a flower farm somewhere in America or the Riviera and having Liebet and Trix and their families to live there with her. She and the two girls had talked lightly about the project that summer and at the time Elizabeth had wisely seen that mothers-in-law are not welcome in even the happiest of marriages. Nevertheless the idea would not entirely lie down and go to sleep.

In the summer of 1925 *Love* was published and Elizabeth started work on *Introduction to Sally*. She decided that her London life was far too frivolous and inclined her to want to see more of Frere than he appeared to want to see of her, so she resolved to spend her time in England in the country. She found a cottage at Wood Green in the New Forest called Six, for it was the sixth house in the lane. It is tiny, like a gingerbread house, thatched and very old with two small rooms up and two down. Nestling under the brow of Castle Hill it enjoyed superb views over the water meadows to the Avon. She invited Ida Baker to come and live with her. The two of them existed for a while in marginal harmony, but Ida Baker did not like having to make sandwiches and canapés for Elizabeth's guests and resented it further when she was not always invited to join them. Frere, whom Elizabeth still clung to, called from time to time but obviously found the duty irksome – he had become exceedingly interested in and good at golf, and a day spent visiting Elizabeth was a day wasted if he could not play. Then the young man was struck with a brilliant idea. Elizabeth, it was clear, needed something to dote on, and for doting purposes, he himself was not available. (He was by then living with a young lady whom Elizabeth did not know of and would never have approved.) What, he decided, she needed was a dog, and there arrived at Six through the post a box, out of which squeezed a woolly but breedless puppy called Pincher. From the moment Elizabeth saw him she began to cheer up. In a few months she and Pincher had had enough of Wood Green and returned to London, leaving Ida Baker behind to live happily at Six for the rest of her life.

Pincher was only a success until he had to be doctored and then he became fat and lethargic. Frere, seeing this, gave Elizabeth another dog, Knobbie, who was a very young fox-terrier. London was obviously no place for them so Elizabeth built a house near the golf club at Wentworth in Virginia Water and named it White Gates or, she joked, as the English would no doubt pronounce it, 'Wiggates'. It was a single-bedroomed cottage with two large garages and a flat above them for staff. Behind it was a magnificent garden divided into three consecutive areas and a little wooden summer-house where Elizabeth worked. Beyond was a wood joined to the garden by a gate where she walked Pincher and Knobbie. While it was being built she stayed from time to time in Venice and Frere joined her there. To the dismay of her daughters she continued to write letters of anticipation about the flower farm she was going to buy, and in the summer she went to the chalet and her guests revolved pleasantly around her.

Frere went to America and Elizabeth arranged for him to see the Doubledays in the hope of getting him work. Nelson gave him a small magazine to sell, which he did with great energy from the back of a motorbike. As a result of this venture he was offered an excellent job on one of Doubleday's recently acquired subsidiary publishing companies in England called William Heinemann. On his return he was in 'one of those moods which seemed to mock the very thought or desire of any affinity'[8] between himself and Elizabeth, but she remained constant and eventually, after a few weeks, they were back to their old routine of seeing each other every three days or so, going out to the theatre, dinner and dancing. When she was away from England she insisted he use the flat or house in Surrey as his own and because he was fond of her and he enjoyed staying at the house and playing golf at the Wentworth Golf Club there seemed no end to the relationship in sight.

Evi, who had had two babies, began to have problems with her husband who did not seem capable of holding down a job. She wrote her mother bitter letters about him and Elizabeth wrote back that she would sell the chalet and look after her if necessary but that she did not see why she should make sacrifices for the sake of a man who was making her daughter unhappy. Eventually 'Useless Eustace'[9] fell so seriously in debt that he had to 'skip the town'.[10] Elizabeth increased the allowance and Evi settled down to a reasonably happy life in Los Angeles looking after her two daughters and writing novels, none of which were ever published. Her mother was wise enough to understand that the life Evi was living was the one she wanted to live and ceased to enjoin her to reform.

Frere gave Elizabeth a cat, some doves and another dog and her family began to refer to her at White Gates as 'Whipsnade'. So she entered upon a fresh lap of loneliness 'decorated with dogs',[11] until one day she had a visit from Bridget Guinness. She was the wife of Benjamin Seymour Guinness, who had augmented the family fortune by investing in American railroad stock among other things and was hugely wealthy. Elizabeth had met them in 1919 in New York and they had seen more of each other since for Bridget was one of London's most elegant hostesses and had given many parties at their house in Ascot and at 11 and 12 Carlton House Terrace in London. In the mid-Twenties they had given their London house to their son, Loel, to avoid death duties, and moved to the Riviera.

> She came to see me, bringing into the room with her that dark afternoon, I thought, all the radiance of the South . . . and wherever she moved I fancied there was delicately shaken into the air a fragrance of sweet flowers . . . [12]

Bridget tried to persuade Elizabeth that she must come to the Riviera, a place which Elizabeth had visited from time to time but had rejected as a solution for her because of the endless parties and the 'gossipy, bored and therefore grabbing people whirling around'. Now that her friend Bridget was there, and also Wells, she thought about living there in a new light.

In the summer of 1926 Charlotte took a villa in Peyloubet and invited her sister to come and stay. It was just across an olive grove from where H. G. Wells lived. He was building an 'enormous sort of Kubla Khan dwelling with maidens and dulcimers no doubt complete', with his new friend Odette Keun, 'a foreign lady of much vitality and very beautiful, slender legs'.[13] Elizabeth strolled over to see them soon after she arrived and was amused to see over the chimneypiece in the hall the inscription: TWO LOVERS BUILT THIS HOUSE. She would have enjoyed her time with Charlotte but, as she wrote to Frere, 'There are no doors in this house, which is really a calamity.' At first she didn't like the Riviera because she was getting no letters from Frere, but as soon as some arrived she began to change her mind. Then she met a man at one of Bridget's lunch parties who lent her his villa and for a few weeks more she enjoyed the glorious sunshine in solitude and with doors. But she came to no decision then about living there, for all her plans were bound up with being near the man she loved, and she knew she would hardly ever see him if she lived in the South of France.

The following summer of 1927 when Elizabeth was, as usual, staying at the chalet, weeks and weeks went by without a letter from Frere and she began to fear he had had an accident. Sick and anxious, she went to Bayreuth with Trix and called on Frau Siegfried Wagner in her 'funny, ugly, stuffy old Mausoleum house' which was just the same as when Elizabeth had visited it thirty-eight years previously with Henning. Frau Siegfried was English by birth, 'but nothing else', Elizabeth commented. They sat on occasion at the Wagners' table with Siegfried sitting there like a death moth and Melchior, 'very sweet and *treuherzig*', devouring huge steaks and onions with his wife sitting by him 'deliciously pretty'.[14] Elizabeth thought that if Tolstoy – not one of her favourite authors – had written opera he would have written *Parsifal*, and hated Bayreuth and everything in it.

By 9 August she was back at the chalet and still no letter from Frere. The summer guests began to arrive relentlessly, oblivious of their hostess's agitation. First there was Maud Ritchie, then Hugh Walpole, closely followed by the cook and then a telegram from Frere on the 11th. Elizabeth was 'immensely relieved'. Two days later he arrived, very brown and sweet and amusing, but after a day or so began shouting out his 'well known views on idle, predatory women'.[15] But the summer was a success in spite of his outbursts and Elizabeth's bouts of sickness which kept her low but of which she never complained.

Middleton Murry's edition of Katherine's journals arrived at the chalet that September, sent by Hugh Walpole, and Elizabeth was saddened when she read of how lonely her cousin had been. When she came to the parts in it about herself which Murry had not had the kindness to omit she wrote in her diary:

> 'She has a vulgar little mind.' If it is true was I not born with it? Can I help it? I was very shy always with her, afraid of her while intensely admiring. Perhaps embarrassment made me say vulgar things. But I don't know – probably she is right. Depressing . . . one has so many sides and it is possible that K.M. drew out the vulgar one.

'I felt so gross when I was with her', she wrote to Murry, 'as if my hands were full of chilblains.'

In London that autumn Frere told her something about the woman with whom he had been living and who was insisting he marry her, 'and the bottom was knocked out of my life. No good pretending it isn't.' The rest of the afternoon and evening were 'knifelike in their cutting pain'. She remembered what Henning had once said in Meran a few weeks before he died: 'Dolly dear, Dolly dear, if only this stupid life were ended – it is nothing but torture and irritation.' She had not agreed with him then but she did now. She heard that she had sold her latest novel, *Expiation*, to a magazine, which would normally have delighted her: 'As it is I only want to die!'[16]

She spent a bleak and unhappy Christmas alone on the Riviera and saw the New Year in holding hands with total strangers and pretending jollity. 'All these days were filled with grief and bewilderment by L.G's strange behaviour,'[17] she wrote, and it would not be too long before she understood the reason for it. The following spring she met Frere by arrangement in Paris on her way back to London from the chalet. They had lunch and walked in the Bois. It was there, sitting on a bench, that Frere told her that he was married. She took the news reasonably quietly and calmly, but when he outlined the circumstances, telling her that his wife's two brothers had more or less frog-marched him to the registry office, Elizabeth told him he was a fool, that she could tolerate everybody except fools and that she never wanted to see him again. She got up and walked away from him. When she got back to England she had a bout of severe sickness, but was seeing Frere regularly again within a few weeks. In June of the following year he fell ill with appendicitis and she flew to his bedside in the nursing home after the operation. Unfortunately she coincided with his wife and was obliged to make her exit as speedily as possible.

Bridget Guinness so much wanted Elizabeth to move to the South of France that she built her a house on her own land which she called L'Enchantement after *The Enchanted April*. It would have been perfect except she forgot to put in the staircase so that it had been rather roughly patched in at the last moment. It was a charming little pink house, but too small, and when Elizabeth went to see it, though touched by her friend's gesture, she felt she could not live in it. Instead she bought a property near Cannes, just below Mougins, which had had a cottage built on it by an English earl* and she engaged an architect to transform it into what she had in mind.

While she was waiting for the villa to be finished she arranged to go to America to see her children, though Frere, when he heard of her plan, was 'astonished and depressed'[18] for he was having much trouble with his wife and needed Elizabeth to advise him. She travelled to Liebet's new house in Vermont. Evi came from California with her children and H.B. and his wife came over for a few days. Elizabeth wrote back to Liebet when she got home, 'Oh it was lovely, and I'll store it up in my heart as a squirrel stores nuts and bring them out on bad days and gloat.'

She was working on a new novel called *Father*, and as a result became thoughtful about her own and her children's experiences of being fathered; for they had all had ones of a Victorian mould and very much the type of man, inevitably, that she was writing about. She corresponded with Liebet about Henning.

> . . . for though he teased you and was fierce as well, he was also very charming often and especially did he love *you*. Still, I understand your point of view about him, and fathers can't begin too young being gentle and loving to their children. My father was terror itself to me all my life, and yet I was very fond of him after I grew up, and much appreciated him and felt he was right not to be able to endure me when I was small.

A few weeks later she sat next to Jung, the psychologist, at one of Hugh Walpole's dinner parties and thought him like a large, genial

---

*The Earl of Sandwich. Later it was bought and transformed into a small palace by the film star Josette Day. Now, as the property of an oil prince, it has marble and onyx bathrooms to each of the seven bedrooms and two swimming pools, while the large kitchen is made entirely of black marble. Of Wells's house there is no trace.

English cricketer. He delighted Hugh with his hatred of hysterics. To Thelma, Elizabeth wrote, 'We met Jung, who is to Freud what cherubim is to seraphim and the Epistles is to the Apostles and Snelgrove is to Marshall . . . We came away from him as full of complexes and suppressions as before.' If she had asked him about what was currently interesting her in fathers and their behaviour to their daughters, she might have discovered that her own inability to enjoy the married state, in spite of all her best intentions, was largely because of her conviction that her father was right not to have been able to endure her as a child.* All children wish to believe their parents right, however tyrannically and unjustly they have been treated, and daughters will project their father's opinion of them on to the man they marry. All her life Elizabeth twisted herself into the most complex emotional contortions in an attempt to *feel* the love that was felt for her by men, with very little success. In the book she was writing the heroine was tyrannized by her father and when he died found true and eternal love, a psychologically unrealistic ending that would be very unlikely to happen in real life.

In February 1929 *Expiation* was published, the greatest contrast to *Introduction to Sally*, her previous book which was in essence a delightful, lighthearted and carefree story about a very pretty girl who is adored by all and ends up being the light of a duke's life. *Expiation* investigates once more the destructive influence on a woman's life of a man like Francis who insists his meals are on time and who punishes his wife, Milly, in a way difficult for her to combat:

> . . . when he was annoyed with her he didn't so much talk as smoulder. She got to know these smoulderings well. They were very punitive in their effect, much more so than a great blaze-up . . . 'Will it be enough when God, at the end, asks me what I have done with my life, to point to Ernest and say, I saw to it that his meals were good?'

In the end Milly has a long-term affair with another man called Arthur 'in whose life she was first an inspiration and later simply

---

*In May 1936 Elizabeth was again pondering on the complicated business of bringing up children and of childhood in general. To Liebet she wrote:
> . . . you emit some wise remarks about the ultimate good effects of feebleness in parents. There is great virture in leaving children alone, I believe. Papa and I as parents were far too zealous . . . My parents on the other hand never gave me a thought . . . [Charlotte] at intervals says to me 'How awful the way Deepa and Granny neglected you.'

someone familiar and vaguely comforting'. Elizabeth also investigated the relationship between widowed sisters with herself and Charlotte in mind. She had recently begun to wonder whether Charlotte did in fact love her as much as she always said she did. The reviewers were, as ever, delighted by yet another book from her distinctive pen. The *Times Literary Supplement* critic wrote:

> You can find the signature of most writers . . . stamped on the pages of their books . . . writers, that is, of any colour and distinction. 'Elizabeth' signs her work with a widow or a bishop, as Whistler signed his with a butterfly; bishop and butterfly are alike characteristic and oddly enough equally audacious and charming.

And the *Birmingham Post* commented. 'Who but "Elizabeth" would write about "happy spats" or fix Mabel in our memory by describing her as a sick monkey whose fur was coming off in patches?'

The summer of 1929 was to be the last house party at the chalet. Frere had not been invited for the first time in spite of an injured letter of protest. Elizabeth's attitude was, 'What can he expect?'[19] But Vernon Lee had asked if her friend, the composer Ethel Smythe, could come and Elizabeth invited her. Ethel Smythe was also a lesbian and usually strode about in heavy tweeds and brogues winter and summer. When she was invited anywhere to dinner she often stuffed her evening clothes into her bicycle basket, pedalled to the house, and changed into them behind a convenient bush. If asked about her work she was liable, as she once did in front of Queen Victoria, to turn into a one-woman band, using plates and knives and forks and wine glasses and even kicking the skirting board to give her effect. Elizabeth found her stimulating and highly amusing, and Miss Smythe wrote her opinion of her hostess to Vernon Lee:

> I think this is one of the most perfect things – I mean the country, the chalet, and the hostess – I ever struck. Elizabeth is . . . well! You know what she is, and will believe the intercourse with her mind has been to me quite a new brand of intellectual adventure; and you know also that some of us – I am one – don't care two straws about such adventures unless the person you are having them with is a person you can get fond of. I find E. more curious than words can say. She continually makes me stretch my eyes and gives me the feeling of standing under a cool and gentle waterfall on an extremely hot day. This apart from the creature's fine, fine skin – the fun of her – her kindness

and the rest of it. She will be, or rather is – a great addition
to my life . . . we are just going off – on an expedition
. . . and I momentarily expect a still small voice from the
garden below . . .

Elizabeth, for her part, found Miss Smythe to be 'the most complete
and perfect human being'[20] she had yet found. The visit was short
and after it both were left with the impression that a new and
beautiful friendship was trembling on the brink of their lives.

The dramas, intrigues and passions of her other guests when they
arrived for August were enough, however, to take Elizabeth's mind
off not only her new friend but her own work as well. The guests were
again mostly women and included Maud Ritchie, Joan Arbuthnot
who was a new and ardent admirer of Elizabeth, Leonora Wodehouse, the stepdaughter of P. G. Wodehouse, and Anna Paues. Some
malignant spirit of change was wreaking havoc emotionally amongst
the guests even more than usual, and the passions that flared up
rocked the mountains back on their foothills. Elizabeth spent as
much of her time as she could away from the house and left Maud
and Joan to cope. Maud understood her desire to get away but the
others resented her withdrawal and when she did appear they
ignored her, behaving as if the place was a hotel. 'There were
moments when their behaviour seemed incompatible with their
evident reluctance to go elsewhere,' commented Liebet, 'and
Elizabeth sadly concluded that they must still, at any rate, appreciate that she did very well by them as far as creature comforts were
concerned.'[21] But the gremlin did not stop with guests, and
Elizabeth started to tease poor Maud about her habit of spending the
whole evening reading her copy of *The Times* which she had sent out
to her every day. When a guest came that Elizabeth particularly
wanted Maud to make friends with she thwarted the poor woman by
locking her paper away. Elizabeth told Maud with glee what she had
done, and Maud told her that she thought it discourteous of her
hostess to have gone on letting her read it night after night if it
displeased her. 'I dare say she was right and so was I,' Elizabeth
wrote in her diary and to soothe her friend she wrote her a poem
which ended,

> Praise God from whom all blessings flow
> Praise him to whom all good guests go,
> Praise Father, Son and Holy Ghost
> And let it here be clearly said
> That of guests living and guests dead

It's Maud I love the most.[22]

Maud and Elizabeth had known each other since soon after the publication of Elizabeth's first book and over the years a profound and lasting friendship was forged which was to endure till the end. Maud was a large and talented lady who could sing and draw and had a lovely sense of humour. Her house in Walton Street was a refuge for many and in particular, in later years, her nephews and nieces who would come to see her and receive the sort of well-considered advice on the matter of their love affairs which parents rarely seem able to give. Judging by the tenor of the correspondence between the two women, there existed between them a deep well of tenderness and affection which grew rather than diminished as time went on.

At the beginning of September all was a great bustle of activity at the chalet, for Teppi came from Germany to help with the moving of Elizabeth's furniture to France. She dazed everybody with her fiery energy and Elizabeth as usual spent most of her time finding her enough jobs to do. Trix had come as well and in the evenings taught Teppi chess so that her mother was able to read quietly. All of the old diaries were exhumed and Elizabeth paused to go through them.

> How happy I've been! Inside so happy. All my unhappi-
> ness, of which I've had my share, came from *people*. Alone
> on a fine day bliss was my portion. Queer little fish,[23]

was Elizabeth's verdict on herself. Frere's letters were her next voyage of reminiscence: 'Some of them very sweet. That has been a funny business! And a sweet one.'[24] On an old blotter which she had kept she came across two limericks which had been voted the best of all the limerick games they had played at the chalet:

> Would you dare to sin
> With Eleanor Glyn
> On a tiger skin?
> Or would you prefer
> To err with her
> On some other fur?

and

> There was a young lady of Loo
> Who had nothing whatever to do.
> So she went to the garret
> And slept with a parrot
> And sent the result to the Zoo.

At the end of September she walked the slopes above the pear tree or, as she now called it, the shrine, 'and sat bewitched by the beauty. Such beauty! I hope it is engraved on my heart – the still brilliance, the misty mauve mountains at the back, the shining steeple of the little church, the autumn crocus . . . ' A few days later she left the chalet for the last time 'very happy to be out of the horrors of the last day'.[25] She had offered it to Trix and Tony to live in but Tony was in the German armed forces and was unable to live abroad. Elizabeth put it up for sale. She hoped it would sell soon, for her house in France was going to cost her more than was estimated, and *Father* had been refused by her publishers, her first experience of a rejection. She had to rewrite her book, and the difficulty was immense, 'like ploughing the sands'.[26]

For some reason setbacks always came in threes in Elizabeth's life, and the third was the worst, for her housekeeper at White Gates fell ill with inoperable cancer and she appeared to have no relatives. Elizabeth had her nursed at home for as long as she was able and then sent her to a private hospital at her own expense – no ordinary hospital would have her because she was incurable. After she died Elizabeth went to the mortuary with a wreath, and into the room where the housekeeper was lying under a sheet. The matron wanted to turn it back, and even though Elizabeth refused she twitched it away. For one instant, before Elizabeth had time to shut her eyes, she saw a terrible, changed face. Later she visited the woman's grave and meditated that the housekeeper had the advantage over the rest of them still alive, lying so quietly in the bird-infested churchyard. Elizabeth paid for the burial and the upkeep of her grave. Many of her friends were also dying and she wrote to Maud: 'How queer it is the way, with the end of the chalet, my friends seem, one after the other, to end too.'

Elizabeth went down to Devonshire alone to work on her book while her house was being fumigated, a Beauchamp custom after there had been illness, and wrote in her diary: 'Extreme loneliness. Too awful being entirely alone and getting old alone. I don't know anybody so alone.' Frere was still a constant visitor at her little house but she ached with anxiety about him when he wasn't there, and found his nerves and headaches and his apparent loathing, now, of all females including herself, trying. His wife, it transpired, had run off with a taxi driver while they had been in Cannes the previous summer. Now she and the taxi driver were back in London calling themselves Mr and Mrs Frere-Reeves and were running up huge bills at shops and hotels all over London, using Frere's charge accounts. There was nothing he could do about it except close down his accounts and change his name, dropping Reeves.

In October the house in France, Le Mas des Roses, was ready and Elizabeth travelled down to stay with Bridget Guinness during the moving in. Trix was to meet her there the day after she arrived. It took two months of dust and exhaustion before they at last were able to move in among the chaos and workmen, while Bridget sent them flowers every day 'to remind us that God is still in his heaven'.[27] Trix was back to her old habit of complaining loudly to anyone who would listen that her mother had no love for her, that her expression of emotion was all sham, and generally continued to wash dirty family linen in public.

Bridget had invited Elizabeth and Trix for a few days on her yacht which Elizabeth declined but Trix accepted. During the trip Trix gained attention for herself by telling terrible stories about her mother's bad behaviour which, as time elapsed, became further and further removed from the truth. By the end Bridget had been entirely alienated from Elizabeth, which state of affairs reached Elizabeth's ears before Trix returned to Le Mas des Roses. She presented her mother proudly with a fish she had caught from the yacht and Elizabeth threw it angrily away saying she did not want a fish. It was not long before this episode was added to Trix's battery of stories showing her mother in a bad light and was interpreted by the intrepid *raconteuse* as an indication that Elizabeth was jealous of her obvious social success.

Elizabeth wrote to Liebet:

> [Trix] had a glorious time . . . and everyone was angelic to her and I took her everywhere, but I think we are really fundamentally apart. She began again the old complaint about the mother business. Her German ideal of a mother isn't a bit like me, and never will be. Indeed, she should rejoice, for if I were what she thinks she would like, I would never do anything but sit still and admire my grandchildren, in which case she wouldn't have one of the charming things I have been able to shower on her. I was surprised when she started on this theme once more, for I thought we were having such a wonderful time together . . .

The disorder, combined with there being no single place of refuge, Elizabeth found as fatiguing spiritually and physically as being perpetually in a noisy railway station. Her only solace was the sun

which 'shone like a fine July in England'.[28] Her furniture from the
chalet was a comfort except that there was always a painter or a
mason in her room. It was only after dark that she could climb on to
her favourite sofa which used to sit in the hall at the chalet, where it
had appeared quite small, but filled up her room as Le Mas des
Roses and looked enormous. She hoped that the house would do the
same thing for her. It was built on the zigzag pattern favoured by the
Chinese to baffle devils, according to one of Elizabeth's favourite
philosophers, Lin Yutang, but this had the added advantage that no
window overlooked any other. She wanted a house that was perfect
and slaved over every detail. In a letter to Liebet she described it:
' . . . I've got three spare rooms, and at a pinch four, and there's a
little study as well as the drawing-room, and my work-room is in the
garden, where I can work and not hear anything . . . '

Everything was decorated in light pastel shades which matched
the flowers in the garden. Violet, pink and light green were her
favourite colours and the drawing-room sofa was piled with silk
cushions in grey and pastel shades against which she knew she
looked fragile, opulent and at her best. When the house was finished
she turned her attention with the same zeal to the garden.

On her first visit back to England Elizabeth drove to Richmond to
fetch Ethel Smythe to tea at White Gates. They had not been back
five minutes when Vernon Lee turned up and was gracious and
sarcastic and, Elizabeth thought, very amusing. Ethel, however,
flew into a wild rage and while Elizabeth and Vernon were in the
garden she got into Vernon's car and went off to the station and
home. Elizabeth was astonished to find her gone but Vernon merely
said, 'Characteristic,' and talked of other things. After she had left,
Elizabeth, who was still taking driving lessons, drove over to Ethel's
house, concerned, for she could not believe that anything that
Vernon had said could cause such wild behaviour. She regretted
doing so for Ethel's rage was transferred on to her, and the next day
Elizabeth received a furious letter from her, more or less winding up
the friendship. Almost immediately the phone rang and Ethel,
having slept on it, regretted what she had written and was 'funny
and dear again. A queer fish,' Elizabeth thought, 'perhaps vain.'[29] A
few weeks later they had tea on Chobham Common. Afterwards
Elizabeth took Ethel home and before letting her out of the car
attempted to turn it round in the narrow drive. Reversing was not,
and never would be, Elizabeth's forte. Ethel became quite maddened during the process, and instructed Elizabeth what to do, even
seizing the wheel.

A few months later they met again and the composer showed Elizabeth a letter she had received from her friend Virginia Woolf, saying that hatred and contempt were written all over Elizabeth's face when she and Virginia had met at a party. Elizabeth was amazed and shocked, and her comment on *A Room of One's Own* in the light of this was, 'A room can't make a writer, not a whole street full of rooms can make a writer.'[30] She and Ethel went for a walk and Ethel berated her for not being a fierce enough feminist. Elizabeth was again astonished that Ethel had not seen what strides she had taken in her work for the cause of female emancipation and felt depressed. Ethel then asked her to drive her somewhere, swearing that there would be no reversing, and left Elizabeth at the end of a small cul-de-sac from which she emerged after having had to back ten times. Oil got on to the gear lever and it began to slip, and Elizabeth arrived home sweating, exhausted and thoughtful. It was a sad episode, but it at least taught Elizabeth not to get herself entangled in the emotions of people who were not of her own inclination. 'What remains of life? Just a few irrelevant memories – very few – to show for all one's strenuous, happy, agonising days. It looks to me very like a bad joke, but I hope I'm wrong.'[31]

That Christmas of 1930 she heard that her friend Bridget Guinness had died after an operation. Elizabeth was greatly saddened, for she loved her dearly and it was to be near her that she had moved down to the South of France, which previously she had disliked. 'There is no place she had been in that is not more beautiful because she once was there, just as there is no person she has met who has not been enriched by coming across her . . . ' Elizabeth said in a brief 'threnody' she wrote about her friend in *The Times*. 'It is hardly to be borne that she has left us.' There was a memorial service in St Martin-in-the-Fields, 'Lilies and black figures. The Saints of God. No hymns seem appropriate to Bridget, who was so alive and didn't in the least want rest and her labours done.'[32]

In January a sadder and wiser Elizabeth returned to her house in France. Friends came round every day with welcome suggestions and cuttings for her garden. It had become, at last, quite delightful, tucked as it was into the steep slopes that climbed to the picturesque hill-top village of Mougins. Behind it were olive groves, in front stately cypresses cut across a magnificent view of the valley and the sea beyond. She lined the terrace with mauve Palladia iris and the walls everywhere as well as the olive trees with pink climbing roses. To Liebet she wrote, 'You know, I feel that this house is the little crown of my career, and the final result of all my toilings at writing books. It is these books got into bricks and mortar, and me, after living inside me for desperate months each, now going to live inside them . . . ' She found it lovely, after the wind-tormented gloom of England, and started work on a new novel called *Jasmine Farm* about Bridget. It was all that her earlier plans to live on a flower farm with her children were to become.

Elizabeth read in *The Times* that Francis was coming to those parts for a fortnight, 'absurd man, chronicling his movements'.[33] This holiday was also to be his last for, in his perversity, as soon as he reached the warmth he developed pneumonia and quickly died of a heart attack. Marie Mallet, her friend from Rapallo, came to commiserate or congratulate. Elizabeth had not heard the news but as her friend walked through the gate she knew that her visit was something to do with Francis. The same feeling of doom fell on her that she had experienced that day at the chalet when he arrived to woo her.

The obituary column listed Francis's accomplishments and praised him for his success as Under Secretary to the Minister of Transport. That appointment had come to an end in 1929 because a studious country clergyman made the disconcerting discovery that there was one too many under-secretaries in the House of Commons. Francis was appointed Indian Under-Secretary in the subsequent shuffling and the next day at a smoking party in Cambridge was overheard to say that he thought 'Dominion status for India would not be possible for a long time' – just when delicate negotiations were going through on the subject. He had been recognized as one of the most skilful debaters in the House of Lords and Elizabeth often used to go and listen to him even after they had separated. The last time she had seen him speaking there she noticed that 'the evil in him had risen up to his face like scum'.[34]

A week after his death she received a letter from Bertrand telling her that Francis had left all his papers and property to Miss Otter, the secretary who was 'the last straw' in his marriage with Elizabeth, which evoked:

> Dearest Bertie,
> How characteristic of Frank.
> I shall make no effort to get my letters back. May Miss Otter read them to her heart's content. They are the record of a great love and a great betrayal.
>> Bless you,
>> Elizabeth

I'm infinitely relieved that ex-Dad is no more, [she wrote to Liebet] and I haven't a shred of sentiment for so cruel and wicked a man. He has left all he has, including his love letters from me, to one of his women – characteristic final act, cutting his brother, and of course odious for me to have my private letters handed over to such a person. Well, he can do no more.

What he did leave Bertrand was the responsibility for paying Mollie her £400 a year, which was not a light burden for the philosopher who himself had an ex-wife to support. To her sister Elizabeth wrote, 'How wonderful the world is cleared and purified; I always feared he might do you some deadly harm; I'm so thankful he has gone; does anyone mourn?'

Having answered the letters of condolence and congratulation on Francis's death, his widow imagined she had nothing more to fear from him. But Miss Otter, on her death not long afterwards, left the love letters to Mollie, thus compounding the last sadistic impulse of the deceased second earl towards his wife. Fortunately Elizabeth was never to know of this.

Santayana sent Elizabeth an extraordinary letter he had received from Francis not long before he died in answer to one from the philosopher asking him about the truth of his feelings for Lionel Johnson.

> . . . It's not really the case that Lionel lies in the limbo of almost incredible things [as Santayana had suggested], on the contrary, all that is the real part of me and my very extensive external activities are to me of the nature of Maya, or an illusion . . . I'm surprised you say I minimise my friendship with Lionel. To all my intimate friends I have always admitted that he was my dearest friend, and the great influence on my life, but I seldom take the public into my confidence about my real feelings. I received two great shocks in my life: the first being when Jowett sent me down. My rage and mortification at being so wronged produced a bitterness and permanently injured my character. Finally, when Elizabeth left me, I went completely dead and have never come alive again. She never realised how I worshipped and loved her . . . Since 1918 I have had neither ambition nor enthusiasm nor interest nor the will to live and I ascribe my bad heart entirely to the year's anguish I suffered after she left me and her

betrayal with a kiss of Judas . . .

His Maya had evidently blinded him to the fact that the 'incredible things' that Santayana referred to were not intended to mean himself; that his character was the result of his lineage and upbringing, and not an admitted mistake of Jowett's, as his brother and the inhabitants of Pembroke Lodge had always known – 'nature not nurture' as Bertrand wrote to Elizabeth – and that his compulsive gambling, dependence on cocaine, ungovernable temper and bad behaviour with women were all individually very good reasons for his wife to have left him.

At the end of March *Father* was published. Elizabeth had not liked the book after she had written it for the second time and nor did the critics although in the United States it was chosen by the Book of the Month Club. It is one of the more serious and thought-provoking of her novels, and the argument in the train between James Ollier and his appalling sister when he breaks free of her tyranny is one of the high points in Elizabeth's art. Rebecca West in the *Daily Telegraph* thought that Elizabeth had written it with 'half her mind', and the critic in the *Observer* found the writing to have the 'terrible defect of coyness'. Vernon Lee remarked to her that it seemed to have been written by somebody else using her pen, which criticism she felt was justified. It was not until two months after her death that Orlo Williams pointed out in the *National Review*, that *Father* had never had all the appreciation it deserved.

But Elizabeth had very little emotional energy to spare for her to be able to spend any time on worrying about the reception of her book for Frere was again making her anxious by not writing to her at all: 'Feel sick with fear about L.G. I don't mind a bit any reason he may have for going dumb if only he stays alive.'[35]

At this time, Frere recalled, she wore a red wig with the curls pulled forward to hide the scars of her face-lift. She powdered her face almost white, wore enormous hats and avoided being photographed. She was extremely thin and her stockings, which weren't small enough for her, wound round her legs like climbing plants. Nevertheless she was still beautiful.

She went back to England, put White Gates on the market, collected her dogs and retired with dignity back to France to await a visit from Liebet and her children. Elizabeth was startled at how fat Liebet's two daughters were, a condition she deplored in anybody, but particularly in children. 'The children have immensely grown'[36] had for her a double meaning which did not escape her daughter.

They left the children with a governess and travelled to Bavaria to see Trix and her two daughters. Evi had also had two daughters and so had H.B. and Elizabeth was beginning to feel fated by the huge preponderance of females in her line. They visited Teppi, who had become the principal of a successful girls' school in Germany (Elizabeth had originally given her the money to set the place up). The family concluded that they had had the perfect summer together.

After Liebet and her children left Elizabeth concentrated her energies on writing and on entertaining her friends, those few of them who were still alive, and some new ones she had met in France and had grown fond of. These included Amy Paget, chatelaine of Garibondy, Eddie Sackville-West, Winifred Fortescue and her ailing husband, John. A constant visitor was Algernon Blackwood, author of many spine-chilling stories such as *The Empty House* and *Prisoner in Fairyland*. Tanis Guinness, the daughter of Bridget, used to go to Le Mas des Roses often with her friends and 'sit at Elizabeth's feet'.[37] Her recollection is that Algernon Blackwood was always there. If so, there is, discreetly, hardly any mention of him in Elizabeth's papers.

Another acquaintance, a rather tiresome society woman called Molly Mount Temple, invited herself to stay, 'to see *you*, Elizabeth dear!' She spent the entire stay going to Cannes every day in Elizabeth's car. She also took Gaston, the chauffeur, and because he was also the cook Elizabeth 'became a little tired of snack lunches'. After her guest had departed Elizabeth inspected the housekeeping accounts and was horrified at the astronomical milk bill. 'How have we drunk all this?' she inquired of Gaston. It had not been drunk at all, Lady Mount Temple had bathed in it. When the same lady wrote the following year and invited herself again Elizabeth replied politely that she would not be able to put her up but would go to the station and wave to her as she went through in the Blue Train. 'I waved and waved, I was *so* delighted to see her pass by.'[38]

Frere surfaced at last and came to see Elizabeth in August, but he was not at all well. He said he was sure he was going to die, that after the war he had been as good as in a lunatic asylum, that he felt any great strain or worry on his brain would make it give way – and generally steeped Elizabeth in wretchedness. 'If he dies the light of my life goes out and I would start dying myself,' she confided in her diary.

He and Betty Clifton came and celebrated Christmas with Elizabeth. To Liebet she wrote:

I'm going to the woods between Grasse and Vence tomor-
row and we will seek out and kidnap a little Xmas tree – a
tiny one. And I'm going to put it on the table in the hall
and Tup [Frere] and Betty Clifton and I, three sophisti-
cated creatures, and me the least sophisticated, will keep
Xmas round it . . .

Betty had been enjoined to bring Elizabeth's furs, which were in
store at Harrods, but forgot to do so. Frere had arrived overworked,
worried and tired as usual and remained in a black mood throughout
except briefly on Christmas Day. His anxiety about his wife, who
had left her taxi driver and come back to him, which he did not like at
all, was supreme amongst the other worries. There was no question
but that he would have to get away from her, but Frere could not
imagine how he was going to do this without causing further upset
and expense. His profound gloom succeeded in making Elizabeth
quite ill.

After he left she was only able to shake off the effect by plunging
into the round of parties always going on at that time of the year on
the Riviera. Arthur Marshall, the journalist and author, remembered seeing her at a party given by Somerset Maugham at his lovely
villa overlooking the sea at St-Jean-Cap-Ferrat. It was a head-
turning gathering of literary figures including G. B. Stern and H. G.
Wells who was with the Baroness Moura Budberg. Elizabeth was
petite and very smart and was complaining that her stomach never
kept to European time and was hungry at half past three while to
everyone else it was only half past two. When all the great men that
were there had had their say her quiet tiny voice 'topped the lot of
them'. She also concentrated on her garden which that Christmas
had in bloom roses, mimosa, irises, stocks, veronica, white broom,
wallflowers, a narcissus or two, a few anemones and oranges hanging
yellow on the trees.

Very early in the new year of 1932 she went to tea with H. G.
Wells. It was a beautiful clear afternoon and she drove right up to the
front door which the two lovers had put, for some reason, at the back
of the house. Wells ran out to meet her and took her up on to the
terrace which had big pine trees and a marvellous view of the bay.
There sat the Aga Khan, the all-conquering, oriental male, and his
Begum, who had her hair in curlers but was otherwise sabled and
jewelled and more or less speechless. Odette Keun was also there,
pleasant, talkative and showing no sign of the rows she had been
having with Wells that morning when she had attempted to instruct

Anthony West, Wells's natural son by Rebecca West, on the birds and the bees. The boy, on holiday from Stowe, sat at tea, uneasy and unnerved by the grandeur of his fellow guests. He was 'very much drawn' to Elizabeth, 'and at the same time a little frightened of her – she was very affable to me, but she was very alert, and, I felt, likely to pounce if given half a chance – I don't suggest anything malicious – but a catlike character: she would be likely, I felt, to scratch automatically if one blundered in her presence. At our first meeting I was frightened of her, but when it was over I felt it had been well worth while and I looked forward to seeing her again.'[39] Elizabeth wondered, as she so often wondered, why such a point had been made of her being there, and was somewhat offended by the boy's presence, seeing that it was his conception that had terminated her liaison with his father. ' . . . to this have I descended,' she recorded in her diary that evening.

> I think there's something wrong with me that I'm happiest when I never go anywhere and never see anybody. Except for my own blood I never want to see a soul. I'm blissfully happy working, and meditating and reading and playing with Chunkie and Knobbie [her two dogs]. Perhaps it's the natural desire of ripeness to adore its shell, anyhow it saves a lot of bother and expense this absence of hankering after parties.

Later in the year Elizabeth received one of Odette Keun's famous long letters, which she wrote constantly in huge, childish pencil scrawls and sent to anybody, regardless of rank or intimacy. After expatiating on her lover's difficult and complex personality, Odette asked to come and see Elizabeth to discuss what she should do about him, whether she should leave him and go and work abroad, although it was common knowledge that she was prepared to do anything to hold on to him. 'I have a conviction that he is mainly to blame for the intolerable conditions of our liaison; I am thoroughly bewildered . . . I do not wish to decide in the state of bitter befuddlement in which I am . . . hardly anyone knows the man's psychological texture . . . ' and much more along the same lines. Elizabeth replied with great caution that she felt she could not involve herself in their affairs and that if a relationship had 'curdled' there was very little to be done. 'One marvels however one could have . . . ' had anything to do with Wells, she wrote in her diary, 'There is something fundamentally wrong with Wells, something mean and base and small. He has grown enormously fat.' And that was her penultimate comment on the 'Great Man' who had owned her heart once, and with whom she had wanted to clamber the mountains of truth for the rest of her life. It was a reflection not on the fickle nature of her vision, nor any disappointment she may have felt at losing him, but on her own blindness about the true nature of the men she fell in love with, a fault which age and experience did not cure.

Elizabeth wrote to George Moore whom she had had no news from for a long time. As she had predicted to Frere, his letter in return was full of the struggles involved in writing fiction. As well, a question:

> Why are the men you portray in your books always disagreeable? You like men; you like me, which is proof that there have been others, and I am now seeking a reason – is the disagreeable man an integral part of your style just as the fat woman was a part of Rubens?

Unfortunately Elizabeth's reply has not been traced.

Elizabeth visited England in the spring of 1932 to see about putting White Gates up for auction as it had not sold. She did not make contact with Frere and concentrated on getting to concerts whenever she could, for she missed music more than anything else on the Riviera. Of course, Frere heard that she was in town and invited her to a party at Heinemann, promising that his wife would not be there. Naturally the wife had other ideas and she turned up, was rude to Elizabeth and made a scene. 'Of all the tiresome undignified situations. I will have none of it!'[40] Elizabeth said she felt ill (which she did), and that she was going home to bed (which she did). A few days later she and Frere went to the theatre together, to see *Tobias and the Angel* by James Bridie. On their return to Whitehall Court, where Elizabeth made him eggs and bacon, he was impossible and they sat in the hall until after midnight 'smashing up everything'. She thought it unlikely, after that, that she would ever see him again. 'Of all the hideous ingratitude.' The next day he rang 'and was decent but never was there anything more obvious and sure than that he doesn't care a rap for me any more'.[41] She thought Frere's protests of devotion in his letters and his complete indifference and rudeness when she was with him so shocking that she couldn't sleep, and she returned to France the next day. Deciding that his unkind ways need no longer be grieved over, she was manifestly grateful to be back in her own home and away from the nonsense that she had let herself in for in London. As soon as she could she drove into Cannes and revoked a codicil in her will which among other things, appointed

Frere her literary executor. 'This is my final cutting him off and high time too. I have been a fool and an exploited one,' she wrote in her diary when she got back.

It was, perforce, a messy end to what had become over the years an untidy relationship, and all of Elizabeth's better thoughts and instincts told her that it was just as well. They had said everything there was to be said, and a lot more besides.* In her hopeful innocence she had not foreseen that they were careering towards an ending of sadness and destruction. She still clung to the hope that somehow all would be civilized and amicable and that, most of all, she could continue to see him sometimes. She did not realize that his wife used his relationship with Elizabeth constantly to jeer at him, and that the wife's friends who were on the fringe of the literary world were fed and revitalized by rows and dissension. Now Elizabeth was left in the undignified position of the cast-off mistress, and her friends, most of whom had nothing better to do than gossip, would soon get to hear of it. It was useless to protest that she was innocent. How could a woman of her age be innocent when clinging to a young man? She had become in the process everything she most despised and feared, spurned, old, pathetic and gossiped about.

Her novels no longer resounded with the clear ring of truth which had made them so popular in her heyday. She clung to them as well, for she could not resist the stir she made whenever a new book came out. She had become used to the discipline of writing every day, not because she particularly wanted to write any more, but because for a short time it erected a fence between her and the emptiness that she knew to be her portion and that of those like her whom she saw everywhere she looked. She envied those of her friends who had been sensible enough to die. Her children were polite and kind and enjoyed the expensive holidays she was able to arrange for them, but she knew they looked on her as a warning and a difficult woman which, in her lonely meditations in Le Mas des Roses that year, she realized was true. Well, she would go on. She would not give in. She would explore this country of old age which had never been explored before in literature, apart from Hugh Walpole's *The Old Ladies* published in 1924 which included a portrait of herself. She would be grateful for the scraps of affection she could glean from her young friends and her dogs. All was not lost as long as she looked resolutely

---

*When Liebet was writing her memoirs she asked Frere if he would mind being mentioned by name. He replied, '. . . since I owe everything in life to her I cannot think of any personal difficulties which may arise on my own account.'[42] In fact, he is referred to throughout the book as 'Mark Rainley'.

towards the future that was still left.

On re-reading *Princess Priscilla's Fortnight* she could exclaim, 'Plainly my things are nothing at all – nothing, nothing. And I used, a few years ago, deluded by the praises of those who don't matter, to think not too badly of them. But it doesn't matter . . .'[43]

To make bad things worse Elizabeth's money was running disastrously short. She had always been generous with it to her friends and those she felt deserved it. She did not trust banks, feeling them to be chilly places, and had preferred property. Now she had three houses and a flat in London, all of them staffed, two of them up for sale, and not a buyer for either in sight. *Father* had not sold at all well and she feared for her financial future as acutely as she feared for her emotional one. She was disappointed when White Gates fetched less at auction than it had cost her to build. The stresses of the past two months had taken their toll on her physically, and she had lost nine pounds, weighing only six stone four and a half pounds, less than ever before in her adult life.

Elizabeth comforted herself in any way that she could. That summer she went often to the beach with her friends, taking a picnic of a hotpot of mutton and vegetables spooned out of a gigantic thermos flask, as she had done on her hikes in Switzerland. 'Queer fare in broiling summer weather,' wrote her friend Winifred Fortescue, 'but she preferred it to all else.' Lady Fortescue shared many of those picnics with her but the most memorable was one at Théoule, when Ernest Shepard was staying with the Fortescues to discuss illustrating Winifred's book *Perfume from Provence*. Elizabeth went into the sea and bobbed up and down, for she couldn't swim or float, looking coquettishly into the face of the tall, thin Kip Shepard, 'who looked like a stick of peppermint rock in his striped swimming-suit, as she uttered her daring witticisms'. After they had come back on to the sand and sat down, Mary Shepard, 'radiant and plump in a rather revealing backless bathing dress' asked Lady Fortescue if she thought Elizabeth would mind if she ate her lunch without changing, and Lady Fortescue suggested she ask her hostess, which she did. 'No, I suppose not, my dear – if you do not mind,' came the rather cold reply, and she cast an icy glance over the young woman's youthful curves. Everyone was therefore staggered when Elizabeth's very tall, dark and good-looking chauffeur appeared to serve the lunch 'clad in only the briefest pair of trunks – today I believe they are called *cache-sexe*,' recalled the astonished Winifred Fortescue. His mistress appeared not to notice.[44]

· 19 ·

Hitler's Victory

Although America had called a moratorium on all war debts to ease the financial situation in Europe, in Germany 1932 was a year of street fighting and political disorder, during which Hitler came to be regarded by the big industrialists and the *Junker* class as their best guarantee against Communism. In May Elizabeth wrote prophetically in answer to Liebet's inquiry as to the safety of their money in Germany.

> ... I believe Germany, as always, is the danger, and should never be surprised if she set us on fire again, at any moment. Not with armies, which she hasn't got, but with a few aeroplanes full of bombs dropped in Paris and London. She has, it appears, a new gas which would do the trick in a few minutes, and as other people can bomb too, the world would then become very noisy for a brief period, then wiped out, except for a few stragglers in caves. That being so and we not able to hinder, let us love and enjoy what we've got while we've got it. Certainly the path to destruction is paved by our own follies. Our policy of piling up tariffs, when the most jealous co-operation is our only hope, is so suicidal as to suggest dementia. It is a pity, isn't it, when we could all be so happy? I utterly agree with your remarks about the way we don't take the trouble to learn a few politics and just let them slide along unchecked to catastrophe, but after all we put people in office to do it for us. Still, we should be more intelligently interested, and as a beginning I am reading everything I can lay my hands on about the [international monetary] crisis. The result so far is that I am a violent free trader and internationalist. Down with all tariffs, away with all

frontiers. Short of a world unit there's no hope, and with a world unit what prosperity and happiness. Meanwhile Hitlerism rages in Germany, and Trixi, who echoes Tony, approves. Those Germans continue to be a danger spot in Europe and therefore America. They never learn. They are just as pure *Junker* as before the war. They'll drag us to hell and themselves too – so meanwhile let us *cultiver notre jardin* and love all the heavenly natural joys that are still ours . . .

And cultivate her garden was what Elizabeth did do, and loved and enjoyed what she had, which was friends, especially a new one, Michael Arlen. She had first met him in the company of Hesketh Bell, a civil servant of the old Empire school, at a party given by a White Russian Princess of enormous wealth with a house 'like an hotel only with flunkeys instead of waiters'.[1] Michael Arlen introduced himself as a friend of Frere, and Elizabeth was delighted to meet him for she had read and enjoyed his novel, the best-selling *The Green Hat*. He was 'so nice' and amusing and told her stories about his escapades with Frere that she had not heard before. There was, for instance, the time they had gone to Bertorelli's in Charlotte Street and were told there was no table for them. They could see that the restaurant was full of theatre-goers up from the suburbs and Arlen held his nose and announced that the train for Blackheath would be leaving in twenty minutes. None of them rushed for their hats as he had hoped.

She invited him and his wife to tea and he gave her the manuscript of his new novel *The Red Bridge* to read. She thought it 'frightfully good'. She went to tea with them the following day where she found Wells, 'rotund and simultaneously haggard with cold evil eyes'.[2] He told Arlen to re-write the second half of the book, and Elizabeth was shocked. It reminded her of the sort of advice her friend George Moore was always giving her. 'How can one, without ceasing to be oneself, make one's work quite different? Idle talk, that is, and Wells is old and stale compared to Arlen . . . '[3] She was not particularly well disposed towards Wells just then, for she had recently heard from a friend, who thought she might like to know, that Wells had described her as having minute but penetrating brains.

At that time she had somehow become entangled with the sixty-five-year-old actress Mrs Patrick Campbell, whom she had met at a tea party given by Stella Cobden-Sanderson. Mrs Pat, as Elizabeth referred to her, brazenly begged to come and stay with her and, taken off guard, Elizabeth could not say no and then regretted it. The next morning she told Mrs Pat she had decided to go to Switzerland instead and 'she positively shameless in her insistence, but naturally, it being my house, she cannot fight her way in'.[4] A solution was found in Notre Dame*, Elizabeth's name for the Guinnesses' house. A week later she invited the actress to supper and she entirely capsized the event by being drunk and noisy and saying 'frightfully indecent things'. Elizabeth realized that parties bored her, for at them she was 'watching a great deal of ugliness, leavened by rare bits of loveliness'. Her opinion was, 'There's nothing for it, when one is old and ugly, or even old and not ugly, or again even ugly and not old, [one must] go in for stern propriety.'[5]

After much prevarication, H.B. decided that he would avail himself of his mother's offer to spend the summer with her. She, of course, would be paying all the expenses including his fares. He was trying to run a chicken farm in Buffalo and not, it seemed, making much of a success at it. His mother did not know how he managed financially and did not dare inquire too closely, feeling sure that she would hear soon enough. It was not for some years that she was shocked and embarrassed to discover that he had been living on his wife's father. He arrived in the middle of July closely followed by a stream of cables from his overseer. The farm was on the brink of bankruptcy and mother and son lived in an 'atmosphere of cables' for several days. It appeared that he might have to return to Buffalo immediately and all their plans dwindle to nothing. Elizabeth saw in her son a 'mixture of squashiness and virtue'. Copybook maxims flowed from him, but also he reminded her, as she never lost an opportunity of commenting in her diary and letters, of Henning, 'The very spit image of him'.[6] With all the cables and anxiety flying around she might have been back in Nassenheide in the middle of imminent financial disaster. Evidently all H.B. needed was a thousand dollars and everything would be saved, and Elizabeth, in her innocence, offered to pay the money, for she would have been sad if the holiday she had prepared had come to nothing. She was to discover the truth later.

She was disappointed that her son had developed an American accent which was so thick that sometimes she could not make out what he was saying at all. 'God and myself gave him such a pleasant voice. Eton showed him how to use it and now it is vanished.'[7] However, they were happy together, for underneath his rather stiff

*'Notre Dame' was Elizabeth's name for the house though it was actually called 'Notre Dame de Vie' and was later bought by Picasso and became his home in the South of France.

and shy exterior he was very like her and they recognized it at every turn and understood each other well. They set out for a motor tour of Switzerland and Germany and ended up in Bavaria to visit Teppi. They stayed at a hotel away from 'all those virgins'[8] at Teppi's school, and walked round every morning so that H.B. could bathe and row on the lake and flirt with the girls. They told him that every night they climbed out of their windows, and went off on motor bikes to Munich to riot till dawn while Teppi innocently slept. Elizabeth sat and imbibed Teppi's 'beautiful, serene wisdom' and in the evening they went to the opera which was doing a season of Wagner which Elizabeth found 'lush and shocking'.[9]

In her old age Teppi had become distinctly idiotic about men. She had embarked on an amorous affair with a man called Schrumpf, having recently broken off another one with a Herr Unold because it was too '*platonisch*'. Elizabeth marvelled at her friend in her Goethe-like multifacetedness, for after she left the von Arnims' employ she had fallen in love with a much older nurse, also called Elizabeth, and it was with her that she had started up the school.

Elizabeth decided to put a finger into her son's future and wrote to Nelson Doubleday to ask if there was a possibility of H.B. working for him. When H.B. arrived in New York he submitted himself for an interview and was turned down. Elizabeth was extremely disappointed and railed against Evi who had got a job as a librarian, having done a course which her mother had paid for, and then simply given it up. Now her mother was forced to continue supporting her and her children, and had no money left to help H.B. and his family as she would have liked.

When she got home Elizabeth settled happily down with her two dogs, who had 'got married' and were shortly expecting a family. 'I'm deeply touched by dogs and their innocence and lowlihood. Really my happiness is almost frightening,' she wrote in her diary. To a bereaved friend she recommended that she get a dog, telling her that they were better than husbands, children and lovers: 'You don't believe me now but you'll see.'[10] After supper one evening Knobbie became very restless and agitated, and before the vet could get there, six puppies were born on the sofa in Elizabeth's bedroom. After two months smothered in puppies, she sold two and kept two (two had been born dead). Her relations were of the opinion that Elizabeth was becoming 'all dog',[11] and there were times when she was inclined to agree with them, but the eighteen months during which all four of them were with her were among the liveliest, if also the most breathless, in her life.

That Christmas Elizabeth was sure she was going to spend alone, and thought of writing a Christmas story called *Alone in Bed*. She wondered if the proper Americans, scenting impropriety a mile off, would publish anything like that. On the other hand, if she were to call it *Not Alone in Bed* they might be justified in getting up on their pure hind legs. In the end Charlotte and her odd son Puddle* arrived for Christmas after much prevarication. Maud came for the New Year and 'So ends 1932. In it, in March, I shed L.G., after nearly twelve years of him. It was high time.'[12]

A new tranquillity entered her life from then onwards, and though she had developed a pronounced quake she still looked, and indeed felt, decades younger than her sixty-eight years. She often aroused 'unsuitable interest' in the young, and 'irrepressible amorousness'[13] in her contemporaries, but simply removed herself with a laugh and continued to cultivate her garden and enjoy her dogs. 'How happy I am now that I have cleared the so-called loves out of my life,' she wrote in her diary. Above the door in her work-room she wrote up PEACE, PERFECT PEACE, WITH LOVED ONES *FAR* AWAY.

And so the months passed. Her salon was always filled with intelligent and charming people, especially men. Among her new guests she counted the Aga Khan, Elsa Maxwell, Sibyl Colefax, Maxine Elliot, the ageing society hostess and one-time mistress of Winston Churchill, Rose Macaulay and Somerset Maugham. Elizabeth busied herself with local fêtes and charities, particularly one of her own for the protection of animals from cruelty. Rudyard Kipling, whom Elizabeth had met often at the Cazalets, came to stay in L'Enchantement and Elizabeth sent him a bunch of flowers and a note asking him if he had any books he wanted to get rid of for the bazaar and might he join her there. He wrote declining on the grounds that he had been sent to the South of France on a regime from which social and other functions were rigidly excluded.

> But there is one thing you might do for us. Please lift these
> low grey skies a little above the English level. We manage
> this present style of sky at home.

She worked slowly at *Jasmine Farm* which was causing her great trouble, keeping in mind what Henry James had once said of a book:

*Charlotte Waterlow OBE, daughter of Sydney, remembered that her namesake and grand-mother Charlotte and her son Puddle lived together in a 'sugary, incestuous relationship' which the rest of the family did not quite like or approve of.

'Let me fumble it gently and patiently out, with fever and fidget laid to rest.'[14] Even so, beneath the calm surface of her life, there throbbed a pulse of anxiety about what she heard of Germany, and even more, what she did not hear but, with her profound understanding of that race, suspected. Trix wrote that she couldn't understand why foreign papers told such lies about Jews being beaten, there was not a word of truth in it. The German press by that time was completely muzzled and she heard nothing of such things. Only the foreign correspondents of English and American newspapers could get any news across.

On a Monday in June she met Frere in the road. He was with a blonde girl and he introduced her to Elizabeth, saying that he was going to be divorced on Tuesday and married on Wednesday. Elizabeth took her hand and looked at her with concern saying, 'Are you going to like that?'[15] In her diary she wrote: 'I am so glad it is she and not I. What perfect grammar.' The girl was Miss Patricia Wallace, daughter of Edgar Wallace, who was to bear Frere three children and live with him happily till the end.

In 1934 Evi sent her mother a photograph of her two daughters, saying 'Aren't they sweet?' Two ogres stared up at their grandmother with teeth splayed in all directions. It was not long, as Elizabeth guessed, before Evi was petitioning her to send money for dentist's and doctor's bills as one of the children was delicate. Her mother decided that the only way to deal with her was to refuse to send her any more money, and suggest she ask Corwin for a loan. She then arranged to pay Corwin secretly anything Evi owed him. Unfortunately, when the requests for money to Corwin bore fruit, Evi became convinced that he had taken a fancy to her and whenever she went to visit she made sheep's eyes at him, alarming him and annoying Liebet. Very soon Evi was banned from Paso Robles and Corwin suggested to his mother-in-law that H.B. take on the duty of Evi. Elizabeth was against the idea, for she had recently heard from Trix that H.B. was constantly petitioning *her* for money, ever since she had been left a small nest egg from her Tante Maggie. The old battle between Elizabeth and her German daughter was rumbling again, for Trix was proudly and defiantly championing her country while her mother was completely unable to agree with anything she said, and did not write at all, finding it difficult to talk about 'dicky-birds and roses' when people were being beaten to death in Trix's fatherland.

Puddle, who was at Monte Carlo, came to see his aunt. Over the years it had become obvious that he had inherited the sad Waterlow family gene of manic-depressive instability, and he was by then pathetically mad. He thought he was the picture of radiant youth, in spite of being quite bald, and his dyed black moustache looked odd with his white eyelashes and *avoirdupois*. They went bathing and Puddle strode up and down the road in his bathing trunks and gloves. He then went back to Marseilles, intending to catch a boat to England, but instead he was certified and locked up there. When Elizabeth drove over to collect him he was walking up and down with the air of a man who had an appointment, a rose in his buttonhole and a meaningless smile on his face. He was finally, and for Elizabeth expensively, deported back to England and Charlotte wrote, a few months later, that he had gone entirely off his head. It had been discovered that in previous periods of mania he had set up expensive mistresses in flats of their own and lost large sums of money on the roulette table, so that his mother was nearly ruined. Poor Charlotte was almost demented herself when her sister hurried to England to comfort her, going over and over the same events, constantly and fruitlessly. Elizabeth went to see Maud Ritchie while she was in London and found her 'refreshingly sane after the welter of dementia prevalent in the family'.[16]

One of the puppies became ill and had to be put down by the vet. The process was an unnecessarily cruel one for the initial injection did not immediately work and Elizabeth could not forgive herself for not having intervened when she saw that the vet was going to smother the dog with chloroform before it was properly unconscious. Then the other puppy, Winkie, was run over while out on a walk. She wrapped him in a cloth and drove home. It was then that she had a moment of truth. It seemed to her as if she saw for the first time the true scale of cruelty and suffering which there is in life, and the 'sure release, the one real consolation' which was death. From having had a good opinion of being alive, for she had been, she thought, a contented and lucky person, she began to 'think highly of being dead. Out of it all.'[17] She passed a donkey on the way which was plodding stoutly along, doing his best for the enormous man sitting on a pile of household goods on its back, hitting it hard and repeatedly. She looked into the man's cruel and insensitive face and realized that for overworked or ill-treated animals this must be a world populated by devils. In the light of this revelation, 'What sort of world was it? . . . Was its loveliness merely mockery? Was it nothing but a bad joke, played off on its helpless children?' she wondered, or was it just a light covering drawn across hell. Perhaps if a corner were lifted something 'so terrible would be seen, such suffering and cruelty, that nobody would ever be at peace again'.[18]

She went home and read *Mein Kampf* in her state of visionary perception, thought its author a gifted savage and was amazed that such things should be said or done. The war news about Mussolini invading Abyssinia entrenched Elizabeth in her view that ' . . . we are utterly mad, and deserve to be annihilated by our beastly inventions for torturing to death. The whole world has gone insane.'[19]

On 19 August 1934 the German people voted by a landslide majority to allow Adolf Hitler, who had previously turned down the Chancellorship, supreme power as their *Führer* (Leader). On October the 9th Alexander of Yugoslavia was assassinated in Marseilles by Macedonian fanatics, and Hitler used this opportunity for a speech that made his intentions unmistakably clear to those who had ears to hear. Elizabeth was one of these, though most of her acquaintances on the Riviera were not. She arranged, on a visit to the still unsold chalet, to meet Trix as near the German border as she dared to go.

Trix appeared philosophical about what was happening, even though she saw husbands of friends suddenly disappearing and leaving their wives with no idea where they were. Everybody she knew, it seemed, was in the power of a servant or someone owing a grudge, for all that was needed for an arrest was a denunciation. Trix told her mother that she had had to rout out all her ancestors in a search for Jews, and of course had immediately come upon Marie Arndt. The Nazi inspector had insisted the name was really Aaron, so that Trix's children would only be allowed to marry into a lower class. 'A pleasing country isn't it?' Elizabeth remarked in a letter to Liebet.

When Elizabeth arrived at the chalet unexpectedly she found it in a terrible state. The overseer's growing family and the chickens had spread into the house, the dog, Mr Fox, was tied up without water and the For Sale notice had been taken down and hidden. She was greatly incensed and understood why the house had not sold: because it was not convenient for the servants. She went down to see the agent and went to bed that night uneasy and angry. Back at Le Mas des Roses, the same thing was happening to her servants there who had also bred and were eating her out of house and home. Everybody else on the Riviera was shutting up their house and going back to England, and, when she gave Gaston notice he was surly and rude. 'How I wish dogs could be servants. They would be such cheerful, delighted and devoted ones.'[20]

In November *Jasmine Farm* was published (by Heinemann this time at Frere's request). The reviews were not good and words such as 'improbable' and 'unconvincing' cropped up, confirming what Elizabeth had secretly feared. She wondered whether she had lost her gift, or had become too old for novel-writing, and she began to think often of suicide and its advantages, not necessarily on her own account but as a precaution against Hitler. She was certain that Europe was like a barrel of gunpowder and that directly after the new year the Germans would apply the match. 'They are such fools, politically and psychologically, that they always mis-reckon, besides not seeing beyond their obvious, truculent noses.'[21] One of them wanted to buy the chalet and, anxious as Elizabeth was to get rid of it, he was so brutal and brow-beating that she was afraid that she would have to break off negotiations. She received a lofty letter from a German publisher who was interested in the translation rights of *Expiation*, but, before he could go any further, he required a certificate that the author was of pure Aryan race and a sworn statement that she would never make unflattering comments on the German government. She wrote back stating briefly that the rights were not for sale. In the evenings she switched on her radio and listened horrified to Hitler's ravings, which were in such contrast to the cool sanity of the BBC. She alarmed Liebet in 1936 by writing that she was not to worry about her, for no German bomb was going to catch her alive – 'I have made all my simple plans.' She had purchased enough narcotics to wipe out her whole family, having preserved since 1929 a cutting from *The Times* which was an account of how Crippen dispatched his victims. He had used a narcotic called Hydrobromide which could be bought over the counter of any chemist. As though the subject of suicide was catching, she heard that Puddle had escaped from the asylum and thrown himself under a train.

Elizabeth's diaries concentrated exclusively on the exact minutiae of daily events as her own stand against insanity. She also started working on her autobiography at Frere's request. When she went back to England to celebrate Christmas with Charlotte, who was greatly troubled, they both went on a tour of churches they had known and loved. Elizabeth gave thanks to God in each of them for her happy life, her dear father and mother and all the 'funny sweet memories'[22] she had of things that had happened to her. Poor Charlotte was in a state of super sensitivity, imagining slights in everything Elizabeth did or said. 'It is like walking on eggs being with her,' Elizabeth complained to Liebet. The sisters went to

Chorleywood to look at the Russell tombs, 'peeping through the windows at all those awful forebears of awful Francis – everywhere prohibition notices – so very Russelly – and barbed wire – again how like. Imagine having barbed wire in one's blood . . . '[23]

At St Paul's she could not hear anything of the sermon and afterwards went up to the preacher in the aisle and asked him if she could have a transcript of it. He said she could not and anyhow it wasn't worth it – 'This is the fourth time in my life I have approached the clergy with all my heart asking for bread and been given a stone. They are a hopeless lot.'[24]

Frere came to see her about her autobiography, *All the Dogs of my Life,* which she called her Dog Book, and she found him 'such a boring little man. But it's because we are all growing old, and the bones of our inadequate minds come through the flesh that hid them.' She left for Cannes in January and there was nobody that time to see her off. 'Solitary I departed – so different from my other departures seen off by friends and adorers! Well, one is old and the old depart alone . . . '[25]

When she had settled down at Le Mas des Roses she started work on her last novel, which she called then *The Birthday Party* but which was finally to be *Mr Skeffington.* It is about old age and especially that most vital of activities, 'letting go'. Her previous books had been about the letting go of inhibitions and preconceptions, loved ones and status, attitudes and reputation, but this one was about the letting go of the allure and good looks that depart with old age. She made this final indignity her province and observed it, as she did everything, with compassion and a large good humour. As a background war rumbled and her hero Mr Skeffington, a Jew, had been imprisoned and tortured by the Nazis. In the end his wife, Fanny Skeffington, is saved the pain of her husband hating her for her ugliness by discovering that he had also been blinded. Elizabeth no longer seemed worried about what, if the book were published during the forthcoming war, the effect would be on Trix.

In August Elizabeth spent most of her time removing her two female dogs, who were on heat, from the attentions of Chunkie who spent his time 'not being able to marry them . . . Ah, if only I could have stopped H.B. as easily as I stop Chunkie from these desperate entanglements. And how deeply he wishes now that I had been able to, poor devil.'[26]

Rebecca West came to tea and the two novelists talked about Wells. Elizabeth thought her 'charming and adorable'[27] and wished she knew her well; she did not know that Rebecca's friendliness was based on the comfort she took in knowing that Elizabeth and Wells were not then on good terms. As her son commented:

> Rebecca West's paranoia made it impossible to get on with anyone she considered a rival, and the only situation in which she could take pleasure in the company of another woman who had been involved with H.G. was that produced by the knowledge that the other woman had parted with him after a quarrel. She was venomous about 'Elizabeth' in private to the end, and seemed to have an especially strong jealousy of her. I imagine that it will have been something to do with class: shabby genteel life in Edinburgh marked those who had to endure it to the bone. I think that 'E' was much envied by her, and brought out feelings of inferiority that she didn't like to have stirred up . . . I would say that something in 'E's' eye told RW that she had been seen right through and placed within an inch.[28]

When her seventieth birthday arrived Elizabeth commented, 'Am now distinctly an old woman, and I must bear it in mind. One is so much used to being young that one goes on taking it for granted. I must remember. And my looking glass helps.'[29] In December 1936 she joined with everyone else in the excitement caused by the events leading up to the abdication of Edward VIII. 'To those who know what Mrs Simpson is like one can feel nothing but shame and regret,' she wrote in her diary. She bumped into the Freres who were on holiday in the South of France. He was doing well at Heinemann and was to become Chairman in 1945, which post he held until 1962. She invited them to stay with her for a few days, and they were delighted and impressed by the opulence of the interior of the house, even down to every sort of towel in each bathroom matching the colour scheme of the room and all covered with a white cloth coroneted in the corner. The bedrooms were designed in the Edwardian manner, one big with a double bed and, 'in case you quarrel',[30] a smaller one with a single bed. Elizabeth's own bedroom, which had french windows leading out on to a balcony with a view of the distant bay, was large with a good-sized bathroom leading off it on one side and a guest bedroom with a concealed interconnecting door which was made to look on both sides like the entry into a hanging cupboard. The Freres took Elizabeth out to Eden Roc for dinner and she thought Pat 'charming' and 'sweet'.[31] The ladies talked and laughed about husbands, and at one point Elizabeth turned to Frere and said, 'You can go if you want to.' It was a spectacularly beautiful evening and there was a forest fire raging in the Esterel mountains on the far side of the bay of Cannes. 'I ought to go and rush into it like Brünnhilde, but I'm not really built for it, am I?' said Elizabeth.[32] Frere requested the orchestra to play the fire music from *The Valkyrie* and this added to the drama of the occasion.

When the Freres' first baby was born Elizabeth was made godmother *in absentia* with Hugh Walpole as the godfather and Mrs Molly Cazalet standing in for Elizabeth. The baby was also called Elizabeth and referred to as 'Little E.2', which her godmother thought sounded as if she were an airship. 'I was clerical, the baby yelled and the parents looked demure,' Hugh wrote to Elizabeth after the ceremony.

> I promised (and so did you) to keep the child from all sensual baits and traps, which is a tall and perhaps unnecessary order. *I* would like to be *your* god-son. I hear from Molly [Cazalet] that you are happy, even radiant. I'm so glad. I am happy too. I would like one day to see you again. Shall I ever?

He never did. Elizabeth replied:

> Indeed I wish too that you were my god-son, or any other sort of son. You are one of the few people I would like to be related to. And I believe you and I are two of the few people who are more often happy than unhappy, and say out loud that they are.

Trix wrote to her mother asking her what she wanted for Christmas and she replied, innocently, on a postcard, that she would like a volume of Heine's poems. She did not know that Heine had recently achieved Hitler's black list and so had she. She travelled to Germany to spend Christmas with the von Hirschbergs at their new house in Murnau near Munich. Trix, as did Liebet, always prepared for her mother's visits as if she were royalty, but as soon as Elizabeth arrived she was aware of a higher pitch of anxiety in the air than before. A few notes survive which were jotted down in preparation for a short story to be called *In a Bavarian Village* which reflect her experience that year.

> 'It's impossible,' I said, shaking myself free of the stupor slowly bearing me down. 'to imagine this Germany as any different from the Germany I knew.'
> 'Oh, but it *is* – ' began my daughter, instantly to be

stopped by her husband with a quick 'Take care – ' for one of the maids had come into the room.

People came singing *Stille Nacht*. I who had read my *Times* and know what is happening to the church in Germany couldn't believe my eyes. 'But – ' I began, as I hung onto my son-in-law's arm.

'Take care,' he quickly whispered, gripping my hand. Take care again, must one forever take so much care? And after all what had I said except 'But'?[33]

Liebet, her husband and their two children came to stay in France the following summer and so did Trix and her slim daughter, Billy, who was pretty, with beautiful red gold hair. A friendship sprang up between her and Elizabeth which infuriated the other girls.

Wells sent Elizabeth his latest novel while they were there and Elizabeth wrote thanking him:

> Thank you so much for *Star Begotten*, a lovely and inspiring book. I cling to it in this deliquescent world where, whichever way one looks, the view is blocked by Mussolini's absurd chin or Hitler's absurd bit of hair, or Stalin's equally absurd and repulsive I am sure I don't know what. I'm embedded in my family – Liebet's husband and two *enormous* children, who plainly have been eating the food of the gods, and Trixi's who is at least a handy size. I don't know why one has to have families. And in hot weather too, Actually I induced myself to go to Germany. I hadn't been there since Hitler. It is an afraid, lowering country, lashed by propaganda into panic, and crouching away there in its beastly corners ready to pounce. Never before did I bless God that I was English . . .

While they were visiting Salzburg Elizabeth's favouritism for Billy caused a rift that was never to be forgiven or forgotten in the family. They planned to go to the opera one evening and out to dinner first, but as nobody appeared to be able to make up their minds where they wanted to eat, Elizabeth took Billy to one of the smarter restaurants, leaving the others to eat wherever they liked. She and Billy had a wonderful time while Trix and the two American grandchildren ate in silence and Liebet wept into her plate. When it was time for Trix, Liebet and their children to leave, which they did simultaneously, Elizabeth saw them off at the station. She ceremoniously presented her hand to the American children to kiss and then bent down and herself kissed Billy on the cheek, an act which is remembered with unabated rancour by all of the children concerned to this day.

In March 1938 Hitler annexed Austria. Elizabeth wrote to Liebet:

> I expect you are horrified by the news of Hitler's goings-on. It is so very clear what he intends to do that I rub my eyes in amazement that there should exist politicians who still think they can come to an understanding with him. When the crash comes nobody will be able to say they haven't been given warning often enough. But I suppose it is very difficult for *gentlemen* to believe in a system of complete dishonourableness and lies. Anyhow, as regards my little Trix and her family, I hope they'll escape to the chalet if and when the worst comes . . . As for me, you needn't give me another thought, darling, because directly the first bombs start I shall put myself to sleep . . . If I were twenty years younger I would see it through, because apart from everything else it will be so *interesting*, and in the long run I'm sure the gangsters will get the worst of it, but it would be absurd to take trouble to hide or get away or things like that at my age, and I shall stay quiet in my garden till the last possible minute, and then, with immense dignity, settle down to sleep . . .

Naturally Liebet was appalled by her mother's cool talk of taking her own life and wrote back a frantic letter begging her to come to America if ever things should get that bad. Meanwhile Elizabeth found refuge from the dreadful days of waiting and wondering what Hitler was going to do next in the simplicity and affection of animals, especially dogs.

That summer Sydney Waterlow, Elizabeth's nephew, came to see her. He had written scholarly works on the Greek classics and Shelley and had been knighted in 1935 while serving as British Minister in Athens. He and Elizabeth had often met since he had been based there and she enjoyed his intelligent conversation. He was a very tall man with a flowing moustache and a kingly manner which earned him the name 'Monarch' in the family, though his bearing ill assorted with his high squeaky voice. He also behaved like royalty, once even ordering his aunt out of his presence with a sweep of his hand when she had visited him in Athens a few years previously. His life, he maintained, had been blighted by not having been elected an Apostle while he was at Cambridge, the most exclusive intellectual coterie there. Its aims were 'the pursuit of truth with absolute devotion and unreserve by a group of intimates and friends'. Sydney was a sincere and deeply thoughtful person with such a high regard for literature and art that it often left his aunt gasping.

He fell in love with and proposed to Virginia Woolf in 1911 soon after he separated from his first wife, but she turned him down with a laugh and had mocked him viciously ever since. 'By God! What a bore that man is!' she wrote to Lytton Strachey, 'I don't know why exactly.' She thought his literary judgements ponderous and ridiculous like an 'elephant in a tea cup', but was fond of him. She wrote to him in 1921,

> . . . You say people drop you, and don't want to see you. I don't agree. Of course I understand that when one feels, as you feel, without a core – it used to be a very familiar feeling to me – then all of one's external relations become febrile and unreal. Only they aren't to other people. I mean, your existence is to us, for example, a real and very important fact. If I treat you as a joke (and my manners are far too haphazard) that's only a method. Of course, one of the things about you I like, admire and find interesting is this sensibility – this introspection – this sense of the importance of things . . .

Elizabeth's own feelings about her tall nephew ran somewhat along the same lines as those of Virginia Woolf, but she was more discreet and had always been fond of him since boyhood. She took his praise or criticisms of her own books as seriously as they were, she knew, intended. After his appointment to Athens in 1933 she saw more of him and heard, through Charlotte, that the King and Mrs Simpson had been entertained to dinner by him on their Mediterranean cruise. The King had shocked Sydney by inquiring who Plato was. Sydney fell in love with a beautiful and talented actress called Katina Paxinou who was described by *The Times* as 'the great tragic actress of all times'. He had taken Elizabeth into his confidence about Katina and was in the habit of seeking his aunt out when matters became complicated, as they had done in 1938. Though Elizabeth was rather shocked at his indiscretions – he had learnt to talk freely about himself when attending the Thursday evening meetings of the Bloomsbury Group at the Café Royal – she was extremely interested, and her conclusion was that he had an unusual, complex personality, very brilliant and delightful but also babyish, forlorn and frightened at heart.

He came to see her in May while it was pouring with rain and immediately he slipped and fell on the wet cement and 'sprained a rib'. She put him up in a spare bedroom and nursed him while he read to her from Shakespeare and Max Beerbohm, and just as he was nearly ready to go home he laughed so much that he sprained the rib again. Elizabeth was coming to the conclusion that he had better go back to Athens, rib or no rib, by the time he was recovered enough to move, when he slipped in his bath and this time broke it in two places. He went entirely to pieces, and his spiritualist religion and brilliant brains seemed to avail him nothing. 'Oh, how glad I am I am a widow . . . I'm glad he is neither my son nor my husband.'[34] Elizabeth decided that her cup had run over enough as far as he was concerned and shipped him off to an English nursing home near Cannes called Sunnybanks.

All of this coincided with the news that Teppi's brother had been interned in a concentration camp: 'They shave them completely bald,' Elizabeth wrote to Liebet, and knowing nothing of the reality of those places she added, 'so when he comes out, how horrible for him. But there are always wigs.' She continued:

> Teppi is perfect . . . I truly love, admire and respect her. She is the *only* woman friend I have of whom I can say these things. I expect you think, and I think too, that intelligence should have an Attic calm. Yet she *is* intelligent and has only just missed by the narrowest margin being outstandingly remarkable. Her large free attitude towards morals and conventions can't be enough admired. It is a wonderful attitude seeing what her [upbringing] and environment are.

H.B. and his wife finally produced a grandson for Elizabeth, the first boy child to be born in the family since his own father and he since his father before him. Elizabeth was not particularly thrilled: 'It is always the poor and unsuccessful that go in for more children than they can afford . . . His silly optimism makes me sick. I am greatly shocked.'[35]

The news of this event coincided with Elizabeth discovering that H.B. had deliberately tricked her into giving him that $1,000 when he came to spend the summer with her. It was terrible to her that he should have inherited his father's unscrupulousness about money when he might just as easily have inherited her own father's rigid and exact honourableness.

Elizabeth commented, when she heard the news that Chamberlain was going to have a meeting with Hitler, that this would probably give the rest of the world a breathing space for a few hours. When, three weeks later, she listened to Hitler raving on the wireless that he was going to occupy the Sudetenland she felt that that was the dogs' and her own death warrant and her heart beat so violently that it kept her awake in bed. She telegraphed Trix to meet her at the chalet, which crossed with a telegram from Trix asking her mother to send enough of the narcotics to kill her and her daughters. It seemed to her that there would be such a conflagration as a result of what was happening that it might be better to die painlessly while she had the choice for her family.

There was great excitement everywhere and Charlotte wrote Elizabeth letters full of capital letters telling her that in a crisis she should turn to her own Flesh and Blood. Later she had a slight stroke and the doctor gave her about a year to live. 'Why, that's over in about five months . . . As you know,' Elizabeth wrote to Liebet, 'I myself am great friends with Death, and think highly of it – but only for myself – and not for other people. I get a pain in my entrails when I think of poor little [Charlotte] disappearing.'

At a lunch party Elizabeth described Trix's despair and started to cry, so that an appalled silence followed. In November she went to meet Trix at a hotel near the German border and found her in a highly nervous state, refusing to speak until they were out in the open, and certain that a man next door, who was typing, was a spy and taking down all she said. She told her mother that a woman had shrieked over her garden fence that she ought be be denounced, that she said dreadful things about Germany abroad, and that, if she did not praise the country, she would have her passport taken away. She was in no doubt, however, that she intended to remain faithful to Toni and Germany whatever happened.

Mougins, near the border of Italy, was full of troops and ambulances, though there was no word about mobilization. Elizabeth had billeted on her eight French officers who were sleeping in her house, twenty-nine soldiers in the garage, a lorry-load of ammunition in her garden, a sentinel with a naked bayonet at the entrance day and night and a soldier crouching behind her rosemary bush with an anti-aircraft gun. The chatelaine made her exits and entrances and the sentinel presented arms to her each time. She bought some balls of wax to stick in her ears in case any of the weapons went off.

Then she received a disturbing letter from Trix's daughter,

Sybilla, or Billy of the red-gold hair, who had been in Berlin to study acting and had lost all of the illusions about her own country that she had ever had. She had smuggled the letter out by diplomatic bag:

> Darling little Granny, I can't go on living in Germany. I hate it . . . I don't know how I dare asking [*sic*] you but could you adopt me and give me an English name? Oh darling, what shall I do here in a war among those awful patriots in a country I hate? Mummy doesn't hate the country and my father is German. Neither of them will ever understand what I feel about this ugly, horrid soldier nation.

Elizabeth was galvanized by this letter to go to the British Consul to see if she could get Billy on her passport, and wrote to Liebet, telling her to expect them both: 'Why not do a final duty in my life and take Billy too?'[36] She did everything she could to get Sybilla out of Germany but in the end Trix made too many conditions, frightened that her daughter might go to America, like it, get married and stay, or that Elizabeth might lose interest in her and leave her somewhere. In the end Elizabeth admitted defeat. She put five of her dogs in a kennel and kept one, a beautiful blue and white cocker spaniel also called Billy that she had fallen in love with in Harrods' pet shop a few years previously. They boarded the *Queen Mary* together at Cherbourg on 17 May, bound for New York.

· 20 ·

The Blasted Heath

America opened its friendly but impersonal arms to the small refugee and her dog. As soon as she arrived she drove to her daughter's house in Connecticut, but the old antagonism immediately sprang up again between her and Corwin, fuelled by Elizabeth's realization that her son-in-law was pro-Nazi. The sight of an exhausted Liebet slaving away at domestic chores while Corwin remained inert behind the *Wall Street Journal* aroused her motherly rage. She soon left Sunset Farm and became a weary traveller, moving from hotel to hotel in search of sunshine and someone 'really' to talk to, and often obliged to move on because Billy whined and yelped inconsolably when she left him alone in her room. Her courage was extraordinary, and despite her homelessness and inevitable loneliness she made friends wherever she went and wrote letters which show an impenetrable façade of stout-heartedness.

The only good news to come from Europe was that a buyer for the chalet had appeared, an order of nuns who had offered 50,000 Swiss francs.* Elizabeth accepted the offer sadly for it had cost her six times that much to build the house. Sybilla had met and fallen in love with a nephew of Maud's, William Ritchie, thus solving all problems in the best possible way. He was working at Barclays Bank in the South of France and later joined the Air Force, but not before marrying Sybilla. Elizabeth was immensely relieved. It was on her conscience that she had not overridden Trix's endless objections to taking her granddaughter to America, and she had grown suspicious (her own word) that Trix profoundly mistrusted her ability to care for anybody for very long. It was a bitter pill for her to swallow: 'Teppi, surely what I have done is not bad, and was it not right for

*£56,000 today.

304

me to be afraid of the responsibility after Trixi opened my eyes?' she wrote to her friend.

As a palliative *Mr Skeffington,* finished in August of the previous year and sold to Doubleday, was published early in 1940 and was well received in England as well as in America. Warner Brothers bought the film rights for $50,000. *Time* magazine did a profile which pleased and flattered her, but she detested the photographs which made her look, she thought, 'like an old crow'.[1] The photographer did some snooping while he was in Beaufort and discovered that Elizabeth had had to move there from another establishment because of the inferior accommodation she demanded for her spaniel. She told him that she had been following with great interest the articles that had been appearing in *Time* about Bertrand. He had caused a scandal in New York because a case had been brought against him for corrupting youth. She couldn't see what all the fuss was about, his morals were all right. 'He's been married several times,' she said, 'but then, so have a lot of Americans.' She also said that *Time* described him as blue-eyed. Her own observation was that he possessed very remarkable brown eyes, 'with orange centres'.

The tenor of *Mr Skeffington* is best summed up by the musings of one of the characters:

> The sorry, she hadn't been able to help observing . . . seemed always to be those who couldn't go on because of no longer being attractive. If they were still attractive, they waited to be sorry till they had lost their looks. And sometimes, in moments of extreme lassitude . . . she wondered what the Kingdom of Heaven, if one did manage to get there after all the trouble, could possibly be like, crowded up with the battered.

The reviews were good, better than she had had for many years. 'This is Elizabeth at her best,' declared the *Times Literary Supplement,* 'and only those who have, for so many years, waited impatiently for each new book know how very good that can be.' It was clear to the author that all the reviewers, and by extension the reading public, held her warmly in their hearts and esteemed her highly as an artist, after all. Knowing this made it marginally easier to cope with the rigours and loneliness of exile.

Poultney Bigelow, a long-standing friend, swam into Elizabeth's orbit and shocked her with his obvious sympathy for the Nazis and his anti-Semitism. He recited the jingle 'How odd of God to choose the Jews' in one of his letters, to which she countered, 'Your views on

Jews shock me. Your E.' She received a reply in violent language from him and what she described in her reply as 'a simply revolting and disgraceful pamphlet of anti-Jew filthy abuse'. She did not know what to do with it: the last thing she wanted was to keep it, and yet even more could she not leave it lying about, and there was no fireplace where she was living. She finally took it into the woods and built a small fire of leaves and twigs and ceremonially burnt it there, vowing she had finished with Poultney Bigelow.

Her diaries are full of her longing to be with Liebet (who was not able to see her very often because of her loyalty to her family) and resoluteness to carry on with life among strangers with dignity, her only companion a dog. It was odd, she reflected, how what she wrote in her novels came true. Unconscious at the time of what was to happen to her in America, she had written in *Mr Skeffington* of the hero and heroine: 'The final summing up of their spectacular lives: one dog.' Hitler's claws were long and reached out even to a harmless dowager, keeping her on the march. She could see no prospect, she wrote to Maud, of anything but ending her days in a foreign land. She longed to see her house in Mougins but steeled her imagination to the prospect of it being looted and ruined. But these things seemed as nothing to her compared with the immense issues of life or death, freedom or slavery, which were being fought for. She remained certain that 'Hitler and all his brood of devils'[2] would one day be destroyed. It was cold comfort to hear that her son-in-law, Tony von Hirschberg, had been twice decorated.

Reading Chateaubriand, she was greatly struck by the resemblance between Napoleon and Hitler – 'except that Napoleon was a great military genius' – but they exhibited the same wild talk and temper tantrums and she hoped they would come to the same end.

> Horrible if every 100 years the world gets scourged by one adventurer. Napoleon was greatly superior though for he never tortured or persecuted. He fought properly. And again, it was England thwarting him that roused his greatest fury. England seems cast for the part of the thorn in the flesh of bullies . . . it is obvious, I think, that she has been cast by fate for the most glorious role of her existence. Whatever mistakes she will make in the future, at this moment she is at the very peak of her glory; a sort of twentieth-century Christ taking the sins of the whole world on her shoulders alone and going to redeem us all . . . We never let go, we shall never be slaves, and I'm

so proud at this moment of being a bit of England . . . [3]

In November 1940 Elizabeth travelled to South Carolina and booked into the Halcyon Inn, Summerville. Because of Billy (or as she called him by that time Belial, because of his wickedness and tendency to howl when left alone) she asked for a place away from the main house and was taken to a small, pale pink cottage in the heart of a sad, sopping wood 'which was yet full of charm'.[4] The windows opened directly on to the trees and a white cat sat aloft on a pedestal, preening itself and majestically ignoring Billy's wild efforts to jump up at her. Elizabeth settled in to spend the winter, and Liebet, who had driven her mother there, motored back home, a distance of about 750 miles. She arrived back with her family in a state of utter exhaustion to begin work on the household chores that had accumulated while she had been away. Unfortunately her daughters were not inclined to exert themselves hugely, and Elizabeth had visions of the three of them, Corwin and the two girls, 'louts' she called them, sitting, watching her beautiful daughter wear herself out in their service like the princess and the goblins. Corwin had been writing to his mother-in-law complaining that it was *her* demands on Liebet that were making her ill (her blood pressure was down to seventy and the doctor was treating her for low vitality) and Elizabeth was acutely conscious that she was an added burden on the poor woman's 'thin shoulders'. Liebet herself was torn between duty and her family and her enormous love and respect for her mother – 'She *adored* her mother,' Sybilla recalled. Liebet appeared not to be able to choose one in favour of the other and neither in favour of her own well-being.

Elizabeth spent Thanksgiving with the Doubledays who lived nearby and who were 'enchantingly kind as usual'.[5] She suspected them of planning to build a cottage for her in their grounds and drove back to her little pale pink abode and her mourning dog laden with books they had given her to read. 'Billy and I will face our winter in, as it were, each others' arms.'[6] She read and meditated and the lines of A. E. Housman ran again and again through her head.

> I, a stranger and afraid
> In a world I never made.

And W. B. Yeats's: 'I am trapped in a dying animal.'

The occasional sortie to a local party was less than uplifting for they were depressingly geriatric in content. Surrounded by silent and beautiful trees, with only a cat and a dog and her own thoughts for company, Elizabeth laid her plans for death. She sent a large sum of money to Evi as a surprise Christmas present and made a gift of one to Liebet too, thus reducing her liquid assets to a little over £6,000, enough to cover the small bequests in her will and to pay for her funeral. She then wrote to Lord Asquith, a High Court judge she had known in the South of France:

> What has happened to 'Mas des Roses', my cottage at Mougins, I do not know. But all these things are details compared with the immense question at stake, which is just simply the survival or destruction of good. I know that if Hitler were to win I would at once kill myself, for nothing would induce me to be a slave. But meanwhile, my passionate wish is to live and see England win . . .

This, of course, appeared to state her intention of doing so but, like Katherine Mansfield, she often left out what was really going on in her mind, what she had planned in spite of her 'passionate wish', sometimes the very opposite of what she had written.

On Christmas Day 1940 Elizabeth had been invited to the Doubledays but was unable to go because of the pelting rain. Solitude and, worst of all, no message or telephone call or present from Liebet or anyone else, combined with the weather to lower her morale. A little lizard came out and 'leaned on its elbows'[7] and gazed at her, and she sat down on the floor next to it to keep it company. She felt extraordinarily desolate and began to cry and was astonished at herself.

> . . . But there was one bright spot – a very bright one, and that was that just as I started crying, I who thought I had dried up for ever, the telephone rang, and I heard Evi's little pipe, so excited she could hardly talk. Naturally, at first, I thought it was [Liebet], and wondered why it sounded so far away. Then it dawned on me that it was Evi, recklessly and beautifully (for it gave me great delight) squandering her few pennies on a talk with me. Each of the children came and talked and I felt so comforted, for this was a real demonstration of affection and also showed an affinity, and I loved the lavishness too, though I dare say I ought to blame it.[8]

A friend, Beatrice Chalner, came on purpose from New York to be with Elizabeth on New Year's Eve. She was a great comfort with her calm wisdom after what Elizabeth described as the 'sound asleep southerners'.[9] They sat around the radio at midnight with a cup of egg-nog and heard the New Year in and Elizabeth prayed for God's blessing on all she loved in the 'terrible, but going to be glorious',[10] coming year.

The first terror of the year was a blemish that grew on her eye, for which she was prescribed X-ray treatment. Then her right hand, the one she used to write with, became crippled with arthritis. In the middle of January she came down with flu and telephoned the doctor who ordered her to bed. She did not go to bed but sat up drinking orange juice, feeling 'weak and queer'. She contacted Liebet who arrived a few days later but, just as Elizabeth was getting better she caught cold, and Liebet caught the flu bug. They were both taking some pills given to them by the doctor which lifted their spirits right up 'and made us feel well when we aren't really, underneath'[11] and produced recklessness in both of them. Elizabeth continued not to feel well for five more days while her daughter stayed with her and convalesced.

On the 29th of January Elizabeth made her last entry in her diary: 'Lovely day but raw, anyhow raw early. Don't feel well.' Soon after writing this she collapsed and Liebet called a doctor. Two nurses were put in charge and the following day she sank into a coma and was taken by ambulance to the Riverside Infirmary in Charleston, where, without ever regaining consciousness, she died on 9 February 1941.

Liebet's grief, exhaustion and the after-effects of flu rendered her unable to see to the funeral arrangements. The Doubledays stepped into the breach and asked Pat Frere, who was staying with them at Barony Hall, Yemassee, at the time, to pick out a coffin. She went to Charleston and chose a pretty dove-grey one with a white satin lining that she was sure Elizabeth would have liked. The Countess Russell had travelled a long road from when little May Beauchamp had spoken her first recorded words, 'Pa, are him bellied?'

She was cremated and laid to rest at Lincoln Fort Cemetery in Washington. In 1947, when her dearest wish had been granted and Hitler had been defeated, she was brought back and as she had requested her ashes were commingled with her brother Sydney Beauchamp's in Tyler's Green churchyard, near Penn in Buckinghamshire. PARVA SED APTA is engraved on the commemorative plaque. Evi travelled over to England in the Fifties and planted a rose tree on the spot where the ashes are buried, but it did not thrive. Even after her death Elizabeth did not cease her wanderings. Her plaque somehow worked itself loose from the wall of the church and spent three placid decades, or more, surrounded by her favourite dandelions and daisies, which is where the author of this book discovered it.

Of her obituaries, the one written by her friend Hugh Walpole for the *Daily Sketch* best captures both her personality and his affection for her:

> A little while ago there died in America, at the age of seventy-three, [she was in fact seventy-four] one of the very few witty women novelists of England.
>
> I said witty – not comic or farcical. There have, I think been only three others – Jane Austen, Rhoda Broughton and Rose Macaulay.
>
> Additions thankfully received. The lady's name was Mary Countess Russell – to all of us she was 'Elizabeth and her German Garden'.
>
> The war has perhaps for the moment dimmed her passing. It will not be for long. English literature is not so crammed with wits that it can spare Elizabeth.
>
> I knew her well. First I hated her and then I loved her.
>
> It amused me to read the final sentence of one obituary: 'Small and blonde, she had good regular features and a frank, gentle expression indicative of the peaceful beauty of her temperament.'
>
> Small and blonde she was, but every other word of this dull category is wrong . . .
>
> Her features were not regular, her nose was too small and her mouth too large. Her expression was never gentle – amused, cynical, ironic, loving, gay, ferocious, cold, ardent – but never gentle.
>
> As to the 'peaceful beauty of her temperament' how she would herself laugh at that! Peaceful! Never!
>
> She had in theory a Wordsworthian gospel for life, but she practised it only when she was alone, and she was rarely alone. Wherever she was there was a whirlwind.
>
> Her friends around her were never in the same position for half an hour at a time – they were in disgrace or in favour, a butt or a blessing.
>
> That is not to say that she did not love loyally and generously. She did. But she was the one who set the tune.
>
> There was always wherever she lived the implication of a Court. You were given your orders for the day.
>
> In that shrill, piping little voice she would call you for

your afternoon walk as she might call her dogs. And then she would set out like a little Madame de Sévigné waiting (not very hopefully) to be entertained . . .

She was loved by all sorts and kinds of people. I knew her first when, as little more than a boy, I went out to her Prussian Baron's Nassenheide to tutor during a vacation her children. They were known then the world over as the April, May and June babies.

I had a horrible summer. She found me a crude country boy, sentimental and sublimely ignorant.

She decided, I suppose, that I should be none the worse for a little training.

When she was cruel she was very cruel, and I was so miserable, so homesick and so stupid that I used to snivel in the cold dark passages of the *Schloss* and ache for home.

I doubt whether any experience in my life did me more good, but dear me, did I suffer!

Later we became great friends and some of my happiest times were when staying with her in the chalet in Switzerland. Here she was a delightful hostess, the company was perfectly chosen and the country most beautiful . . .

Later when she lived on the Riviera, I saw little of her. I hated the Riviera, and she knew that I did. But I always loved her.

She was as unique as one of Benvenuto Cellini's salt-cellars.

I hate to think that I shall never hear that high-pitched voice again or see her, befurred to the ears, marching across the snow, or watch the gentle kindliness steal into her eyes.

But there! I've used the word 'gentle' myself. The point is not, however, her character, but rather what does she leave behind her?

She leaves, undoubtedly, some of the wittiest novels in the English language. What should anybody read?

The original *Elizabeth and her German Garden* and *The Solitary Summer*, its sequel. *Fräulein Schmidt and Mr Anstruther*, *Elizabeth in Rügen* and her latest and last *Mr Skeffington*.

I don't care for her sentiment and therefore I won't recommend you *The Enchanted April*, perhaps her most popular work. Her wit was acid, her sentiment was very sweet and English.

She was not a novelist in the creative sense. All her novels were sooner or later autobiography.

The two books of hers that I love best are *Fräulein Schmidt* and *Elizabeth in Rügen* . . .

If anyone wants to know at this particular moment of time why the Germans are lovable and detestable, let them read these two books. Everything is here, the jollity, the guzzling, the brutality and the sentiment.

But wherein exactly lay Elizabeth's wit? What is the quality of this that makes it so rare?

Wit is, I think, in English people very rare, because it must spring both from cruelty and tenderness. English people hate to be cruel, and are ashamed of being tender.

P. G. Wodehouse is never cruel – never more than a school boy is cruel to guinea pigs.

Miss Delafield would like to be cruel, but can't be. Rose Macaulay is sometimes cruel and knows it.

Elizabeth could be so cruel (as in *The Caravaners*) that you blush for her a little, but this gives her uniqueness in England.

And figures like Fräulein Schmidt and the heroine of *Mr Skeffington* show her exquisite tenderness of heart, her delicacy and fragile artistry.

One or two of her books will remain, I think, as minor classics.

Afterword

In her will, made in 1937, Elizabeth's first and major concern was to instruct the vet, step by step, on the least distressing manner of despatching her dogs in France, and, of course, Billy. 'He (the vet) is to put all my dogs to sleep by *picure* and when asleep he is to put them to death by means of another *picure*, the greatest care being taken that the dogs should suffer neither fear nor pain . . . ' She left Le Mas des Roses to Liebet and the chalet to Trix. There were other minor bequests after which she decreed that the residue of her estate be converted into cash and the income was to be shared between Evi and H.B. with the capital entailed to their children. In the event, no doubt intentional, because of the sale of the chalet Trix received hardly anything at all. This was a state of affairs which Elizabeth could have remedied in a codicil she made in 1941 but, possibly because of the hard feelings engendered by the episode of Sybilla and much else, Elizabeth failed to do this. Liebet was appointed executor of all of her estate in lieu of Frere and was given the power to destroy 'whatever she thinks should be destroyed . . . '

In the mid Fifties, when the horror of the war years had receded, Liebet gathered all of her mother's personal papers and letters, recalling as many of those in other people's possession as they could be persuaded to part with, and had the voluminous diaries typed – a major task undertaken with care and devotion to detail. Out of this came her version of Elizabeth's life, *Elizabeth of the German Garden*, published in 1958 by Frere's company, William Heinemann. According to Elizabeth's wishes everything that might threaten 'the eyes and reason of the biographer' was destroyed in 'the great bonfire' of 1957 and much else besides. The rest was deposited in the vaults of the Huntington Library, San Marino, California, where it has slumbered, undisturbed until recently.

Evi was incensed when she read her sister's book for she felt that much had been omitted and misrepresented about her mother's life and that the book was primarily a 'whitewash job'. She embarked on her own version of her youth with the aid of her diaries, calling it *Ten Times Round,* and what remains of the manuscript, saved from the fire, charred and patchy, is intimate, well written and affectionate.

Trix was imprisoned for six months before the end of the war for alleged anti-German activities and it is likely that the Germans suspected her (erroneously) of providing her mother with details of their brutality which formed the background of *Mr Skeffington*.

Elizabeth's novels and reputation went into eclipse after her death, astonishingly so considering her popularity when she was alive: 'Does anyone read her books now, and if not why not? How odd is fame . . . ' George Lyttelton wrote to Sir Rupert Hart-Davis in 1956. Her light, pre-war banter, and 'Beauchamp waggishness' as she once described her particular brand of wit to H. G. Wells, reminded people of the carefree past which it was useless to contemplate in the times of inflation, cold war and hardship suffered by most of her public in the decades that followed her death. Katherine Mansfield, by contrast, gained in reputation and appreciation, deservedly, for she better reflects the doubtful and introspective ethos of the post-war years, while Elizabeth's 'thin flute' continued to play in an empty, Edwardian afternoon, all alone.

All of Elizabeth's books have been out of print since the war but a new generation are beginning to hear at least rumours of the excellence and perception of her writing. Virago has reissued *Elizabeth and her German Garden, Fräulein Schmidt and Mr Anstruther, Vera,* and *The Enchanted April* and *The Pastor's Wife* will appear in 1987. Her new public will find in her work an undated lightness and relevance to the issues of relationships between men and women written with power that is not strident, wit that never becomes brittle and compassion without sentimentality. They will find that her work deserves the renaissance in recognition that will place it once again in the forefront of English letters.

Acknowledgements

My key indebtedness is to A. S. Frere without whose consent, encouragement, friendship and untiring help this book would have been written by somebody else.

His wife, Pat Frere, with equal dedication, fed me, answered my questions and letters, provided photographs and, when the time came, turned around the finished manuscript with dispatch and professionalism although she was at the time recovering from the blow of her husband's death.

The staff at the Huntington Library, San Marino, California, which houses Elizabeth's vast collection, deserve many thanks for their good manners and patience while harbouring such an eccentric researcher as myself. Also the good friends I made there who bolstered my morale in the face of what seemed, at one time, an impossible task.

My cousin Jinny Ross, whose hospitality and charm is famous over two continents, will never know the extent of my debt to her for her patience and generosity to me while I commuted daily for sometimes months on end to the library.

My dear friends Lesley Cunliffe and Stan Gebler Davies talked me through the worst of the perplexities of this book and much else with high good humour and I here express my heartfelt gratitude. No stumbling pilgrim has ever had a richer source of wit and wisdom, sense and nonsense, warmth and loyalty as I have been fortunate enough to strike in these two people.

Noel Picarda Kemp has acted in turn as my rock, my spur, my friend and most valiant supporter and has always opened the way before me if it was within his power to do so, without stint or thought for himself.

My editor, Jill Black, who has nursed my manuscript into some semblance of order and method with good humour and fortitude, will no doubt dismiss my thanks as unnecessary and her own contribution as simply part of her job. In half a lifetime of experience of editors, good, excellent and efficient, I have never come across one of such calibre and professionalism.

Caroline Dawnay, my most excellent agent, steered me through the pitfalls and snares of this book with great diligence and foresight.

I should like to thank Elizabeth's family, both in England and America, for their hospitality, integrity and alacrity; her reputation is excellently guarded by them. In particular my gratitude to Jackie (Graves) Harris, Evi's daughter, whose efficiency and real understanding of the problems facing a biographer could not have been more helpful to me, and also for pulling out all the stops and finishing the translation of Teppi's memoirs from the German in time for me to take it back to England. Ann Hardham cheerfully accepted the disruption in her life that my demands made on her and was helpful in every way. My thanks to G. W. Arnim for his charming and helpful letters; Beatrix von Hirschberg for her most illuminating conversations and letters about her mother, and Sybilla and William Ritchie for their hospitality and helpfulness.

My own family, particularly my mother and father, have been a constant source of encouragement and unstinting help for the most laborious tasks in spite of their own busy timetable. I here express my gratitude not only for what they have done but for who they are.

Of the other people who have helped me, my thanks to: Antony Alpers, Rosemary Billington, Morchard Bishop, Margaret Birkinshaw, John and Peggy Booker, Piers Brendon, Gerald Brenan, Judith Burnley, Mel Calman, Thelma Cazalet-Keir, Margaret Chester, Barbara Cartland, Lady Diana Cooper, Richard Crawshaw, Peter Day, Jean Frere, Winifred Fortescue, Nick Furbank, Roland Gant, Betty Galton, Jonny Gathorne Hardy, Lady Cynthia Gladwyn Jebb, Rosemary Graham, Brian Guinness, Sir Rupert Hart-Davis, Michael Holroyd, Mrs Keith Miller-Jones, David Machin, James Moore, Colin Murry, David Nathan, Stanley Olsen, Henrietta Partridge, Tanis Phillips, Jeanne Renshaw, Dr Alice Roughton, Geoffrey Roughton, Bernard Stone, Jessica Strang, Frank Swinnerton, E. Warren Smythe, Henry and Pam Usborne, Andrew and Bridget Usborne, Tommy and Gerda Usborne, Anna Verrender, Geoffrey Wheatcroft, Alec Waugh, Dr Martin Wells, Anthony West, Rebecca West and Gordon Williams.

The majority of the quotations in this book are from the Countess Russell collection at the Huntington Library for which I would like to thank both the library and Ann Hardham for permission to reproduce them. Ann also kindly allowed me to quote from her grandmother Liebet Butterworth's book, *Elizabeth of the German Garden*. Jackie Harris has allowed me to quote from her mother Evi's diaries, her memoir *Ten Times Round* as well as Teppi's recollection. Sir Rupert Hart-Davis has allowed me to quote from Hugh Walpole's diaries as well as from his own excellent biography of Walpole and his published correspondence with George Lyttelton.

For further copyright material my thanks for permission to quote go to: A. P. Watt for *The New Machiavelli*; Chatto and Windus for *Mr Britling Sees it Through*; Faber & Faber for *H. G. Wells in Love*, and Dr Martin Wells for the Wells estate; Macmillan Publishing Company in New York for Lady Maude Warrender's *My First Sixty Years*; Olivia Swinnerton for Frank Swinnerton's *Background With Chorus* and *The Georgian Literary Scene*; the Society of Authors and King's College, Cambridge for E. M. Forster's diaries and letters (New E. M. Forster texts © 1986. The Provost and Scholars of King's College Cambridge); The National Trust for an extract from Rudyard Kipling's letter to Elizabeth; David Higham Associates Limited for a letter written by Ethel Smythe to Vernon Lee; Elizabeth Jane Howard for fragments from her biography of Bettina von Arnim; Susan Lowndes Marques and William Heinemann for Mrs Belloc Lowndes' *The Merry Wives of Westminster*; The Bertrand Russell Foundation for his autobiography and Allen and Unwin for *The Amberley Papers*; Dover Publications for George Santayana; the *New Statesman* for the review of *Vera* by Rebecca West.

The rest of the material I quote is either out of copyright or brief enough individually and in aggregate to permit publication under the normal conventions of 'fair dealing'.

The BBC Hulton Picture Library has given me permission to reproduce photographs from their archives of Wells and Hugh Walpole; Thelma Cazalet-Keir for photographs from her albums; the University of London Courtauld Institute of Art for Sir William Sargent's charcoal portrait of the Countess Russell from their library of negatives at the Witt Library; Rupert Hart-Davis for the photograph of Elizabeth, Hugh Walpole and Rudyard Kipling with the Cazalets at Fairlawn from his biography of Hugh Walpole; the Bertrand Russell Peace Foundation and Dr David Lewis Hodgson for the photograph from Bertrand Russell's election address in 1907; Eric Schall/*Life Magazine* © 1940 Time Inc/Colorific for the photograph of Elizabeth at the Golden Eagle; The Huntington Library, San Marino, California for the photograph of Elizabeth and

Wells; Ann Hardham for photographs from Liebet Butterworth's biography and albums; Jackie Harris for photographs from her mother's albums; the University of Illinois at Urbana-Champaign for the photograph of the caravan tour; The Mansell Collection for the photograph of Hugh Walpole as a young man and Antony Alpers for the photograph of Katherine Mansfield from his biography of her published by Viking Press.

My thanks also to the Alexander Turnbull library in Wellington for sending me copies of the letters of Katherine Mansfield, John Middleton Murry and Elizabeth; the London Library for all their help and for allowing me the use of their projector; the University of Illinois at Urbana-Champaign for sending me relevant copies of documents from the H. G. Wells collection at their library; the Macmaster University at Ontario for sending me documents of Bertrand and Francis Russell and extracts of Lionel Johnson's diaries and letters; the Westminster City Library for allowing me to look up back numbers of *The Times*; the manuscript department at the British Library for providing me with photocopies of Katherine Mansfield's letter to Elizabeth in their possession and King's College Library, Cambridge for allowing me to study the Forster collection. Last, but by no means my least debt of gratitude is to the hard working employees of the *Telegraph* Information Service who saved me much work.

Selected Bibliography

Alpers, Antony: *The Life of Katherine Mansfield*, Viking Press 1980
  Katherine Mansfield, a Biography, Jonathan Cape 1954.
Anderson, Margaret: *The Unknowable Gurdjieff*, Routledge & Kegan Paul 1962
Arnim, Elizabeth von: *Elizabeth and her German Garden*, Macmillan 1898. Virago 1985.
  The Solitary Summer, Macmillan 1899.
  The April Baby's Book of Tunes, Macmillan 1900.
  The Benefactress, Macmillan 1901.
  The Adventures of Elizabeth in Rügen, Macmillan 1904.
  Princess Priscilla's Fortnight, Smith & Elder 1905.
  Fräulein Schmidt and Mr Anstruther, Smith & Elder 1907. Virago 1983.
  The Caravaners, Smith & Elder 1909.
  Priscilla Runs Away (Play). Unpublished, 1910.
  The Pastor's Wife, Smith & Elder 1914. Virago 1987.
  (Alice Cholmondely): *Christine*, Macmillan 1917.
  Christopher and Columbus, Macmillan 1919.
  In the Mountains, Macmillan 1920.
  Vera, Macmillan 1921. Virago 1983.
  The Enchanted April, Macmillan 1922. Virago 1986.
  Love, Macmillan 1925.
  Introduction to Sally, Macmillan 1926
  Expiation, Macmillan 1929.
  Father, Macmillan 1931.
  Jasmine Farm, Heinemann 1934.
  All the Dogs of my Life, Heinemann 1936.
  Mr Skeffington, Heinemann 1940.
Bagnold, Enid: *Autobiography*, Heinemann 1969.
Beauchamp, Sir Harold: *Reminiscences and Recollections*, New Plymouth, N.Z. 1937.
Bell, Quentin: *Bloomsbury*, Futura 1974.
Belloc Lowndes, Mrs: *The Merry Wives of Westminster*, Macmillan 1946.
  A Passing World, Macmillan 1948.
Bennett, Arnold: *Journals 1896–1928*, Ed. Newman Flower (3 vols), Cassell 1932–3.
Bennett, J. G. (Ed): *Gurdjieff, Making a New World*, Turnstone Books 1973.
Bredsdorff, Dr Elias: *Some Personal Reminiscences of Bertrand Russell*. Unpublished.
Buxton Forman, Maurice (Ed): *The Letters of John Keats*, Oxford University Press 1947.
Carswell, John: *Lives and Letters*, Faber & Faber 1978.
Cavitch, David: *D. H. Lawrence and the New World*. Oxford University Press 1947.
Cazalet-Kier, Thelma: *From the Wings*, The Bodley Head 1964.

Charmes, Leslie de: *Elizabeth of the German Garden*, Heinemann 1958.

Clark, Ronald: *Bertrand Russell and his World*, Thames and Hudson 1981.
  The Life of Bertrand Russell, Jonathan Cape 1975.

Cobden-Sanderson, Thomas James: *Journals 1879–1922*, Thavies Inn 1926.

Compton-Rickett, Arthur: *A History of English Literature*, Jaek 1929.

Cooper, Diana: *The Light of Common Day*, Rupert Hart-Davis 1959.

Cory, Daniel (Ed): *The Letters of George Santayana*, Constable 1956.

Daphne in Paris, by the anonymous author of *Daphne in the Fatherland*, Andrew Melrose 1912.

Davies, Stan Gebler: *James Joyce: A Portrait of the Artist*, Granada 1982.

Dickson, Lovat: *H. G. Wells, His Turbulent Life and Times*, Macmillan 1969.

Dukes, Sir Paul: *The Unending Quest*, Cassell 1950.

Engen, Rodney: *Kate Greenaway, a Biography*, Macdonald 1981.

Fisher, Henry W: *The Private Lives of William II and his Consort, A Secret History of the Court of Berlin*, Heinemann 1904.

Forster, E. M.: *Where Angels Fear to Tread*, Blackwood 1905.
  The Longest Journey, Blackwood 1907.

Furbank, P. N.: *E. M. Forster, a Life*, Secker & Warburg 1977–78

Fussell, Paul: *The Great War of Modern Memory*, Oxford University Press 1975.

Gathorne Hardy, Robert (Ed): *Lady Ottoline at Garsington*, Faber & Faber 1973.

Glenavy, Lady Beatrice: *Today We Will Only Gossip*, Constable 1964.

Gregor-Dellin, Martin, and Mack, Dietrich: *Cosima Wagner's Diaries*, Collins 1978.

Gurdjieff, G. I.: *Meetings With Remarkable Men*, Routledge & Kegan Paul 1963.

Hart-Davis, Rupert: *Hugh Walpole, a Biography*, Macmillan 1952.

Hartmann, Thomas: *Our Life with Gurdjieff*, Cooper Sq Publishers (New York) 1964.

Helps, Arthur and Howard, Elizabeth Jane: *Bettina von Arnim, a Portrait*, Chatto and Windus 1957.

Hynes, Samuel: *The Edwardian Turn of Mind*, Princeton University Press 1968.

James, Henry: *Notes on Novelists*, Dent 1914.

Jepson, Edgar: *Memories of a Victorian*, Victor Gollancz 1933.
  Memories of an Edwardian and Neo-Georgian, Richards Press 1937.

Joysmith, Georgina: *The Memories of L.M.*, Michael Joseph 1971.

Kent, George O.: *Arnim and Bismarck*, Oxford University Press 1968.

Lago, Mary and Furbank, P. N.: *Selected Letters of E. M. Forster*, Collins 1983.

Lee, Vernon: *The Handling of Words*, The Bodley Head 1923.

Mackenzie, Norman and Jean: *The Time Traveller*, Weidenfeld and Nicolson 1973.

Malleson, Constance: *The Coming Back*, Jonathan Cape 1931.
  After Ten Years, a Personal Record, Collins 1936.

Mansfield, Katherine: *Collected Stories*, Constable 1945.
  A Scrapbook, Constable 1939.
  The Letters, Constable 1939.

Marse, L. J.: *Politicians on the Warpath*, National Review 1920.

Marsh, Edward: *A Number of People*, Hamish Hamilton 1939.

Marwick, Arthur: *The Deluge. British Society in World War One*, Bodley Head 1967.

Maugham, W. Somerset: *Cakes and Ale*, Heinemann 1930.
  Strictly Personal, Heinemann 1942.
  A Vagrant Mood, Heinemann 1952.

Meyers, Jeffrey: *Katherine Mansfield, a Biography*, Hamish Hamilton 1978.

Middleton Murry, John (Ed): *The Journals of Katherine Mansfield*, Constable 1927.
  Novels and Novelists, Constable 1930.

Moore, George: *Conversations in Ebury Street*, Heinemann 1924.

Mullaly, Frederick: *The Silver Salver*, Granada 1981.

Nichols, Beverley: *25: Being a Young Man's Candid Recollections of his Elders and Betters*, Jonathan Cape 1925.

Nicolson, Nigel and Trautmann, Joanne: *Virginia Woolf's Letters, 1888–1935*, Chatto and Windus 1976.

Priestley, J. B.: *The Edwardians*, Heinemann 1970.

Ray, Gordon N.: *H. G. Wells and Rebecca West*, Macmillan 1974.

Russell, Bertrand: *Autobiography*, George Allen & Unwin 1967.

Russell, Bertrand and Patricia (Ed): *The Amberley Papers*, Hogarth Press 1937.

Russell, Dora: *The Tamarisk Tree*, Elek 1975.

Russell, John Francis: *Lay Sermons*, Thomas Burleigh 1902.

   Divorce, Heinemann 1912.

   My Life and Adventures, Cassell 1923.

Russell, Mollie: *Five Women in a Caravan*, Everleigh Nash 1911.

Santayana, George: *My Host the World*, Cresset Press 1953.

   The Middle Span, Constable 1947.

Showalter, Elaine: *A Literature of Their Own*, Virago 1978.

Stead, C. K. (Ed): *Letters and Journals of Katherine Mansfield*, Allen Lane 1977.

Swinnerton, Frank: *Background With Chorus*, Hutchinson 1956.

   The Georgian Literary Scene, Heinemann 1935.

Usborne, Richard (ed): *A Century of Summer Fields*, Methuen 1964.

Walpole, Hugh: *The Old Ladies*, Macmillan 1924.

Wells, H.G.: *Experiment in Autobiography*, Victor Gollancz 1934.

   Mr Britling Sees it Through, Cassell 1916.

   H. G. Wells in Love, Faber and Faber 1984.

West, Anthony: *H. G. Wells*, Hutchinson 1984.

West, Geoffrey: *H. G. Wells*, Gerald Howe Ltd. 1930.

Yutang, Lin: *The Importance of Living*, Reynal & Hitchcock 1938.

References

KEY (in order of appearance)

HB'sJ: Henry Herron Beauchamp's journals

EoftheGG: *Elizabeth of the German Garden* by Leslie de Charmes, William Heinemann 1958.

SirHB'sRec: *Reminiscences and Recollections* by Sir Harold Beauchamp, published privately by New Plymouth, N.Z. 1937.

E'sDofL: *All the Dogs of My Life* by 'Elizabeth', William Heinemann 1936.

RecSvH: From conversations with Sybilla (von Hirschberg) Ritchie.

RecEMF: 'Recollections of Nassenheide' by E. M. Forster, published in the *Listener* 1959.

RecASF: Many conversations with Alexander Stuart Frere.

E'sD: Elizabeth's diaries at the Huntington Library, San Marino, California.

RecFS: Recollections of Frank Swinnerton in *Background with Chorus*, Hutchinson 1956 and *Georgian Literary Scene*, William Heinemann 1935.

E'sB: *The Benefactress* by 'Elizabeth', Macmillan 1901.

E'sC: *The Caravaners* by 'Elizabeth', Smith & Elder 1909.

BbyH&H: *Bettina (von Arnim): a Portrait* by Arthur Helps and Elizabeth Jane Howard, Chatto & Windus 1957.

E'sPW: *The Pastor's Wife* by 'Elizabeth', Smith & Elder 1914.

Evi'sJ: The unpublished journals of Evi (von Arnim) Graves.

ML&AbyFR: *My Life and Adventures* by Earl Russell, Cassell 1923.

AmbP EdB&PR: *The Amberley Papers* The diaries and letters of Lord and Lady Amberley, edited by Bertrand and Patricia Russell, Volumes One and Two published by Leonard and Virginia Woolf at the Hogarth Press 1932.

BR'sA: *Bertrand Russell's Autobiography*, George Allen & Unwin 1967.

E'sGG: *Elizabeth and her German Garden* by 'Elizabeth', Macmillan 1898.

E'sSS: *The Solitary Summer* by 'Elizabeth', Macmillan 1899.

TTRbyEG: *Ten Times Round* by Evi Graves, unpublished.

RecBvH: From conversations with Beatrice (von Arnim) von Hirschberg.

RecJR: From conversations with Jeanne Renshaw (Beauchamp).

RecT: Recollections of Teppi as written in *Remembrances of the Author of Elizabeth and her German Garden*. Unpublished.

RecMrsBL: *The Merry Wives of Westminster* by Mrs Belloc Lowndes, Macmillan 1946 and *A Passing World* 1948.

E'sC&C: *Christopher and Columbus* by 'Elizabeth', Macmillan 1919.

EMF'sJ: The Journal of EMF (unpublished) King's College, Cambridge.

E'sPPF: *Princess Priscilla's Fortnight* by 'Elizabeth', Smith & Elder 1905.

E'sFS&MrA: *Fräulein Schmidt and Mr Anstruther* by 'Elizabeth', Smith & Elder 1907.

TCRbyJDD: The Cambridge Review by James Duff Duff.

FrofLL: Fragments of love letters to Elizabeth from Stuart, Wells, Francis Russell etc.

HW'sD: Hugh Walpole's unpublished diaries.

E'sAdd.inHW'sD: Elizabeth's additions to Walpole's diaries.

E'sITM: *In the Mountains* by 'Elizabeth', Macmillan 1920.

RecMW: Recollections of Lady Maude Warrender.

HGWinL by HGW: *H. G. Wells in Love* by H. G. Wells, Faber & Faber 1984.

HGWandRW by GR: *H. G. Wells and Rebecca West* by Gordon N. Ray, Macmillan 1974.

RecGS: Recollections of Elizabeth by George Santayana as published in *My Host the World*, Cresset Press 1953 and *The Middle Span*, Constable 1947.

RecMB: From conversations with Margaret Birkinshaw.

KM'sJ: *Katherine Mansfield's Journals* edited by John Middleton Murry, Constable 1927.

RecTC-K: From conversations with Thelma Cazalet-Keir.

C-S'sJ: *The Journals of Cobden-Sanderson*, R. Cobden-Sanderson 1929.

RecBN: Recollections of Beverley Nichols as published in *25: Being a Young Man's Candid Recollections of his Elders and Betters*, Jonathan Cape 1925.

E'sEA: *The Enchanted April* by 'Elizabeth', Macmillan 1923.

RecLCG-J: From conversations with Lady Cynthia Gladwyn-Jebb.

RecIB: Recollections of Ida Baker from her book *Katherine Mansfield: the Memories of Ida Baker*, Taplinger, New York 1971.

E'sL: *Love* by 'Elizabeth', Macmillan 1925.

Unpub.frag.: Unpublished fragments of Elizabeth's work.

RecTP: From conversation with Tanis (Guinness) Phillips.

RecBC: From correspondence with Barbara Cartland.

PfrPbyWF: *Perfume from Provence* by Winifred Fortescue

E'sBV unpub.: 'In a Bavarian Village', unpublished story by Elizabeth.

Abbreviations of correspondence (in order of appearance)

FL: Frederick Lassetter
RevL: Reverend Lassetter
LL: Louey Lassetter
HB: Henry Herron Beauchamp
LB: Louey Beauchamp (Lassetter)
JL: Jesse Lassetter
HW: Hugh Walpole
E: Elizabeth
KM: Katherine Mansfield
EMF: Edward Morgan Forster

M: Edward Morgan Forster's mother
CW: Charlotte Waterlow
Ch: Children
CM: Charles Marriott
HGW: H. G. Wells
Evi: Evi von Arnim
FR: Francis Russell
L: Liebet von Arnim (Mrs Corwin Butterworth)
JW: Jane Wells
AW: Anthony West

KU: Karen Usborne
GS: George Santayana
LOM: Lady Ottoline Morrell
BR: Bertrand Russell
Mrs BL.: Mrs Belloc Lowndes

ASF: Alexander Stuart Frere
DB: Dorothy Brett
JMM: John Middleton Murry
MR: Maud Ritchie
RHD: Sir Rupert Hart-Davis

Chapter One
1 HB'sJ
2 EoftheGG
3 Sir HB'sRec
4 HB'sJ
5 E'sDofL
6 EoftheGG
7 LfrFL-RevL
8 LfrLL-HB
9 RecSvH
10 E'sDofL
11 LfrFL-HB
12 HB'sJ
13 ibid
14 E'sDofL
15 HB'sJ

Chapter Two
1 HB'sJ
2 E'sDofL
3 HB'sJ
4 E'sDofL
5 HB'sJ
6 E'sDofL
7 RecEMF
8 E'sDofL
9 HB'sJ
10 ibid
11 ibid
12 LfrHB-LB
13 E'sDofL
14 HB'sJ
15 E'sDofL
16 HB'sJ
17 LfrLB-JL
18 EoftheGG
19 HB'sJ
20 RecASF
21 EoftheGG
22 E'sD
23 E'sDofL
24 HB'sJ
25 ibid
26 E'sD
27 RecASF

28 RecFS
29 HB'sJ

Chapter Three
1 E'sD
2 E'sDofL
3 E'sB
4 E'sDofL
5 HB'sJ
6 ibid
7 E'sDofL
8 ibid
9 EoftheGG
10 E'sDofL
11 RecASF
12 LfrLB-JL
13 ibid
14 LfrLB-JL
15 LfrHW-E
16 LfrLB-JL
17 HB'sJ
18 LfrLB-JL
19 HB'sJ

Chapter Four
1 HB'sJ
2 E'sDofL
3 E'sC
4 E'sDofL
5 ibid
6 BbyH&H
7 EoftheGG
8 E'sPW
9 ibid
10 HB'sJ
11 Evi'sJ
12 ML&AbyFR
13 ibid
14 AmbP EdB&PR
15 ML&AbyFR
16 BR'sA
17 AmbP EdB&PR
18 ML&AbyFR
19 ibid
20 BR'sA

21 BR'sA
22 ibid
23 ML&AbyFR
24 E'sDofL
25 EoftheGG

Chapter Five
1 E'sGG
2 ibid
3 ibid
4 RecEMF
5 E'sGG
6 BbyH&H
7 E'sD
8 E'sGG
9 E'sD
10 HB'sJ
11 E'sD
12 E'sGG
13 E'sD
14 E'sSS
15 E'sGG
16 E'sD
17 E'sGG
18 E'sD
19 E'sSS
20 ibid
21 ibid
22 E'sD
23 ibid
24 RecEMF
25 E'sD

Chapter Six
1 E'sD
2 ibid
3 ibid
4 E'sSS
5 ibid
6 ibid
7 ibid
8 ibid
9 E'sGG
10 E'sD
11 E'sDofL

324

REFERENCES

12 ibid
13 E'sGG
14 E'sD
15 HB'sJ
16 E'sD
17 E'sB

Chapter Seven
1 AmbPEdbyB&PR
2 BR'sA
3 ML&AbyFR
4 HB'sJ
5 E'sDofL
6 ibid
7 E'sD
8 ibid
9 ibid
10 Evi'sJ
11 TTRbyEG
12 HB'sJ
13 LfrE-HB
14 RecBvH
15 Evi'sJ
16 ibid
17 TTR byEG
18 RecEMF
19 E'sDofL
20 EoftheGG
21 ibid
22 RecJR
23 TTR byEG
24 RecBvH
25 EoftheGG

Chapter Eight
1 RecT et seq.
2 RecEMF
3 RecMrsBL
4 RecEMF
5 LfrKM-?
6 E'sD
7 E'sC&C
8 RecEMF
9 E'sGG
10 RecEMF
11 EMF'sJ
12 RecEMF
13 EMF'sJ
14 RecEMF
15 EMF'sJ
16 LfrEMF-M
17 ibid
18 ibid

19 ibid
20 ibid
21 RecEMF
22 ibid
23 E'sD
24 LfrE-CW
25 RecBvH
26 TTRbyEG
27 Evi'sJ
28 TTRbyEG

Chapter Nine
1 E'sPPF
2 RecT
3 LfrE-Ch
4 RecBvH
5 E'sFS&MrA
6 E'sDofL
7 E'sFS&MrA
8 HB'sJ
9 RecT
10 TCRbyJDD, 1917
11 RecT
12 FroLL-E
13 LfrE-HW
14 HW'sD
15 ibid
16 RecASF
17 EoftheGG
18 LfrHW-CM
19 E'sAdd in HW'sD
20 RecT
21 HW'sD
22 EoftheGG
23 ibid

Chapter Ten
1 TTRbyEG
2 E'sD
3 RecT
4 TTRbyEG
5 EMF'sJ
6 ibid
7 RecT
8 E'sITM
9 EoftheGG
10 RecMW
11 ibid
12 EMF'sJ
13 ibid
14 TTRbyEG
15 Evi'sJ
16 HGWinL by HGW

17 TTRbyEG
8 RecT
19 E'sDofL
20 RecT

Chapter Eleven
1 RecT
2 E'sD
3 E'sDofL
4 Evi'sJ
5 EoftheGG
6 Evi'sJ
7 E'sDofL
8 BR'sA
9 Evi'sJ
10 HGWinLbyHGW
11 RecT
12 EoftheGG
13 Evi'sJ
14 ibid
15 ibid
16 ibid
17 ibid
18 TTRbyEG
19 Evi'sJ
20 TTRbyEG
21 Evi'sJ
22 ibid
23 ibid
24 RecT
25 Evi'sJ

Chapter Twelve
1 LfrHGW-JW
2 HGWinL by HGW et seq.
3 LfrE-L
4 E'sDofL
5 LfrE-L
6 RecFS
7 RecASF
8 RecT
9 HGWinL by HGW
10 RecASF
11 E'sD
12 HGWandRW by GR
13 HGWinL by HGW
14 RecT
15 HGWinL by HGW
16 RecT
17 RecFS
18 HGWinL by HGW
19 LfrAW-KU
20 E'sD

21 RecT
22 FrofLL
23 E'sD
24 E'sDofL
25 HGWinL by HGW
26 RecFS
27 E'sDofL
28 HGWinL by HGW
29 RecT
30 LfrAW-KU
31 E'sDofL
32 RecT
33 E'sDofL
34 HGWinL by HGW
35 ibid

Chapter Thirteen
1 HGWinL by HGW
2 Evi'sJ
3 E'sD
4 FrofLL
5 E'sD
6 E'sDofL
7 E'sD
8 E'sDofL
9 RecFS
10 FrofLL
11 LfrE-L
12 LfrE-L
13 E'sD
14 RecGS
15 FrofLL
16 RecFS
17 ibid
18 EoftheGG
19 ML&AbyFR
20 E'sDofL
21 E'sD
22 ibid
23 RecT
24 EoftheGG
25 E'sD
26 Evi'sJ
27 Evi'sJ
28 ibid
29 ibid
30 E'sD
31 Evi'sJ
32 E'sD
33 ibid
34 LfrE-T
35 ibid
36 LfrE-L

37 E'sD
38 LfrGS-FR
39 E'sD
40 ibid
41 ibid
42 RecASF
43 RecGS
44 E'sD
45 ibid
46 ibid
47 LfrE-L
48 E'sD
49 LfrE-L
50 E'sD
51 BR'sA
52 E'sD
53 ibid
54 EoftheGG
55 LfrFR-GS, 1916
56 RecASF
57 E'sD
58 ibid

Chapter Fourteen
1 E'sD
2 ibid
3 RecASF
4 E'sD
5 ibid
6 ML&AbyFR
7 E'sD
8 LfrE-L
9 ibid
10 ibid
11 E'sD
12 LfrE-L
13 RecT
14 LfrE-L

Chapter Fifteen
1 E'sD
2 LfrE-L
3 E'sD
4 LfrBR-LOM, 1916
5 E'sD
6 EoftheGG
7 LfrE-L
8 ibid
9 RecFS et seq
10 ibid
11 BR'sA
12 RecGS
13 ibid

14 RecMB
15 ibid
16 RecMrsBL
17 LfrE-L
18 LfrE-L
19 E'sD

Chapter Sixteen
1 E'sITM
2 E'sD
3 LfrE-L
4 E'sD
5 ibid
6 RecJR
7 LfrKM-MrsBL
8 KM'sJ
9 RecASF
10 LfrE-L
11 RecTC-K
12 LfrE-ASF
13 C-S'sJ
14 LfrE-BR
15 RecASF
16 ibid
17 ibid
18 RecBN
19 ibid
20 ibid
21 ibid
22 RecFS
23 E'sD
24 EoftheGG
25 ibid
26 E'sD
27 E'sEA
28 RecASF
29 E'sD
30 LfrKM-E
31 LfrKM-DB
32 EoftheGG
33 E'sD
34 LfrE-HW
35 RecLCG-J
36 E'sD
37 KM'sJ
38 RecASF
39 E'sD
40 LfrJMM-IB
41 RecASF
42 ibid
43 HGWinL by HGW
44 E'sD

Chapter Seventeen
1 LfrE-KM
2 ibid
3 BR'sA
4 LfrE-KM
5 LfrE-ASF
6 SirHBRec
7 RecJR
8 E'sD
9 E'sDofL
10 E'sD
11 KM'sJ
12 ibid
13 ibid
14 E'sD
15 LfrKM-E
16 E'sD
17 KM'sJ
18 LfrJMM-KM
19 LfrE-HW
20 E'sD
21 LfrE-L
22 LfrE-ASF
23 E'sD
24 RecASF
25 E'sD
26 ibid
27 RecASF
28 LfrKM-E
29 RecJR
30 LfrKM-E
31 LfrE-KM
32 LfrE-L
33 LfrE-ASF
34 RecMrsBL
35 E'sD
36 LfrE-ASF
37 RecASF
38 E'sD
39 ibid
40 LfrE-CW
41 KM'sJ
42 RecIB
43 LfrE-JMM

Chapter Eighteen
1 E'sL

2 LfrE-ASF
3 RecT
4 E'sD
5 LfrE-ASF
6 ibid
7 LfrASF as MrA
8 EoftheGG
9 LfrE-L
10 LfrEvi-E
11 LfrE-ASF
12 E'sDofL
13 E'sD
14 ibid
15 ibid
16 ibid
17 ibid
18 ibid
19 ibid
20 ibid
21 EoftheGG
22 LfrE-MR
23 E'sD
24 ibid
25 ibid
26 ibid
27 LfrE-MR
28 E'sD
29 ibid
30 unpub.frag.
31 E'sD
32 ibid
33 ibid
34 LfrE-L
35 E'sD
36 EoftheGG
37 RecTP
38 RecBC
39 LfrAW-KU
40 E'sD
41 ibid
42 LfrL-RHD
43 E'sD
44 LinPbyWF

Chapter Nineteen
1 E'sD
2 ibid

3 ibid
4 ibid
5 ibid
6 LfrE-L
7 ibid
8 E'sD
9 LfrE-L
10 LfrE-Ellen
11 EoftheGG
12 E'sD
13 EofheGG
14 E'sD
15 RecASF
16 E'sD
17 ibid
18 E'sDofL
19 E'sD
20 ibid
21 ibid
22 ibid
23 LfrE-L
24 E'sD
25 ibid
26 ibid
27 ibid
28 LfrAW-KU
29 E'sD
30 RecASF
31 E'sD
32 RecASF
33 E'sBV unpub.
34 LfrE-L
35 E'sD
36 LfrE-L

Chapter Twenty
1 E'sD
2 LfrE-L
3 ibid
4 E'sD
5 ibid
6 ibid
7 LfrE-L
8 ibid
9 E'sD
10 ibid
11 ibid

Index

Doubleday, Nelson 167, 244, 245, 289
Doubleday, publishers 183, 305, 307, 308
Douglas, Norman 227
Doves Press 49
Dresden 40, 106
Dumas, Alexandre 47
Duomo (Florence) 35

East Kent Yeomanry 217
East Lodge, Acton 26, 29, 30, 31, 32
Easton Glebe 16
L'Ecole Industrielle Nationale 19
Eden Roc 296
Edensor 132
Edward VIII 296, 300
Egypt 217
Eliot, George 55
Eliot, T. S. 246
Elise 139, 145
Elizabeth: (Mary Annette Beauchamp, or May, Countess von Arnin, Countess Russell) birth 5, 7, 8, 9; her first words 10, 11; and Toady 12; walks with Henry 13; in church 14; with her mother 15; hay fever 16; ill 18; in the schoolroom 19; fat 23; her first dog; Cinderella, her talent 25; accompanies Harry 26; at fifteen 27; at school 28; failed Cambridge entrance 29; at twenty-one 30; still single 31; feminist 32; playing Bach 35; engagement 36, 37, 38; learning German 40; taking initiative 41; honeymoon 42, 43; expecting a baby 44, 45, 46, 47; friendship with Francis 48, 49; Teutons 53; resolve to write 54; as an author 56; moving flat 56; at Nassenheide 57; decorating 58, 59, 60; coping with the castle 61, 63; as hostess 64; influenced by the Poet Laureate 65; her books 66; views on being fat 67; called Elizabeth 69, 70; philanthropy 72; her manifesto 73; her pseudonym 74; her fame 75; another baby 76; and her sister 77; to England 78; H's arrest 79; letter to Henry 80; children's book 82; recommends Kate Greenaway 83; silent diary 85; Stanley salon 86; F

to gaol 88; girls educated like boys 88; searching for a subject 89; pregnant again 91; her two youngest 92; holiday 93, (94n); Trix elopes 95; her gaiety 96; punishments 97; the tutors 98; like 'a sweet smiling fairy' 100, 101; at breakfast 102; relationship with Teppi 104, 105; E. M. Forster 106, 107, 108, 109; her views 110; as Mrs Failing 112, 113, 114; *Princess Priscilla's Fortnight* 115; Miss Armstrong 116, 117; C. E. Stuart in love 118; teasing Hugh Walpole 121; and Stuart 122, 123; fear of thunder 125, 126; holiday 127, 129, 130; highland fling 131; discussions with Henning 132, 133, 134, 136, (136n), 137; leaving Nassenheide 138, 140; unhappy 141; receiving calls 143, 144; the only breadwinner 145; her views on God 146; friends with Stephen Reynolds 148, 150, 151, 152; husband dies 153, 154, 155; H. G. Wells 157, 158, (158n), 159; not writing 160, 161; teasing Wells 163; dissatisfied with Wells 164, 165; other facets of her personality 166, 167; Rebecca West's child 168; in Wells's novels 169, 170; Francis Russell 171, 172, 173; in love 174; having doubts 177; Martin's punishment 178, 179; escape 180; England 182; not heeding reviews 183; doubts about F 184, 186, 187, 188; her complex personality 189; after the wedding 190; cultivating not caring 191, 192, 193; life unbearable 194; F's adultery 195; escape 196, 197; on West Coast 198, 199; in New York 200; in 'bath of love' 201; Bertrand Russell's character 202; as a grandmother 203; go-between 204; friendship with Santayana 205; 206 her revenge 207; exchange of letters 208; flees 210; exhausted 211; law case 212; back to the chalet 214; visits K.M. 218; A. S. Frere 219; fond of C. Allen 221; Beverley Nichols 222; with Frere 224; escaping Frere 225; MSS 227; K.M. 228; *Vera* published 231, 233; not

INDEX

Rose Marie, (from *Fr. Schmidt and Mr Anstruther*) 117, 118, 119
Rothermere, Lady 257
Routledge, George 83
Royal, Francis Russell's yacht 53, 86
Royal Automobile Club 185
Royal College of Music 26, 29
Rügen 70, 102
Rupprecht, Crown Prince of Bavaria 214
Russell family (Pembroke Lodge) 49, 52
Russell, Lady Agatha 247
Russell, Bertrand 3, 49, 50, 52, 85, 174, 186, 187, 188, 189, 190, 195, 198, 201, 202, 203, 204, 208, 211, 212, 215, 219, 221, 233, 237, 247, 250, 263, 277, 278, 279, 305
Russell, Dora 237, 250
Russell, John Francis Stanley 1, 13, 47, 49, 50, 52, 53, 85, (85n), 87, 91, 92, 93, 143, 148, 149, 158, 163, 171, 172, 173, 174, 177, 178, 182, 183, 184, 186, 187, 188, 189, 190, 191, 192, 194, 195, 196, 199, 200, 201, 202, 203, 204, 205, 206, 207, 208, 209, 211, 212, 213, 215, 216, 218, 221, 222, 229, 235, 236, 246, 251, 253, 269, 277, 278, 295
Russell, Lord John, Earl Russell 5, 48, 49
Russell, Rachel 49
Russell, Rollo 5

Sackville-West, Edward 280
Sadawa, Battle of 5
St Paul's School for Girls 113, 116, 150
Sanderson, Thomas (Cobden-Sanderson) 49
Sandgate near Folkestone, Kent 123, 125, 126, 127
Sandwich, the Earl of (268n)
San Salvadore 226
San Ysidro 198, 199, 209
Santa Barbara 197
Santayana, George, 2, 53, 85, (85n), 172, 184, 185, 188, 204
Sapins, Chalet des 227, 231, 241, 242
La Scala 32
Schiff, Violet 218, 244

Schlagenthin 93, 133, 136, 137, 138, 150, 151, 154, 155, 193, 245
Schleck, Herr (Pope) 60
Schleck, Frau (The Popess) 60, 61, 63
Scott, Edith 53, 86, 87
Scott, Lady 53, 86
Second Reform Bill 48
Second World War 2, 31
Selfridges 113
Sévigné, Madame de 2
Sgambacti, Signor 33, 34
Shakespeare, William 98, 228, 236, 258, 301
Shakespeare & Company 244
Sharp, William 259
Sharp, Miss 41, 94
Shaw, G. B. 2, (86n), 156, 164, 221
Shelley, P. B. 247
Shepard, Ernest 285
Shepard, Mary 285
Shepheard & Co. 24
Shoolbred & Shoolbred 211, 212
Sierre 178, 179, 227, 240
Simpson, Mrs 296, 300
Smedley, The Honourable Constance 120, 123, 125
Smith & Elder 225
Smythe, Ethel 270, 275, 276
Somerville, Marion (Molly, Countess Russell) 86, 87, 143, 148, 149, 158, 171, 172, 184, 188, 192, 253, 278
Something Childish by Katherine Mansfield 263
South of France 290, 296, 304, 308
South Wind by Norman Douglas 227
Spade House 127, 157
Spalding 49, 50
Spectator 102, 115, 183
Stäel, Madame de 54, 262
Stanley, Kate 48
Stanley, Miss Maude 47, 49, 85, 87, 88, 91, 113, 133, 182
Star Begotten by H. G. Wells 298
Stein, Frau von 184, 205
Steinweg, Herr 98, 108, 121
Stern, G. B. 281
Stettin 56, 81, 90
Stokoe, Mr 98
Stokoe, Miss 98
Stone, Ann 6, 16